ACCA

PRACTICE & REVISION KIT

PAPER P6

ADVANCED TAXATION (UK)
FA 2008

In this January 2009 new edition

- We discuss the **best strategies** for revising and taking your ACCA exams
- We show you how to be **well prepared** for your exam
- We give you **lots of great guidance** on tackling questions
- We show you how you can **build your own exams**
- We provide you with **three** mock exams including the **December 2008 exam**

Our **i-Pass** product also supports this paper.

FOR EXAMS IN 2009

BPP
LEARNING MEDIA

First edition 2007
Third edition January 2009

ISBN 9780 7517 6671 4
(previous ISBN 9780 7517 4695 2)

British Library Cataloguing-in-Publication Data
A catalogue record for this book
is available from the British Library

Published by

BPP Learning Media Ltd
BPP House, Aldine Place
London W12 8AA

www.bpp.com/learningmedia

Printed in the United Kingdom

Your learning materials, published by BPP Learning
Media Ltd, are printed on paper sourced from
sustainable, managed forests.

We are grateful to the Association of Chartered Certified
Accountants for permission to reproduce past
examination questions. The suggested solutions in the
exam answer bank have been prepared by BPP Learning
Media Ltd, except where otherwise stated.

Contents

Question index

The headings in this checklist/index indicate the main topics of questions, but questions are expected to cover several different topics.

Mock exam 1

Mock exam 2

Mock exam 3 (December 2008)

Planning your question practice

Our guidance from page xvii shows you how to organise your question practice, either by attempting questions from each syllabus area or **by building your own exams** – tackling questions as a series of practice exams.

Topic index

Listed below are the key Paper P6 syllabus topics and the numbers of the questions in this Kit covering those topics.

If you need to concentrate your practice and revision on certain topics or if you want to attempt all available questions that refer to a particular subject, you will find this index useful.

Syllabus topic	Question numbers
Administration of tax – individuals	11,18
Administration of tax – companies	20, 25, ME3 Qu2
Capital allowances	8, 19, 38
Chargeable gains – reliefs	6, 12, 13, 15, 16, 17, 18, 22, 31, 32, 33, 34, 35, 39, ME1 Qu1, ME1 Qu2, ME1 Qu3, ME3 Qu3
Chargeable gains – companies	22, 29
Chargeable gains – individuals	6, 10, 12, 13, 14, 15, 16, 17, 18, 30, 31, 32, 33, 35, 39, ME1 Qu1, ME1 Qu2, ME1 Qu3, ME2 Qu2, ME3 Qu3
Companies – calculation of tax	19, 20, 21, 29, ME1 Qu5, ME2 Qu1, ME2, Qu3
Companies – close/investment	8, 21, ME1 Qu5
Companies – groups and consortia	19, 23, 24, 25, 26, 27, 28, ME1 Qu4, ME2 Qu1,ME3 Qu2,
Companies – liquidation	39, ME1 Qu5
Companies – losses	23, 28
Companies – overseas aspects	24, 26, 33, ME1 Qu2
Companies – personal service	ME3 Qu4
Companies – repurchase of shares	16, 36
Ethics	25, 26, ME3 Qu1, ME3 Qu1
Financial management	40
Income tax computation	10, 11, ME1 Qu3, ME2 Qu2
Individuals – employment income	3, 4, 5, 6, 11, 15, 17, 18, 21, 34, ME1 Qu2, ME3 Qu4
Individuals – property income	ME3 Qu5
Individuals – trading income	6, 7, 8, 38, ME1 Qu3, ME2 Qu3
Individuals – losses	7, 8
Individuals – overseas aspects	2, 10, 16, 29, 32, ME3 Qu1, ME3 Qu5
Inheritance tax	10, 12, 13, 14, 18, 31, 35, 39, 40, ME1 Qu1, ME2 Qu1, ME2 Qu4, ME3 Qu1, ME3 Qu1, ME3 Qu3
National insurance contributions	7, 38, ME2 Qu3
Partnerships	8
Stamp duties	26
Tax efficient investments	1, 2, 30, 35, 37, 38, ME1 Qu2, ME2 Qu4
Tax planning	30, 31, 32, 33, 34, 35, 36, 37, 38, ME2 Qu5
Trusts	17, ME3 Qu1
Value added tax	5, 6, 7, 11, 19, 20, 23, 24, 25, 26, 28, 29, 33, 37, 38, ME1 Qu2, ME1 Qu4, ME2 Qu2, ME3 Qu1, ME 3 Qu2

ME1 is Mock Exam 1

ME2 is Mock Exam 2

ME3 is Mock Exam 3

Using your BPP Learning Media Practice and Revision Kit

Tackling revision and the exam

You can significantly improve your chances of passing by tackling revision and the exam in the right ways. Our advice is based on feedback from ACCA examiners.

- We look at the dos and don'ts of revising for, and taking, ACCA exams
- We focus on Paper P6; we discuss revising the syllabus, what to do (and what not to do) in the exam, how to approach different types of question and ways of obtaining easy marks

Selecting questions

We provide signposts to help you plan your revision.

- A full **question index**
- A **topic index** listing all the questions that cover key topics, so that you can locate the questions that provide practice on these topics, and see the different ways in which they might be examined
- **BPP's question plan** highlighting the most important questions and explaining why you should attempt them
- **Build your own exams**, showing how you can practise questions in a series of exams

Making the most of question practice

At BPP Learning Media we realise that you need more than just questions and model answers to get the most from your question practice.

- Our **Top tips** included for certain questions provide essential advice on tackling questions, presenting answers and the key points that answers need to include
- We show you how you can pick up **Easy marks** on some questions, as we know that picking up all readily available marks often can make the difference between passing and failing
- We include **marking guides** to show you what the examiner rewards
- We include **examiners' comments** to show you where students struggled or performed well in the actual exam
- We refer to the **Finance Act 2008 BPP Study Text** (for exams in June and December 2009) for detailed coverage of the topics covered in questions

Attempting mock exams

There are three mock exams that provide practice at coping with the pressures of the exam day. We strongly recommend that you attempt them under exam conditions. **Mock exams 1 and 2** reflect the question styles and syllabus coverage of the exam; **Mock exam 3** is the December 2008 paper.

Passing P6

BPP Learning Media is committed to giving you the best possible support in your quest for exam success. With this in mind, we have produced **guidance** on how to revise and techniques you can apply to **improve your chances of passing** the exam. This guidance can be found on the BPP Learning Media web site at the following link:

www.bpp.com/acca/examtips/revising-for-ACCA-exams.doc

A paper copy of this guidance is available by writing to learningmedia@bpp.com.

As well as written guidance, an excellent presentation entitled '**Exam technique – advice from the experts at BPP Learning Media**' is available at the following link:

http://www.bppprofessionaldevelopment.com/elearning/Assets/audiovisual/ACCAExamSkills/NewSyllabus/player.html?cmp=get_ataste

Topics to revise

That said, you must have sound knowledge in the following fundamental areas if you are to stand a chance of passing the exam. You should therefore revise the following areas particularly well.

- Proformas for income tax (including capital allowances), capital gains, inheritance tax (IHT) and corporation tax computations so that you can calculate tax liabilities quickly. Make sure that you can also calculate NIC and VAT liabilities without difficulty.

- The calculation of benefits from employment so that you can make sensible comparisons between remuneration packages. Make sure you can advise on tax free benefits too.

- The reliefs available for the different taxes. For example, EIS relief for income tax and capital gains tax (CGT) and business property relief for IHT. There are, of course, many more reliefs to consider; you must be familiar with them all to be able to provide sound tax advice. Reliefs are the foundation of any tax planning.

- All aspects of corporation tax groups including the impact of associated companies on corporation tax liabilities, loss relief, chargeable gains groups, the effect of group VAT registration and stamp duty groups. You should pay particular attention to the impact on corporate restructuring.

- The special VAT schemes available for small businesses so that you can advise if and when they might be appropriate.

- Overseas issues for income tax, CGT, IHT, corporation tax and VAT.

- Investment opportunities for clients, taking into account their objectives and attitude to risk.

Question practice

Question practice under timed conditions is essential, so that you can get used to the pressures of answering exam questions in **limited time** and practise not only the key techniques but allocating your time between different requirements in each question. Our list of recommended questions includes 23 to 39 mark Section A questions and Section B questions of various marks.

Passing the P6 exam

Displaying the right qualities

The examiner expects students to display the following qualities.

Qualities required	
Knowledge development	Basic knowledge of the core taxes from Paper F6 is key, extended to encompass further overseas aspects of taxation, capital taxes (IHT and trusts, stamp duty and stamp duty land tax), and additional exemptions and reliefs.
Knowledge application	You must be able to apply your knowledge to the issues commonly encountered by individuals and businesses. You will be expected to consider more than one tax at any one time and to identify planning issues and areas of interaction of the taxes.
Skill development	Paper P6 seeks to develop the skills of analysis and interpretation. You must be able to interpret and analyse the information provided in the question, keeping your answers focused and as accurate as possible, while avoiding waffle.
Communication skills	Paper P6 also seeks to develop the skill of communication. It is no good having the knowledge but not being able to communicate it effectively, so ensure you keep your communication appropriate to the intended audience. Practise using the appropriate terminology in your answers: you will need to be more technical when communicating with a tax manager (eg using technical terms for loss relief) and less so when speaking to a client (who may not understand 'early years loss relief'!)
Keeping current	The examiner expects you to advise using established tax planning methods in the exam. Fortunately he does not expect you to invent new ones. However, you must be aware of current issues in taxation.
Computation skills	Computations are not the focus of the P6 exam. However they may be required in support of explanations. It is therefore essential that you can complete calculations of tax liabilities speedily and without difficulty to provide numerical evidence for your tax advice.

You will not always produce the exact same solution as we have in our answer section. This does not necessarily mean that you have failed the question, as marks are often available for any other relevant key points you make.

Avoiding weaknesses

We give details of the examiner's comments and criticisms (at various points throughout this Kit. His reports always emphasised the need to demonstrate a fairly wide syllabus knowledge, but also to identify and justify the availability (or non-availability) of particular reliefs and exemptions. There are various things you can do on the day of the exam to enhance your chances. Although these all sound basic, the examiner has commented that scripts show:

- A failure to read the question and requirements properly and answer the question set, instead churning out irrelevant 'set pieces'

- Clear evidence of poor time management

- Tendency to confuse CGT and IHT and even personal and corporation tax issues

Make sure you attempt only four questions (as only four will be marked) and start each question on a new page, clearly labelled.

Finally, never ever cross your workings out. These may be correct and you will not be given credit if you have crossed the working out.

Reading time

You will have 15 minutes reading time for Paper P6. Here are some helpful tips on how to best utilise this time.

- Ignore the compulsory questions.

- Speed read through the optional questions, paying particular attention to the requirements, to enable you to decide which two questions to choose from the three. Jot down any ideas that come to you about either of them.

- Cross out the question that you have **not** decided to attempt.

- Decide the order in which you're likely to tackle the other two questions (probably easier question first, more difficult question last).

- Spend the remainder of the time reading the question you'll do first in detail, jotting down answer plans and proformas for supporting calculations (any plans or proformas written on the question paper should be reproduced in the answer booklet).

- When you can start writing, get straight on with the question(s) you've planned in detail.

The reason for attempting the optional questions first is, in the examiner's own words:

'The majority of…candidates appeared to attempt the compulsory questions first, and overrun the time allocation, which they may have regretted later when they reached some relatively straightforward areas in the Section B questions, but didn't have time to have a reasonable attempt at them.'

Doing these questions first should mean that you can manage your time more effectively and not run out of time answering the longer compulsory questions. Attempting the easier question first means that you will have been generating ideas and remembering facts for the more difficult question.

Choosing which questions to answer first

You will need to answer the two compulsory questions in Section A and two out of the three optional questions in Section B, with a larger number of marks awarded for the first two questions.

- The optional questions will be for equal marks. Answer the question on your most comfortable topic but be strict with timing. It is all too tempting to tell the examiner everything you know about your favourite topic. Don't!

- When answering the two compulsory questions, the marks may be allocated unevenly between them. Many students prefer to answer the question with the larger number of allocated marks first. Others again prefer to answer a question on their most comfortable topic.

- Whatever the order, make sure you leave yourself **sufficient time** to tackle all the questions. Don't get bogged down in the more difficult areas, or re-write your answer two or three times. Instead move on and try the rest of the question as there may be an easier part. You do not want to be in a position where you have to rush the rest of the paper.

- Allocate your time carefully between different question parts. If a question is split into a number of requirements, use the number of marks available for each to allocate your time effectively.

Tackling questions

You'll improve your chances by following a step-by-step approach along the following lines.

Step 1   Read the requirement

Identify the knowledge areas being tested and see precisely what the examiner wants you to do. This will help you focus on what's important in the question.

Step 2   Check the mark allocation

This helps you allocate time.

Step 3   Read the question actively

You will already know which knowledge area(s) are being tested from having read the requirement so whilst you read through the question underline or highlight key words and figures as you read. This will mean you are thinking about the question rather than just looking at the words blankly, and will allow you to identify relevant information for use in your advice and supporting calculations.

Step 4   Plan your answer

You may only spend five minutes planning your answer but it will be five minutes well spent. Identify the supporting calculations (and appropriate proformas) you will need to do, if any. Plan the structure of your written answer, even if it is only a series of bullet points, or maybe a spider diagram, using suitable headings and sub headings. Determine whether you can you use bullet points in your answer or if you need a more formal format.

Step 5   Write your answer

Stick carefully to the time allocation for each question, and for each part of each question.

Gaining the easy marks

There are two main ways to obtain easy marks in the P6 exam.

Supporting calculations

Although computations will not be required in isolation in Paper P6 as the focus is on written explanations and advice, there will always be marks available for calculating figures which will support your recommendations. Often you cannot provide any sensible advice until you know the tax cost of a course of action so make sure you can readily set out proformas and fill in the numbers from the question. Make it easy for yourself to pick up the easy marks.

Answer the question set

If you need to consider alternative planning strategies in a question and provide advice on which is the most suitable, do exactly that. If you do not advise on the most suitable plan you'll be losing easy marks. Similarly, if you are asked to consider CGT and IHT in a requirement, don't think that by including some income tax considerations you will pick up extra marks – you won't. Show the examiner you have read his question and requirements carefully and have attempted to answer them as expected – not how you would like to.

Exam information

Format of the exam

Time allowed: 3 hours (with 15 minutes reading time)

Tax rates and allowances and information on certain reliefs will be provided in the examination paper.

Paper P6 is split into sections A and B each comprising scenario based questions which will usually involve consideration of more than one tax, together with some elements of planning and the interaction of taxes. The focus is on explanations and advice rather than computations.

Section A contains two compulsory questions for a total of between 50 and 70 marks, which may be unevenly allocated between the two questions.

Section B consists of three questions, two of which must be answered, for the same number of marks.

Examiner's general comments

If you are preparing to sit Paper P6 you should pay particular attention to the following in order to maximise your chances of success.

1   *Know your stuff*

   - Successful candidates are able to demonstrate sufficient, precise knowledge of the UK tax system.

   - Knowledge and understanding of the technical content of Paper F6 is vital if you are to be successful at paper P6.

   - This knowledge must be up to date. Candidates sitting the exam in 2009 must familiarise themselves with the many changes introduced by the Finance Act 2008 as summarised in the Finance Act article published in Student Accountant magazine and on the website.

2   *Address the requirement*

   - Read the requirement carefully – then read it again; it's important.

   - The requirement of each question is carefully worded in order to provide you with guidance as regards the style and content of your answers. You should note the command words within the requirement (calculate, explain etc), any matters which are not to be covered and the precise issues you have been asked to address.

   - Pay attention to the number of marks available – this provides you with a clear indication of the amount of time you should spend.

3   *Don't provide general explanations or long introductions.*

   - There is no need to explain what you are going to do before you do it; just get on with it.
   - Think before you write. Then write whatever is necessary to satisfy the requirement.
   - Apply your knowledge to the facts by reference to the requirement.

4   *Be brave*

   - Don't be put off by a situation that you have not seen before.

   - Follow the instructions in the question and the requirement and apply your knowledge of the tax system to the facts of the situation.

5   *Manage your time*

   - Ensure that you allow the correct amount of time for each question.

Marks available in respect of professional skills

In order to earn marks for professional skills such as report writing, candidates first have to satisfy the requirement in relation to the format of the document requested. Further marks are then available for the clarity of the answer, including the ease with which it can be marked and the degree to which the conclusions reached follow logically from the explanations and calculations provided. These latter marks are more likely to be earned by those candidates who think about the manner in which they intend to satisfy the requirement such that there is a sense of purpose and a coherency to their answers.

December 2008

Question in this kit

Section A

1   Expansion (employees or sub-contractors), VAT partial exemption, IHT on inheritance, ethical issues   Mock exam 3 Qu 1

2   Sale of group company, payment of corporation tax by group, VAT group, transfer pricing   Mock exam 3 Qu 2

Section B

3   Sale of capital assets by individual, IHT for unmarried couple   Mock exam 3 Qu 3

4   Redundancy package, personal service company   Mock exam 3 Qu 4

5   Overseas aspects of CGT and IT for individual   Mock exam 3 Qu 5

June 2008

Question in this kit

Section A

1   Loss relief for group, capital gains group, stamp duty   26

2   Tax return errors, income tax and CGT computations for married couple, VAT registration, trust income   11

Section B

3   Repurchase of own shares, company – overseas aspects   36

4   IHT on gifts, employment income – overseas aspects   18

5   Tax efficient investments, VAT on commercial building   37

Examiner's comments

Candidates appeared to be comfortable with the style of the paper with a good proportion of them spending an appropriate period of time on the optional questions. There was further evidence of some candidates starting their exam with the shorter, optional questions in Section B.

December 2007

Examiner's comments

It was pleasing to see a good proportion of candidates spending an appropriate period of time on the optional questions. Candidates should be aware that they are more likely to be successful if they manage their time throughout the exam and allow the correct amount of time for each question.

Some candidates started with the shorter, optional questions in Section B. This is an approach that all candidates should at least consider as these questions provide a more gentle introduction to the exam than those in section A.

Pilot paper

Useful websites

The websites below provide additional sources of information of relevance to your studies for *Strategic Financial Management*.

- www.accaglobal.com

  ACCA's website. The students' section of the website is invaluable for detailed information about the qualification, past issues of Student Accountant (including technical articles) and even interviews with the examiners.

- www.bpp.com

  Our website provides information about BPP products and services, with a link to the ACCA website.

Using your BPP Learning Media products

This Kit gives you the question practice and guidance you need in the exam. Our other products can also help you pass:

- **Learning to Learn Accountancy** gives further valuable advice on revision

- **Passcards** provide you with clear topic summaries and exam tips

- **Success CDs** help you revise on the move

- **i-Pass CDs** offer tests of knowledge against the clock

- **Learn Online** is an e-learning resource delivered via the Internet, offering comprehensive tutor support and featuring areas such as study, practice, email service, revision and useful resources

You can purchase these products by visiting www.bpp.com/mybpp.

Visit our website www.bpp.com/acca/learnonline to sample aspects of Learn Online free of charge. Learn Online is hosted by BPP Professional Education.

Planning your question practice

We have already stressed that question practice should be right at the centre of your revision. Whilst you will spend some time looking at your notes and Paper P6 Passcards, you should spend the majority of your revision time practising questions.

We recommend two ways in which you can practise questions.

- Use **BPP Learning Media's question plan** to work systematically through the syllabus and attempt key and other questions on a section-by-section basis

- **Build your own exams** – attempt questions as a series of practice exams

These ways are suggestions and simply following them is no guarantee of success. You or your college may prefer an alternative but equally valid approach.

BPP Learning Media's question plan

The BPP Learning Media plan below requires you to devote a **minimum of 30 hours** to revision of Paper P6. Any time you can spend over and above this should only increase your chances of success.

Step 1   **Review your notes** and the chapter summaries in the Paper P6 **Passcards** for each section of the syllabus.

Step 2   **Answer the questions** for that section which have boxes round the question number in the table below. You should complete your answers without referring to our solutions.

Step 3   For some questions we have suggested that you prepare **answer plans or do the calculations** rather than full solutions if you are short of time. Planning an answer means that you should spend about 40% of the time allowance for the questions brainstorming the question and drawing up a list of points to be included in the answer.

Step 4   Attempt **Mock exams 1, 2 and 3** under strict exam conditions.

Syllabus section	Passcards chapters	Questions in this Kit	Comments	Done ☑
Revision period 1/2 Income tax computations, pensions and other investments	1, 2, 3	1	This is a useful introductory question. Make sure you plan your answer carefully. If short of time, work through alongside the answer.	☐
Revision periods 3/4 Employees & NIC	2, 4, 5, 6, 19, 22, 28, 30	3, 4, 5, 7	You must be comfortable comparing the tax benefits of taking additional salary versus benefits. The new areas of termination payments and share remuneration are key. Useful questions. Answer Q3 and Q4 in full. Q5 is a Pilot paper question so worth looking at carefully. You should concentrate only on the termination payment in Q7 then return to the rest of the question after you have completed the next revision period.	☐
Revision periods 5/6 Trading profits and losses for individuals & NIC	4, 5, 6, 7, 8, 12, 19, 22, 28, 29	6, 7, 9	These are key questions testing fundamental topics covered in F6 but with a planning focus. Have a go at the income tax aspects of Q6 on incorporation at this stage. Work through alongside the answer if your time is short. Ignore the VAT for now. You can now return to Q7 and almost answer it in full (you still need to revise VAT – see how essential it is for your exam?). Come back to both of these questions after you have completed revision period 26/27. Question 9 covers both unincorporated and incorporated businesses.	☐
Revision period 7 Partnerships	6, 7, 8, 9	8	Partnerships essentially revise the trading income rules again! You should find this question quite straightforward, although you may like to return to the ethics when you have completed revision period 28/29/30.	☐
Revision period 8 Overseas aspects of income tax	1, 4, 5, 6, 8, 10, 12, 14, 17, 18	2, 10	Overseas aspects is a new topic. Q2 is a recent question so worth a close look. Q10 deals with overseas aspects of income tax, CGT and IHT, so you may want to return to this question once you have completed revision period 13/14/15.	☐
Revision period 9/10/11 Capital gains, shares and securities, reliefs	11,12, 13, 14, 17, 18, 19	13, 14, 15	It is unlikely that you will be examined only on capital gain tax. It is often tested alongside inheritance tax (IHT) for individuals and the questions in this section therefore contain both taxes. Focus **only** on the CGT aspects the first time you work through the questions, then return to the IHT aspects once you have completed the relevant revision period. Q14 is a recent question so well worth a close look at.	☐

Syllabus section	Passcards chapters	Questions in this Kit	Comments	Done ☑
Revision period 12 Self-assessment for individuals and partnerships	15	11	The administration rules will not be tested in isolation but will make up some of the marks on a number of questions. Whenever you are advising a client they must be aware of their responsibilities so giving submission and payment deadlines is always valid. Question 11 covers a number of areas but also involves tax administration.	☐
Revision period 13/14/ 15 IHT valuation, reliefs, death estate and additional aspects	11, 13, 16, 17	12, 16, 18	This is a completely new topic so it will almost certainly be tested. Do you understand the interaction between CGT and IHT? You must be clear about this as the two taxes are often examined together. Useful questions. Work in full.	☐
Revision period 17 Trusts and stamp duties	5, 6, 7, 12, 18, 28	17	Q17 revisits topics you have seen earlier in your revision. Important question.	☐
Revision periods 18/19/ 20 Computing PCTCT and corporation tax, administration	20, 21, 22, 23, 28, 29	19, 20	Important questions. Leave the VAT in both questions for now but return to them after you complete revision period 26/27. Also ignore the corporation tax group elements of Q19.	☐
Revision period 21/ 22 Corporation tax losses, close and investment companies	12, 14, 20, 21, 22, 25, 30	21, 22	Important questions. Work through carefully.	☐
Revision period 23/ 24 Groups and consortia	11, 12, 20, 21, 22, 24, 26, 27, 28, 29	23, 24, 26	Useful questions. Answer in full. Do you understand the topics tested?	☐
Revision period 25 Overseas aspects of corporation tax	7, 20, 21, 22, 23, 24, 26, 27, 28	25, 27	Useful questions. Answer in full.	☐
Revision period 26/27 VAT	1, 6, 7, 11, 15, 16, 17, 19, 20, 21, 22, 24, 26, 27, 28, 29	28, 29	Important questions. Note that VAT can be tested for an individual or company.	☐

Syllabus section	Passcards chapters	Questions in this Kit	Comments	Done ☑
Revision period 28/29/30 Tax planning	All	30, 31, 32, 33, 34, 35, 36, 37	If you are short on time work through alongside the answers. Essential questions. All questions in the exam will test more than one tax and possibly the interaction of those taxes. You have revised all of the topics now (apart from personal and corporate financial management) so if there are any areas you are unhappy with make sure you revisit them now.	☐
Revision period 31 Personal and corporate financial management	All	38, 39, 40	Essential questions. These test your ability to bring together all your knowledge in a scenario.	☐

Build your own exams

Having revised your notes and the BPP Passcards, you can attempt the questions in the Kit as a series of practice exams. You can organise the questions in the following ways.

- Either you can attempt complete past exam papers; recent papers are listed below:

	Pilot paper Question in kit	December 07 Question in Kit	June 08 Question in kit
1	28	40	26
2	5	9	11
3	15	27	36
4	16	2	18
5	34	14	37

- Or you can make up practice exams, either yourself or using the suggestions we have listed below.

	Practice Exam					
	1	2	3	4	5	6
1	7	28	23	28	17	11
2	22	8	35	16	19	26
3	15	18	39	1	24	36
4	27	34	31	25	10	14
5	34	36	13	6	20	2

Questions

TAXATION OF INDIVIDUALS

Questions 1 to 11 cover the taxation of individuals. This is the subject of Chapters 1 to 10 in the BPP study text.

1 Styrax   38 mins

You have recently been approached to act as an accountant for Styrax, aged 32, who is self-employed.

The following information has been extracted from client files and from meetings with Styrax. You should assume that today's date is 15 March 2009.

Styrax:

- Annual trading profits have been fairly constant at approximately £20,000 for the last few years.
- Has building society savings amounting to around £6,000 which generate gross annual interest of approximately £300.
- Wife, Salvia, is aged 28, is expecting their first child and has recently given up employed work.
- The couple has no other sources of income.
- Disposable income is about £3,000 pa after paying their mortgage and living expenses.

Investment strategy:

- Neither Styrax nor his wife have made, and for the present do not wish to start making, any pension provision.
- Risk averse.

Stryax's brother, Taxus:

- Single.
- Prepared to take medium to high risk in his investments.
- Already has a portfolio of investments and wishes to shelter some of his gains.
- Considering investing in the Enterprise Investment Scheme (EIS) and in Venture Capital Trusts (VCTs).

Required

(a) (i) Prepare notes for a meeting with Styrax setting out any measures that could be undertaken by the couple in order to reduce their income tax and national insurance liabilities following Salvia leaving her employment.

You should assume that Styrax does not wish to incorporate his business and that Salvia does not wish to join him in partnership.

Detailed income tax computations are not required in this question part.   **(8 marks)**

(ii) Explain the options open to the couple regarding making future pension provision.   **(3 marks)**

You should assume that the tax rates and allowances for 2008/09 apply throughout.

(b) Write a memorandum to Taxus setting out the features of the EIS and VCTs. You should include details of the risk and taxation implications of each type of investment.   **(10 marks)**

(Total = 21 marks)

2 Coral (ATAX 12/07)   32 mins

Coral is the owner and managing director of Reef Ltd. She is considering the manner in which she will make her first pension contributions. In November 2009 she inherited her mother's house in the country of Kalania.

The following information has been extracted from client files and from telephone conversations with Coral.

Coral:

- 1973 – Born in the country of Kalania. Her father, who died in 2004, was domiciled in Kalania.
- 2001 – Moved to the UK and has lived and worked here since then.
- 2003 – Subscribed for 100% of the ordinary share capital of Reef Ltd.
- Intends to sell Reef Ltd and return to live in the country of Kalania in 2014.
- No income apart from that received from Reef Ltd.

Reef Ltd:

- A UK resident company with annual profits chargeable to corporation tax of approximately £70,000.
- Four employees including Coral.
- Provides scuba diving lessons to members of the public.

Payments from Reef Ltd to Coral in 2009/10:

- Director's fees of £460 per month.
- Dividends paid of £14,250 in June 2009 and £14,250 in September 2009.

Pension contributions:

- Coral has not so far made any pension contributions in the tax year 2009/10 but wishes to make gross pension contributions of £9,000.
- The contributions are to be made by Reef Ltd or Coral or a combination of the two in such a way as to minimise the total after tax cost.
- Any contributions made by Coral will be funded by an additional dividend from Reef Ltd.

House in the country of Kalania:

- Beachfront property with potential rental income of £550 per month after deduction of allowable expenditure.
- Coral will use it for holidays for two months each year.

The tax system in the country of Kalania:

- No capital gains tax or inheritance tax.
- Income tax at 8% on income arising in the country of Kalania.
- No double tax treaty with the UK.

Required

(a)   With the objective of minimising the total after tax cost, advise Coral as to whether the gross pension contributions of £9,000 should be made:

- wholly by Reef Ltd; or
- by Coral to the extent that they are tax allowable with the balance made by Reef Ltd.

Your answer should include supporting calculations where necessary.   **(9 marks)**

(b)   (i)   Explain, by reference to Coral's residence, ordinary residence and domicile position, how the rental income arising in respect of the property in the country of Kalania will be taxed in the UK in the tax year 2009/10. State the strategy that Coral should adopt in order to minimise the total income tax suffered on the rental income.   **(7 marks)**

(ii)   Explain how the inclusion of rental income in Coral's UK income tax computation could affect the income tax due on her dividend income.   **(2 marks)**

You are not required to prepare calculations for part (b) of this question.

Note: you should assume that the tax rates and allowances for the tax year 2008/09 and for the Financial Year to 31 March 2009 will continue to apply for the foreseeable future.

(Total = 18 marks)

3 Benny Fitt

Your manager has had a meeting with Benny Fitt, the managing director of Usine Ltd, and has sent you a copy of the following memorandum.

To	The files
From	Tax manager
Date	20 December 2008
Subject	Usine Ltd

(a) Provision of employment benefits to Benny Fitt (BF)

Petrol company car

Provided on 1 October 2008. Car has list price of £28,400 and CO_2 emission figure of 222g/km. Sun-roof has been added costing £700. BF made a capital contribution of £2,500 towards the cost of the car.

Company credit card

During 2008/09 this will be used to pay for:

- motor repairs   £460
- business accommodation   £380
- customer entertaining   £720
- petrol   £425

Included in the figure for petrol is £180 in respect of private mileage which is not reimbursed to Usine Ltd.

Lap top computer

Cost £3,000. Provided on 6 April 2008, for private use and occasional business use.

(b) Sales director changes

On 10 December 2008 Usine Ltd dismissed their sales director and paid him a lump sum redundancy payment of £45,000. This consisted of the following.

	£
Statutory redundancy pay	2,100
Payment in lieu of notice	3,100
Holiday pay	2,800
Ex gratia compensation for loss of office	34,000
Agreement not to work for a rival company	3,000
	45,000

A new sales director is to commence employment on 1 January 2009. She is to be paid a lump sum payment of £10,000 upon the commencement of employment. The new director currently lives 120 miles from Usine Ltd's head office, so the company has offered her two alternative arrangements.

(i) Usine Ltd will pay £9,500 towards the cost of the director's relocation, and will also provide an interest free loan of £50,000 in order for the director to purchase a property.

(ii) Usine Ltd will provide accommodation for the director. The company owns a house which has an annual value of £4,400, is currently valued at £99,000, and has recently been furnished at a cost of £10,400. Usine Ltd will pay for the annual running costs of £3,200.

An extract from an email from your manager is set out below.

Please prepare a letter to Benny Fitt setting out the following:

1   Employment benefits

        Advise both Benny Fitt and Usine Ltd of the tax implications arising from the provision of the company car, the credit card and the laptop computer.

        Explain why it would be beneficial if Benny paid Usine Ltd £180 for his private petrol.

        You can ignore the VAT implications.

2   Sales director changes

        Explain the income tax implications of the lump sum payments of £45,000 and £10,000.

        Explain the income tax implications of the two alternative arrangements offered to the new sales director.

        You do not need to consider the tax implications for Usine Ltd and you should confine your statements to the implications for 2008/09.

3   Share option scheme

        Outline the conditions required for the scheme to obtain HMRC approval.

You have extracted the following further information from client files.

*   Usine Ltd is an unquoted trading company.
*   It is a small company for the purposes of the Companies Acts.
*   Benny Fitt is aged 39 and is paid a salary of £45,000 per annum.
*   Usine Ltd purchased the house available to the new sales director in 1996 for £86,000. It was improved at a cost of £8,000 during 2005.

Required

Prepare the letter requested by your manager.

Marks are available for the components of the letter as follows:

1	Tax treatment of the employment benefits for Benny Fitt and Usine Ltd.	**(8 marks)**
2	Tax implications of the payments (and benefits) provided to the two sales director.	**(9 marks)**
3	The conditions for the share option scheme to be approved.	**(4 marks)**

Appropriateness of the format and presentation of the letter and the effectiveness with which its content is communicated.   **(2 marks)**

You may assume that the rates and allowances for the 2008/09 tax year and Financial Year 2008 continue to apply for the foreseeable future. The official rate of interest for 2008/09 is 6.25%.

(Total = 23 marks)

4 Benny Korere

Benny Korere has been employed as the sales director of Golden Tan plc since 1994.

The following information has been extracted from client files and from meetings with Benny.

Benny

- Age 42.
- Receives rental income of £4,000 (net of deductible expenses) each year.

Current remuneration package with Golden Tan plc:

- Annual salary of £32,000.
- Petrol company car with list price of £22,360 and CO_2 emission rate of 182g/km. Paid a £6,100 capital contribution towards the cost of the car. Pays £18 per month as a condition of being able to use the car for private purposes.
- Golden Tan plc does not pay for any of Benny's private petrol.

Redundancy package:

- Will be made redundant on 28 February 2009.
- Will be paid his final month's salary together with a payment of £8,000 in lieu of his six-month notice period in accordance with his employment contract.
- Will also be paid £17,500 in return for agreeing not to work for any of Golden Tan plc's competitors for the six-month period ending 31 August 2009.

New remuneration package with Summer Glow plc:

- Summer Glow plc is one of Golden Tan plc's competitors and one of the most innovative companies in the industry, although not all of its strategies have been successful.
- Has been offered a senior management position leading the company's expansion into Eastern Europe.
- Would join Summer Glow plc on 1 September 2009 for an annual salary of £39,000.
- Will be granted an option to purchase 10,000 ordinary shares in the company for £2.20 per share under an unapproved share option scheme.
- Can exercise the option once has been employed for six months but must hold the shares for at least a year before he sells them.

Relocation:

- Will be required to spend a considerable amount of time in London.
- Summer Glow plc has offered exclusive use of a flat, purchased by the company on 1 June 2005 for £165,000, which will be available from 1 September 2009.
- All utility bills, furnishing and maintenance costs will be paid by the company.
- Summer Glow plc has suggested that the company could sell the existing flat and buy a more centrally located one, of the same value, with the proceeds.

Capital transactions:

- Intends to sell 5,800 shares in Mahana plc, a quoted company, for £24,608 on 15 March 2009.
- Transactions in the company's shares have been as follows:

		£
2 June 1988	Purchased 8,400 shares	6,744
14 February 1996	Sale of rights nil paid	610
10 April 2005	Purchased 1,300 shares	2,281

- The sale of rights nil paid was not treated as a part disposal of Benny's holding in Mahana plc.
- Shareholding represents less than 1% of the company's issued ordinary share capital.
- Will not make any other capital disposals in 2008/09.

Required

(a)   Calculate Benny's employment income for 2008/09.   **(3 marks)**

(b)   (i)   Advise Benny of the income tax implications of the grant and exercise of the share options in
             Summer Glow plc on the assumption that the share price on 1 September 2009 and on the day he
             exercises the options is £3.35 per share. Explain why the share option scheme is not free from risk
             by reference to the rules of the scheme and the circumstances surrounding the company. **(4 marks)**

      (ii)   List the additional information required in order to calculate the employment income benefit in
             respect of the provision of the furnished flat for 2009/10 and advise Benny of the potential income tax
             implications of requesting a more centrally located flat in accordance with the company's offer.

                                                                                                               (4 marks)

(c)   Calculate Benny's capital gains tax liability for 2008/09.   **(4 marks)**

You should assume that the rates and allowances for the tax year 2008/09 apply throughout this question.

The official rate of interest is 6.25%.

                                                                                                    (Total = 15 marks)

5 Pilar Mareno (Pilot Paper)   **45 mins**

Your manager has had a meeting with Pilar Mareno, a self-employed consultant, and has sent you a copy of the
following memorandum.

To   The files
From   Tax manager
Date   31 May 2009
Subject   Pilar Mareno – Business expansion

Pilar Mareno (PM) has been offered a contract with DWM plc, initially for two years, which will result in fees of
£80,000 plus VAT per annum.

In order to service this contract, PM would have to take on additional help in the form of either a part-time
employee for two days a week, or the services of a self-employed contractor for 100 days per year. She would also
have to acquire a van, which would be used wholly for business purposes. PM has decided that she will only enter
into the contract if it generates at least an additional £15,000 per annum, on average, for the family after all costs
and taxes.

PM's annual profitability and the profit generated by the contract (before taking into account the costs of the part-
time employee/contractor and the van) are summarised below.

	Existing business £	New contract £
Sales	210,000	80,000
Less: Materials, wages and overheads	(120,000)	(35,000)
Profit per accounts and taxable profit	90,000	45,000

Supplies made under the contract will be 65% standard rated and 35% exempt for value added tax (VAT) purposes;
this is the same as for PM's existing business. £31,500 of the costs incurred in relation to the contract will be
subject to VAT at the standard rate. The equivalent figure for PM's existing business is £100,000.

PM has identified Max Wallen (MW) as a possible self-employed contractor. MW would charge £75 per day plus
VAT for a contract of 100 days per year, with a rate of £25 per day plus VAT in respect of any days when he is ill (up
to a maximum of eight days per year). PM has a spare copy of the specialist software that MW would need but MW
would use his own laptop computer.

Alternatively, PM could employ her husband, Alec (AM), paying him a gross annual salary of £7,600. AM would have to give up his current full-time job, but would expect to do other part-time employed work earning a further £10,000 (gross) per annum.

PM estimates that a second hand van will cost £7,800 plus VAT or alternatively, a van could be leased for £300 plus VAT per month. We can assume that if the van is purchased, it will be sold at the end of the two-year contract for £2,500 plus VAT.

Tax manager

An extract from an email from your manager is set out below.

Please prepare a memorandum for me, incorporating the following:

1   Calculations to demonstrate whether or not Pilar's desired annual after tax income from the new contract will be achievable depending on:

- whether she leases or buys the van; and
- whether she employs Alec or uses Max Wallen.

You may find it easier to:

(i)   work out the after tax cost of buying or leasing the van. (When calculating the annual cost of the van, assume that the total cost can be averaged over the two years of the contract.)

and then to consider:

(ii)   the after tax income depending on whether Alec is employed or the self-employed contractor, Max, is used.

2   A rationale for the approach you have taken and a summary of your findings.

3   Any other issues we should be considering in respect of Pilar employing Alec, including any alternative to employment.

4   It seems to me that HM Revenue and Customs may be able to successfully contend that Max Wallen would be an employee, rather than a self-employed contractor. Prepare your figures on the basis that he is self-employed but include a list of factors in your memorandum, based on the information we have, that would indicate either employed or self-employed status.

Take some time to think about your approach to this before you start. Also, as always when working on Pilar's affairs, watch out for the VAT as it can get quite tricky. I suspect the VAT will affect the costs incurred so you'll need to address VAT first. Pilar's estimate of the profit on the contract will have ignored these complications.

Tax manager

You have extracted the following further information from Pilar Mareno's client file.

- None of Pilar's VAT inputs is directly attributable to either standard rated or exempt supplies.
- Alec has worked for a UK bank for many years and is currently paid an annual salary of £17,000.
- The couple have no sources of income other than those set out above.

Required

Prepare the memorandum requested by your manager.

Marks are available for the four components of the memorandum as follows:

(1)   Relevant calculations.   **(16 marks)**

(2)   Rationale for the approach taken and summary of findings.   **(2 marks)**

(3)   Other issues in respect of Pilar employing Alec, together with any suggestions as to an alternative to employment.   **(2 marks)**

(4)   The employment status of Max Wallen.   **(3 marks)**

Appropriateness of the format and presentation of the memorandum and the effectiveness with which the information is communicated. **(2 marks)**

You may assume that the rates and allowances for the tax year 2008/09 will continue to apply for the foreseeable future.

(Total = 25 marks)

6 Alex Zong

29 mins

Alex Zong, aged 38, commenced self-employment as a builder on 1 October 2005.

The following information has been extracted from client files and from meetings with Alex.

Alex Zong:

- Has capital losses of £12,500 resulting from the sale of investments in 2008/09.
- Is registered for VAT; does not operate the cash accounting scheme.
- Drives 12,000 miles per year, of which 4,800 are for private purposes.
- Plans to incorporate the trade into a new limited company, Lexon Ltd, on 31 December 2008.

Tax adjusted trading profits (*after* capital allowances):

- Period ended 30.6.06 – £19,950
- Year ended 30.6.07 – £41,612
- Year ended 30.6.08 – £49,993
- Estimated profits for the period ended 31.12.08 – £29,000

Capital assets:

The tax written down values at 30 June 2008 were as follows:

- Main pool – £4,275
- Expensive car, used by Alex Zong – £10,500

Planned incorporation details:

- All the assets of the business will be transferred to Lexon Ltd.
- Consideration will consist of 1,000 £1 ordinary shares in Lexon Ltd and a loan account balance of £10,000.
- The estimated market value of the business assets at 31 December 2008 are as follows:

	£
Goodwill	40,000
Freehold premises	75,000
Lorry	4,300
Plant	8,200
Motor car	11,500
Net current assets	21,000
	160,000

- The freehold premises had been purchased for £32,000 on 1 October 2005, and subsequently extended on 10 December 2007 at a cost of £6,700.

VAT issues for return for quarter ended 30 November 2008:

- Completed a contract for a customer on 20 May 2008, and raised an invoice for £9,400 (inclusive of VAT) on 15 June 2008. Customer paid £2,350 on 30 June 2008, and the balance was due to be paid within 10 days of the invoice date. Now considered to be a bad debt.

- Has not been claiming the input VAT on plant which is leased for £475 (inclusive of VAT) per month. The same amount has been paid since commencement of business on 1 October 2005.

- Invoiced a customer for £3,400 (excluding VAT) on 30 September 2008. Was offered a 5% discount for payment within 30 days. This was not taken and full amount was paid on 28 November 2008.

Required

(a)   (i)   Calculate Alex's trading profits assessment for 2008/09. You should ignore NIC.   **(4 marks)**

      (ii)   Advise Alex of the capital gains tax implications of incorporating his business on 31 December 2008.
                (5 marks)

      (iii)   Advise Alex of the VAT implications of incorporating his business on 31 December 2008.   **(2 marks)**

      You should include any tax planning points that you consider relevant.

(b)   Advise Alex how he should deal with the VAT issues for the return for the quarter ended 30 November 2008.
                (5 marks)

                (Total = 16 marks)

7 Anne Parr   **70 mins**

Anne Parr was made redundant from Cleves plc on 1 April 2008. Anne received £88,000 on 15 September 2008 made up of a bonus of £14,000 in respect of the year ended 31 March 2008 and an unexpected *ex gratia* payment of £74,000 as compensation for loss of office.

On 1 October 2008 Anne set up her own consultancy business from home. She had submitted a business plan to her bank on the basis that she would be self-employed which showed the following projected profit figures.

Period 1 October 2008 – 30 June 2009	£27,750 (net of depreciation of £3,200)
Year to 30 June 2010	£42,800 (net of depreciation of £2,560)

The depreciation charges relate to the purchase of a motor car for £11,000 and office equipment costing £5,000 in October 2008. The private use of the motor vehicle is 70%. No other items included in the net profit figures require adjustment for trading income purposes.

In the business plan Anne also forecast the following pattern of standard-rated supplies (exclusive of VAT).

1 October 2008 – 31 March 2009	£4,200 per month
1 April 2009 onwards	£6,300 per month

She has negotiated a six-month contract with Longhorn Ltd, for a fixed fee of £36,000. Anne was not in a position to undertake any other work during the assignment. A large part of the current assignment was carried out at Longhorn Ltd's premises and the company provided Anne with the use of an assistant while she was there. Anne was expected to report on the progress of her assignment on a weekly basis to the managing director. Anne has not so far obtained any firm promises of work from other companies, but Longhorn Ltd has indicated that it might well be in a position to offer her further work.

Longhorn Ltd is a trading company, with no associates, which is expected to pay corporation tax at the small companies' rate. It is expected to make standard-rated supplies of £220,000 pa, zero-rated supplies of £30,000 pa, and exempt supplies of £70,000 pa for VAT purposes (all amounts are stated exclusive of any VAT). Longhorn Ltd's annual input VAT (disregarding any payments to Anne) is currently expected to be £34,743 of which £4,700 will be directly attributable to the exempt supplies and £8,900 will relate to general overheads.

All payments to Anne would be regarded as part of general overheads for VAT purposes. All of the company's input VAT relates to expenditure which is allowable in computing taxable profits.

Longhorn Ltd's draft profit before tax figure for the year ended 31 March 2009 has been calculated at £149,000, after crediting or deducting the following items.

	£
Depreciation of fixed assets	16,225
Amortisation of intangible asset acquired 1 July 2008	3,650
Directors' remuneration	
(including £14,000 accrued but not due to be paid until 31 March 2010)	56,000
Medical insurance paid for employees	9,250
Fine in respect of breach of trading standards	3,850
Release of specific provision for bad debts	4,500
Profit on sale of office	
(capital gain computed for tax purposes is £28,070)	42,875
Profit on sale of government security	850
Gifts of £250 each to employees passing professional examinations	2,000
Gifts of brandy to customers (costing £14 per customer)	2,268
Subscription to political party which has promised	
to reduce costs for UK businesses	10,000
Advisers' fees in relation to issue of new shares	3,750
Interest paid on loan to acquire overseas investment	3,020
Dividend received from overseas investment	
(gross amount – inclusive of 10% foreign withholding tax)	4,800
Bank interest receivable from non-trade funds	2,850

No capital allowances were due in respect of plant and machinery for the period. Any potential tax implications arising from payments to Anne are to be disregarded for these purposes.

In August 2007 Longhorn Ltd bought a site costing £175,000, including legal fees of £8,750; in the course of the year, the company built a sports pavilion on the site for its employees at a cost of £280,000, including architect's fees of £14,000. All of the costs were capitalised in the accounts of the company.

In October 2008 the company made a qualifying investment of £27,000 under the Corporate Venturing Scheme.

Required

(a) Explain the taxation treatment of the two sums received by Anne, indicating whether your analysis would be different if she had been contractually entitled to receive the payment of £74,000. **(3 marks)**

(b) Prepare a report for Anne concerning her consultancy business. The report should be in three sections, addressing the issues set out below, and should, where appropriate, include supporting calculations.

  (i) Self-employed status

  Discuss whether Anne is likely to be classified as employed or self-employed in respect of her contract with Longhorn Ltd.

  Explain the factors that HMRC are likely to consider. **(7 marks)**

  (ii) Projected taxable trading income

  Advise Anne what her trading income assessments will be for the first three tax years of her business assuming that she is classified as self-employed in respect of her consultancy activities.

  You should also indicate the amount of any overlap profits arising and how they can be relieved. **(6 marks)**

  (iii) VAT

  State the date from which Anne would be obliged to register for VAT and the date on which she should start charging VAT.

  You should assume that the current VAT registration threshold will remain unchanged.

  Indicate the main consequence for Anne if she fails to register by the due date. **(4 marks)**

(c) Compare the annual after-tax cost to Longhorn Ltd of using Anne's services on the alternative assumptions that:

   (i) Anne is an employee of the company who will receive a salary of £36,000 pa and who will not be contracted out for NIC purposes, and

   (ii) Anne is a self-employed contractor who will charge the company annual fees of £36,000 plus VAT.

   (7 marks)

(d) Compute the corporation tax payable by Longhorn Ltd for the accounting period ended 31 March 2009, briefly explaining why you have allowed or disallowed each item of expenditure and income.

   You should assume that all amounts are stated inclusive of any irrecoverable VAT. **(10 marks)**

Appropriateness of the format and presentation of the report and the effectiveness with which its advice is communicated. **(2 marks)**

You may assume that the tax rates and allowances for the tax year 2008/09 and the Financial Year to 31 March 2009 will continue to apply for the foreseeable future.

(Total = 39 marks)

8 Ming Khan and Nina Lee

49 mins

Your manager has had a meeting with Ming Khan and Nina Lee, who are in partnership running a music recording studio, and has sent you a copy of the following meeting notes.

To	The files
From	Tax manager
Date	1 November 2009

Subject Ming Khan and Nina Lee – partnership

This was the first meeting with Ming Khan (MK) and Nina Lee (NL). They provided the following information:

MK and NL – background

MK was previously employed by a music company with an annual salary of £42,000. She was made redundant on 28 February 2008, and received an *ex gratia* redundancy payment of £60,000.

NL was previously a student. She had inherited an investment property on the death of her parents and sold this for £125,000 on 31 March 2008 in order to finance her partnership capital. The disposal resulted in a chargeable gain of £39,600. Until March 2008 NL received rental income of £6,250 pa.

Partnership – background

The partnership commenced trading on 1 May 2008. Profits and losses are shared between MK and NL 60:40.

The partnership is registered for VAT and all of its supplies are standard rated.

Their first accounts for the 15 month period to 31 July 2009 show a tax adjusted trading loss (*before* capital allowances) of £71,250.

Capital expenditure

On 12 May 2008 the partnership purchased a freehold building and converted it into a recording studio during May and June of 2008 at a cost of £211,500, made up as follows:

	£
Land and building	69,500
Recording equipment	70,300
Installation of electrical system for the recording equipment	19,400
Sound insulation	13,200
Replacement doors and windows	2,500
Heating system	5,100
VAT	31,500
	211,500

MK and NL have decided not to claim the AIA in respect of any or the above expenditure but will claim full writing down allowances for the fifteen month period to 31 July 2009.

Partnership's financial position

The partnership needs to purchase computer equipment costing £61,100, but does not have sufficient funds to do so outright. The computer equipment can either be leased for three years at a cost of £28,200 pa or can be bought on hire-purchase for an initial payment of £11,100 (including VAT of £9,100), followed by 35 monthly payments of £2,000.

The computer equipment will be replaced after three years' use, at which time it will be worthless. MK and NL want to know the tax implications of each alternative method of financing the computer equipment.

All figures are inclusive of VAT where relevant.

Tax manager

An extract from an email from your manager is set out below.

Please prepare a memorandum for me, incorporating the following:

1   Calculations to show how the partnership's trading loss for the 15-month period to 31 July 2009 will be allocated between MK and NL for 2008/09 and 2009/10.

2   State the possible ways of relieving the trading loss.

3   Advise MK and NL on the most beneficial loss relief claims for them. Calculate the tax refunds that they will receive.

4   Advise MK and NL of the income tax and the VAT implications of acquiring the computer equipment by hire purchase or leasing.

Tax manager

Required

(a)   Prepare the memorandum requested by your manager.

Marks are available for the four components of the memorandum as follows:

1   Calculation of the partnership's trading loss for the 15-month period and its allocation to the 2008/09 and 2009/10 tax years.

Your calculations should be made on a monthly basis.   **(3 marks)**

2   Stating the options for relieving the trading loss   **(4 marks)**

3   Advising on the most beneficial claims for MK and NL and calculating the tax refunds that will be due to them.

You should ignore the possibility of any repayment supplement being due.   **(9 marks)**

4   Explaining the income tax and VAT implications for the partnership of hire purchasing or leasing the computer equipment.

You should ignore the implications of SSAP 21: *Accounting for leases and Hire-Purchase Contracts*.

(6 marks)

Appropriateness of the format and presentation of the memorandum and the effectiveness with which the information is communicated.
(2 marks)

You may assume that the rules, rates and allowances for the tax year 2008/09 apply for all relevant years.

(b)   Set out briefly the steps you would take when commencing to act for MK, NL and the partnership. **(3 marks)**

(Total = 27 marks)

9 Kara Weddell (ATAX 12/07)   63 mins

You have received the following email from your manager, Kara Weddell.

From:	Kara Weddell
Date:	3 December 2009
To:	Tax senior
Subject:	Banda Ross

I've put a copy of a letter from a potential new client, Banda Ross, on your desk. I've arranged a meeting with Banda for Friday this week to discuss the most appropriate structure for her new business, 'Aral'.

I spoke to Banda yesterday and obtained the following additional information.

- Banda has owned the whole of the ordinary share capital of Flores Ltd since 1 January 2006.
- Flores Ltd pays Banda a salary of £11,700 per annum and pays dividends to her of £20,250 on 31 July each year.
- Banda does not intend to take any income from Aral until the tax year 2012/13 at the earliest.
- Flores Ltd is Banda's only source of income.

Banda also mentioned that Flores Ltd made some sort of 'informal loan' to her in 2006 of £21,000 to pay for improvements to her house. I decided not to press her about this over the phone but I need to discuss with her what she meant by 'informal' and whether or not the loan has been disclosed to HM Revenue and Customs.

Please prepare the following schedules for me to use as a basis for our discussions. I will give Banda copies of schedules (a) and (b) but not schedule (c), as some of its contents may be sensitive.

(a)   Calculations of the anticipated tax adjusted trading profit/loss of Aral for its first three trading periods.

(b)   Explanations, together with relevant supporting calculations, of the tax relief available in respect of the anticipated trading losses depending on whether the business is run as a sole trader or a limited company. When considering the use of a limited company, don't forget that it could be owned by Banda or by Flores Ltd.

Please include a recommendation based on your figures but do not address any other issues regarding the differences between trading as a sole trader and as a company; I just want to focus on the losses for the moment.

(c)   Explanatory notes of the tax implications of there being a loan from Flores Ltd to Banda and whether or not such a loan might affect our willingness to provide her with tax advice.

Take some time to think about your approach to this before you start; I want you to avoid preparing any unnecessary calculations and to keep the schedules brief.

Thank you

Kara

The letter referred to in Kara's email is set out below.

Dear Kara

Aral business

I am the managing director of Flores Ltd, a company that manufactures waterskiing equipment. I am looking for a tax adviser to help me with my next business venture.

When I began the Flores business in 2004 it was expected to make losses for the first year or so. I was advised not to form a company but to trade as a sole trader and to offset the losses against my income of earlier years. I followed that advice and transferred the business to Flores Ltd on 1 January 2006, once it had become profitable.

Flores Ltd has made taxable trading profits of approximately £120,000 each year since it was formed. It prepares accounts to 30 June each year.

For the past few months I have been researching the windsurfing market. I must have spent at least £6,000 travelling around the UK visiting retailers and windsurfing clubs (half of which was spent on buying people lunch!).

However, it was all worth while as on 1 January 2010 I intend to start a new business, 'Aral', manufacturing windsurfing equipment.

The budgeted results for the first three trading periods of the Aral business are set out below:

		£
6 months ending 30 June 2010	Trading loss	(12,500)
Year ending 30 June 2011	Trading loss	(13,000)
Year ending 30 June 2012	Trading profit	77,000

The figures above have been adjusted for tax purposes but take no account of the tax relief available in respect of the premises and equipment to be acquired on 2 January 2010.

I have negotiated the purchase of a small industrial unit. The building was constructed at a cost of £160,000. This included £50,000 for the cost of the land.

The business will also purchase equipment (machinery, computers, shelving etc) in January 2010 at a cost of £33,500. The equipment should last approximately three years so there will be no further acquisitions until the year ending 30 June 2013.

The next decision I need to make is whether the new business should trade as a company or as an unincorporated entity. It would make more sense commercially to form a company immediately but I would be willing to use the same approach as I used when establishing the Flores business if this maximises the relief obtained in respect of the trading losses. I want to obtain relief for the losses now; I do not want the losses carried forward for relief in the future unless there are no other options available.

Yours sincerely

Banda

Required

Prepare the schedules requested by Kara.

Marks are available for the three schedules as follows:

(a) Tax adjusted trading profit/loss of the new business (Aral) for its first three trading periods. **(6 marks)**

(b) The tax relief available in respect of the anticipated trading losses, together with supporting calculations and a recommended structure for the business. **(16 marks)**

(c) Explanatory notes, together with relevant supporting calculations, in connection with the loan. **(10 marks)**

Additional marks will be awarded for the appropriateness of the format and presentation of the schedules, the effectiveness with which the information is communicated and the extent to which the schedules are structured in a logical manner. **(3 marks)**

Notes:

1. You should assume that the tax rates and personal allowance for the tax year 2008/09 and for the Financial Year to 31 March 2009 apply throughout the question.
2. You should ignore value added tax (VAT).

(Total = 35 marks)

10 Amy (ATAX 12/04)   40 mins

Amy is 43 years old. She is single and does not have any children.

The following information has been extracted from client files and from meetings with Amy. Assume that today's date is 1 May 2009.

Amy:

- Resident and ordinarily resident in the UK since 2003/04.
- Domiciled overseas.
- Pays £5,000 into personal pension each year.
- Has not made any lifetime transfers of assets before this year.
- Concerned about future inheritance tax liabilities.

2008/09 remuneration package:

- Salary of £23,000 (PAYE deducted of £5,085).
- Diesel company car, list price of £15,000 and an emission rate of 170 grams per km.
- Fuel for both private and business use.

Investment income:

- National Savings & Investments easy access account interest of £180 (amount received).
- UK bank deposit account interest of £400 (amount received).
- Overseas bank interest of £10,000 (amount received) withholding tax of 20% has been deducted at source. None of this interest was remitted to the UK.
- Dividend of £1,800 (amount received) from 50,000 £1 ordinary shares in Red plc, a UK quoted company.
- Dividend of £1,300 (amount received) from Black Inc, a company quoted overseas. Withholding tax of 35% had been deducted at source. Only £650 of this net dividend was remitted to the UK.

Property business income:

Overseas property

- £850 rent per month.
- Withholding tax of 15% deducted at source.
- Full net amount remitted to the UK.
- Gifted to her brother, Michael, on 6 November 2008 (see below).

UK property

- £1,340 rent per month (net of letting expenses).
- Not her main residence and has never been used as a business asset.
- £140 per month interest paid on loan taken out to purchase the property.
- Gifted to her brother, Michael, on 6 January 2009 (see below).

Gifts made to her brother, Michael, during the year to 5 April 2009:

- *1 June 2008:* 50,000 £1 ordinary shares in Red plc, quoted at 221–229p, with daily bargains of 219p, 220p and 225p. Inherited in April 2006 (probate value £20,000) from her aunt, who bought them in March 2001 for £17,200. Amy has never worked for Red plc and holds less than 5% of the shares.
- *6 November 2008:* the overseas property, market value £245,000; purchased August 2003 for £220,000.
- *6 January 2009:* the UK property, market value £125,000; purchased in June 1995 for £67,000.

Future plans:

- Intends to gift her main residence to her niece, Erica, on 1 June 2009.
- Current market value is £400,000; purchased in January 2002 for £235,000.
- Has always been Amy's main residence and intends to continue to live there after the gift.

Required

(a) (i) State the basis on which Amy will be charged to income tax (IT), capital gains tax (CGT) and inheritance tax (IHT) given her UK residence and ordinary residence and non-UK domicile status.

(3 marks)

(ii) Calculate Amy's IT, CGT and IHT payable for 2008/09, assuming she makes any beneficial claims and clearly identifying any actions she can take to defer the chargeable gains that have arisen. **(13 marks)**

(b) (i) Explain the inheritance tax (IHT) implications of Amy making the gift of her main residence to her niece, and calculate the IHT arising if Amy should die on 1 September 2013. Assume that the value of the property will still be £400,000, that Amy retains her non-UK domicile for the purpose of inheritance tax and that the tax rates and allowances for 2008/09 apply throughout. **(5 marks)**

(ii) Suggest a way by which the IHT liability calculated in (i) above could be reduced and indicate any other tax implications arising from this advice. **(1 mark)**

(Total = 22 marks)

11 John Robinson (ATAX 6/08)   67 mins

You have received the following memorandum from your manager, Irwin Allen.

To:	Tax senior
From:	Irwin Allen
Date:	2 June 2011
Subject:	John and Maureen Robinson

I had a meeting with John Robinson and his wife Maureen yesterday. They have two children; Will, aged seven and Penny, aged nine. John and Maureen have made a number of errors in their income tax returns and Maureen requires advice in connection with her business.

Errors in income tax returns

John inherited a portfolio of quoted shares, an investment property and a large sum of cash in May 2008. Whilst completing his tax return for 2008/09 he decided to 'give' all the income arising from the shares, property and cash deposits to his wife for tax purposes. Accordingly, he omitted the income from his own tax return and included it in that of his wife. He did the same thing in 2009/10.

John has since realised that such a 'gift' has no effect for tax purposes and has decided to notify HM Revenue and Customs (HMRC) of his mistake.

In January 2009 John gave the investment property to Maureen who sold it a week later. The gift to Maureen was the subject of a legitimate legal conveyance but, after the sale, Maureen gave the sales proceeds to John in accordance with an agreement they had made prior to the gift. Maureen declared the capital gain of £13,470 in her 2008/09 income tax return. John used his annual exemption for 2008/09 on a disposal in September 2008.

John has asked us to calculate the additional tax payable as a result of his mistaken declaration to HMRC. A schedule prepared by John summarising the family's income for the two years 2008/09 and 2009/10 together with details of the investment property is on your desk. The gain on the sale of the investment property was the couple's only capital gain in the last four years.

Maureen's business

Maureen began trading as Robinson Mapping on 1 November 2008. She registered for value added tax (VAT) immediately and prepared her first accounts to 30 September 2009. A schedule prepared by Maureen summarising the results of the business is also on your desk.

Maureen supplies specialised maps to businesses in the leisure industry. All of her customers are registered for VAT. The business has recoverable input tax of approximately £300 per quarter. Despite accounting for VAT on an annual basis, Maureen is finding the administration of the tax very time consuming and is considering deregistering unless the amount of administration can be reduced.

Please prepare the following for me.

(a) A calculation of the additional taxes payable by John Robinson in respect of the tax years 2008/09 and 2009/10 as a result of disclosing to HMRC the errors in his tax returns.

There's quite a bit to do here; please ensure that your calculations are clear and logical so that they are easy to follow. You'll need to work out the extra tax payable by John on the investment income and compare it with the tax paid by Maureen (probably a fairly small amount as most if no all of her income will have fallen into her basic rate band).

Please **do not** address the issue of interest and penalties for the moment.

(b) Advice for Maureen on her ability to deregister for the purposes of VAT together with the procedure she should follow and implications of deregistration. Include details of any alternative strategy that might solve her problem.

I do not want you to write a letter or to prepare illustrative calculations; just write the necessary paragraphs for me to incorporate in a letter that will cover a number of other issues.

Thank you

Irwin

The schedule summarising all of the family's income, with the exception of that relating to Maureen's business, is set out below.

Robinson Family – Income received in tax years 2008/09 and 2009/10			
	Notes	*2008/09* £	*2009/10* £
Income arising on inherited assets:			
Dividend income received in respect of share portfolio		8,856	9,108
Rental income in respect of investment property		2,550	–
Bank interest income received in respect of cash deposits		2,424	2,576
John – other income:			
Salary		29,400	30,500
Company car	1		
Trust income received	2	720	780
Maureen – other income:			
Unincorporated business	3		
Will – bank deposit interest received	4	Nil	88
Penny – bank deposit interest received	4	Nil	144

Notes

1 I have had use of the car since 1 August 2008 for both business and private use. I also receive free petrol in respect of all of my mileage. The car had a list price when new of £17,400 and has a CO_2 emission rate of 182 grams per kilometre.

2 The trust is a discretionary trust established by my uncle.

3 Maureen will provide you with a summary of the results of her business.

4 I transferred cash from my bank account to two new accounts for the children on 1 June 2009. The interest is credited gross as there is no tax liability on the children's income.

The schedule summarising the result of Maureen's business is set out below.

Maureen Robinson – Robinson Mapping

- Began trading on 1 November 2008.

- Purchased a computer and other equipment for £55,850 (excluding value added tax (VAT)) in the first month of trading.

- Tax adjusted trading profits, before deduction of capital allowances.

Period ended 30 September 2007	£73,729
Year ended 30 September 2008	£31,998

Required

(a) Prepare a calculation of the additional taxes payable by John and Maureen Robinson in respect of the tax years 2008/09 and 2009/10 as a result of disclosing to HMRC the errors in their tax returns. **(26 marks)**

Additional marks will be awarded for the clarity with which the information is presented and the extent to which the calculations are structured in a logical manner. **(2 marks)**

(b) Advise Maureen on deregistration for the purposes of valued added tax (VAT) and any possible alternative strategy. **(8 marks)**

An additional mark will be awarded for the effectiveness with which the information is communicated. **(1 mark)**

Assume that the tax rates and allowances for 2008/09 apply to subsequent years.

(Total = 37 marks)

CAPITAL TAXES

Questions 12 to 18 cover capital taxes. This is the subject of Chapters 11 to 19 in the BPP study text.

---

12 Rowan Sorbus   38 mins

Rowan Sorbus, aged 47, died on 23 March 2009.

The following information has been extracted from client files and from meetings with Rowan.

Rowan Sorbus:

- Rowan made no gifts during his lifetime, other those detailed below.

Domestica Limited shares:

- Owned 30% of the £1 ordinary shares of this unquoted trading company at the date of his death.
- Remaining shares were held as follows:

National Charity	25%
Rowan's son	10%
Unconnected persons	35%

- Originally acquired a 65% holding in April 2007 for £650,000.
- Neither Rowan nor his son have ever been employed by Domestica Limited nor been an officer of the company.
- Gifted the charity's shareholding to it on 10 July 2008.
- Gifted his son's shareholding to him on 20 July 2008.
- Values of the shares have been agreed by HMRC as follows:

% holding	July 2008 £	March 2009 £
65%	2,100,000	2,250,000
55%	1,450,000	1,500,000
40%	850,000	900,000
30%	650,000	700,000
25%	500,000	550,000
10%	150,000	175,000

Other assets owned at date of death:

- 100% of the shares in Aria Limited, an unquoted trading company. Acquired for £1,000 in October 2005. Value on 23 March 2009 has been agreed by HMRC at £100,000.
- Property used in Domestica Limited's trade, acquired in April 2007 for £200,000. Valued in March 2009 at £750,000.
- Property used in Aria Limited's trade, acquired in September 2006 for £100,000. Valued in March 2009 at £175,000. Outstanding mortgage of £75,000.
- Other net assets valued for IHT purposes on 23 March 2009 at £650,000, after taking account of outstanding personal tax liabilities owed at this date.

Other information:

- Residue of estate left to his son.
- Son sold all his shares in Domestica Limited in December 2009 for £1,500,000.

Required

(a) Explain the inheritance tax implications resulting from Rowan's death on 23 March 2009. Your answer should include a calculation of any inheritance tax liabilities arising and also an explanation of the basis for valuing his shares in Domestica Limited and of any reliefs which are available. **(13 marks)**

(b) Explain the capital gains tax implications arising as a result of the gifts in July 2008 and the sale by Rowan's son in December 2009. Your answer should include a calculation of any chargeable gains arising, assuming that all reliefs available to minimise these gains are claimed, and include an explanation of those reliefs and why they are beneficial.

You should assume that the rates and allowances for 2008/09 apply throughout this part of the question.
(8 marks)

(Total = 21 marks)

13 Christopher (ATAX 6/06) **36 mins**

Christopher died suddenly on 5 February 2009.

The following information has been extracted from client files and from meetings.

Christopher:

- Widower, aged 76.
- One child, Eleanor, who is 44 years old and single.

Lifetime gifts:

- *9 August 2001:* Gift of property worth £262,000 to a discretionary trust.
- *10 April 2004:* Gift of £75,000 cash into the same discretionary trust.
- Christopher paid any tax due on the gifts.

Probate values of assets in death estate:

- Residence – £550,000.
- ISA account – £12,000.
- Cash deposits – £40,000.
- Shares in Penfold Limited – £85,000.
- Shares in Boise plc (see below).

Cash deposits and Penfold Limited shares:

- Received £30,000 in cash and 5,000 shares in Penfold Limited, with a probate value of £14 each, from his deceased uncle's estate in August 2007. Inheritance tax of £5,000 was paid by the estate in respect of Christopher's legacy.
- Penfold Limited is an unquoted UK trading company.
- The 5,000 shares (which had been owned by Christopher's uncle for five years prior to his death) represent 5% of the company's share capital.

Boise plc shares:

- 15,000 ordinary £1 shares in Boise plc, a UK quoted company.
- Holding represents 2% of the company's issued share capital.
- Cum dividend price per share on 5 February 2009 was 700p – 708p, with marked bargains at 701p, 702p and 707p.
- A dividend of 18p per share had been declared on 15 January 2009.
- This was received on 20 February 2009.

Eleanor:

- Sole beneficiary of Christopher's estate.
- Wealthy in her own right paying income tax at the higher rate.
- Intends to gift assets worth £50,000 to her friend, Sam and is considering three options (see below).
- Has made no previous lifetime gifts.

Three options for gift to Sam:

- Three paintings valued at £50,000. Eleanor paid £25,000 for a set of four paintings in June 1996. Sold one painting for £9,000 in January 2003, when remaining paintings were valued at £31,000.
- Cash of £50,000 from the inheritance she is shortly to receive following the death of her father.
- 5,000 shares worth £50,000 representing a 5% holding in Grange Limited, an unquoted UK trading company. Acquired by Eleanor for £17,500 in May 1994.

Required

(a) Calculate the inheritance tax (IHT) liability arising as a result of Christopher's death. **(11 marks)**

(b) Evaluate the capital gains tax (CGT) and inheritance tax (IHT) implications of each of the three options being considered by Eleanor, and recommend the most tax efficient solution. Assume that any gift will be made in June 2009, that Eleanor will have already utilised her CGT and IHT annual exemptions for the tax year 2009/10 and that gift relief will not be claimed. **(9 marks)**

You should assume that the rates and allowances for the tax year 2008/09 apply throughout this question.

(Total = 20 marks)

14 Noland (ATAX 12/07) **32 mins**

Crusoe has contacted you following the death of his father, Noland. Crusoe has inherited the whole of his father's estate and is seeking advice on his father's capital gains tax position and the payment of inheritance tax following his death.

The following information has been extracted from client files and from telephone conversations with Crusoe.

Noland – personal information:

- Divorcee whose only other relatives are his sister, Avril, and two grandchildren.
- Died suddenly on 1 October 2009 without having made a will.
- Under the laws of intestacy, the whole of his estate passes to Crusoe.

Noland – income tax and capital gains tax:

- Sales of quoted shares resulted in:
- Chargeable gains of £7,100 and allowable losses of £17,800 in the tax year 2009/10.
- Chargeable gains of approximately £14,000 each tax year from 2002/03 to 2008/09.

Noland – gifts made during lifetime:

- On 1 December 2001 Noland gave his house to Crusoe.
- Crusoe has allowed Noland to continue living in the house and has charged him rent of £120 per month since 1 December 2001. The market rent for the house would be £740 per month.
- The house was worth £240,000 at the time of the gift and £310,000 on 1 October 2009.
- On 1 November 2006 Noland transferred quoted shares worth £247,000 to a discretionary trust for the benefit of his grandchildren.

Noland – probate values of assets held at death:

	£
Portfolio of quoted shares	370,000
Shares in Kurb Ltd	38,400
Chattels and cash	22,300
Domestic liabilities including income tax payable	(1,686)

- It should be assumed that these values will not change for the foreseeable future.

Kurb Ltd:

- Unquoted trading company
- Noland purchased the shares on 1 December 2007.

Crusoe:

- Long-standing personal tax client of your firm.
- Married with two young children.
- Successful investment banker with very high net worth.
- Intends to gift the portfolio of quoted shares inherited from Noland to his aunt, Avril, who has very little personal wealth.

Required

(a) Prepare explanatory notes together with relevant supporting calculations in order to quantify the tax relief potentially available in respect of Noland's capital losses realised in 2009/10. **(4 marks)**

(b) State the immediate tax implications of the proposed gift of the share portfolio to Avril and identify an alternative strategy that would achieve Crusoe's objectives whilst avoiding a possible tax liability in the future. State any deadline(s) in connection with your proposed strategy. **(5 marks)**

(c) On the assumption that the administrators of Noland's estate will sell quoted shares in order to fund the inheritance tax due as a result of his death, calculate the value of the quoted shares that will be available to transfer to Avril. You should include brief notes of your treatment of the house and the shares in Kurb Ltd. **(9 marks)**

Note: you should assume that the tax rates and allowances for the tax year 2008/09 apply throughout this question.

(Total = 18 marks)

15 Stanley Beech (Pilot Paper)   32 mins

Stanley Beech, a self-employed landscape gardener, intends to transfer his business to Landscape Ltd, a company formed for this purpose.

The following information has been extracted from client files and from meetings with Stanley.

Stanley:

- Acquired a storage building for £46,000 on 1 July 2000 and began trading.
- Has no other sources of income.
- Has capital losses brought forward from 2004/05 of £11,400.

The whole of the business is to be transferred to Landscape Ltd on 1 September 2009:

- The market value of the assets to be transferred is £118,000.
- The assets include the storage building and goodwill, valued at £87,000 and £24,000 respectively, and various small pieces of equipment and consumable stores.
- Landscape Ltd will issue 5,000 £1 ordinary shares as consideration for the transfer.

Advice given to Stanley in respect of the sale of the business:

- 'No capital gains tax will arise on the transfer of your business to the company.'
- 'You should take approximately 30% of the payment from Landscape Ltd in shares with the balance left on a loan account payable to you by the company, such that you can receive a cash payment in the future.'

Advice given to Stanley in respect of his annual remuneration from Landscape Ltd:

- 'The payment of a dividend of £21,000 is more tax efficient than paying a salary bonus of £21,000 as you will pay income tax at only 25% on the dividend received, whereas you would pay income tax at 40% on a salary bonus. The dividend also avoids the need to pay national insurance contributions.'
- 'There is no tax in respect of an interest free loan from an employer of less than £5,000.'
- 'The provision of a company car is tax neutral as the cost of providing it is deductible in the corporation tax computation.'

Stanley's proposed remuneration package from Landscape Ltd:

- An annual salary of £40,000 and an annual dividend of approximately £21,000.
- On 1 December 2009 an interest free loan of £3,600, which he intends to repay in two years' time.
- A company car with a cost when new of £11,400. The only costs incurred by the company in respect of this car will be lease rentals of £300 per month and business fuel of £100 per month.
- The annual employment income benefit in respect of the car is to be taken as £3,420.

Landscape Ltd:

- Will prepare accounts to 31 March each year.
- Will pay corporation tax at the rate of 21%.

Required

(a) (i) Explain why there would be no capital gains tax liability on the transfer of Stanley's business to Landscape Ltd in exchange for shares. Calculate the maximum loan account balance that Stanley could receive without giving rise to a capital gains tax liability and state the resulting capital gains tax base cost of the shares.   **(8 marks)**

(ii) Explain the benefit to Stanley of taking part of the payment for the sale of his business in the form of a loan account, which is to be paid out in cash at some time in the future.   **(1 mark)**

(b) Comment on the accuracy and completeness of the advice received by Stanley in respect of his remuneration package. Supporting calculations are only required in respect of the company car.   **(9 marks)**

Ignore value added tax (VAT) in answering this question.

You may assume that the rates and allowances for the financial year to 31 March 2009 and the tax year 2008/09 will continue to apply for the foreseeable future.

(Total = 18 marks)

16 Claus Rowen (Pilot Paper)   32 mins

Mahia Ltd is an unquoted, UK resident trading company formed in May 2002. One of its shareholders, Claus Rowen, intends to sell his shares back to Mahia Ltd on 31 July 2009. Another shareholder, Maude Brooke, intends to give some of her shares to her daughter, Tessa.

The following information has been extracted from client files and from meetings with the shareholders.

Mahia Ltd:

- In May 2002 the company issued 40,000 shares at £3.40 per share as follows:

Claus Rowen	16,000
Charlotte Forde	12,000
Olaf Berne	12,000

- Olaf sold his 12,000 shares to Maude Brooke on 1 October 2007 when they were worth £154,000.

Claus and Charlotte:

- Have always lived in the UK.
- Are higher rate taxpayers who use their capital gains tax annual exemption every year.

Maude:

- Was born in the UK, but moved to Canada on 1 April 2005 with her daughter, Tessa.
- Has not visited the UK since leaving for Canada, but will return to the UK permanently in December 2014.
- Is employed in Canada with an annual salary equivalent to £70,000.

Sale of shares by Claus:

- Charlotte and Maude want to expand the company's activities in the UK but Claus does not. The shareholders have been arguing over this matter for over a year. Claus resigned as a director of the company on 1 July 2008.
- In order to enable the company to prosper, Claus has agreed to sell his shares to the company on 31 July 2009.

Gift of shares by Maude:

- Maude will gift 4,000 shares in Mahia Ltd to her daughter, Tessa, on either 1 August 2009 or 1 June 2010.
- She will delay the gift until 1 June 2010 (Tessa's wedding day) if this reduces the total tax due.
- The tax due in Canada will be the same regardless of the date of the gift.
- She has made no previous transfers of value for UK inheritance tax purposes.
- For the purposes of this gift, you should assume that Maude will die on 31 December 2013.

Market values of shares in Mahia Ltd on all relevant dates are to be taken as:

Size of shareholding %	Market value per share £
< 25	10.20
25 – 35	14.40
> 35	38.60

Market values of the assets of Mahia Ltd on all relevant dates are to be taken as:

	£
Land and buildings used within the trade	1,400,000
Three machines of equal value used within the trade	15,000
Motor cars used by employees	45,000
Quoted shares	42,000
Inventory, trade receivables and cash	145,000

Required

(a) Advise Claus on the tax treatment of the proceeds he will receive in respect of the sale of his shares to Mahia Ltd. Prepare a calculation of the net (after tax) proceeds from the sale based on your conclusions. **(8 marks)**

(b) Advise Maude on the UK tax consequences of gifting the shares to Tessa and prepare computations to determine on which of the two dates the gift should be made, if the total UK tax due on the gift is to be minimised. Your answer should consider all relevant taxes. **(10 marks)**

You may assume that the rates and allowances for the tax year 2008/09 will continue to apply for the foreseeable future.

(Total = 18 marks)

17 Paul and Sharon (ATAX 6/06)   52 mins

Your manager has had a meeting with Paul and Sharon Potter and has sent you a copy of the following memorandum.

To	The files
From	Tax manager
Date	12 July 2009
Subject	Paul and Sharon Potter – Tax issues

Paul Potter (PP)

- Resigned from Memphis plc on 1 June 2009.
- Holds options over 5,000 company shares, granted to him on 25 June 2006.
- The options are part of an approved company share option plan (CSOP), and the exercise price was agreed at £3.50 per share. The current market value of the shares is £6, and this is unlikely to change in the short-term.
- Has one month from the date of his resignation in which to exercise the share options and sell the shares, which are not transferable. Intends to do so as soon as possible.

Sharon Potter (SP)

- Has been running a business as a sole trader for the past three years.
- Wishes to incorporate the business and will hold 100% of the shares issued.
- Would like part of the consideration for the business to be in cash, but only if no tax is payable as a result.
- PP will work for the newly incorporated company.
- SP estimates that the business is worth £120,000, comprising the following assets:

Asset	Market value £	Indexed gain £
Cash	10,000	–
Goodwill	40,000	40,000
Property	70,000	40,000
Stock	10,000	–
Creditors	(10,000)	–

Trust planning

- PP wishes to set up a discretionary trust in the next few months for their children by gifting a residential property into the trust.
- This property was acquired for £70,000 in August 2007 and has a current market value of £160,000.

An extract from an email from your manager is set out below.

Please prepare a report from me to Paul and Sharon Potter setting out the following:

1   The condition that would need to be satisfied for the exercise of Paul's share options to be exempt from income tax and the tax implications if this condition is not satisfied.

       Calculate Paul's tax liability if he exercises the share options in Memphis plc and subsequently sells the shares immediately.

       Advise Paul how he may reduce this tax liability.

2   The conditions that must be satisfied if Sharon's business is to be sold to a company without incurring an immediate charge to capital gains tax (CGT).

       Advise Sharon whether or not she will be able to take advantage of such relief.

       Regardless of this advice calculate the maximum amount of cash she could receive on incorporation, without triggering a CGT liability.

       Are there any disadvantages to this relief that Sharon should be aware of?

       Is there an alternative relief she could use?

3   All of the capital taxation issues Paul needs to be aware of for the discretionary trust for the children.

Tax manager

You have extracted the following further information from client files.

- Paul and Sharon are both aged 38.
- Have two children, Gisella, aged 5 and Gavin aged 2.
- Both Paul and Sharon are higher rate taxpayers
- Neither Paul nor Sharon has made any capital disposals in the tax year 2009/10.
- Paul made a gross chargeable transfer of £212,000 in May 2005.
- The property acquired by Paul in August 2007 generates net rental income of £4,000 per annum.

Required

Prepare the report for Paul and Sharon requested by your manager. The report should be in three sections, addressing the issues set out below, and should, where appropriate, include supporting calculations.

(1)   Paul's share options

       State the condition that would need to be satisfied for the exercise of Paul's share options in Memphis plc to be exempt from income tax and the tax implications if this condition is not satisfied.

       Calculate Paul's tax liability if he exercises the share options in Memphis plc and subsequently sells the shares in Memphis plc immediately, as proposed, and show how he may reduce this tax liability. **(6 marks)**

(2)   Incorporation of Sharon's business

       State the conditions that must be satisfied if Sharon's business is to be sold to a company without incurring an immediate CGT charge, and advise Sharon whether or not she will be able to take advantage of such relief.

       Assuming the relief **is** available, advise Sharon on the maximum amount of cash she could receive on incorporation, without triggering a CGT liability.

       State any disadvantages to the relief that Sharon should be aware of, and identify and describe another relief that she might use. **(10 marks)**

(3)   Capital tax implications of the discretionary trust

Explain the capital tax issues that Paul needs to be aware of when he sets up a trust for Gisella and Gavin and the potential charges that could arise whilst the trust is in existence. Calculate the stamp duty land tax on the gift into the trust.   **(11 marks)**

Appropriateness of the format and presentation of the report and the effectiveness with which its advice is communicated.   **(2 marks)**

You may assume that the rates and allowances for the tax year 2008/09 continue to apply for the foreseeable future.

(Total = 29 marks)

18 Galileo (ATAX 6/08)   30 mins

Assume it is July 2008.

Kepler gave his nephew, Galileo, 600 shares (a 30% holding) in Messier Ltd on 1 June 2004. On 1 May 2008 Kepler died and left the remaining 1,400 shares in Messier Ltd to Galileo. Galileo intends to move to the UK from the country of Astronomeria to participate in the management of Messier Ltd.

The following information has been obtained from client files and meetings with the parties involved.

Kepler:

- Died on 1 May 2008
- Has two nephews; Galileo and Herschel
- In his will he left 1,400 shares in Messier Ltd valued at £546,000 to Galileo and the residue of his estate valued at £480,000 to Herschel

Kepler – Lifetime gifts:

- 1 February 2003   Gave a house to Herschel valued at £298,000
- 1 July 2003   Gave a watch costing £900 to each of his two nephews
- 1 June 2004   Gave 600 shares in Messier Ltd to Galileo (owned by Galileo at 1 May 2008)

Messier Ltd:

- Unquoted company that transports building materials
- Incorporated on 1 February 1996 when Kepler subscribed for 2,000 share, the whole of its share capital

Messier Ltd – Value of an ordinary share:

- As at:

	1 June 2004	1 May 2008
	£	£
As part of a 100% holding	485	570
As part of a 70% holding	310	390
As part of a 30% holding	230	260

Messier Ltd – Asset values:

- As at 1 June 2004

	£
Premises	900,000
Surplus land rented to third party	480,000
Vehicles	100,000
Current assets	50,000

Galileo:

- Resident, ordinary resident and domiciled in the country of Astronomeria where he has lived since birth
- Lives in rented accommodation in Astronomeria
- Intends to sell two paintings in order to provide funds to go towards the cost of relocating to the UK and purchasing a house here
- Has a full time employment contract with Messier Ltd commencing on 1 September 2008
- Intends to stay in the UK for at least five years

The two paintings:

- Are situated in Astronomeria and are worth approximately £20,000 each
- Have been owned by Galileo since 1 May 1994; their cost is negligible and can be ignored

Employment contract with Messier Ltd:

- Galileo will be paid an annual salary of £52,000
- Messier Ltd will assist Galileo with the cost of relocating to the UK

Required

(a) (i) Calculate the inheritance tax payable (if any) by Galileo in respect of (1) the gift of shares in June 2004 and (2) the inheritance of shares in May 2008. **(7 marks)**

(ii) Explain why Galileo is able to pay the inheritance due in instalments, state when the instalments are due and identify any further issues relevant to Galileo relating to the payments. **(3 marks)**

(b) Prepare a reasoned explanation of how any capital gains tax arising in the UK on the sale of the paintings can be minimised. **(2 marks)**

(c) (i) Explain how Messier Ltd can assist Galileo with the cost of relocating to the UK and/or provide him with interest-free loan finance for this purpose without increasing his UK income tax liability. **(3 marks)**

(ii) State, with reasons, whether Messier Ltd can provide Galileo with accommodation in the UK without giving rise to a UK income tax liability. **(2 marks)**

(Total = 17 marks)

TAXATION OF COMPANIES

Questions 19 to 27 cover the taxation of companies. This is the subject of Chapters 20 to 27 of the BPP study text.

---

19 Miller Plc   49 mins

Your manager has had a meeting with Fred Kildow, the finance director of Miller plc, and has sent you a copy of the following memorandum.

To	The files
From	Tax manager
Date	1 June 2009
Subject	Miller Plc

To simplify the group finance function Fred Kildow has moved all companies in the group to the same accounting year end. Miller plc's accounting date during 2009 has therefore changed from 31 July to 31 March.

1 August 2008 to 31 March 2009

The profit and loss account for the period from 1 August 2008 to 31 March 2009 shows a profit of £450,000 after accounting for the following items:

	£
Loss on disposal of machinery (Note 1)	30,000
Gift Aid donation accrued (paid 1 April 2009)	10,000
UK rental income	45,000
Advertising (Note 2)	60,000
Interest charged on overdue corporation tax	3,000
Dividend income (Note 3)	75,000
Debenture interest receivable (Note 3)	9,000

Note 1

The machinery had been used in the business and capital allowances had been claimed. It had originally cost £86,000 in January 1999 and was sold for £62,800 in October 2008. At the time of purchase, installation costs of £10,000 were charged in addition to the purchase price.

Note 2

The advertising included £37,750 for the hire of a corporate entertainment box at a sporting event. The cost was for the hire of the box and all food and drink. During the event, Miller plc displayed its corporate logo in the window of the box.

Note 3

In September 2008, Miller plc received a dividend of £13,500 from Bode Ltd, £27,000 from Hillman Ltd and £34,500 from Vogtli Inc. The dividend from Vogtli Inc was received gross as it was not subject to any withholding tax. Miller plc also received interest of £9,000 on a debenture loan to Bode Ltd.

Items not included in the profit and loss account

Miller plc incurred general expenses of £11,550 from the management of its various investments.

Miller plc sold its entire holding in Vogtli Inc for £120,000 on 31 January 2009.

Capital acquisitions

Miller plc purchased a Mercedes car on 1 August 2008 for £28,000. The Mercedes car was purchased for one of the directors with estimated private usage of 25%. On 1 September 2008 Miller plc also purchased a low carbon dioxide emission Jaguar car for £30,000 and new office furniture at a cost of £61,250. The annual investment allowance for the group is to be claimed by Miller plc.

Forecast group results – year ended 31 March 2010

Fred Kildow will be sending a copy of the group's forecast results for the year ended 31 March 2010.

He advised that Bloom Ltd is likely to break even in 2011. From 2012 onwards Bloom Ltd expects to reach trading profit levels of at least £500,000 per annum.

The other group companies do not expect their income levels to change.

The capital loss shown for Weinbrecht Ltd arose on the sale of an office building in November 2009 to a non-associated company.

Tax manager

An extract from an email from your manager is set out below.

Please prepare a report to Fred Kildow setting out the following:

1   Corporation tax liability

Provide a calculation of Miller plc's corporation tax liability for the period ended 31 March 2009.

I have calculated the indexed rise on the holding in Vogtli Inc from March 1999 to January 2009 to be £9,725.

You have extracted the following further information from client files.

● The Miller plc group operates a variety of related businesses aimed at retail customers.

● The group is as follows:

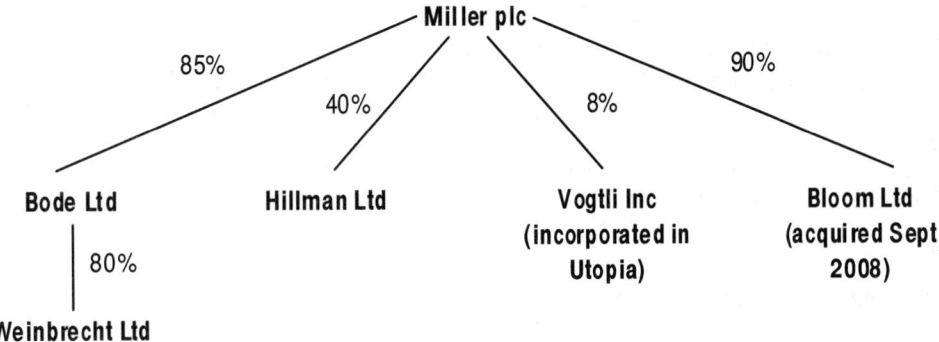

● Miller plc had brought forward trading losses of £95,000 at 1 August 2008.
● Miller plc qualifies as a medium-sized enterprise for capital allowances purposes.
● The tax written-down value of Miller plc's main pool on 1 August 2008 was £450,000.
● The holding in Vogtli Inc was acquired in March 1999 at a cost of £35,000.
● For VAT purposes Miller plc, Bode Ltd, and Hillman Ltd all make wholly standard rated supplies within the UK.
● 95% of Bloom Ltd's sales are to large businesses in the European Union.
● Weinbrecht Ltd specialises in the supply of insurance services and is therefore wholly exempt from VAT.

A copy of the forecast results arrives showing the following.

	Miller plc	Bode Ltd	Hillman Ltd	Weinbrecht Ltd	Bloom Ltd
	£	£	£	£	£
Trading profit / (Loss)	320,000	125,000	76,000	101,000	(600,000)
Chargeable gains / (Loss)	100,000			(45,000)	35,000
Property business income	70,000				
Interest income	10,000	60,000			20,000
Trading losses b/f					(50,000)

Required

Prepare the report requested by your manager to Fred Kildow. Marks are allocated as follows.

(a)   Corporation tax liability

Calculate Miller plc's corporation tax liability for the period ended 31 March 2009.   **(11 marks)**

(b) Group issues

State, with reasons, the nature of the relationships that exist between the various companies for corporation tax purposes in the year ending 31 March 2010 and briefly outline the consequences. **(4 marks)**

Explain the options available to utilise the losses within the group in the year ending 31 March 2010 and state the optimum use for each loss. **(5 marks)**

(c) VAT

Advise on the benefits of a VAT group.

Explain which companies, if any, should or should not be included in a VAT group registration. **(5 marks)**

Appropriateness of the format and presentation of the notes and the effectiveness with which their content is communicated. **(2 marks)**

You may assume that the rates and allowances for the Financial Year 2008 continue to apply for the foreseeable future.

(Total = 27 marks)

20 Flop Ltd (ATAX 6/05)   40 mins

You have recently been approached by Fred Flop. Fred informs you that he is experiencing problems in dealing with aspects of his company tax returns. The company accountant has been unable to keep up-to-date with matters, and Fred also believes that mistakes have been made in the past. Fred needs assistance.

The following information has been extracted from client files and from meetings with the shareholders. Assume that today's date is 10 May 2010.

Fred Flop:

- 100% shareholder of Flop Limited.
- Managing director.

Flop Limited:

- UK trading company.
- Taxable profits of £595,000 in the year ended 31 March 2008.
- Has one wholly owned subsidiary.
- Both companies have a 31 March year-end.

Corporation tax return (CT600) for the year ended 31 March 2008:

- The corporation tax return for this period was not submitted until 2 November 2009, and corporation tax of £123,500 was paid at the same time. Profits chargeable to corporation tax were stated as £741,800.
- A formal notice (CT203) requiring the company to file a self-assessment corporation tax return (dated 1 February 2009) had been received by the company on 4 February 2009.

Examination of the accounts and tax computation for the year ended 31 March 2008:

- A £10,000 repairs provision was made; there is no supporting information.
- £46,500 legal and professional fees allowed in full without any explanation. Fred has subsequently produced the following analysis:

Analysis of legal & professional fees

	£
Legal fees on a failed attempt to secure a trading loan	5,000
Debt collection agency fees	12,800
Obtaining planning consent for building extension	5,700
Accountant's fees for preparing accounts	14,000
Legal fees relating to a trade dispute	9,000

- No enquiry has yet been raised by HMRC.

CT600 for the year ended 31 March 2009:

- Has not been submitted yet.
- Accounts are late and nearing completion, with only one change still to be made.
- A notice requiring the company to file a self-assessment corporation tax return (CT203) dated 27 July 2009 was received on 1 August 2009. No corporation tax has yet been paid.
- Computation currently shows profits chargeable to corporation tax of £815,000 before accounting adjustments.
- A company owing Flop Ltd £50,000 (excluding VAT) has gone into liquidation, and it is unlikely that any of this money will be paid. The money has been outstanding since 3 September 2008, and the impairment loss (bad debt) will need to be included in the accounts.
- Computer equipment totalling £50,000 had been expensed in the accounts. No adjustment has been made in the tax computation. The annual investment allowance has already been used during the year ended 31 March 2009.

VAT issues:

- VAT return for the quarter ended 31 March 2010 was submitted on 5 May 2010, and VAT of £24,000 was paid at the same time.
- Previous return to 31 December 2009 was also submitted late.
- No account has been made for VAT on the bad debt.
- VAT return for 30 June 2010 may also be late. Estimated VAT liability is £8,250.

Required

(a) (i)   Calculate the revised corporation tax (CT) payable for the accounting periods ending 31 March 2008 and 2009 respectively. Your answer should include an explanation of the adjustments made as a result of the information which has now come to light and the practical steps needed to correct the position. **(6 marks)**

    (ii) State, giving reasons, the due payment date of the corporation tax (CT) and the filing date of the corporation tax return for each period, and identify any interest and penalties which may have arisen to date. **(7 marks)**

    Assume that the rates and allowances for Financial Year 2008 apply throughout this part and interest on overdue tax is 7.5%.

(b) Explain the consequences of filing the VAT returns late and advise Fred how he should deal with the underpayment and bad debt for VAT purposes. Your explanation should be supported by relevant calculations. **(9 marks)**

(Total = 22 marks)

21 Bargains Ltd

29 mins

Bargains Ltd is a close company that buys and sells antiques.

The following information has been extracted from client files and from meetings with the shareholders.

Shareholders:

- Rodney, Reggie and Del Rotter each own one third of Bargains Ltd's ordinary share capital.
- Rodney and Reggie are company directors.
- Del is not a company director or an employee.

Bargains Ltd:

- Incorporated 1 August 2008.
- Incurred advertising campaign expenditure on 1 February 2009.
- Commenced purchasing antiques for resale on 1 March 2009, but the business premises (see below) were not opened until 1 April 2009.
- On the same day the company registered for VAT and made its first sale.
- Accounts have been prepared for the period 1 August 2008 to 31 December 2009.

Capital acquisitions:

- Acquired business premises, which were in a bad state of repair, on 1 January 2009. Immediately started to repair and refurbish them.

- Bought three new motor cars costing £10,575 each (including VAT), on 1 July 2009 for the business and private use of Rodney, Reggie and Del.

- CO_2 emissions for the cars are 162 g/km. No private fuel is provided.

Interest free loan to Del:

- The company made an interest free loan of £42,000 to Del on 1 October 2009.
- Del used funds to purchase a holiday villa in Spain.
- The loan has not yet been repaid.

Required

(a) (i) Set out the accounting periods for Bargains Ltd up to, and including, 31 December 2009.

   (ii) How will Bargains Ltd's expenditure on its advertising campaign and the refurbishment of its business premises be treated for the purposes of corporation tax and VAT? **(6 marks)**

(b) What are the tax implications, for both Bargains Ltd and the Rotter brothers, arising from the provision of the three company motor cars? You should ignore the implications of NIC. **(6 marks)**

(c) Advise both Bargains Ltd and Del of the tax implications arising from the provision of the interest free loan.

(4 marks)

(Total = 16 marks)

22 Lorna Mill Ltd

45 mins

Your manager has had a meeting with the directors of Lorna Mill Ltd and has sent you a copy of the following memorandum.

To	The files
From	Tax manager
Date	1 June 2009
Subject	Lorna Mill Ltd

Tax position for year ended 31 March 2009

The directors informed me of the following information:

Adjusted trading profit for the year is £255,000, before considering the matters referred to below.

11 May 2008: £20,000 was spent restoring a country cottage to be lived in by Sam Bradley. It was estimated that £11,000 related to improvements, although the full expenditure had been written off in the profit and loss account.

20 February 2009: a loan of £7,100 to John Harmer, son of Frank Harmer, to assist him in purchasing a racing yacht. John will pay a market rate of interest on 30 June each year.

30 September 2008: the sale of a leasehold building for £125,000. This building was acquired by the company on 1 July 1999 for £100,000, when the lease had 30 years to run (indexed rise = 0.232).

Dividends received during the year from non-group companies were £27,000.

Proposed takeover

The directors of Lorna Mill Ltd have recently been approached by representatives of Evergreen plc who want to take over the company. They are offering a package of either cash or a combination of shares and loan stock (which will be qualifying corporate bonds) in exchange for either the shares held by the members of Lorna Mill Ltd or the trade itself from the company.

Tax manager

An extract from an email from your manager is set out below.

Please prepare a letter from me to the directors of Lorna Mill Ltd, setting out the following:

1	Calculations to show the corporation tax position for the company and its directors for the year ended 31 March 2009.

The appropriate lease percentage figures you will need to work with are:

30 yrs: 87.330
21 yrs: 74.635
20 yrs: 72.770

2   Explanations of your treatment of each item.

3   Advice on the tax considerations arising out of the takeover offers from Evergreen plc.

4   Other issues arising in respect of the proposed takeover offers.

You have extracted the following further information from Lorna Mill Ltd's client files.

- Lorna Mill Ltd was formed in 1985.

- The ordinary issued share capital of Lorna Mill Ltd is as follows:

Don Bradley FCA	(Chairman)	13,500
Sam Bradley	(Sales Director, brother of Chairman)	3,000
Mrs Anne Bradley	(Director, wife of Chairman)	2,000
Frank Harmer ACA		4,000
Chris Justice	(Production Director)	2,500
20 unrelated members of the public		2,500
Carol Laker	(Chairman's niece, not employed by the company)	2,500
Ordinary £1 shares		40,000

- All shareholders/ directors are higher rate taxpayers.

- The building sold on 30 September 2008 had been acquired using £100,000 of the proceeds from the sale of a freehold building. The freehold building had been acquired in May 1991 for £40,000 and was sold on 28 October 1998 for £130,000 (indexed rise = 0.310).

Required

Prepare the letter requested by your manager.

Marks are available for the components of the letter as follows:

1	Relevant calculations.	**(6 marks)**
2	Clear and concise explanations of your treatment of each item.	**(6 marks)**
3	The tax considerations of Evergreen plc's takeover offer.	**(7 marks)**
4	Any other considerations for the company in respect of the takeover proposals.	**(4 marks)**

Appropriateness of the format and presentation of the letter and the effectiveness with which the information is communicated. **(2 marks)**

You may assume that the rates and allowances for the tax year 2008/09 and Financial Year 2008 continue to apply for the foreseeable future.

(Total = 25 marks)

23 Trent Plc

Your firm has acted for many years as taxation advisors to Trent plc, which trades as a transportation company throughout the south of England.

The partner who deals with Trent plc's affairs has just received the following letter from Sally Kosar, the managing director.

STRICTLY PRIVATE AND CONFIDENTIAL

1 July 2009

Dear Nicholas

Proposed acquisition of Ivan Ltd

We are currently involved in negotiations with Reznik plc to purchase one of its 100% subsidiaries, Ivan Ltd, a removals firm. I would like your advice on certain aspects of this proposed acquisition and some other matters.

Method of acquisition

We have agreed in principle with Reznik plc to buy Ivan Ltd for a total of £35 million. We hope to effect the acquisition on 31 August 2009.

Ivan Ltd prepares accounts to 30 June each year, and preliminary figures suggest that as at 30 June 2009 it will have the following tax losses available to carry forward:

Trading losses	£16 million
Capital losses	£2 million
Total	£18 million

Once Trent plc has acquired Ivan Ltd we would intend to refocus its operations gradually so that it would concentrate less on their traditional residential removals market and more on supplying commercial customers. The intention would be to get to the point after about two or three years when Ivan's outlets would be engaged in much the same activities as our existing 'Trent' outlets. At that point we would want to merge the activities of the two companies so that one company could operate under a single name. We would be indifferent whether the outlets would be operated by Ivan Ltd or Trent plc.

Our financial forecasts indicate that Ivan Ltd will continue to make losses for the next two to three years so that by the time of the merger of the trades of Trent plc and Ivan Ltd I would expect the total trading losses in Ivan Ltd to have risen to £20 million.

Machinist House

We hope to be able to use a surplus freehold property, 'Machinist House', owned by Ivan Ltd, to create a further capital loss which Trent plc will be able to utilise against its anticipated capital gains.

Machinist House was purchased by Ivan Ltd for £12 million on 28 February 2002 and is currently worth about £7 million. Our valuers have indicated that they do not expect this value to change in the foreseeable future.

Trent plc has just commissioned builders to commence the construction of a new freehold headquarters for the group which will cost a total of £9 million exclusive of VAT. This new office is scheduled to be ready for occupation in the early part of the summer of 2010, and we anticipate being able to vacate and to sell our existing headquarters on or around 31 August 2010. We expect to sell the existing headquarters for a total of £13 million and would anticipate realising a capital gain on this sale of about £8 million after indexation allowance.

What I hope to do is to transfer Machinist House to Trent plc immediately after we have acquired Ivan Ltd so that it can be sold, and the capital loss realised, at about the same time we realise the capital gain on the sale of our existing headquarters. In this way I would hope to be able to shelter the bulk of the capital gain arising on the sale of the headquarters with the capital loss arising on the sale of Machinist House and the capital losses carried forward in Ivan Ltd.

Finally, our new office block will contain rather more office accommodation than we are going to need for many years. We are therefore negotiating to sub-let the surplus space and we have identified an insurance company which seems to be willing to rent this surplus from us. I understand that we are permitted to opt to tax the new building for VAT purposes and would appreciate your advice on the procedure and on the advantages and disadvantages of doing so.

It occurs to me that I have not as yet sought any tax advice on the Ivan Ltd acquisition and in particular I have assumed all of our business plans can be put into practice without any tax disadvantages and that we will have considerable freedom to use Ivan Ltd's tax losses as we wish. I do not know to what extent my assumptions are correct and I should be grateful if you could write to me and explain the tax position in relation to the various matters referred to in this letter.

Yours sincerely

Sally Kosar

Required

Draft a reply to Ms Kosar's letter. Your reply should:

(a) Explain the ways in which the various tax losses in Ivan Ltd are capable of being utilised following the acquisition of Ivan Ltd by Trent plc. **(9 marks)**

(b) Explain whether and if so to what extent Trent plc will be able to shelter its forecast capital gain on the sale of its existing headquarters using the forecast loss on the sale of Machinist House as anticipated by Ms Kosar and provide advice on alternative methods of sheltering this gain. **(7 marks)**

(c) Advise how the merger of the trades of Ivan Ltd and Trent plc should be effected, and provide advice on possible ways of improving the corporation tax position in which the Trent plc group would find itself following the acquisition of Ivan Ltd. **(9 marks)**

(d) Answer Ms Kosar's queries in relation to VAT. **(7 marks)**

Appropriateness of the format and presentation of the notes and the effectiveness with which their content is communicated. **(2 marks)**

You may assume that the rates and allowances for the Financial Year 2008 continue to apply for the foreseeable future.

(Total = 34 marks)

24 Irroy (ATAX 12/05)   40 mins

Irroy is aged 45, and owns 75% of the ordinary share capital of two companies, Aqua Limited and Aria Limited. Her brother, Irwin, owns the remaining 25% of the shares in both companies. Assume today's date is 1 May 2009.

The following information has been extracted from client files and from meetings with the shareholders.

Aqua Ltd and Aria Ltd:

- Both companies have a 31 March year end.
- Aqua Limited makes water tanks for aquariums and has been trading for five years.
- Aria Limited makes loudspeakers and started trading on 1 April 2008.

Trading results:

- The trading profits/(losses) results for the two companies are as follows:

Year ended 31 March	2009	2010 (estimated)	2011 (estimated)
	£	£	£
Aqua Limited	140,000	175,000	200,000
Aria Limited	(30,000)	(60,000)	(20,000)

- Irroy would like to obtain tax relief for Aria Limited's trading losses as soon as possible.

Overseas expansion plans:

- In April 2010 Aqua Ltd will incorporate a subsidiary, Green Limited, in the Republic of Ireland.
- It will sell water tanks supplied by Aqua Limited from the UK.
- Year ended 31 March 2011: estimated combined taxable profits of the two companies will increase from £200,000 to £275,000.
- The group currently qualifies as a small and medium sized enterprise (SME) under European Union (EU) definitions.
- Irroy believes this will continue to be the case after incorporating Green Limited.

Republic of Ireland tax rates and information:

- Standard rate of corporation tax (CT) = 12.5%.
- Standard rate of value added tax (VAT) = 21%.
- A double tax treaty exists between the UK and the Republic of Ireland, based on the OECD model.
- Both countries are part of the EU.

Required

(a) (i) Explain why the current corporate structure prevents the early relief of Aria Limited's losses. Advise Irroy of two alternative ways in which the current structure can be amended so as to obtain such early relief. **(5 marks)**

 (ii) Illustrate the benefit of revising the corporate structure by calculating the corporation tax (CT) payable for the year ended 31 March 2010, on the assumptions that:

 (1) no action is taken; and
 (2) an amended structure as recommended in (i) above is implemented from 1 June 2009.

(3 marks)

 Assume that the corporation tax rates for the Financial Year 2008 apply throughout.

(b) Explain the corporation tax (CT) and value added tax (VAT) issues that Irroy should be aware of, if she proceeds with her proposal for the Irish subsidiary, Green Limited. Your answer should clearly identify those factors which will determine whether or not Green Limited is considered UK resident or Irish resident and the tax implications of each alternative situation.

 You need not repeat points that are common to each situation. **(14 marks)**

(Total = 22 marks)

25 Dovedale Ltd (ATAX 12/06)   38 mins

Dovedale Ltd, a company with no subsidiaries, has been a client for several years, as has Belgrove Ltd.

The following information has been extracted from client files and from meetings with directors.

Proposed group:

- Intends to purchase 65% of the ordinary share capital of Hira Ltd from Belgrove Ltd on 1 January 2009.
- Belgrove Ltd currently owns 100% of the share capital of Hira Ltd and has no other subsidiaries.
- All three companies have head offices in the UK and are UK resident.

Hira Ltd:

- Has £18,600 trading losses brought forward at 1 April 2008.
- Had no income or gains in the year ended 31 March 2008.
- Expects to make further tax adjusted trading losses of £55,000 before deduction of capital allowances, and to have no other income or gains in the year ended 31 March 2009.
- Tax written down value brought forward of the plant and machinery pool at 1 April 2008 was £96,000. There will be no fixed asset additions or disposals in the year ending 31 March 2009.
- A small tax adjusted trading loss is anticipated in the year ending 31 March 2010.
- Will surrender the maximum possible trading losses to Belgrove Ltd and Dovedale Ltd.

Dovedale Ltd:

- Expected tax adjusted trading profit for year ended 31 March 2009 is £875,000 and will continue at this level in the future.

- Will sell a small office building, purchased for £210,000 in March 2007, to Hira Ltd on 1 February 2009 for its market value of £234,000.

- Sold a factory in October 2006 for £277,450 making a capital gain of £74,331. A claim was made to roll over the gain on the sale of the factory against the acquisition cost of the office building.

Belgrove Ltd:

- The profits chargeable to corporation tax of Belgrove Ltd are expected to be £38,000 for the year ending 31 March 2009 and to increase in the future.

Planned overseas expansion:

- Dovedale Ltd intends to acquire the whole of the ordinary share capital of Atapo Inc, an unquoted company resident in the country of Morovia on 1 April 2009.

- Atapo Inc sells components to Dovedale Ltd as well as to other companies in Morovia and around the world.

- Atapo Inc's estimated profit before tax (and taxable profits) for year ended 31 March 2010 is £160,000 and it will pay a dividend to Dovedale Ltd of £105,000.

- The rate of corporation tax in Morovia is 9%. There is a withholding tax of 3% on dividends paid to non-Morovian resident shareholders. There is no double tax agreement between the UK and Morovia.

Required

(a) Advise Belgrove Ltd of any capital gains that may arise as a result of the sale of the shares in Hira Ltd. You are not required to calculate any capital gains in this part of the question.   **(3 marks)**

(b) Explain by reference to Hira Ltd's loss position why it may be beneficial for it not to claim any capital allowances for the year ending 31 March 2009. Support your explanation with relevant calculations.

(5 marks)

(c) Calculate the expected corporation tax liability of Dovedale Ltd for the year ending 31 March 2009 on the assumption that all available reliefs are claimed by Dovedale Ltd but that Hira Ltd will not claim any capital allowances in that year.   **(3 marks)**

(d) Comment on your position as accountant to both Dovedale Ltd and Belgrove Ltd.   **(2 marks)**

(e) Explain whether or not Dovedale Ltd, Hira Ltd and Atapo Inc can register as a group for the purposes of value added tax.   **(3 marks)**

(f) Explain in detail how the profits of Atapo Inc, both distributed and non-distributed, will be taxed in the UK. You are not required to produce any calculations for this part of the question.   **(5 marks)**

You should assume that the corporation tax rates and allowances for the Financial Year 2008 apply throughout this question.

Relevant retail price index figures are:

March   2007   204.4
February   2009   219.8 (estimated)

(Total = 21 marks)

26 Daniel Dare (ATAX 6/08)   53 mins

An extract from an email from your manager is set out below.

I had a telephone conversation with Daniel Dare (DD), the managing director of Saturn Ltd, first thing this morning. We discussed the anticipated results of the Saturn Ltd group of companies and the proposed acquisition of a majority holding in Tethys Ltd. All the relevant details are included in the attached memorandum.

I need for the following:

(i)   A memorandum that I can use to prepare for my telephone call to DD. I realise that DD did not give me all of the information we need so please identify any additional information that you think could have an effect on our advice.

(ii)   A summary of the information we need and any action we should take before agreeing to become tax advisers to the Saturn Ltd group.

Tax manager

The memorandum attached to the email is set out below.

To: Internal filing
From: Tax manager
Date: 2 June 2009
Subject: Saturn Ltd group of companies

This memorandum sets out the matters discussed with Daniel Dare (DD), the managing director of Saturn Ltd, earlier today.

Group structure

Saturn Ltd has three wholly-owned subsidiaries: Dione Ltd, Rhea Ltd and Titan Inc. Titan Inc trades in and is resident in the country of Galactica. The other three group companies are resident in the UK. Saturn Ltd has owned all three subsidiary companies for many years.

Budgeted results for the year ending 30 June 2009

It is estimated that Dione Ltd will make a tax adjusted trading loss of £187,000 in the year ending 30 June 2009; it will have no other income or capital gains in the period. The budgeted profits chargeable to corporation tax of the other companies in the group are set out below.

	£
Saturn Ltd	385,000
Rhea Ltd	590,000
Titan Ltd	265,000

Rhea Ltd paid a dividend of £240,000 to Saturn Ltd on 1 May 2009.

Proposed acquisition of 65% of Tethys Ltd

On 1 August 2008, Saturn ltd will purchase 65% of the ordinary share capital of Tethys Ltd for £235,000 from the personal representatives of George Jetson. the whole of the balance of the company's share capital is owned either by Edith Clanger or by her family company, Clangers Ltd; DD cannot remember which.

It is anticipated that Tethys Ltd will make a tax adjusted trading loss of approximately £80,000 in the year ending 31 December 2009.

In early 2010, Tethys Ltd will sell its manufacturing premises for £240,000 and move to a rented factory. The premises where acquired new on 1 May 1999 for £112,000 and immediately brought into industrial use. The tax written down value for the purposes of industrial buildings allowances as at 31 December 2009 will be £62,720. We agreed that the indexation factor on the disposal can be assumed to be 27%.

Required

Prepare the memorandum requested by your manager.

(a)   Prepare the memorandum requested by your manager. The memorandum should include explanations together with supporting calculations and should identify any further information that you think is required. the following marks are available for the four components of the memorandum:

(i)   The amount of tax that can be saved via the use of the loss of Dione Ltd;   **(7 marks)**

(ii)   The use of the trading loss of Tethys Ltd for the year ending 31 December 2009;   **(6 marks)**

(iii)   Advice in connection with the sale of the manufacturing premises by Tethys Ltd;   **(7 marks)**

(iv)   The stamp duty and/or stamp duty land tax payable by the Saturn Ltd group.   **(2 marks)**

Additional marks will be awarded for the appropriateness of the format and presentation of the memorandum and the effectiveness with which the information is communicated   **(2 marks)**

(b)   A summary of the information needed to satisfy our obligations under the money laundering legislation and any action that should be taken before agreeing to become tax advisers to the Saturn Ltd group   **(5 marks)**

(Total = 29 marks)

27 Palm plc (ATAX 12/07)   32 mins

Palm plc recently acquired 100% of the ordinary share capital of Nikau Ltd from Facet Ltd. Palm plc intends to use Nikau Ltd to develop a new product range, under the name 'Project Sabal'. Nikau Ltd owns shares in a non-UK resident company, Date Inc.

The following information has been extracted from client files and from a meeting with the Finance Director of Palm plc.

Palm plc:

•   Has more than 40 wholly owned subsidiaries such that all group companies pay corporation tax at 28%.
•   All group companies prepare accounts to 31 March.
•   Acquired Nikau Ltd on 1 November 2009 from Facet Ltd, an unrelated company.

Nikau Ltd:

- UK resident company that manufactures domestic electronic appliances for sale in the European Union (EU).
- Large enterprise for the purposes of the enhanced relief available for research and development expenditure.
- Trading losses brought forward as at 1 April 2009 of £195,700.
- Budgeted taxable trading profit of £360,000 for the year ending 31 March 2010 before taking account of 'Project Sabal'.
- Dividend income of £38,200 will be received in the year ending 31 March 2010 in respect of the shares in Date Inc.

'Project Sabal':

- Development of a range of electronic appliances, for sale in North America.
- Project Sabal will represent a significant advance in the technology of domestic appliances.
- Nikau Ltd will spend £70,000 on staffing costs and consumables researching and developing the necessary technology between now and 31 March 2010. Further costs will be incurred in the following year.
- Sales to North America will commence in 2011 and are expected to generate significant profits from that year.

Shares in Date Inc:

- Nikau Ltd owns 35% of the ordinary share capital of Date Inc.
- The shares were purchased from Facet Ltd on 1 June 2005 for their market value of £338,000.
- The sale was a no gain, no loss transfer for the purposes of corporation tax.
- Facet Ltd purchased the shares in Date Inc on 1 March 1996 for £137,000.

Date Inc:

- A controlled foreign company resident in the country of Palladia.
- Annual chargeable profits arising out of property investment activities are approximately £120,000, of which approximately £115,000 is distributed to its shareholders each year.

The tax system in Palladia:

- No taxes on income or capital profits.
- 4% withholding tax on dividends paid to shareholders resident outside Palladia.

Required

(a) Prepare detailed explanatory notes, including relevant supporting calculations, on the effect of the following issues on the amount of corporation tax payable by Nikau Ltd for the year ending 31 March 2010.

    (i) The costs of developing 'Project Sabal' and the significant commercial changes to the company's activities arising out of its implementation. **(8 marks)**

    (ii) The shares held in Date Inc and the dividend income received from that company. **(7 marks)**

(b) Explain why making sales of Sabals in North America will have no effect on Nikau Ltd's ability to recover its input tax. **(3 marks)**

Notes:

1. You should assume that the corporation tax rates and allowances for the Financial Year to 31 March 2009 will continue to apply for the foreseeable future.

2. You should ignore indexation allowance.

(Total = 18 marks)

VAT

Questions 28 and 29 cover VAT. This is the subject of Chapters 28 and 29 in the BPP study text.

28 Hutt plc (Pilot Paper)   70 mins

Hutt plc has owned the whole of the ordinary share capital of Rainbow Ltd and Coronet Ltd since 1998. All three companies are resident in the UK. Their results for the year ended 31 March 2009 are as follows:

	Hutt plc £	Rainbow Ltd £	Coronet Ltd £
Taxable trading profit/(loss)	(105,000)	800,000	63,000
Capital gain	144,000	–	–
Rental income	65,000	–	–
UK bank interest receivable	2,000	57,000	18,000

Hutt plc's rental income of £65,000 per annum arises in respect of Hutt Tower, an office building acquired on 1 April 2008.

In the year ended 31 March 2008 Hutt plc had a trading profit of £735,000, UK bank interest receivable of £2,000 and a capital loss of £98,000, which was carried forward as at 31 March 2008.

Hutt plc and Coronet Ltd both carry on trades in the UK. Rainbow Ltd conducts both its manufacturing and trading activities wholly in the country of Prismovia. The system of corporation tax in Prismovia is mainly the same as that in the UK although the rate of corporation tax is 26%. There is no double taxation agreement between the UK and Prismovia.

Hutt plc has agreed that it will purchase the whole of the share capital of Lucia Ltd, a UK resident engineering component manufacturing company, on 1 July 2009 for £130,000.

Hutt plc will need to take out a loan to finance the purchase of Lucia Ltd. The company intends to borrow £190,000 from BHC Bank Ltd on 1 July 2009. BHC Bank Ltd will charge Hutt plc a £1,400 loan arrangement fee and interest at 7.25% per annum. Hutt plc only needs £130,000 of the loan to buy the share capital of Lucia Ltd and intends to use the balance of the loan as follows: £45,000 to carry out repairs to Hutt Tower; and the remainder to help fund the company's ongoing working capital requirements.

Lucia Ltd is a UK resident company. The scale of its activities in the last few years has been very small and it has made tax adjusted trading losses. As at 31 March 2009 Lucia Ltd has trading losses carried forward of £186,000. The company's activities from 1 April 2009 to 30 June 2009 are expected to be negligible and any profit or loss in that period can be ignored. Because of the small scale of its activities Lucia Ltd has not been registered for value added tax (VAT) since March 2008. In arriving at the purchase price for the company, the owners of Lucia Ltd have valued the company's trading losses at £39,060 (£186,000 at 21%), as Lucia Ltd has always been a small company.

On the purchase of Lucia Ltd, Hutt plc has plans to return the company to profitability and the budgeted turnover of Lucia Ltd for the nine months ended 31 March 2010 is as set out below. All amounts relate to the sales of engineering components and are stated exclusive of VAT. It can be assumed that all categories of turnover will accrue evenly over the period.

		£
UK customers:	– VAT registered	85,000
	– non-VAT registered	25,000
European Union customers:	– VAT registered	315,000
	– non-VAT registered	70,000
Other non-UK customers		180,000
		675,000

Lucia Ltd will incur input VAT of £7,800 per month from 1 July 2009 in respect of purchases from UK businesses. It will also purchase raw materials from Dabet Gmbh for £17,000 in November 2009. Dabet Gmbh is resident and registered for VAT in Germany.

Lucia Ltd owns a factory that was built in May 1972 at a cost of £210,000. The factory was acquired by Lucia Ltd on 30 June 2005, for £270,000. It can be assumed that the factory's current value of £80,000 will not change in the foreseeable future. On 1 January 2010, Lucia Ltd will sell this factory and take out a short lease on a new, larger one. The indexation allowance applicable to the period June 2005 to January 2010 can be assumed to be £27,000.

It is proposed that an office building owned by Coronet Ltd be sold to Lucia Ltd in May 2010 at its market value. This building will then be sold on by Lucia Ltd, to Vac Ltd, an unconnected third party in June 2010, giving rise to a capital gain of £92,000. The intention is that this gain will be reduced by the capital loss arising on the sale of the factory.

Required

(a)   Describe and evaluate the options available in respect of the trading losses of Hutt plc for the year ended 31 March 2009. Your answer should include a recommendation on the most tax efficient use of these losses, together with details of and time limits for any elections or claims that would need to be submitted, assuming that the losses are to be used as soon as possible and are not to be carried forward.   **(13 marks)**

(b)   Prepare a report for the management of Hutt plc concerning the acquisition of Lucia Ltd. The report should be in three sections, addressing the three sets of issues set out below, and should, where appropriate, include supporting calculations.

   (i)   The purchase price

           Comment on the valuation placed on Lucia Ltd's trading losses, by the owners of Lucia Ltd.

           Provide an explanation of the tax treatment of the loan arrangement fee and the interest payable on the loan of £190,000, assuming that Hutt plc continues to have bank interest receivable, in the year ended 31 March 2010, of £2,000.   **(9 marks)**

   (ii)   VAT issues

           Provide an explanation of the date by which Lucia Ltd will be required to register for VAT in the UK and any other relevant points in respect of registration.

           Provide a calculation of the VAT payable by, or repayable to, Lucia Ltd in respect of the period from registration to 31 March 2010.

           With reference only to the facts in the question, suggest ONE disadvantage of Lucia Ltd entering into a group VAT registration with Hutt plc.   **(6 marks)**

   (iii)   The office building

           Advise on the tax implications of the proposed sale of the office building by Coronet Ltd to Lucia Ltd in May 2010. Your answer should consider all relevant taxes.

           Evaluate the proposed strategy to reduce the capital gain arising on the sale of the office building by offsetting the capital loss on the sale of the factory, on the assumption that both Lucia Ltd and Coronet Ltd will pay corporation tax at the rate of 28%, for the year ended 31 March 2011. **(9 marks)**

Appropriateness of the format and presentation of the report and the effectiveness with which its advice is communicated.   **(2 marks)**

You may assume that the tax rates and allowances for the Financial Year to 31 March 2009 and for the tax year 2008/09 will continue to apply for the foreseeable future.

(Total = 39 marks)

29 Tay Limited (ATAX 6/06)

Assume today's date is 1 May 2009.

Tay Limited is an unquoted trading company with a 31 March year end. It acquired 100% of the shares of another company, Trent Limited, on 1 September 2008. Both companies manufacture engine components.

The following information has been extracted from client files and from meetings with shareholders.

Tay Limited:

- £250,000 trade profits in year ended 31 March 2009.
- Incurred expenditure of £250,000 on intellectual property on 1 January 2009. Does not depreciate this amount so has not claimed any writing down allowances for the expenditure.
- Lacks capacity to take on more work, so intends to transfer several orders to Trent Limited.
- Planning to sell a capital asset in September 2009 that will realise a capital gain of £75,000. Has suggested that Trent Limited sell its building (see below) at the same time to take advantage of the capital loss that would arise.

Trent Limited:

- At 1 January 2008 had tax losses of £300,000 (including £60,000 relating to the year ended 31 December 2007).
- Losses for year ended 31 December 2008 are £120,000.
- Anticipated profits, following transfer of orders, are £50,000 for the year to 31 December 2009, with greater profits expected in subsequent years. Hopes to utilise its existing corporation tax losses.

Building owned by Trent Limited:

- Purchased in September 1998 for £400,000. Tax life had expired at this date.
- Always used for trade purposes.
- Valued at £300,000 on 1 September 2008.
- Current market value is £250,000.

Proposed overseas investment by Tay Limited:

- Has recently identified an opportunity to purchase either the shares or the assets of Tagus LDA, an engineering company based in Portugal.
- Tagus LDA's business will remain Portuguese resident irrespective of the acquisition route taken.
- Portuguese companies and businesses pay tax on profits at the rate of 27.5%

Trent Limited's VAT return for quarter ended 31 March 2009:

- Recent investigation by Trent Limited's finance director has revealed an error in this return.
- Input VAT was correctly calculated at £40,000, but the output VAT was under declared by £55,000 as £87,500.
- The additional VAT due has not yet been paid.

Required

(a) (i) State, giving reasons, whether or not Tay Limited is entitled to claim a tax allowance in respect of the purchased intellectual property. **(2 marks)**

　　 (ii) Calculate the corporation tax (CT) payable by Tay Limited for the year ended 31 March 2009, taking advantage of all available reliefs. **(3 marks)**

　　 (iii) Explain the potential corporation tax (CT) implications of Tay Limited transferring work to Trent Limited, and suggest how these can be minimised or eliminated. **(2 marks)**

(b) Advise on the capital gains implications should Trent Limited's old building be sold as proposed. Support your advice with relevant calculations. **(3 marks)**

(c)   Briefly outline the corporation tax (CT) issues that Tay Limited should consider when deciding whether to acquire the shares or the assets of Tagus LDA. You are not required to discuss issues relating to transfer pricing. **(6 marks)**

(d)   Advise Trent Limited of the consequences arising from the submission of the incorrect value added tax (VAT) return, assuming that the company has previously had a good compliance record with regard to accounting for VAT, and comment on any action you should take. **(5 marks)**

(Total = 21 marks)

TAX PLANNING

Questions 30 to 37 cover tax planning. This is the subject of Chapter 30 in the BPP study text.

30 Andrew (ATAX 6/06)   38 mins

Andrew is aged 38 and is employed as a consultant by Bestadvice & Co.

The following information has been extracted from client files and from meetings with Andrew.

Andrew:

- Single.
- Has earnings of £300,000.
- Contributes 6% of his annual salary to the Bestadvice & Co registered occupational pension scheme. The firm contributes 8%.
- Is considering investing in a new business, Scalar Limited, so has recently disposed of a number of assets to fund the investment.

Capital disposals:

- *12 May 2009:*   Assigned short leasehold interest in a residential property for £90,000. Originally paid £50,000 for a 47 year lease in May 1998.

- *14 March 2009:*   Sold £10,000 7% Government Stock for £11,250. Originally purchased on 1 June 2002 for £9,980. Interest is payable half-yearly on 20 April and 20 October.

Scalar Limited:

- UK based manufacturing company.
- Three investors (including Andrew) have been identified to subscribe for ordinary shares in the company, but a fourth investor may also be invited to subscribe for shares.
- Investors are all unconnected, and would subscribe equally for shares.
- Has advised investors that they can take advantage of various tax reliefs on this investment.
- Will raise £450,000 in this way and a further £50,000, in the form of loans, from the investors.

Required

(a)   (i)   Calculate the chargeable gain arising on the assignment of the residential property lease in May 2009. **(1 marks)**

        (ii)   Advise Andrew of the tax implications arising from the disposal of the 7% Government Stock. **(3 marks)**

(b)   (i)   Advise Andrew of the income tax (IT) and capital gains tax (CGT) reliefs available on his investment in the ordinary share capital of Scalar Limited, together with any conditions which need to be satisfied. Your answer should clearly identify any steps that should be taken by Andrew and the other investors to obtain the maximum relief. **(12 marks)**

        (ii)   State the taxation implications of both equity and loan finance from the point of view of a company. **(2 marks)**

(c)   Advise Andrew of the maximum contributions he may make to a personal pension, together with any limits he should be aware of both now and in the future, and how he may obtain tax relief for both the occupational and personal pension contributions.   **(3 marks)**

You should assume that the rates and allowances for the tax year 2008/09 apply throughout this question.

Relevant extracts from the leasehold depreciation tables are as follows:

36 years	92.761
47 years	98.902

(Total = 21 marks)

31 Bluetone Ltd   36 mins

Bluetone Ltd is an unquoted trading company that manufactures compact discs.

The following information has been extracted from client files and from meetings with shareholders.

Bluetone Ltd:

• Has four full-time working directors, each of whom owns 25% of its share capital of 200,000 £1 ordinary shares.

• Shareholdings are currently valued as follows:

Shareholding	Value per share £
15%	9.00
25%	11.00
35%	12.50
50%	15.00

• Forecast profits chargeable to corporation tax for year ended 31 March 2009 are £1,100,000.

• Has no chargeable non-business assets.

Melody Brown:

• Recently appointed a director of Bluetone Ltd after inheriting 50,000 shares from her father, Tony.
• Melody wants to retain the full 25% holding so she will personally account for any IHT liability (see below).

Tony Brown's death estate:

• Died on 15 February 2009.
• Owned the following assets at date of death:

Asset	Value
50,000 Bluetone Ltd shares, purchased 12 November 2008	See above
42,000 50p ordinary shares in Expanse plc	Quoted at 312p – 320p Bargains of 282p, 288p, 306p and 324p.
26,000 units in World-Growth, a unit trust.	Bid price: 80p; offer price 84p
Building society deposits	£29,000
Mini-cash ISA with building society	£3,000
Main residence	£125,000 (outstanding repayment mortgage of £42,000)
Life assurance policy on his own life	£53,000 open market value £61,000 proceeds received on 4 March 2009

• Had an income tax liability of £6,600, gambling debts of £1,200 and funeral expenses came to £3,460.

Tony Brown's will:

- Bluetone Ltd shares left to Melody bearing their own IHT.
- Residue left to Melody's brother.

Tony Brown's lifetime gifts:

- *10 February 2005:* £30,000 to Melody on her wedding day.
- *4 June 2005:* £184,000 to a discretionary trust.

Liam and Opal White

- Married, aged 37 and 32 respectively.
- Have been directors and shareholders of Bluetone Ltd since its incorporation on 1 October 1991; acquired their shares at par.
- On 20 March 2009 Liam will sell 30,000 of his shares in Bluetone Ltd to their son for £75,000.
- Liam is a 40% taxpayer.
- Has not previously made any lifetime gifts of assets.

Noel Green

- Aged 52.
- Has been a director and shareholder of Bluetone Ltd since its incorporation on 1 October 1991; acquired the shares at par.
- For the past two years he has disagreed with the other directors of Bluetone Ltd over the company's business policies.
- Will resign as a director on 31 March 2009.
- Has been agreed that Bluetone Ltd will purchase his shareholding for £550,000. HMRC has given advance clearance that the purchase qualifies for the special treatment applying to a company's purchase of its own shares, and can therefore be treated as a capital gain.
- 40% taxpayer.

Required

(a)   Calculate Melody's IHT liability and state when this will be due.   **(8 marks)**

(b)   Advise Liam of the CGT and IHT implications of selling the 30,000 shares in Bluetone Ltd to his son. You should assume that reliefs are claimed in the most favourable manner on the basis that Liam wishes to defer gains where possible.   **(8 marks)**

(c)   Advise both Bluetone Ltd and Noel of whether it will be beneficial to have the purchase of Noel's 25% shareholding treated as a capital gain under the special treatment, rather than as a distribution by Bluetone Ltd.   **(4 marks)**

The rates and allowances for 2008/09 should be used throughout.

(Total = 20 marks)

32 Graeme (ATAX 12/05)   **36 mins**

Graeme, aged 57, is married to Catherine, aged 58. Graeme has come to you for some tax advice.

The following information has been extracted from client files and from meetings with Graeme.

Graeme's family:

- Both Graeme and Catherine work as medical consultants.
- Both are higher rate taxpayers.
- Have one son, Barry, aged 32.
- All are UK resident, ordinarily resident and domiciled.

Graeme's Thistle Dubh Limited shareholdings:

- *December 1987:* inherited 10,000 £1 ordinary shares on the death of his grandmother. Probate value 360p per share.

- *March 1993:* took up a 1 for 2 rights issue. The price paid for the rights shares was £10 per share.

- *October 2008:* company underwent a reorganisation whereupon Graeme received 'T' and 'D' ordinary shares (details below).

- *May 2009:* sold 12,000 'T' shares. The market values for the 'T' shares and the 'D' shares on that day were 300p and 600p per share respectively.

- *October 2009:* Graeme sold all of his 'D' shares for £85,000.

October 2000 share reorganisation:

- The ordinary shares were split into two new classes of ordinary share – 'T' shares and 'D' shares, each with differing rights.

- Graeme received two 'T' and three 'D' shares for each original Thistle Dubh Limited share held.

- The market values for the 'T' shares and the 'D' shares on the date of reorganisation were 135p and 405p per share respectively.

Thistle Dubh Limited:

- Unquoted UK trading company.
- Provides food supplies for sporting events.
- Current market value of the 'T' shares is 384p per share.
- Graeme has never been an employee or officer of the company.

Holiday cottage:

- Graeme and Catherine own a UK holiday cottage let out as furnished holiday accommodation.
- Considering selling the cottage and purchasing a holiday villa abroad.
- Plan to let villa out on a furnished basis.
- Following their anticipated retirement, expect to occupy the property for a significant part of the year themselves, possibly moving to live in the villa permanently.

Required

(a) Calculate the total chargeable gains arising on Graeme's disposals of 'T' and 'D' ordinary shares in May and October 2009 respectively. **(4 marks)**

(b) Explain the capital gains tax (CGT) and inheritance tax (IHT) implications of Graeme gifting his remaining 'T' ordinary shares at their current value either:

    (i) to his wife, Catherine, or
    (ii) to his son, Barry.

Your answer should be supported by relevant calculations and clearly identify the availability and effect of any reliefs (other than the CGT annual exemption) that might be used to reduce or defer any tax liabilities arising. **(8 marks)**

(c) Advise Graeme of the potential CGT and income tax implications of selling the UK country cottage and replacing it with a holiday villa abroad as proposed.

You are not required to discuss the income tax treatment of the UK country cottage. **(8 marks)**

(Total = 20 marks)

33 Reisling Ltd
52 mins

Reisling Ltd is a trading company that produces German wine in the UK. It also produces special shaped bottles that are characteristic of German wine, the majority of which are distributed to other manufacturers. This has been a very successful business which looks set to continue, although the wine production business has not proved so efficient. The rising costs of importing grapes have created substantial losses in the past four years.

The company has been a client for several years, as have the directors who each have significant shareholdings.

On 23 October 2008, the board of Reisling Ltd are approached by Chardonnay Ltd, a very successful company in the wine producing business, and negotiations have commenced for the purchase of the wine production trade.

The company has always kept information separate for the two trades and the following information relates only to the wine production side of the business:

Losses brought forward at 1 January 2008 were £290,000, and the adjusted trading loss for the year ended 31 December 2008 are expected to be £60,000.

At 1 January 2008, there were capital losses brought forward of £42,000.

**Projected Balance sheet of Reisling Ltd as at 31 December 2008
(wine production only)**

	£'000
Fixed assets	
Freehold factory	80
Freehold winery	40
Plant and machinery	30
Motor vehicles	30
	180
Net current assets	70
	250

Originally the freehold factory had been used for bottle production but it was replaced 3 years ago by a larger factory with all the latest technology. The factory was then transferred to the wine production side of the business and had been used for storing the finished goods before distribution.

The proposals are as follows:

Step 1   On 1 January 2009 a wholly owned subsidiary, Plonk Ltd, will be formed and the assets and undertaking of the wine production trade will be hived down.

Step 2   All assets will be transferred to Plonk Ltd except the freehold winery which Chardonnay Ltd will sell to a third party for £50,000.

Step 3   The consideration for the trade transferred will be the issue of shares in Plonk Ltd, which will be immediately sold to Chardonnay Ltd for £475,000.

Following the disposal of the wine production business, the directors are considering increasing the range of bottles produced, and exporting them. Some of the exports will be to manufacturers in the EU, and some to manufacturers in the New World.

Required

Prepare notes for a forthcoming meeting with the board of Chardonnay Ltd outlining the tax and other implications of the above proposals. Your notes should be in four sections, addressing the four sets of issues set out below, and should, where appropriate, include supporting calculations.

(a)   The transfer of Reisling Ltd's wine production trade to Plonk Ltd

Comment on the tax position for Reisling Ltd if the transfer of Reisling Ltd's wine production trade to Plonk Ltd (steps 1 and 2 of the hive down, above) takes place.

Explain how the trading losses and the capital losses may be used by Plonk Ltd, if at all. You should not consider any anti-avoidance rules at this stage. **(9 marks)**

(b)   The sale of Plonk Ltd to Chardonnay Ltd

Advise the company of the tax consequences of this aspect of the proposal.

Evaluate the likelihood of any anti-avoidance rules applying to the transaction.   **(6 marks)**

(c)   Other considerations

Advise the company of the effects of the proposal on existing staff, customers and suppliers.

At this point, you should also comment on any other issues that you think may be relevant to the disposal of the production business.   **(8 marks)**

(d)   Export of wine bottles

Explain the VAT implications of exporting wine bottles.   **(4 marks)**

Appropriateness of the format and presentation of the notes and the effectiveness with which the information is communicated.   **(2 marks)**

You may assume that the rates and allowances for the tax year 2008/09 and Financial Year 2008 continue to apply for the foreseeable future.

(Total = 29 marks)

34 Vikram Bridge (Pilot Paper)   32 mins

Vikram Bridge has been made redundant by Bart Industries Ltd, a company based in Birmingham. He intends to move to Scotland to start a new job with Dreamz Technology Ltd.

The following information has been extracted from client files and from meetings with Vikram.

Vikram Bridge:

- Is unmarried, but has been living with Alice Tate since 1997. The couple have four young children.
- Receives dividends of approximately £7,800 each year and makes annual capital gains of approximately £1,200 in respect of shares inherited from his mother.
- The couple have no sources of income other than Vikram's employment income and the £7,800 of dividends.

Made redundant by Bart Industries Ltd on 28 February 2009:

- Vikram's employment contract entitled him to two months' notice or two months' salary in lieu of notice. On 28 February 2009 the company paid him his salary for the two-month period of £4,700, and asked him to leave immediately.
- On 30 April 2009 the company paid him a further £1,300 in respect of statutory redundancy, together with a non-contractual lump sum of £14,500, as a gesture of goodwill.

Job with Dreamz Technology Ltd:

- Starts on 1 October 2009 with an annual salary of £42,500.
- The company will contribute £9,400 in October 2009 towards Vikram's costs of moving to Scotland.
- In November 2010, the company will issue free shares to all of its employees. Vikram will be issued with 200 shares, expected to be worth approximately £2,750.

Moving house:

- Vikram's house in Birmingham is fairly small; he intends to buy a much larger one in Glasgow.
- The cost of moving to Glasgow, including the stamp duty land tax in respect of the purchase of his new house, will be approximately £12,500.
- To finance the purchase of the house in Glasgow Vikram will sell a house he owns in Wales, in August 2009.

House in Wales:

- Was given to Vikram by his mother on 1 September 2001, when it was worth £145,000.
- Vikram's mother continued to live in the house until her death on 1 May 2009, when she left the whole of her estate to Vikram.
- At the time of her death the house had severe structural problems and was valued at £140,000.
- Vikram has subsequently spent £18,000 improving the property and expects to be able to sell it for £195,000.
- Vikram is keen to reduce the tax payable on the sale of the house and is willing to transfer the house, or part of it, to Alice prior to the sale if that would help.

Required

Prepare explanations, including supporting calculations where appropriate, of the following issues suitable for inclusion in a letter to Vikram.

(a) (i) The capital gains tax payable on the sale of the house in Wales in August 2009, together with the potential effect of transferring the house, or part of it, to Alice prior to the sale. **(3 marks)**

(ii) Calculate Vikram's taxable income for 2009/10 briefly explaining the treatment of the termination payment received from Bart Industries Ltd. **(4 marks)**

(b) The inheritance tax implications in respect of the house in Wales on the death of Vikram's mother. **(2 marks)**

(c) The income tax treatment of the receipt by Vikram of the shares in Dreamz Technology Ltd. **(3 marks)**

(d) How Vikram's job with Dreamz Technology Ltd will affect the amount and date of payment of the income tax due on his dividend income for 2011/12 and future years. **(6 marks)**

Ignore national insurance contributions in answering this question.

You may assume that the rates and allowances for the tax year 2008/09 will continue to apply for the foreseeable future.

(Total = 18 marks)

35 Stuart and Rebecca (ATAX 12/05)   47 mins

Your manager has had a meeting with Stuart and Rebecca Lundy and has sent you a copy of the following memorandum.

To   The files
From   Tax manager
Date   21 November 2009
Subject Stuart and Rebecca Lundy – Estate planning

Stuart has recently been diagnosed with a serious illness. He is expected to live for another two or three years only. He is concerned about the possible inheritance tax that will arise on his death. Rebecca is in good health.

In November 2009 Stuart sold a house in Plymouth for £422,100. Stuart had inherited the house on the death of his mother on 1 May 1997 when it had a probate value of £185,000. The subsequent pattern of occupation was as follows:

1 May 1997 to 28 February 1998   Occupied by Stuart and Rebecca as main residence
1 March 1998 to 31 December 2001   Unoccupied
1 January 2002 to 31 March 2004   Let out (unfurnished)
1 April 2004 to 30 November 2004   Occupied by Stuart and Rebecca
1 December 2004 to 30 November 2009   Used occasionally as second home

Both Stuart and Rebecca had lived in London from March 1998 onwards. On 1 March 2004 Stuart and Rebecca bought a house in London in their joint names. No other capital disposals were made by Stuart in the tax year 2009/10. He has £29,650 of capital losses brought forward from previous years.

Stuart intends to invest the gross sale proceeds from the sale of the Plymouth house, and is considering two investment options, both of which he believes will provide equal risk and returns. These are as follows:

(1)   acquiring shares in Omikron plc, a listed UK trading company, with 50,250,000 shares in issue. Its shares currently trade at 42p per share, or

(2)   acquiring further shares in Omega plc. The issued share capital of Omega plc is currently 10,000,000 shares. The share price is quoted at 208p – 216p with marked bargains at 207p, 211p, and 215p

Stuart and Rebecca's assets (following the sale of the Plymouth house but before any investment of the proceeds) are as follows:

Assets	Stuart £	Rebecca £
Family house in London	450,000	450,000
Cash from property sale	422,100	–
Cash deposits	165,000	165,000
Portfolio of quoted investments	–	250,000
Shares in Omega plc	see files	see files
Life insurance policy	note	note

Note. The life insurance policy will pay out a sum of £200,000 on the death of the first spouse to die.

Tax manager

An extract from an email from your manager is set out below.

Please prepare a letter from me to Stuart incorporating the following:

1   State the taxable capital gain on the sale of the Plymouth house in November 2009, setting out the amounts of any reliefs claimed.

2   Given his recent diagnosis, advice for Stuart on which of the two proposed investments (Omikron plc/Omega plc) would be the more tax efficient alternative.

      Give reasons for your choice.

3   Assuming that Stuart:

      (i)   uses proceeds from the house sale to purchase 201,000 shares in Omega plc on 3 December 2009; and

      (ii)   dies on 20 December 2011,

      calculations of the potential IHT liability which would arise if Rebecca were to die on 1 March 2012, and no further tax planning measures were taken.

      Assume that all asset values remain unchanged.

4   Advice on any lifetime IHT planning that could be undertaken to help reduce the potential liability calculated above.

Tax manager

You have extracted the following further information from client files.

- Stuart is a self-employed business consultant aged 58. He is married to Rebecca, aged 55.
- They have one child, Sam, who is aged 24 and single.
- Both Stuart and Rebecca have wills whose terms transfer all assets to the surviving spouse.
- On 1 January 2005 Stuart and Rebecca elected for their London house to be their principal private residence with effect from that date, up until that point the Plymouth property had been their principal private residence.
- Omega plc was formerly Omega Ltd and Stuart and Rebecca helped start up the company. The company was formed on 1 June 1990, when they each bought 24,000 shares for £1 per share. The company became listed on 1 May 1999. On this date their holding was subdivided, with each of them receiving 100 shares in Omega plc for each share held in Omega Ltd.
- Neither Stuart nor Rebecca has made any previous chargeable lifetime transfers for IHT purposes.

Required

Prepare the letter requested by your manager.

Marks are available for the four components of the letter as follows:

1   Relevant calculations of the taxable capital gain on the sale of the Plymouth house in November 2009.

(8 marks)

2   Advice on which of the two proposed investments would be more tax efficient alternative.   **(3 marks)**

3   Calculations of the potential IHT liability which would arise if no further tax planning measures are taken and Rebecca dies in March 2012.   **(6 marks)**

4   Advice on any lifetime IHT planning that could be undertaken for both Stuart and Rebecca to help reduce their potential IHT liability (in three above).   **(7 marks)**

Appropriateness of the format and presentation of the report and the effectiveness with which its advice is communicated.   **(2 marks)**

You may assume that the rates and allowances for the tax year 2008/09 continue to apply for the foreseeable future.

(Total = 26 marks)

36 Spica (ATAX 6/08)   30 mins

Assume it is July 2008.

Spica, one of the director shareholders of Acrux Ltd, has been in dispute with the other shareholders over plans to expand the company's activities overseas. In order to resolve the position it has been agreed that Spica will sell her shares back to the company. Once the purchase of her shares has taken place, the company intends to establish a number of branches overseas and acquire a shareholding in a number of companies that are resident and trade in overseas countries.

The following information has been obtained from client files and meetings with the parties involved.

Acrux Ltd:

- An unquoted UK resident company
- Share capital consists of 50,000 ordinary shares issued at £1.90 per share in July 2001
- None of the other shareholders has any connection with Spica

The purchase of own shares:

- The company will purchase all of Spica's share for £8 per share
- The transaction will take place by the end of 2008

Spica:

- Purchased 8,000 shares in Acrux Ltd for £2 per share on 30 September 2003
- Has no income in the tax year 2008/09
- Has chargeable capital gains in the tax year 2008/09 of £3,800
- Has houses in the UK and the country of Solaris and divides her time between them

Investment in non-UK companies:

- Acrux Ltd will acquire between 15% and 20% of each of the non-UK resident companies
- The companies will not be controlled foreign companies as the rates of tax in the overseas countries will be between 23% and 42%
- There may or may not be a double tax treaty between the UK and overseas countries in which the companies are resident. Where there is at treaty, it will be based on the OECD model treaty
- None of the countries concerned levy withholding tax on dividends paid to UK companies
- The directors of Acrux Ltd are concerned that the rate of tax suffered on the profits of the overseas companies will be very high as they will be taxed in both the overseas country and in the UK.

Required

(a) (i)   Prepare detailed calculations to determine the most beneficial tax treatment of the payment Spica will receive for her shares.   **(7 marks)**

(ii) Identify the points that must be confirmed in order to determine if the capital treatment will apply to the transaction.   **(4 marks)**

(b) Provide the directors of Acrux Ltd with a detailed explanation of the maximum rate of tax that will be suffered on both the distributed and non-distributed profits of the non-UK resident investee companies where:

(1) There is a double tax treaty between the UK and the country in which the individual companies are resident, and

(2) There is no such double tax treaty.

Note: you are not required to explain the position of the overseas resident branches.   **(6 marks)**

(Total = 17 marks)

37 Gagarin (ATAX 6/08)   **30 mins**

Assume it is July 2008.

Gagarin wishes to persuade a number of wealthy individuals who are business contacts to invest in his company, Vostok Ltd. He also requires advice on the recoverability of input tax relating to the purchase of computer equipment.

The following information has been obtained from a meeting with Gagarin.

Vostok Ltd:

- An unquoted UK resident company
- Gagarin owns 100% of the company's ordinary share capital
- Has 18 employees
- Provides computer based services to commercial companies
- Requires additional funds to finance its expansion

Funds required by Vostok Ltd:

- Vostok Ltd needs to raise £420,000
- Vostok Ltd will issue 20,000 shares at £21 per share on 31 August 2008
- The new shareholder(s) will own 40% of the company
- Part of the money raised will contribute towards the purchase of new premises for use by Vostok Ltd.

Gagarin's initial thoughts:

- The minimum investment will be 5,000 shares and payment will be made in full on subscription
- Gagarin has a number of wealth business contacts who may be interested in investing
- Gagarin has heard that it may be possible to obtain tax relief for up to 60% of the investment via the enterprise investment scheme

Wealthy business contacts:

- Are all UK resident higher rate taxpayers
- May wish to borrow the funds to invest in Vostok Ltd if there is a tax incentive to do so

New premises:

- Will cost £446,500 including value added tax (VAT)
- Will be used in connection with all aspects of Vostok Ltd's business
- Will be sold for £600,000 plus VAT in six year's time
- Vostok Ltd will waive the VAT exemption on the sale of the building

The VAT position of Vostok Ltd:

- In the year ending 31 March 2009, 28% of Vostok Ltd's supplies will be exempt for the purposes of VAT
- This percentage is expected to reduce over the next f
- Irrecoverable input tax due to the company's partially exempt status exceeds the *de minimis* limits

Required

(a) Prepare notes for Gagarin to use when speaking to potential investors. The notes should include:

(i)   The tax incentives immediately available in respect of the amount invested in share issued in accordance with the enterprise investment scheme. **(5 marks)**

(ii) The answers to any questions that the potential investors may raise in connection with the maximum possible investment, borrowing to finance the subscription and the implications of selling the shares **(7 marks)**

Note: you should assume that Vostok Ltd and its trade qualify for the purposes of the enterprise investment scheme and you are not required to list the conditions that need to be satisfied by the company, its shares or its business activities.

(b) Calculate the amount of input tax that will be recovered by Vostok Ltd in respect of the new premises in the year ending 31 March 2009 and explain, using illustrative calculations, how any additional recoverable input tax will be calculated in future years. **(5 marks)**

(Total = 17 marks)

PERSONAL AND CORPORATE FINANCIAL MANAGEMENT

Questions 38 to 40 cover personal and corporate financial management. This is the subject of Chapter 31 of the BPP study text.

---

38 Karen Wade   63 mins

Your manager has had a meeting with Karen Wade, who runs her own catering business, and has sent you a copy of the following memorandum.

To   The files
From   Tax manager
Date   1 June 2010
Subject   Karen Wade – tax issues

(1) *Year ended 31 December 2009*

Karen Wade (KW) provided a copy of the accounts for the year ended 31 December 2009 (see attached).

She also provided the following information in connection with the accounts.

(i)   Both her nephew and son work for her. Her nephew works full-time earning £9,600 (employer's NICs are £560). Her son, aged 19, works approximately 40 Saturdays each year from 8 am until 6 pm. He will shortly be going to university to study engineering.

(ii) Electricity and other household expenses represent the allowable percentage agreed with HMRC of the total costs at Karen's home.

(iii) Motor expenses represent the total costs, excluding depreciation, of the car and the van.

(2) *Motor vehicle*

Karen uses her car for both business and private use.

Her annual mileage figures are 12,500 for business and 2,500 private.

(3) *Capital purchases*

Recent purchases of assets are as follows.

2009		£
January	Delivery van – 100% business use	5,000
February	New office equipment	2,000
August	Motor car (to replace Karen's original car which was sold for £7,600)	9,600
September	New refrigerator	800
October	New coffee machine	300
November	Computer and printer	1,300

(4) *Other income*

	£
Dividends from quoted shares – amounts received	22,536
Dividends on shares within an ISA	4,000
Interest on National Savings & Investments Bank – investment account	4,015
Premium Bond prize	500

(5) *New contract*

From 1 January 2010 Karen will commence a new contract to supply catering to a local hotel at £3,725 per month for the next twelve months. She will not need additional staff but, to assist with deliveries, she has agreed that from 1 July 2010 her nephew will be allowed to use the van for travel to and from work and at weekends.

(6) *Investment strategy*

Karen has surplus income of approximately £10,000 per annum. Nearly all of her wealth is invested in quoted shares and she is concerned that they may fall in value. She is considering selling a proportion of her portfolio in order to acquire an investment property.

Her brother-in-law has suggested contributing to a personal pension scheme.

Accounts for the year ended 31 December 2009

	£	£
Turnover		44,710
Expenses		
Wages		
Self	12,000	
Nephew	10,160	
Son	1,600	
Electricity	1,400	
Other household expenses	2,243	
Catering materials	1,307	
Depreciation		
Equipment	1,300	
Car	700	
Van	500	
Loss on sale of car	200	
Motor expenses		
Car	800	
Van	1,200	
		(33,410)
Profit		11,300

An extract from an email from your manager is set out below.

Please find attached a copy of the notes from the meeting with Karen Wade, along with a copy of her accounts for the year ended 31 December 2009.

Please prepare a report from me to Karen setting out the following:

1 VAT

- The rules for determining when she will need to register for VAT.
- Let her know specific dates and her administrative responsibilities.
- Explain how her VAT liability will be calculated.

2 Income tax and NIC

- Advise on the income tax consequences of the change of use of the van from 1 July 2010.
- Provide a calculation of her assessable trading income for 2009/10.
- Prepare computations of her income tax and National Insurance contributions payable for 2009/10.

3 Investment strategy

- Advise Karen which of her personal circumstances may impact the investment strategy she should adopt for investing the surplus £10,000.
- Provide details of the issues to consider depending on whether she invests in quoted shares or commercial property.
- Outline the main issues of which Karen should be aware with regard to a personal pension scheme.

Tax manager

You have extracted the following further information from client files.

- Karen is 42 and divorced.
- Started the business in 1998.
- Customers include private individuals and businesses.
- The tax written-down values for capital allowances purposes at 1 January 2009 are:

Miscellaneous equipment pool	£12,000
Karen's motor car	£7,000

- Karen has made a payment of £360 pa to Oxfam, a registered charity, for the past three years. A copy of the signed gift aid declaration is on file.
- Karen has never made any pension contributions.

Required

Prepare a report for Karen as requested by your manager. The report should be in three sections, addressing the three sets of issues set out below, and should, where appropriate include supporting calculations.

(a) VAT

Advise Karen when she needs to register for VAT and of her associated administrative responsibilities.

Explain how her VAT liability for the year ended 31 December 2010 will be calculated. **(6 marks)**

(b) Income tax and NIC

Advise on the income tax consequences of the change of use of the van from 1 July 2010. **(2 marks)**

Compute her assessable trading income for 2009/10. **(6 marks)**

Prepare computations of the income tax and National Insurance contributions payable in respect of Karen's income for 2009/10. **(6 marks)**

(c)   Investment strategy

    (i)   Investing the surplus £10,000

        Advise Karen which of her personal circumstances may impact the investment strategy she should adopt.

        Identify any further personal information required.   **(3 marks)**

    (ii)   Investment in quoted shares compared with commercial property

        Provide Karen with details of the issues to consider depending on whether she invests in quoted shares or commercial property.

        You should consider all aspects of the investments including the taxation treatment of each.

                                                                   (6 marks)

    (iii) Personal pension schemes

        Outline the main issues of which Karen should be aware with regard to a personal pension scheme.

                                                                  (4 marks)

Appropriateness of the format and presentation of the notes and the effectiveness with which their content is communicated.   **(2 marks)**

You may assume that the rates and allowances for the tax year 2008/09 continue to apply for the foreseeable future.

                                                              (Total = 35 marks)

39 Alasdair (ATAX 12/05)   36 mins

Alasdair is considering investing in property, as he has heard that this represents a good investment.

The following information has been extracted from client files and from meetings with Alasdair.

Alasdair:

- Aged 42 and is single.
- Wants to extract cash from his personal company, Beezer Limited, with the minimum amount of tax payable, to raise funds to buy a property.
- Partner at a marketing firm, Gallus & Co.
- Estimated profit share for 2009/10 will be £32,000.
- Has not made any capital disposals in the current tax year.
- Has never been a director or employee of Beezer Ltd.

Beezer Ltd:

- Formed on 1 May 2001 with £1,000 of capital issued as 1,000 £1 ordinary shares.
- Alasdair sold the trade and related assets on 1 January 2009.
- Only asset is cash of £120,000.
- Makes up accounts to 31 December.

Extraction of profits from Beezer Ltd:

- Option 1: paying Alasdair a dividend of £120,000 on 31 March 2010.
- Company would have no assets and be wound up.
- Option 2: leaving the cash in the company and then liquidating the company.
- Costs of liquidation would be £5,000.

Property investment:

- Unsure whether to invest directly in residential or commercial property, or do so via some form of collective investment.
- Gallus & Co is looking to rent a new warehouse which could be bought for £200,000.
- May buy the warehouse himself and lease it to his firm.
- Will need to borrow additional funds to buy the property.

Required

(a) Advise Alasdair whether or not a dividend payment will result in a higher after-tax cash sum than the liquidation of Beezer Limited. Assume that either the dividend would be paid on 31 March 2010 or the liquidation would take place on 31 March 2010. **(7 marks)**

Assume that Beezer Limited has always paid corporation tax at or above the small companies' rate of 21% and that the tax rates and allowances for 2008/09 apply throughout this part.

(b) (i) Advise Alasdair of the tax implications and relative financial risks attached to the following property investments:

      (1) buy to let residential property,
      (2) commercial property, and
      (3) shares in a property investment company/unit trust. **(9 marks)**

    (ii) State, giving reasons, the inheritance tax (IHT) and capital gains tax (CGT) reliefs that would be available to Alasdair if he acquires the warehouse and leases it to Gallus & Co, rather than to an unconnected tenant. **(4 marks)**

(Total = 20 marks)

40 Adam Snook (ATAX 12/07)   52 mins

Your manager has had a meeting with Adam Snook and has sent you a copy of the following memorandum.

To	The files
From	Tax manager
Date	1 December 2009
Subject	Adam Snook

Adam Snook (AS) has been entertaining children at parties as a hobby for the last two years. On 1 June 2009 his aunt gave him shares in Brill plc, a quoted company, worth £88,040. As a result, AS intends to give up his job on 31 December 2009 (he is a regional sales manager with Rheims Ltd) and purchase a small theatre from which he will carry on a business of providing entertainment for children's parties.

The business

AS will begin advertising and charging for attending children's parties on 1 January 2010. He estimates that his net profit for the first five months (until the theatre opens) will only be £400 per month. Accordingly, he has agreed to work part-time for his existing employer from 1 January 2010 until 31 May 2010 for a salary of £1,050 per month.

AS will purchase the theatre on 1 April 2010. He estimates that it will take six weeks or so to renovate the theatre such that it should be ready for business by 1 June 2010 at the latest. AS will seek to rent out the theatre for the days when it is not required for his business.

We agreed that the business should prepare accounts to 31 March each year. AS does not wish to form a limited company.

The supply of entertainment at the theatre will be standard rated for the purposes of value added tax (VAT) and AS will register for VAT on 1 June 2010.

The finance required

The costs of establishing the business, exclusive of recoverable VAT, are set out below.

	£
Purchase price of the theatre	215,000
Renovation of the theatre	45,000
Equipment and other costs	50,000
Finance required	310,000

The finance available

AS sold 42,600 shares in Snapper plc for £104,370 on 1 December 2009 and intends to sell £25,000 6% Snapper plc non-convertible loan stock next week for £29,900. He will use the net proceeds of these sales to finance the business and obtain the balance of the funds required via a bank overdraft at an annual interest rate of 15%.

The shares and loan stock in Snapper plc were acquired as follows:

- AS was given 14,200 shares in Brill plc by his aunt on 1 June 2009. At that time the shares were worth £88,040.
- On 1 November 2009 Brill plc was acquired by Snapper plc. Both Brill plc and Snapper plc are UK resident trading companies.
- AS received 42,600 shares in Snapper plc together with £25,000 6% Snapper plc non-convertible loan stock (a qualifying corporate bond) in exchange for his shares in Brill plc.
- The shares and the loan stock were worth £97,980 and £28,400 respectively as at 1 November 2009.

Other background information

AS is 35 years old. His full time salary with Rheims Ltd is £25,200 per annum. He is provided with a diesel company car which had a list price when new of £13,950 and a CO2 emission rate of 177 grams per kilometre.

He is not provided with free fuel. He will return the car to the company on 31 December 2009.

AS's aunt is 71 years old and is domiciled in the UK. This is the first substantial gift that she has made to AS although he suspects that she has made similar gifts to other relatives in the past.

Tax manager

An extract from an email from your manager is set out below.

Please prepare a memorandum for me, incorporating the following:

(a) (i) Calculations to support the amount of external finance required by Adam including a note of any assumptions made. Don't forget to take his capital gains tax liability into account but ignore any possible inheritance tax liability.

(ii) • A proposal which will increase the after tax proceeds from the sale of the Snapper plc loan stock together with the amount of the increase.

• A reasoned recommendation of a more appropriate form of external finance for the business.

(b) Explanations of the following matters:

(i) Adam's liability to income tax in 2009/10.

(ii) Adam's liability to class 2 and class 4 national insurance contributions in 2009/10.

(iii) The income tax relief available in respect of both the cost of purchasing and renovating the theatre.

(iv) For value added tax (VAT) purposes: the effect of renting out the theatre on Adam's ability to recover input tax, the implications of opting to tax the theatre and the factors affecting the decision to opt to tax.

(c) An explanation of the inheritance tax payable by Adam in respect of the gift from his aunt depending on when his aunt dies.

We will be under significant fee pressure on this job so please don't do any unnecessary work – I'm sure that time spent thinking about what needs to be done before you start will save you time in the long run.

Tax manager

Required

Prepare the memorandum requested by your manager.

Marks are available for the components of the memorandum as follows:

(a) (i) Calculations to support the amount of external finance required. You should state any assumptions you have made in preparing the calculations;   **(6 marks)**

   (ii) A proposal which will increase the after tax proceeds from the sale of the Snapper plc loan stock and a reasoned recommendation of a more appropriate form of external finance.   **(3 marks)**

(b) Explanations of the various matters.   **(14 marks)**

(c) The inheritance tax payable by Adam in respect of the gift from his aunt.   **(4 marks)**

Additional marks will be awarded for the appropriateness of the format and presentation of the memorandum and the effectiveness with which the information is communicated.   **(2 marks)**

Note: you should assume that the tax rates and allowances for the tax year 2008/09 will continue to apply for the foreseeable future.

(Total = 29 marks)

Answers

1 Styrax

Text references. Chapter 30 covers basic tax planning such as utilising the personal allowance. Pensions and other tax efficient investments are dealt with in Chapter 2.

Top tips. Your financial planning suggestions must be practical. Styrax and Salvia do not have much disposable income so it would be inadvisable for them to make large pension payments.

Marking scheme

				Marks
(a)	(i)	Salvia's PA wasted	1	
		Styrax needs to transfer income	1	
		Employment of Salvia	1	
		Tax savings	2	
		Use of ISAs	2	
		Tax savings	1	
				8
	(ii)	Personal pension provision	1	
		Maximum contributions	1	
		Occupational scheme	1	
		Suitability	1	
		Max		3
(b)		*Enterprise Investment Scheme*		
		Aim of scheme	1	
		Income tax reducer	2	
		Withdrawal of relief	1	
		CGT on disposal	1	
		CGT deferral relief	1	
		Risk	1	
		Venture Capital Scheme		
		Aim of scheme	1	
		Risk	1	
		Income tax reducer	1	
		Dividends	1	
		CGT	1	
		Withdrawal of relief	1	
		Max		10
				21

(a)   (i)   **Notes for meeting with Styrax**

Use of Salvia's personal allowance

Now that Salvia has given up employed work, she does not have any source of income. This means that her personal allowance (£6,035) is being wasted. It is not possible to transfer the benefit of this to Styrax. Therefore, Styrax needs to transfer some of his income to Salvia. Styrax could do this by employing Salvia in his business (the question states that she does not want to be a partner so this is not considered).

Salvia's salary must be commercially justifiable for the work that she will do. Styrax will then be able to deduct the salary from his trading profits. This will save income tax at 20% and also reduce his Class 4 NICs at 8%.

The salary up to £6,035 will be free of income tax and Class 1 NICs. This will therefore save tax and NICs of 28%.

If Styrax were to pay anything above the level of the personal allowance to Salvia, this would be subject to 20% income tax and employee 11% Class 1 NICs in the hands of Salvia. Styrax will also have to pay 12.8% employer Class 1 NICs. Therefore the overall tax rate is 43.8%. However, Styrax would also save income tax and NICs at approximately the rate of 31.8% (income tax of 20%, Class 4 NICs at 8%, and income tax and Class 4 NICs on the employer's Class 1 contributions which would be 12.8% × (20% + 8%) = 3.584%). Therefore, it would not be advantageous to pay this additional amount.

Therefore if the salary exceeded the personal allowance for Salvia, this would not be tax efficient as both Styrax and Salvia would be basic rate tax payers and the Class 1 NIC costs would outweigh the tax saving for Styrax.

Savings income

The couple should take advantage of Individual Savings Accounts.

Each of them can invest up to £7,200 per tax year. They can invest up to a maximum of £3,600 in a cash component, with the balance up to the maximum in stocks and shares. The income generated by the accounts is tax free as are any gains on shares.

Since the couple are risk adverse, shares are not a suitable investment for them. Each of them should open an ISA and invest the maximum amount allowable in the cash component. (Styrax would need to transfer £3,600 to Salvia). This would save income tax of £3,600 × 20% = £720.

(ii)   **Future pension provision**

Styrax and Salvia could both start personal pensions.

The maximum tax relievable contributions that Styrax could make would be the higher of:

(1)   £3,600 or
(2)   the amount of his earnings

Salvia could make contributions up to £3,600 even though she has no earnings.

Alternatively, if Salvia becomes an employee of Styrax, he could set up an occupational pension scheme for her.

Since the couple only have disposable income of £3,000 per year, they would probably not wish to spend all of it on pension provision! Possibly both of them could try to invest a small amount per month (say £50).

(b)   **Memorandum**

Enterprise Investment Scheme

The Enterprise Investment Scheme (EIS) is designed to promote enterprise and investment. It helps high-risk, unlisted trading companies raise finance by issuing ordinary shares to unconnected individuals.

If you subscribe for EIS shares you may be entitled to both income tax and capital gains tax reliefs. For income tax, you can claim a tax reduction of the lower of:

(i)   20% of the amount subscribed for qualifying investments (maximum qualifying investments are £500,000 in 2008/09) and
(ii)   your tax liability for the year after deducting VCT relief (described below).

For example, if you subscribed the maximum of £500,000, you could claim a tax reduction of £500,000 × 20% = £100,000. However, if your tax liability is less than £100,000, you can only bring that liability down to nil.

You must hold the shares for at least three years if the income tax relief is not to be withdrawn or reduced. The main reason for the withdrawal of relief will be the sale of the shares by you within the three year period mentioned above.

Where shares qualify for EIS income tax relief there are also special rules for capital gains purposes:

(i)   Where shares are disposed of after the three year period any gain is exempt from CGT. If the shares are disposed of within three years any gain is computed in the normal way.

(ii)   If EIS shares are disposed of at a loss at any time, the loss is allowable but the acquisition cost of the shares is reduced by the amount of EIS relief attributable to the shares. The loss is eligible for a special type of loss relief which enables you to set the loss off against income.

EIS deferral relief may be available to defer chargeable gains if you invest in EIS shares in the period commencing one year before and ending three years after the disposal of an asset. The deferred gain will become chargeable, for example when the shares are disposed of (subject to a further claim for the relief being made). It is not necessary for the shares acquired to be subject to the EIS income tax relief.

The amount of the gain that can be deferred is the lower of:

(i)   The amount subscribed by the investor for his shares, which has not previously been matched under this relief, and

(ii)   The amount specified by the investor in the claim. This can take into account the availability of losses, taper relief and the annual exemption.

The gain may come back into charge, for example if you dispose of the shares or if you become non resident, broadly within three years of the issue of the shares (except if employed full time abroad for up to three years and retaining the shares until your return to the UK).

EIS investments are high risk because there is total exposure to unquoted companies engaged in risky trades.

Venture capital trusts (VCTs)

Venture capital trusts (VCTs) are listed companies which invest in unquoted trading companies and meet certain conditions. The VCT scheme differs from EIS in that you can spread your risk over a number of higher-risk, unquoted companies. However, it is still a moderately high risk investment.

If you invest in a VCT, you will obtain the following tax benefits on a maximum qualifying investment of £200,000 in 2008/09:

(i)   A tax reduction of 30% of the amount invested.

(ii)   Dividends received are tax-free income.

(iii)   Capital gains on the sale of shares in the VCT are exempt from CGT (but losses are not allowable).

If the shares in the VCT are disposed of within five years of issue, then:

(i)   If the shares are not disposed of under a bargain made at arm's length, the tax reduction is withdrawn.

(ii)   If the shares are disposed of under a bargain made at arm's length, the tax reduction is withdrawn, up to the disposal proceeds × 30%.

There is no deferral relief available for VCT investments.

If a VCT's approval is withdrawn within three years of the issue any tax reduction given is withdrawn.

2 Coral

Marking scheme

				Marks
(a)	*Reef Ltd makes the pension contributions*			
	Amount of contributions to be made	1		
	Corporation tax saving	1		
	No income tax or NIC for employee	1		
	Coral and Reef Ltd make the pension contributions			
	Maximum contribution by Coral	½		
	Relevant earnings	1		
	Dividend required by Reef Ltd to Coral	1½		
	Corporation tax implications of dividend	½		
	Income tax implications of dividend	1½		
	Contribution from HMRC	½		
	Contribution by Reef Ltd	½		
	Corporation tax saving	½		
	Conclusion	1		
		Max		9
(b) (i)	UK resident	1		
	UK ordinarily resident	1		
	Non-UK domicile of origin	1		
	No UK domicile of choice	1		
	Rental income potentially taxable on the remittance basis	1		
	Remittance basis charge	2		
	UK tax rate on income on arising basis	1		
	Double taxation relief	1		
		Max		7
(ii)	Dividend income pushed into higher rate band	1		
	Increase in tax rate on dividend income	1		
				2
				18

(a) **Minimising the total after tax cost of the pension contributions**

Reef Ltd makes the pension contributions

The pension contributions will not give rise to any national insurance implications and are an exempt benefit for the purposes of income tax.

	£
Contributions made by Reef Ltd	9,000
Reduction in corporation tax liability (£9,000 × 21%)	(1,890)
Total after tax cost	7,110

Coral and Reef Ltd make the pension contributions between them

The maximum gross tax allowable pension contributions that can be made by Coral are equal to her relevant UK earnings of £5,520 (£460 × 12). The dividend income and any rental income from the overseas property are not relevant earnings. The overseas property cannot be a furnished holiday letting because it is situated outside the UK.

Coral will make the contributions net of 20% income tax. Accordingly, her contributions will be £4,416 (£5,520 × 80%) and she will require a dividend from Reef Ltd of this amount. HMRC will contribute £1,104 (£4,416 × 20/80) such that the gross contributions will be £5,520.

The dividend will not be allowable for the purposes of corporation tax.

The dividend will not give rise to an income tax liability as Coral's basic rate band will be extended by the gross amount of pension contributions made (£5,520) which is more than the taxable dividend income received of £4,907 (£4,416 × 100/90). Accordingly, the dividend income will be taxed at 10% with a 10% tax credit.

	£
Contributions made by Coral	4,416
Contributions made by Reef Ltd (£9,000 – £5,520)	3,480
Reduction in corporation tax liability (£3,480 × 21%)	(731)
Total after tax cost	7,165

The calculations indicate that Coral and Reef Ltd should make the contributions between them as this results in the lower tax cost.

(b) (i) **UK tax on the rental income**

Coral is UK resident in 2009/10 because she is present in the UK for more than 182 days.

Coral is ordinarily resident in the UK in 2009/10 as she is habitually resident in the UK.

Coral will have acquired a domicile of origin in Kalania from her father. She has not acquired a domicile of choice in the UK as she has not severed her ties with Kalania and does not intend to make her permanent home in the UK.

Therefore, Coral is resident and ordinarily resident in the UK, but she is not domiciled in the UK.

As Coral has been resident in the UK for seven of the nine tax years preceding 2009/10 and has unremitted income from Kalania in excess of £2,000 then she can only use the remittance basis for overseas income if she makes a claim. If she makes the claim she would have to pay the remittance basis charge of £30,000. Given her low level of overseas income it would not be worth making the remittance basis claim.

If Coral does not make a remittance basis claim, all rental income from Kalania will be taxed on Coral on an arising basis. The income will fall into the basic rate band and will be subject to income tax at 20% on the gross amount (before deduction of Kalanian tax). Unilateral double tax relief will be available in respect of the 8% tax suffered in Kalania. The effective rate of tax suffered by Coral in the UK on the grossed up amount of income will be 12%.

(ii) **The effect of taxable rental income on the tax due on Coral's dividend income**

Taxing the rental income in the UK on an arising basis will cause some of Coral's dividend income currently falling within the basic rate band to fall within the higher rate band.

The effect of this would be to increase the tax on the gross dividend income from 0% (10% less the 10% tax credit) to 22½% (32½% less 10%) (an effective rate of tax of 25% on the dividend income).

3 Benny Fitt

Marking scheme

				Marks
(a)	*Employment benefits*			
	Car benefit		2	
	Other benefits		2	
	Expense claim		1	
	Income tax liability		1	
	Usine Ltd			
	Capital allowances		2	
	Deductible expenses		1	
	Class 1A NIC		1	
	Private petrol			
	Tax saving		1	
		Max		8
(b)	*Lump sum payments*			
	Wages in lieu of notice		1	
	Taxable amount		2	
	Lump sum on taking up employment			
	Beneficial loan		1	
	Relocation costs		2	
	Accommodation			
	Annual benefit/additional benefit		2	
	Furniture/running costs		1	
				9
(c)	CSOP conditions (1 mark for each relevant point)	Max		4
	Format/ presentation			2
		Max		23

PRIVATE AND CONFIDENTIAL

[Our address]

[Your address]
[Date]

Dear Benny

USINE LTD – BENEFITS FOR EMPLOYEES

This letter deals with the income tax implications of providing various benefits to you, as managing director. It also covers the tax treatment of payments made to the departing sales director and those payments and benefits provided to the new sales director. Finally the conditions for a share option scheme to be approved are detailed.

(a) **Employment benefits**

Benny Fitt

You will have a total taxable benefit charge in respect of the provision of the company car, credit card and computer of £8,660 (see Appendix 1).

You will be able to claim a deduction from your general earnings for the expense payments of £1,100.

The total tax due on these benefits for 2008/09 will be £3,024 (£8,660 – £1,100 = £7,560 @ 40%).

There is no NIC for you as an employee on the value of the benefits.

Usine Ltd

Capital allowances are available to Usine Ltd on the cost of the motor car. The writing-down allowance on the car cannot exceed £3,000 per annum as it costs more than £12,000.

Capital allowances will be available for the expenditure on the computer. It will either be fully relieved via the annual investment allowance or obtain allowances at 20%.

The credit card expenses of £1,265 (£460 + £380 + £425) are allowable deductions from trading profits. However, the cost of client entertaining is not deductible.

Class 1A NIC of £968 will be due on 19 July 2009.

Private petrol

If you reimburse Usine Ltd the £180 paid for your private petrol there would be no assessable fuel benefit.

This would reduce your income tax liability by £1,082 (£2,704 at 40%). The net saving for you would therefore be £902 (£1,082 – £180).

Usine Ltd's Class 1A NIC liability will also be reduced by £346 (£2,704 at 12.8%).

(b) **Sales director changes**

Redundancy payment to departing sales director

Each component of the redundancy payment is treated differently for tax purposes.

The statutory redundancy element is completely exempt from income tax and NIC.

Any payment that the sales director was contractually entitled to is taxable income. This means that the holiday pay is subject to income tax and NIC.

The agreement not to work for a rival company is a 'restrictive covenant'. This is taxable. Income tax and NIC are due on this amount.

Unless there is a contractual entitlement to receive a payment in lieu of notice such payments are treated as 'ex gratia'. The first £30,000 of ex gratia payments are exempt. However any statutory redundancy payment received reduces this amount.

Consequently £15,000 of the £45,000 redundancy payment is taxable (see Appendix 2).

Payments and benefits on new sales director taking up employment

(i) Lump sum payment

The lump sum payment of £10,000 to the new sales director will be taxable as a 'golden hello' unless the payment represents compensation for a right or asset given up on taking up the employment.

(ii) Beneficial loan

In 2008/09 there will be a taxable benefit of £781 (£50,000 × 6.25% × 3/12).

(iii) Relocation costs

There will be no taxable benefit in respect of eligible removal expenses up to £8,000. The exemption covers such items as legal and estate agents' fees, stamp duty land tax, removal costs, and the cost of new domestic goods where existing goods are not suitable for the new residence.

(iv) Accommodation

There will be a taxable benefit in respect of the accommodation in 2008/09 of £2,795 (Appendix 2).

(c) **Company Share Option Plan**

To obtain HMRC approval, a Company Share Option plan must satisfy the following conditions:

(i) The shares over which the options are granted must be fully paid ordinary shares.

(ii) The price of the shares must not be less than their market value at the time of the grant of the option.

(iii) Participation must be limited to employees and full-time directors but not all such individuals need be eligible to participate.

(iv) An employee can only hold options up to a market value of £30,000.

(v) If the company has more than one class of shares, the majority of shares of the class over which the scheme operates must not be held by directors/employees (except for an employee controlled company) nor a holding company (unless scheme shares are quoted).

(vi) Anyone who has, within the preceding 12 months held over 25% of the shares of a close company whose shares may be acquired under the scheme, must be excluded from the scheme.

If you can provide any further information please let me know.

Yours sincerely

Tax manager.

Appendix 1 – Benny Fitt

Employment benefits

	£
Car benefit (£28,400 + £700 − £2,500) × 32% (W) × 6/12	4,256
Fuel benefit (£16,900 × 32% × 6/12)	2,704
Expense payments (£380 + £720)	1,100
Computer £3,000 × 20%	600
	8,660

Working

Taxable car benefit percentage

220 (rounded down) − 135 = 85 ÷ 5 = 17% + 15% = 32%

Class 1A NIC for Usine Ltd

Taxable benefits (£8,660 − 1,100 =) £7,560 at 12.8%   £968

Appendix 2 – Sales director payments and benefits

Redundancy payment to departing sales director

	£	£
General earnings		
Holiday pay	2,800	
Restrictive covenant	3,000	5,800
Specific employment income		
Payment in lieu of notice (if not contractual)	3,100	
Compensation	34,000	
	37,100	
Less: exempt £(30,000 – 2,100)	(27,900)	9,200
Taxable as employment income		15,000

Accommodation benefit for new sales director

	£
Annual value (£4,400 × 3/12)	1,100
Additional benefit (£99,000 – £75,000) = £24,000 at 6.25% × 3/12	375
Furniture (£10,400 × 20% × 3/12)	520
Running costs (£3,200 × 3/12)	800
	2,795

4 Benny Korere

Text references. Employment income aspects in Chapters 4 and 5. CGT liability covered in Chapter 11. Shares are dealt with in Chapter 12. The income tax computation is covered in Chapter 1.

Top tips. You would be best to look at each section of the requirements carefully and separately. Work through each part one by one. Keep your answers well presented, clear and well spaced out.

Easy marks. Three marks for standard employment income computation. It is well worth getting to grips with this topic as there can be lots of easy marks available.

Marking scheme

				Marks
(a)		Salary	½	
		Payment in lieu of notice taxable in full	½	
		Payment for agreeing not to work for competitors	½	
		Car benefit	1½	
				3
(b)	(i)	Grant of option – no income tax	½	
		Exercise of option:		
		Amount chargeable to tax	1	
		Tax year/rate of tax	½	
		Risk exposure:		
		Identification of potential problem	1	
		Shares could be worth less than price paid	½	
		Income tax paid	½	
				4
	(ii)	Additional information – 5 × ½	2½	
		Flat in different location:		
		Recognition that benefit is likely to increase	1	
		Statement of how increase calculated	1	
			Max	4

(c) Share pool: Proceeds   1
                     Cost   1
                     Sale of rights   1
     Annual exemption   ½
     CGT at 18%   ½
                                                                          $\frac{4}{15}$

(a) **Employment income for 2008/09**

	£
Salary (£32,000 × 11/12)	29,333
Payment in lieu of notice (Note)	8,000
Payment for agreeing not to work for competitors	17,500
Car benefit (W)	3,621
Employment income	58,454

Note. As the payment in lieu of notice is made in accordance with Benny's contractual arrangements with Golden Tan plc, it will be treated as a payment in respect of services provided and will be taxable in 2008/09, the year in which it is received.

Working

Car benefit

	£
List price (£22,360 – £5,000)	17,360
Percentage (180 – 135)/5 = 9	
15 + 9	× 24%
	× 11/12
	3,819
Contributions for private use (£18 × 11)	(198)
	3,621

> **Top tips.** Although Benny paid £6,100 as a capital contribution towards the car only £5,000 can be deducted from the cost of £22,360.

(b) (i) **The share options**

There are no income tax implications when the share options are granted.

In the tax year in which Benny exercises the options and acquires the shares, the excess of the market value of the shares over the price paid, ie £11,500 ((£3.35 – £2.20) × 10,000) will be subject to income tax.

Benny's financial exposure arises due to the rule of the share option scheme obliging him to hold the shares for a year before he can sell them. If the company's expansion into Eastern Europe fails, and its share price consequently falls to below £2.20 before Benny has the chance to sell the shares, Benny's financial position may be summarised as follows:

- Benny will have paid £22,000 (£2.20 × 10,000) for shares which are now worth less than that.
- He will also have paid income tax of £4,600 (£11,500 × 40%).

(ii) **The flat**

The following additional information is required in order to calculate the employment income benefit in respect of the flat.

- The flat's annual value.
- The cost of any improvements made to the flat prior to 6 April 2009.
- The cost of power, water, repairs and maintenance etc borne by Summer Glow plc.
- The cost of the furniture provided by Summer Glow plc.
- Any use of the flat by Benny wholly, exclusively and necessarily for the purposes of his employment.

Note. The market value of the flat is not required as Summer Glow plc has owned it for less than six years.

One element of the employment income benefit in respect of the flat is calculated by reference to its original cost plus the cost of any capital improvements prior to 6 April 2009. If Benny requests a flat in a different location, this element of the benefit will be computed instead by reference to the cost of the new flat, which in turn equals the proceeds of sale of the old flat.

Accordingly, if, as is likely, the value of the flat has increased since it was purchased, Benny's employment income benefit will also increase. The increase in the employment income benefit will be the flat's sales proceeds less its original cost less the cost of any capital improvements prior to 6 April 2009 multiplied by 6.25%.

(c) **Capital gains tax liability – Sale of shares in Mahana plc**

Share pool

	£
Disposal proceeds	24,608
Less: Cost (W)	(5,032)
	19,576
Less: Annual exemption	(9,600)
Taxable gains	9,976
Capital gains tax at 18%	1,796

Working

Share pool

		No.	Cost £
June 1988	Acquisition	8,400	6,744
February 1996	Sale of rights (Note)		(610)
		8,400	6,134
April 2005	Acquisition	1,300	2,281
		9,700	8,415
March 2009	Sale	(5,800)	(5,032)
		3,900	3,383

Note. The proceeds from the sale of the rights are regarded as small because they are less than £3,000. Accordingly, there is no disposal and the proceeds are deducted from the cost in the pool.

5 Pilar Mareno

Text references. Income tax computations are dealt with in Chapter 1. Employment income is dealt with in Chapter 4 and sole traders in Chapter 6. Irrecoverable VAT is covered in Chapter 29.

Top tips. Make sure you read the whole of the question carefully before starting. There was a very useful guide to how to tackle this question in the e-mail from your manager. If you followed this method you should have scored reasonable marks .

Easy marks. The factors for employment versus self-employment should have been easy marks as this is basic book knowledge.

Marks

(1) Calculations
Employ Alec:

Net profit of contract	½
Irrecoverable VAT/purchase of van	½
Alec's salary and class 1 secondary NIC	1½
Tax and NIC saved	½

Effect on Alec's income:

Identification of issue	1
Calculation	1½

Offer Max a contract:

Fees paid	½
Irrecoverable VAT on fees	½
Tax and NIC saved	½

Supporting calculations
Irrecoverable VAT:

Identification of issue	1
Current partial exemption position	1
Application of *de minimis*	1
Irrecoverable amount with new contract	1

Purchase of van:

Net cost	½
Irrecoverable VAT	1
Tax and NIC saved	1
Cost per year	½

Leasing van

Rentals	1½
Irrecoverable VAT	1
Tax and NIC saved	1

Max   16

(2) Rationale and summary

Reference to Pilar's family income criterion	1
Conclusion re van and implications	1
Summary of findings	1

Max   2

(3) Alec's employment

Use of partnership	2
Secure job, short-term contract	1½
Alec would be a separate client from Pilar	1

Max   2

(4) Max's employment status

Each valid factor – ½ mark (max 5 factors)	2½
Depends on all of the facts	½

3

Appropriate style and presentation	1
Effectiveness of communication	1

2

25

MEMORANDUM

To: The files
From: Tax assistant
Date: [date]
Subject: Pilar Mareno – Business expansion

This memorandum covers tax issues relating to Pilar Mareno's (PM's) proposed business expansion.

Rationale

PM will only take on the new contract if it generates at least £15,000 for her and her family. It has therefore been necessary to determine the true cost of the contract and the effect on the whole family.

PM needs to know whether it is more beneficial to employ her husband, Alec, as her assistant or to take on a contractor. In addition she would need to have the use of a van and would like to know whether it would be better from a tax perspective to purchase the van outright or to lease it over a period of, say, two years.

Workings 2 and 3 below show that it is more beneficial to purchase the van outright and therefore this route only has been incorporated into the illustrative calculations in the attached Appendices.

Appendix 1 shows the position if Alec is employed and Appendix 2 shows the position if Max Wallen contracts as PM's assistant.

Other issues regarding employing Alec

As Alec and PM are married, it may be a better decision to enter into a partnership agreement. An appropriate profit share ratio can be decided upon so that Alec receives sufficient income. In addition, they may decide that Alec should receive more than the equivalent of the proposed salary in order to better balance the amount of income taxed in PM's and Alec's hands, as Alec is a basic rate taxpayer.

This would mean that more of the family's income would be taxed at 20% rather than 40%. In addition, Alec's rate of NIC would reduce from 11% (Class 1 primary) to 8% (Class 4). However, the converse of this is that PM's rate of NIC would only be 1% as she is liable at the additional rate.

This would provide more stability for Alec who it is proposed will give up his steady employment for less money and a possible part-time position that he has not even found yet.

Alec should take advice about his own personal situation. As Alec and Pilar are spouses there may be a conflict of interest if we offer advice to each. We need to point this out to both clients, but may continue to act if we monitor the situation to ensure that there is not threat to our integrity.

Max Wallen: employed v self-employed

There are a number of factors that HMRC would look at to determine whether Max Wallen is a self-employed contractor or an employee.

These include:

- Max provides his own equipment, which indicates he is self-employed
- However, he will use PM's own software which could indicate that he an employee
- Max must perform the work himself and cannot send a substitute, which indicates that he is an employee
- He receives sick pay – another indicator that he is an employee
- He is paid by the day with no particular contract tasks – this again would indicate that he is an employee rather than self-employed

No one factor is enough in itself to indicate employment or self employment position and therefore HMRC will look at the facts of the individual case to decide Max's status.

Summary of findings

Whether PM employs Alec or offers a contract position to Max Wallen, both routes will generate over £15,000. It is therefore up to PM to make a decision based on all of the information contained in this memorandum.

Tax assistant

APPENDIX 1 – EMPLOY ALEC AND BUY VAN

	£
Contract profit	45,000
Less:	
irrecoverable VAT (W1)	(8,054)
Alec's salary	(7,600)
Class 1 secondary NIC on Alec's salary £(7,600 – 5,435) @ 12.8%	(277)
Net profit	29,069
Less:	
Income tax: £29,069 @ 40%	(11,628)
NIC: £29,069 @ 1%	(291)
	17,150
Less: Van costs (W2 and W3)	(1,705)
	15,445
Effect on Alec's income (W4) (Note)	414
Total post-tax income	15,859

Note. Pilar has stated that she will enter into the contract if it generates an additional £15,000 for the *family* – Alec's position therefore also needs to be considered.

APPENDIX 2 – OFFER MAX WALLEN A CONTRACT AND BUY VAN

	£
Contract profit	45,000
Less:	
irrecoverable VAT (W1)	(8,054)
Max Wallen's fees: £75 × 100 (No NIC due from Pilar)	(7,500)
irrecoverable VAT on fees:	
£7,500 × 17.5% × 35%	(459)
Net profit	28,987
Less:	
Income tax: £28,987 @ 40%	(11,595)
NIC: £28,987 @ 1%	(290)
	17,102
Less: Van costs (W2 and W3)	(1,705)
Pilar's post-tax income	15,397

Workings

(1)   *Irrecoverable VAT*

      We are told to deal with VAT first by Tax Manager

      EXISTING CONTRACT

      Exempt supplies: £100,000 × 17.5% × 35%   £6,125

      This is less than ½ of the total VAT and is below the *de minimis* limit of £625 × 12 = 7,500. As a result all of this is recoverable in full.

      WITH NEW CONTRACT

	£
Existing contracts (as above)	6,125
New contract: £31,500 × 17.5% × 35%	1,929
Total	8,054

      This is less than ½ of the total VAT but exceeds the *de minimis* limit of £(625 × 12 =) 7,500. As a result none of this VAT will be recoverable.

(2)   *After tax cost of buying the van*

	£	£
Cost	7,800	
Less: sale value	(2,500)	5,300
Add: irrecoverable VAT		
£7,800 × 17.5% × 35% (Note 1)		478
Less:		
income tax saved: £(5,300 + 478) × 40%	(2,311)	
NIC saved: £(5,300 + 478) × 1%	(58)	
		(2,369)
Total		3,409
Averaged over two years		£1,705

Notes

1   Although the van will be used wholly for business purposes, we are told that exempt supplies will amount to 35% of the contract and therefore this proportion of VAT will not be recoverable.

2   As the van will be sold at a loss, full relief for the expenditure will be allowed through the capital allowances computation and will therefore be fully deductible for income tax purposes.

(3)   *After tax cost of leasing the van*

	£
Lease payments: 12 × £300	3,600
Add: irrecoverable VAT	
£3,600 × 17.5% × 35%	221
Less:	
income tax saved: £(3,600 + 221) × 40%	(1,528)
NIC saved: £(3,600 + 221) × 1%	(38)
Annual cost	2,255

As the cost of buying the van outright (W2) is cheaper than leasing the van, all calculations in the Appendices have been made on the basis that the van is purchased.

(4)   *Effect on Alec's income*

	£
Original salary	17,000
New income	
working for Pilar	(7,600)
other part-time work	(10,000)
Additional income	600
Less:	
additional income tax: £600 @ 20%	(120)
additional NIC: £600 @ 11%	(66)
Net additional income	414

6 Alex Zong

Text references. Trading profits are covered in Chapter 6. Incorporation of a business is covered in Chapter 30. The VAT aspects of the question are in Chapters 28 and 29.

Top tips. Consider how much of this question requires nothing more than your basic Paper F6 tax knowledge.

Easy marks. The trading profits calculation in part (a) should have been very easy marks, so long as you knew your basis period rules for opening, continuing and closing years. If you pick up these easy marks you do not have to score so highly on the more complex incorporation and VAT issues.

					Marks
(a)	(i)	Trading income		1½	
		Overlap profits		1	
		2008/09 trading income		1	
		Capital allowances		2	
			Max		4
	(ii)	Gains		1	
		Incorporation relief		1	
		Losses		1	
		Use of entrepreneurs' relief/AE		3	
			Max		5
	(iii)	TOGC		1	
		VAT number		1	
					2
(b)		Bad debt		2	
		Refund of VAT		2	
		Discount		1	
					5
					16

(a)   (i)   **Trading profits assessments**

The trading profits for each accounting period are:

		£
2005/06	1.10.05 – 5.4.06 (6/9 × £19,950)	13,333
2006/07	12 m/e 30.9.07	
	£19,950 + (3/12 × £41,612)	30,353
2007/08	y/e 30.6.07	41,612

Overlap profits on commencement were.

	£
1.10.05 to 5.4.06 (£19,950 × 6/9)	13,300
1.7.06 to 30.9.06 (£41,612 × 3/12)	10,403
	23,703

Alex's taxable trading profits assessment for 2008/09 will be as follows.

	£
y/e 30.6.08	49,993
p/e 31.12.08	29,000
	78,993
Relief for overlap profits	(23,703)
	55,290

Capital allowances

Alex should elect to transfer plant to Lexon Ltd at its written-down value. This avoids the balancing charges that would otherwise arise in the final period. The market values of the lorry and plant (£4,300 + £8,200 = £12,500) and the motor car (£11,500) both exceed their respective written-down values. A balancing charge of £8,225 (£4,275 – £12,500) would arise on the main pool; and one of £600 (£10,500 – £11,500) × 60%) would arise on the private use expensive car.

(ii) **Capital gains tax**

The assets will be deemed to be disposed of at their market values:

	£	£
Goodwill		
Proceeds		40,000
Cost		(nil)
Capital gain		40,000
Freehold premises		
Proceeds		75,000
Cost	32,000	
Enhancement expenditure	6,700	
		(38,700)
Gain		36,300

Total gains total £76,300 (40,000 + 36,300).

Incorporation relief applies automatically as the business is being transferred as a going concern, and all of the business assets are being transferred. However since Alex is receiving some shares and some cash (loan account) not all of the gain can be rolled over. Alex will have a chargeable gain of £4,769 (£76,300 × 10,000/160,000) which will be completely extinguished by the capital losses made in the year.

However, Alex could also make a claim for entrepreneurs' relief and make use of his annual exemption for 2008/09 by increasing the amount of the loan account to £83,418.

	£
Gain before incorporation relief	76,300
Less: incorporation relief (W)	(36,520)
Gain after incorporation relief	39,780
Less: entrepreneurs' relief	
4/9 × £39,780	(17,680)
Gain after entrepreneurs' relief	22,100
Less: loss	(12,500)
Net gain	9,600
Less: annual exemption	(9,600)
Taxable gain	nil

Working

	£
Annual exemption	9,600
Add losses	12,500
Gain before entrepreneurs' relief	22,100
Add entrepreneurs' relief	
4/5 × £22,100	17,680
Gain	39,780
Less total gain	(76,300)
Incorporation relief required	36,520

Share consideration required:

$$£160,000 \times \frac{36,520}{76,300}$$

76,582

Loan account should therefore be:
£(160,000 − 76,582)

83,418

(iii) **Value added tax**

The incorporation of a business as a going concern is outside the scope of VAT. This means there will be no VAT charged on any assets transferred to Lexon Ltd.

Lexon Ltd will be able to take over Alex's VAT registration number if it wishes. However, if this is done then the company assumes Alex's VAT liabilities.

(b)   (i)   **Bad debt**

Bad debts relief is given six months after the time that payment was due, provided that the debt has been written-off. Since an invoice was not raised until 15 June 2008, bad debt relief cannot be claimed in the VAT return for the quarter ended 30 November 2008. The amount of the relief to be claimed in the following VAT return will be £1,050 ([9,400 – 2,350] × 17.5/117.5) .

(ii)   **Refund of VAT**

A claim must be made for the repayment of the VAT under-claimed. The amount due cannot just be put through on the next VAT return, since the error exceeds £2,000. Claims for the refund of VAT are subject to a three-year time limit, and so the claim will cover the period 1 December 2005 to 30 November 2008. The repayment will be for £2,547 (£475 × 36 × 17.5/117.5).

(iii)   **Discount**

Where a discount is offered for prompt payment, VAT is due on the net amount even if the discount is not taken. The output VAT due is £565 (£3,400 × 95% × 17.5%).

7 Anne Parr

Text references. Chapter 5 covers the taxation of termination payments. The employment vs self-employment factors are discussed in Chapter 4. Trading income is in Chapter 6. The basic VAT rules are in Chapter 28 and the partial exemption rules are in Chapter 29. Chapters 20 and 22 cover the calculation of corporation tax liabilities, with capital allowances in Chapter 7.

Top tips. The requirement for part (b) provides you with three useful headings to use in your report so use them to help structure your answer.

Make sure you do the calculations for part (c) before you jump in and write your answer so that you can compare the results of each option and write a sensible conclusion.

Easy marks. Part (d) required a calculation for ten marks. Do your workings first, such as the capital allowances, and reference them in clearly to pick up all the available marks.

Marking scheme

		Marks	
(a)	**Compensation payment**		
	Bonus = reward for services	½	
	Taxable 2008/09	½	
	Ex gratia partially exempt	1	
	£30,000 exempt	1	
	If contractual = taxable	½	
	Max		3
(b)	**Employment vs self-employment**		
	Contract of/ for services	½	
	No single factor conclusive	½	
	Factors – 1 mark per sensible comment	6	
	Conclusion	1	
	Max		7
	Taxable trading income		
	Adjusted profits	1	
	Capital allowances	1½	
	2008/09	1	
	2009/10	1	
	2010/11	½	
	Overlap profits	1	
	When can be relieved	1	
	Max		6

VAT dates

Threshold exceeded	1	
Register by 30 November	1	
Charge from 1 December	1	
Liable for VAT if fails to register	1	
		4
Format/ presentation		2

(c) **After-tax cost of using Anne's services**

Employer's NIC	½	
Partial exemption percentage	1	
Irrecoverable VAT – excluding Anne's services	2½	
Irrecoverable VAT – including Anne's services	3½	
Corporation tax saving	1	
Max		7

(d) **Longhorn Ltd CT liability**

Adjusted trading profits (½ mark for each correct adjustment)	5½	
IBAs	2	
Interest income	1½	
Overseas income	½	
Gains	½	
CT rates	½	
DTR	1	
CVS relief	½	
Max		10
		39

(a) **Compensation payment**

The bonus due to Anne forms part of her normal earnings as it is a reward for past services performed and will be fully liable to tax. It will be taxable in the tax year of receipt, ie 2008/09.

The *ex gratia* payment does not arise from her employment contract but is instead made in respect of the loss of her employment. Only the excess of the payment over £30,000 (ie £44,000) is taxable.

If Anne were to receive a contractual termination payment, this would again be fully taxable since it would arise from her employment.

(b) **Report**

To:	Anne Parr
From:	A Adviser
Date:	[date]
Subject:	Self-employment status

This report covers tax issues relating to:

(i) Factors in deciding employment or self-employment
(ii) Projected taxable trading income
(iii) VAT registration

(i) **Factors in deciding employment or self-employment**

The key test of employment as against self-employment is the existence of a contract *of* service, compared with a contract *for* services. There are a number of other factors which should be considered. No single factor is likely to be conclusive.

HMRC is likely to consider the following factors:

- Degree of control
- Mutuality of obligations
- Correction of work
- Degree of financial risk
- Provision of equipment
- Conditions of pay
- Client portfolio
- Integration into business organisation

Factors indicating self-employment

With regard to your own circumstances, you appear to be acting as an external consultant, as opposed to performing an integral function in Longhorn Ltd's business.

You are receiving a fixed fee for work done, rather than payment for time spent on the company's behalf.

While Longhorn Ltd is currently your only paymaster you are not formally tied to it beyond the span of your six-month assignment and it appears that you are seeking other clients; this probably outweighs the fact that in practice you cannot currently work for others.

You have no obligation to accept further work from Longhorn Ltd nor does Longhorn Ltd have to provide such work. This shows there is no mutual obligation.

Longhorn Ltd does not seem to have control over the conduct of your work, assuming that your presence on the premises is merely a practical requirement; the obligation to report to the managing director does not appear to imply supervision of your work as such.

Factors indicating employment

Office space and assistance is provided by Longhorn Ltd. However, you will presumably also make use of your home office. It is therefore arguable that these are temporary arrangements which are a necessary feature of this particular line of work.

Conclusion

Taking all these factors into account, it therefore seems likely that you would be regarded as having self-employed status.

(ii) **Projected taxable trading income**

Your first tax year of trade will be 2008/09 when the taxable trading profits will be £16,970. The taxable trade profits in 2009/10 and 2010/11 will be £36,665 and £44,799 respectively.

The overlap profits that will arise as a result of double taxation of trade profits in 2008/09 and 2009/10 will be £28,170, which you will be able to offset either on a change of accounting date or when the business ceases.

Please see Appendix 1 for my calculations of the above figures.

(iii) **VAT registration**

You will exceed the registration threshold of £67,000 by the end of October 2009 as follows:

		£
October 2008 – March 2009	6 × £4,200	25,200
April 2009 – October 2009	7 × £6,300	44,100
Exceeds threshold		69,300

You will be required to register with HMRC by 30 November 2009.

You should start charging VAT on your supplies from 1 December 2009.

Failure to register for VAT

If you to fail to register on time you would still be liable to account for VAT due on supplies made from the date on which you were obliged to register (from 1 December 2009).

(c) **After-tax cost to Longhorn Ltd of using Anne's services**

As an employee, the cost to the company comprises Anne's salary and Class 1 secondary contributions, both of which are allowable deductions in the company's corporation tax computation.

As a self-employed contractor the company will pay her fees, but will consequently incur irrecoverable input VAT relating to general business overheads. Both costs are allowable deductions in the company's corporation tax computation.

The after tax cost to the company will be £3,145 (£34,675 – £31,530) greater if it hires Anne on a self-employed basis (see Appendix 2).

(d) **Longhorn Ltd – Corporation tax computation – period ended 31 March 2009**

	£
Taxable trading profits (W1)	142,338
Interest (W3)	680
Overseas income (dividends)	4,800
Chargeable gains	28,070
PCTCT	175,888
Corporation tax (£175,588 × 21% (W4))	36,936
Less Double tax relief (W5)	(480)
	36,456
Less Corporate Venturing Scheme relief (£27,000 × 20%)	(5,400)
Corporation tax payable	31,056

Workings

(1)   *Taxable trading profits*

	£	£
Profit per accounts		149,000
Add back		
Depreciation of fixed assets (Note (i))	16,225	
Directors' remuneration (Note (ii))	14,000	
Fine for breach of law	3,850	
Gifts of drink to customers	2,268	
Subscription to political party	10,000	
Fees in relation to issue of shares	3,750	
Interest on loan to acquire investment	3,020	
		53,113
Deduct		
Non-trade interest	2,850	
Profit on sale of office	42,875	
Profit on gain of government security	850	
Dividend from overseas investment	4,800	
		(51,375)
Adjusted profit before capital allowances		150,738
Less IBAs (W2)		(8,400)
Taxable trading profits		142,338

Notes

(i)   The amortisation of intangible assets is an allowable deduction for companies.

(ii)   The directors' remuneration is allowable if paid within nine months of the year end. As £14,000 is not paid within nine months, it must be disallowed in this period's computation, but will be allowed in the following year when paid.

(2) *IBAs allowances on sports pavilion*

Sports pavilions provided for the welfare of employees qualify for industrial buildings allowances.

Building costs (including fees but excluding cost of land) (£280,000 × 3%)   £8,400

(3) *Interest (loan relationships)*

	£
Bank interest	2,850
Profit on sale of government security	850
Interest paid on loan to acquire overseas investment	(3,020)
Interest	680

The income/expenditure and profits/losses on all loan relationships entered into for non-trade purposes are aggregated. A net credit is taxed as interest income.

(4) *Corporation tax rate – 12 months ended 31 March 2009*

PCTCT = 'profits'   £175,888

The company has not received any franked investment income and the 'profits' are therefore the same as the PCTCT

FY2008

Upper limit	£1,500,000
Lower limit	£300,000
	Small companies' rate applies

(5) **Double tax relief**

	£	£
Double tax relief available on the overseas dividend is the lower of:		
(i) Foreign tax suffered (£4,800 × 10%)	480	
(ii) UK tax on overseas income (£4,800 × 21%)	1,008	
Double tax relief		480

Appendix 1

Taxable trading profits

	£
2008/09	
1 October 2008 – 5 April 2009 (actual basis)	
£25,455 (W1) × $^6/_9$	16,970
2009/10	
1 October 2008 – 30 September 2009 (first 12 months)	
£25,455 + (£44,799 × $^3/_{12}$)	36,655
2010/11	
Year ended 30 June 2010 (current year basis)	44,799

Overlap profits

	£
1 October 2008 to 5 April 2009 (£25,455 × $^6/_9$)	16,970
1 July 2009 to 30 September 2009 (£44,799 × $^3/_{12}$)	11,200
	28,170

Workings

(1)   *Adjusted profits*

	Nine months to 30 June 2009 £	*Year ended 30 June 2010* £
Profits	27,750	42,800
Add Depreciation	3,200	2,560
Less Capital allowances (W2)	(5,495)	(561)
Tax adjusted profits	25,455	44,799

(2)   *Capital allowances*

	AIA £	*Private use car* £	*Allowances* £
9 months ended 30.6.09			
Additions qualifying for AIA			
10.08 Office equipment	5,000		
AIA (Max £50,000 × $^9/_{12}$)	(5,000)		5,000
Additions not qualifying for AIA			
10.08 Car		11,000	
WDA @ 20% × $^9/_{12}$		(1,650) × 30%	495
TWDV c/f		9,350	
Allowances			5,495
y/e 30.6.10			
WDA @ 20%		(1,870) × 30%	561
TWDV c/f		7,480	
Allowances			561

Appendix 2

After-tax cost to Longhorn Ltd of using Anne's services

	Employee £	*Self-employed* £
Payment – salary/fees	36,000	36,000
Employer's NIC (W1)	3,912	
Irrecoverable VAT cost (W2)		7,892
	39,912	43,892
Less Corporation tax saving @ 21%	(8,382)	(9,217)
After-tax cost to the company	31,530	34,675

Workings

(1)   *Employer's NIC*

Class 1 secondary contributions = (£36,000 – £5,435) × 12.8% = £3,912

Note. For annual calculations the primary threshold of £5,435 should be used in the examination.

(2)   *Irrecoverable VAT cost*

Recoverability of input VAT

Excluding supplies from Anne as a VAT registered trader

	Total £	*Recoverable* £	*Irrecoverable* £
Re exempt supplies	4,700		4,700
Re general overheads (W3)	8,900	7,031	1,869
Re taxable supplies (balancing fig)	21,143	21,143	
	34,743	28,174	6,569

Average exempt input tax falls below £625 per month and is less than 50% of the total input tax. Therefore all exempt input VAT is recoverable, ignoring Anne's supplies.

Taking Anne's supplies into account

	£	Total £	Recoverable £	Irrecoverable £
Re exempt supplies		4,700		4,700
Re taxable supplies		21,143	21,143	
Re general overheads				
As before	8,900			
Supplies from Anne				
(£36,000 × 17.5%)	6,300			
Allocation (79%:21%) (W3)		15,200	12,008	3,192
		41,043	33,151	7,892

Exempt input tax is now in excess of *de minimis* limits so no exempt input VAT is recoverable. Recoverable VAT would be £33,151.

Irrecoverable VAT of £7,892 represents an additional cost to the company but, as it relates to general business overheads, it is an allowable deduction for corporation tax purposes.

(3) *Indirectly attributable input VAT*

Recoverable input VAT on general overheads = $\dfrac{220,000 + 30,000}{220,000 + 30,000 + 70,000} \times 100\%$

Recoverable input VAT on general overheads = 79% (round up to nearest whole %)

Irrecoverable input VAT on general overheads = 21%

8 Ming Khan and Nina Lee

Text references. Partnerships are covered in Chapter 9. Capital allowances are in Chapter 7. Loss relief is in Chapter 8. Ethics are in Chapter 30.

Top tips. Chargeable gains are taxed at a flat rate of 18%.

Easy marks. There are a lot of different things to do in this question. You do not have to answer the question in order. For example, part (b) is a stand alone part. For easy marks tackle the parts of a question you feel most comfortable with first. However, allocate your time carefully between the sections.

Marking scheme

					Marks
(a)	(1)	Capital allowances		2	
		Allocation of loss		2	
			Max		3
	(2)	Carry forward trade loss relief		1	
		Trade loss relief against general income on gains		2	
		Early trade loss relief		1	
					4
	(3)	*Ming Khan*			
		Loss relief claims		1	
		Refund 2007/08		3	
		Refund 2006/07		2	
		Nina Lee			
		Refund 2007/08		3	
		Loss relief claims		1	
			Max		9

(4)	*Computer equipment – Hire-purchase*		
	Capital allowances	2	
	Finance charge	1	
	VAT	1	
	Computer equipment – Leasing		
	Lease rental payments	1	
	VAT	1	
			6

Format/ presentation   2

(b)	Client identification	1	
	Communication with previous accountant	1	
	Engagement letter	1	
	Conflict of interest	1	
	Max		3
			27

(a)

To	The files
From	Tax assistant
Date	[date]
Subject	Ming Khan and Nina Lee – partnership

This memorandum covers tax issues relating to the partnership run by Ming Khan (MK) and Nina Lee (NL).

Allocation of partnership trading loss

The trading loss is £98,250 (71,250 + 27,000 (W)).
This is shared £58,950 to MK and £39,300 to NL, and allocated to tax years as follows.

	Ming (60%) £	Nina (40%) £
2008/09 (1.5.08 to 5.4.09)		
£58,950/£39,300 × 11/15	43,230	28,820
2009/10 (Balance of loss)	15,720	10,480
	58,950	39,300

The trading profit assessments for 2008/09 and 2009/10 will be nil.

Working

Capital allowances	*Pool* £
Recording equipment	70,300
Electrical system	19,400
Sound insulation	13,200
Heating system	5,100
	108,000
WDA 20% × 15/12	(27,000)
TWDV carried forward	81,000

The building is not an industrial building hence no IBAs are due on its cost.

Use of trading losses

The trading losses can be relieved in the following ways:

(i)   Carrying it forward to set against future trading profits.

(ii)   Claiming relief against general income. The loss for 2008/09 can be set against general income for 2008/09 and/or 2007/08. The loss for 2009/10 can be set against general income for 2009/10 and/or 2008/09. Provided, in any particular year, that a claim to offset the loss against general income is made first, a claim could also be made to extend the set off to chargeable gains of the same year.

(iii)   Claiming early trade losses relief against general income of the three years preceding the year of the loss, earliest year first. Thus the 2008/09 loss can be carried back to: 2005/06, 2006/07 and 2007/08 and the 2009/10 loss can be carried back to 2006/07, 2007/08 and 2008/09

Specific loss relief claims and repayments generated

Ming Khan

MK should claim to set the loss of £43,230 for 2008/09 against her total income for 2007/08.

	£	£
Employment income – Salary (£42,000 × 11/12)		38,500
Compensation	60,000	
Exemption	(30,000)	
		30,000
		68,500
Less: Loss relief		(43,230)
		25,270
Personal allowance		(6,035)
Taxable income		19,235

This will result in a tax repayment of:

£	£
15,565 (£34,800 – £19,235) @ 20%	3,113
27,665 @ 40%	11,066
43,230	14,179

MK does not have any income for 2008/09 or 2009/10, and so a claim to offset the loss against general income of the year of the loss and/or the prior year in respect of her loss for 2009/10 is not available. She should therefore make a claim for early trade losses relief against her total income for 2006/07.

	£
Employment income – Salary	42,000
Loss claim	(15,720)
	26,280
Personal allowance	(6,035)
Taxable income	20,245

This will result in a tax repayment of:

	£
£14,555 (£34,800 – £20,245) @ 20%	2,911
£1,165 @ 40%	466
15,720	3,377

Nina Lee

NL's taxable income for 2005/06 and 2006/07 is £215 (£6,250 – £6,035). A claim for early trade losses relief is not beneficial as it would waste personal allowances in these years and only save a small amount of tax.

NL should utilise her loss of £28,820 for 2008/09 by claiming against her total income for 2007/08. Although this does waste personal allowances it also allows her to set the loss against her chargeable gain and obtain an immediate repayment of CGT.

	£
Rental income	6,250
Less: Loss relief	(6,250)
	nil
Tax refund: £215 at 20%	43

	£
Chargeable gain	39,600
Less: Loss relief (£28,820 – £6,250)	(22,570)
	17,030
Less: Annual exemption	(9,600)
Taxable gain	7,430

	£
Capital gains tax due:	
£7,430 × 18%	1,337
Previously paid on £30,000 (£39,600 – £9,600)	
£30,000 × 18%	(5,400)
Repayment due	(4,063)

NL's loss of £10,480 for 2009/10 should be carried forward to set against her trading profits for 2010/11 (year ended 31 July 2010).

Acquisition of computer equipment

Hire-purchase

The partnership will be able to claim capital allowances on the cost of the computer equipment of £52,000 (£61,100 × 100/117.5). Dependent on the level of other capital expenditure, up to £50,000 AIA may be available and a writing down allowance of 20% pa will be available on the balance not covered by the AIA.

The finance charge of £20,000 (36 × £2,000 = £72,000 – £52,000) will be a deductible expense for the partnership, and will be allocated to periods of account using normal accounting principles.

The input VAT of £9,100 will be reclaimed on the VAT return for the period in which the computer equipment is purchased.

Leasing

The lease rental payments of £24,000 pa (£28,200 × 100/117.5) will be a deductible expense for the partnership, and will be allocated to periods of account in accordance with the accruals concept.

The input VAT of £4,200 (£28,200 × 17.5/117.5) included in each lease rental payment will be reclaimed on the tax return for the period during which the appropriate tax point occurs.

No capital allowances can be claimed by the partnership.

Tax assistant

(b)   When commencing to act for MK, NL and the partnership you must:

- Obtain proof of identity. For MK and NL this would be one item of photographic ID, such as a passport, and proof of address, eg a recent utility bill. A partnership need have no formal documentation, but you should obtain some proof of existence such as a bank statement, or certificate of registration for VAT. You have already confirmed the identities of the partners.

- Communicate with the former accountant, if any. If either MK or NL has previously had a tax adviser you should request permission to write to them, and you should ask MK or NL to authorise the previous adviser to communicate with you. If this permission is not forthcoming you need to decline to act.

- Prepare a letter of engagement for each of MK, NL and the partnership setting out your own and their responsibilities.

- In instances where you are acting for all the parties you need to ensure that no conflict of interest arises. You will need to monitor the situation regularly to ensure that you identify any threat as soon as it arises.

9 Kara Weddell

Text references. Chapters 6 and 7 deal with computation of trading profits and capital allowances. Losses for a sole trader are covered in Chapter 8. Corporation tax losses are dealt with in Chapter 24 and group relief in Chapter 26. Close companies are covered in Chapter 25 and taxable employment benefits in Chapter 4. Ethics are covered in Chapter 30.

Top tips. It was very important to follow the order of the schedules set out in the question. You needed to calculate the losses available for relief in part (a) first and then apply loss relief in part (b).

Easy marks. The calculation of the losses and profits and the application of basis periods to tax years was knowledge that you should have been familiar with from the F6 syllabus. You should also have been able to state some basic rules on loss relief.

Examiner's comments. In part (a) candidates were required to calculate the tax adjusted trading profit/loss of the new business. This required a relatively tricky calculation of industrial buildings allowances which was not done well.

Part (b), representing almost half of the question, required candidates to determine the tax relief available in respect of the anticipated trading losses depending on the legal structure of the venture. This necessitated some clear thinking, ideally communicated to the examiner via the use of subheadings, such that a distinction was drawn between operating as an unincorporated trader and operating as a company. In many cases there was little evidence of such thinking taking place.

The majority of candidates either ignored the opening year rules for the unincorporated trader or failed to apply them to the situation. To be fair this was a relatively tricky situation due to the presence of the losses but it did seem as though many candidates had forgotten the basic rules governing the taxation of an unincorporated trader.

In order to calculate the potential tax relief it was necessary to determine the taxpayer's income tax liability for the years in which loss relief was available. Candidates had no problems calculating the income but were unsure how to proceed from there. In particular there was a lack of thought with many candidates performing calculations for all years rather than recognising that the income was the same in each year such that only one calculation was necessary.

Answers improved when considering the position of a company but there was a lack of precision when describing the loss reliefs available. There was also some confusion as to whether group relief would be available if the two companies were owned personally by the individual taxpayer (it wouldn't). Finally, there was a general unwillingness to satisfy the requirement and calculate the 'tax relief available'.

The final part of the question concerned a loan from a close company to a participator. Candidates did well in identifying the tax implications of the loan but many ignored the ethical considerations inherent within the question.

		Marks
(a)	Pre-trading expenditure	1
	Capital allowances on plant and machinery	1½
	Industrial buildings allowance:	
	Cost excluding land	1
	allowances available to Arral business	1
	Tax adjusted profit/(losses)	1½
		6
(b)	*Business run as sole trader*	
	Basis periods	1½
	Losses	2½
	Available loss reliefs	2
	Set against general income	1
	Dividend tax credit not repayable	1
	Tax saving each year	2
	Overall tax relief	1
	Business run as company	
	Allowable losses	1½
	Loss relief if Aral Ltd owned by Banda	1½
	Loss relief if Aral Ltd owned by Flores Ltd	2
	Recommendation	1
	Max	16
(c)	*Tax implications of loan*	
	Tax payable to HMRC on close company loan	1
	Due date	½
	Reason for tax being due	1½
	Repayment of tax by HMRC if loan ceases	1
	Taxable employment benefit	½
	Report on P11D	1
	Income tax due	1
	Interest and penalties	1
	Willingness to act for Banda	
	Threat to fundamental principles	1
	Requirement for full disclosure	1
	Deliberate concealment	1
	Max	10
Appropriate style and presentation		1
Effectiveness of communication		1
Logical structure		1
		3
		35

(a) Tax adjusted profit/(loss) of the Aral business

	Period ending 30 June 2010 £	Year ending 30 June 2011 £	Year ending 30 June 2012 £
Budgeted profit/(loss)	(12,500)	(13,000)	77,000
Less: pre trading expenditure			
(£6,000 × 1/2) (note)	(3,000)		
capital allowances: (working 1)	(25,850)	(1,530)	(1,224)
IBAs (working 2)	(1,650)	(3,300)	(3,300)
Tax adjusted profit/(loss)	43,000	(17,830)	72,476

Note

Expenditure incurred in the seven years prior to the start of trading is treated as if incurred on the first day of trading. Entertaining expenditure is not allowable.

Workings

1   *Capital allowances on plant and machinery*

	AIA £	Pool £	Allowances £
6 months ending 30 June 2010			
Cost in January 2010	33,500		
AIA £50,000 × 6/12	(25,000)		25,000
Transfer balance to pool	8,500	8,500	
Writing down allowance @ 20% × 6/12		(850)	850
TWDV c/f		7,650	
Allowances			25,850
Year ending 30 June 2011			
Writing down allowance @ 20%		(1,530)	1,530
TWDV c/f		6,120	
Year ending 30 June 2012			
Writing down allowance @ 20%		(1,224)	1,224
TWDV c/f		4,896	

2   *Industrial buildings allowance*

	£
£(160,000 – 50,000)	110,000
Writing down allowance 6 m/e 30.6.10	
£110,000 × 3% × 6/12	(1,650)
Writing down allowances y/e 30.6.11 and 30.6.12	
£110,000 × 3%	(3,300)

(b)   **Banda Ross**

Tax relief available in respect of the anticipated trading losses

(i)   *Business run as a sole trader*

The anticipated allowable losses for the business are set out below.

	Trading income £	Allowable loss £
2009/10 (1 January 2010 to 5 April 2010)		
Allowable loss £43,000 × 3/6	0	(21,500)
2010/11 (1 January 2010 to 31 December 2010)		
Allowable loss £43,000 – £21,500 + (£17,830 × 6/12)	0	(30,415)
2011/12 (Year ending 30 June 2011)		
Allowable loss £17,830 – (£17,830 × 6/12)	0	(8,915)

Banda can use the losses by deducting the losses:

- from her general income in the year of loss and/or the previous year; or
- from her general income in the three years preceding the year of loss, starting with the earliest year, under early years trading loss relief

All of the losses can be used in this way and therefore the possibility of carrying the losses forward has not been considered.

Banda's income throughout the years in which the losses can be relieved (2006/07 to 2011/12) consists of her salary and dividends from Flores Ltd. In any year in which she claims loss relief, she will save the income tax on her employment income only. There will be no saving in respect of her dividend income because Banda is a basic rate taxpayer and the 10% tax credit is not repayable.

The income tax position of Banda before taking account of loss relief is as follows:

	Non-savings income £	Dividend income £	Total £
Salary	11,700		
Dividend income (£20,250 × 100/90)		22,500	
Total/Net income	11,700	22,500	34,200
Less: personal allowance	(6,035)		
Taxable income	5,665	22,500	28,165

Tax

	£
£5,665 × 20%	1,133
£22,500 × 10%	2,250
Tax liability	3,383
Less: tax credit on dividend	(2,250)
Tax payable	1,133

The total tax saved would be £1,133 × 3 = £3,399 as the losses would be set off against non-savings income in preference to dividend income.

The best use of relief would be to use the losses under early years trading loss relief as this would give the earliest tax relief (in 2006/07, 2007/08 and 2008/09).

Tutorial note

The examiner did not expect you to provide any more detailed computations than those shown above, but you might find it easier to understand why the loss relief applies in this way if you look at the following computations.

Banda could use the loss of 2009/10 against general income in 2006/07 as follows:

	Non savings income £	Dividend income £	Total £
Salary	11,700		
Dividend income (£20,250 × 100/90)		22,500	
Total income	11,700	22,500	34,200
Less: early years loss relief	(11,700)	(9,800)	(21,500)
Net income	0	2,700	12,700
Less: personal allowance	(0)	(6,035)	(6,035)
Taxable income	0	6,665	6,665

Tax

	£
£6,665 × 10%	666
Less: tax credit on dividend	(666)
Tax payable	0
Tax saved £(1,133 − 0)	£1,133

Banda could use the loss of 2010/11 against general income in 2007/08 as follows:

	Non savings income £	Dividend income £	Total £
Salary	11,700		
Dividend income (£20,250 × 100/90)		22,500	
Total income	11,700	22,500	34,200
Less: early years loss relief	(11,700)	(18,715)	(30,415)
Net income	0	3,785	3,785
Less: personal allowance	(0)	(3,785)	(3,785)
Taxable income	0	0	0

Tax saved £(1,133 – 0)   £1,133

Banda could use the loss of 2011/12 against general income in 2008/9 as follows:

	Non savings income £	Dividend income £	Total £
Salary	11,700		
Dividend income (£20,250 × 100/90)		22,500	
Total income	11,700	22,500	34,200
Less: early years loss relief	(8,915)	(0)	(8,915)
Net income	2,785	22,500	25,285
Less: personal allowance	(2,785)	(3,250)	(6,035)
Taxable income	0	19,250	19,250

Tax

	£
£19,250 × 10%	1,925
Less: tax credit on dividend	(1,925)
Tax payable	0

Tax saved £(1,133 – 0)   £1,133

(ii) **Business run as a company – Aral Ltd**

The anticipated allowable losses for Aral Ltd are as follows:

	Trading income £	Allowable Loss £
6 months ending 30 June 2010	0	(43,000)
Year ending 30 June 2011	0	(17,830)

Aral Ltd owned by Banda

The losses would have to be carried forward and deducted from the trading profits of the year ending 30 June 2012.

Aral Ltd cannot offset the loss in the current period or carry it back as it has no other income or gains.

Aral Ltd owned by Flores Ltd

The two companies will form a group relief group if Flores Ltd owns at least 75% of the ordinary share capital of Aral Ltd. The trading losses could be surrendered to Flores Ltd in the year ending 30 June 2010 (note) and the year ending 30 June 2011.

The total tax saved would be £(43,000 + 17,830) × 21%   £12,774

Note

The whole of the loss for the period ending 30 June 2010 can be surrendered to Flores Ltd as it is less than that company's profit for the corresponding period, ie £60,000 (£120,000 × 6/12).

Recommended structure

The Aral business should be established in a company owned by Flores Ltd.

This will maximise the relief available in respect of the trading losses and enable relief to be obtained in the period in which the losses are incurred.

(c) **Tax implications of there being a loan from Flores Ltd to Banda**

Flores Ltd should have paid tax to HMRC equal to 25% of the loan, ie £5,250. The tax should have been paid on the company's normal due date for corporation tax in respect of the accounting period in which the loan was made, which was 1 April following the end of the accounting period.

The tax is due because Flores Ltd is a close company that has made a loan to a participator and that loan is not in the ordinary course of the company's business.

HMRC will repay the tax when the loan is either repaid or written off.

Flores Ltd should also have included the loan on Banda's Form P11D in order to report it to HMRC because it is a taxable benefit as the loan is tax-free.

Banda should have paid income tax on an annual benefit equal to 6.25% of the amount of loan outstanding during each tax year as follows:

£21,000 × 6.25% × 20%   <u>£263</u>

Interest and penalties may be charged in respect of the tax underpaid by both Flores Ltd and Banda and in respect of the incorrect returns made to HMRC.

Willingness to act for Banda

We would not wish to be associated with a client who has engaged in deliberate tax evasion as this poses a threat to the fundamental principles of integrity and professional behaviour.

Accordingly, we should refuse to act for Banda unless she is willing to disclose the details regarding the loan to HMRC and pay the ensuing tax liabilities.

Even if full disclosure is made, we should consider whether the loan was deliberately hidden from HMRC or Banda's previous tax adviser and, if so, should refuse to act for her.

10 Amy

Text references. Income tax elements of question dealt with in Chapters 1 to 4 with the overseas aspects covered in Chapter 10. CGT, including the overseas aspects, is covered in Chapters 11 to 14. IHT knowledge contained in Chapters 16-18.

Top tips. Part (a) (ii) required you to deal with three different taxes. In questions like this ensure that you do deal with all of the taxes mentioned otherwise you will throw away many easy marks.

Easy marks. If you knew the answer to part (b)(ii) it was worth doing this early on to ensure you picked up the mark available. However, remember you only have about 1½ minutes to spend on one mark.

				Marks
(a)	(i)	Income tax	1	
		Capital gains tax	1	
		Inheritance tax	1	
				3
	(ii)	*Income tax:*		
		Car benefit	1	
		Fuel benefit	½	
		UK rental income	½	
		Overseas rental income	1	
		NS&I interest	½	
		Bank interest	½	
		UK dividends	½	
		Overseas dividends	1	
		Income tax (before DTR) including W3	2	
		DTR (½ + ½)	1	
		Tax deducted at source	½	
		CGT:		
		June gain (½ + ½)	1	
		November – no gain	½	
		January gain (½ + ½)	1	
		Tax liability	½	
		IHT	½	
		Deferral of gains:		
		Not eligible for gift relief	½	
		Qualifies for EIS relief	½	
		EIS deferral relief details	½	
		Max		13
(b)	(i)	Gift with reservation – identification	½	
		– treatment	1	
		Potential double charge	½	
		Calculate ignoring PET:		
		June – annual exemptions	½	
		November – not chargeable	½	
		Estate at death – liability	½	
		Calculation with gift as PET:		
		Annual exemption	½	
		Tax liability	½	
		Taper relief	½	
		Higher charge used	½	
		Max		5
	(ii)	Pay market rent	½	
		IHT saving as not GWR	½	
		Rent charge	½	
		Max		1
		Total		22

(a) (i) **Basis of charge to tax:**

Income tax – Amy will be chargeable to income tax on all of her UK source income but as she is not UK domiciled she will only be liable to income tax on such amount of her foreign income as is remitted to the UK, if she claims the remittance basis. However, she will not be entitled to a personal allowance.

If she does not claim the remittance basis she will be assessed to UK income tax on her foreign income on an arising basis. In this case, she will be entitled to the personal allowance.

Since Amy has not been resident in the UK for more than seven of the last ten tax years, the remittance basis charge will not apply.

Capital gains tax – Amy will be chargeable to capital gains tax on any gains made on the disposal of UK situated assets but as she is not UK domiciled she will be liable to capital gains tax on any gains on the disposal of non-UK situated assets that are remitted to the UK, if she claims the remittance basis. In this case, the annual exemption will not apply. If she does not claim the remittance basis, the gains will be assessed on an arising basis.

Inheritance tax – As Amy is not UK domiciled she is only liable to inheritance tax on transfers of assets that are situated in the UK. As Amy has not been UK resident for seventeen out of the last twenty tax years she will not be treated as UK domiciled.

(ii) **Amy income tax computation 2008/09**

	Non-savings income	Savings Income	Dividend income	Total
	£	£	£	£
Salary	23,000			
Benefits (W1)	7,975			
NS&I easy access		180		
Deposit interest (£400 × 100/80)		500		
UK Dividends (£1,800 × 100/90)			2,000	
Foreign dividends (£650 × 100/65) (remittance basis)	1,000			
Foreign rents £850 × 7 × 100/85	7,000			
UK rents ((£1,340 − 140) × 9)	10,800			
Net income/Taxable income	49,775	680	2,000	52,455

Amy should make a claim for the remittance basis as she has unremitted overseas income in excess of the personal allowance.

Income tax liability	£
£41,050 (W2) × 20%	8,210
£8,725 × 40%	3,490
£680 × 40%	272
£2,000 × 32.5%	650
	12,622
Less DTR	
On dividends £1,000 × 32.5% (UK tax lower)	(325)
On rent £7,000 × 15% (overseas tax lower)	(1,050)
	11,247
Less tax deducted:	
PAYE	(5,085)
Bank interest	(100)
Dividends	(200)
Income tax payable	5,862

Capital gains tax computation 2008/09

	£
Red plc shares	
Proceeds (market value) 50,000 × £2.22 (W3)	111,000
Cost (probate value)	(20,000)
Gain	91,000

Overseas property

The property is gifted to Michael so no proceeds are remitted to the UK and no chargeable gain arises because the remittance basis has been claimed.

UK property

	£
Proceeds (market value)	125,000
Cost	(67,000)
Gain	58,000

	£
Total gains £(91,000 + 58,000) (no AE – remittance basis claim)	149,000
CGT payable £149,000 × 18%	£26,820

As neither the shares nor the UK property qualify as business assets, gift relief is not available. The only way in which Amy can defer the gains arising is by subscribing for shares under the enterprise investment scheme (EIS). The investment must be made within three years of the disposal, and the amount of the gain that can be deferred is the lower of the amount invested, the amount of the gain, or the amount claimed.

IHT: the gifts to Michael are PETs and will only be chargeable to IHT should Amy die within seven years of the gifts.

Workings

(1) **Benefits**

	£
Car benefit (170 − 135)/5 = 7 + 15 = 22 + 3 (diesel) = 25%	
Benefit £15,000 × 25%	3,750
Fuel benefit £16,900 × 25%	4,225
	7,975

(2) **Basic rate band**

Contributions: £5,000 ×100/80 = £6,250 gross

Basic rate band = £34,800 + £6,250 = £41,050

(3) **Market value**

¼ up 221 + ¼ × (229 − 221) =223

Average bargain ½ × (225 + 219) = 222

(b) (i) If Amy gives her main residence to her niece Erica on 1 June 2009 but continues to live in the property, then this will be treated as a gift with reservation of benefit. However as a lifetime gift to an individual it is treated as a PET. Also, as Amy dies without having moved out of the property the house is treated as part of her estate on death.

There will be an IHT charge, being the higher of:

• the charge on the PET ignoring the house in the death estate, and
• the charge on the house in the death estate ignoring the PET.

IHT computation

Lifetime transfers	£
1 June 2008 Red plc shares	
Value	111,000
Less annual exemptions 2008/09	(3,000)
2007/08	(3,000)
	105,000

Covered by nil rate band. No IHT payable.

6 November 2008 Overseas property

The gift is not chargeable as Amy is not UK domiciled.

6 January 2009 UK property

Value £125,000

Covered by nil rate band. No IHT payable.

GWR

Charge PET and ignore house in estate

1 June 2009 House

	£
Value	400,000
Less annual exemption 2009/10	(3,000)
	397,000

£105,000 + £125,000 = £230,000 of nil band used, £82,000 remaining	£
£82,000 @ Nil	–
£315,000 @ 40%	126,000
Less taper relief (4 – 5 years) 40% × £126,000	(50,400)
	75,600

Ignore PET and charge house in estate

1 September 2013 House

	£
Value	£400,000

£105,000 + 125,000 = £230,000 of nil band used, £82,000 remaining	£
£82,000 @ Nil	
£318,000 @ 40%	127,200
The highest charge will apply so the IHT payable is	127,200

(ii)   If Amy paid Erica a full market rental for occupying the house it would not be a gift with reservation of benefit, it would be a PET and would not be in Amy's estate on death. The IHT payable as a result of Amy's death would be £75,600.

Erica would be liable to income tax on the rent receivable, less any expenses that she incurred.

11   John Robinson

Text references. Income tax and employment income is covered in Chapter 1 to 5. Trade profits are in Chapter 6. Basic chargeable gains is in Chapter 11.

Top tips. Be methodical. You needed to consider the tax liability of each person for both years assuming that the income had been both correctly and incorrectly treated in order to compute the error. Whilst there are a lot of calculations to do they were quick once you got started. A lot of marks could be scored quickly

Easy marks. Listing out the income tax computations for each year for each person should have been straightforward.

Examiner's comments. Part (a) of this question required candidates to carry out a series of calculations to determine the income tax underpaid where the income of one spouse was incorrectly declared on the tax return of the other. This is an example of a question that tests fundamental tax knowledge (brought forward from Paper F6) in a Paper P6 context.

There was a large number of marks here for dealing with basic aspects of investment income, employment income and trading income and the calculation of income tax liabilities. Most of these matters were handled well by the majority of candidates although knowledge of the trading income opening years rules and capital allowances was noticeably weaker than that relating to other matters.

Further marks were then available for determining the additional tax due on the income declared in the incorrect tax return. This could be handled most efficiently by working at the margin; calculating the tax on the additional income only and comparing it with the tax already paid on that income. However, this approach was not taken by the majority of students who wasted time preparing full income tax computations both with and without the incorrectly declared income.

Part (b) required candidates to explain the implications of deregistration for the purposes of VAT and to identify an alternative strategy that would assist in reducing the administration of VAT. Although the rules regarding deregistration were known by many candidates, a considerable amount of time was wasted by some who went on to describe the advantages and disadvantages of being registered in detail. The identification of an alternative strategy was not done particularly well, with many candidates providing a comprehensive list of VAT schemes rather than identifying the flat rate scheme as the one which would genuinely help the client.

Marking scheme

		Marks
(a)	The additional income:	
	Interest – ½ mark for each year	1
	Dividends – ½ mark for each year	1
	Property income	½
	Children's interest – identification of issue	1
	De minimis	1
	John's income tax:	
	2008/09	
	Car benefit	1
	Fuel benefit	½
	Trust income	1
	Personal allowance	½
	Remainder of basic rate band	½
	Additional tax liability	2
	Tax credits	1
	Comparison with the tax paid by Maureen	½
	2009/10	
	Car	½
	Fuel benefit	½
	Trust income	½
	Personal allowance	½
	Remainder of basic rate band	½
	Additional tax liability	2
	Tax credits	1
	Comparison with the tax paid by Maureen	½
	Maureen's income tax:	
	Trading income:	
	Capital allowances	2
	2008/09 assessment	1
	2009/10 assessment	1½

Tax on investment income:

2008/09	2½	
2009/10	2½	
Additional capital gains tax due:		
Annual exemption	½	
Additional tax	1½	
Total additional tax due	½	
	Max	26
Clarity of presentation and use of headings	1	
Logical structure	1	
		2

(b)
Conditions for voluntary deregistration	1	
Effective date	½	
Deemed supply	1	
De minimis limit	1	
Stop charging VAT	½	
Cannot recover input tax	½	
Deductible for income tax	½	
Need to monitor turnover	1	
Suggestion of flat rate scheme	1	
Operation of the scheme	2	
Possible financial advantage	½	
	Max	8
Effectiveness of communication		1
		37

(a) **John and Maureen Robinson – Additional tax payable**

Additional income tax payable – 2008/09

£	£
2,550 × 20% (property income (W1))	510
2,197 × 20% (interest income (W1))	439
4,747 (remainder of basic rate band (W2))	
833 × 40% (interest income (£3,030 – 2,197))	333
9,840 × 32.5% (dividend income (W1))	3,198
	4,480
Less: Tax credits	
£3,030 × 20%	(606)
£9,840 × 10%	(984)
	2,890
Tax paid by Maureen (W3)	(510)
Additional income tax payable	2,380

Additional capital gains tax payable – 2008/09

Additional capital gains tax payable £9,600 × 18% (Note)	1,728

Note. The gift of the property to Maureen would not be effective for capital gains tax purposes due to the prior agreement whereby Maureen gave the sales proceeds to John. Therefore an amount equal to Maureen's unused annual exemption becomes taxable.

Additional income tax payable – 2009/10

	£
803 × 20% (interest income (W1))	161
803 (remainder of basic rate band (W2))	
2,417 × 40% (interest income (£3,220 – £803))	967
144 × 40% (interest income – Penny (W1))	58
10,120 × 32.5% (dividend income (W1))	3,289
	4,475
Less: Tax credits	
£3,220 × 20%	(644)
£10,120 × 10%	(1,012)
	2,819
Tax paid by Maureen (W4)	(246)
Additional income tax payable	2,573
Total additional tax payable (£2,380 + £1,728 + £2,573)	6,681

Workings

1   John - Additional taxable income

	2008/09	2009/10
	£	£
Arising on inherited assets:	2,550	–
Property income	3,030	3,220
Interest income (£2,424/£2,576 × 100/80)	9,840	10,120
Dividend income (£8,856/£9,108 × 100/90)		
Children's bank accounts:		
Will – below *de minimis* limit of £100	–	–
Penny	–	144

2   John – Reminder of basic rate band

	2008/09	2009/10
	£	£
Salary	29,400	30,500
Car benefit:		
15 + (180 – 135)/5 = 24%		
£17,400 × 24% × 8/12	2,784	
£17,400 × 24%		4,176
Fuel benefit:		
£16,900 × 24% × 8/12	2,704	
£16,900 × 24%		4,056
Trust income (£720/£780 × 100/60)	1,200	1,300
Less: Personal allowance	(6,035)	(6,035)
Taxable income	30,053	33,997
Basic rate band	(34,800)	(34,800)
Remainder of basic rate band	4,747	803

3   Maureen – Tax paid on investment income 2008/09

	£
Trading income (W5)	11,845
Property income	2,550
Interest income (W1)	3,030
Dividend income (W1)	9,840
	27,265
Less: Personal allowance	(6,035)
Taxable income	21,230
Tax on property income (Note)	
£2,550 × 20%	510

Note: All of the investment income fell into the basic rate band. The tax liability in respect of the interest and dividend income was covered by the related tax credits. Accordingly, in respect of the income arising on the inherited assets, only the property income gave rise to income tax payable.

4   Maureen – Tax paid on investment income 2009/10

	£
Trading income (W5)	28,590
Interest income (W1)	3,220
Dividend income (W1)	10,120
	41,930
Less: Personal allowance	(6,035)
Taxable income	35,895
Tax on dividend income in higher rate band (Note)	
£1,095 × 32.5%	356
Less: Tax credit	
£1,095 × 10%	(110)
	246

Note: The tax liability in respect of the investment income that fell into the basic rate band was covered by the related tax credits. Accordingly, income tax was payable in respect of the dividend income that fell into the higher rate band only, ie £1,095 (£35,895 – £34,800).

5   Maureen – Trading income

	Period ended 30 September 2009 £	Year ended 30 September 2010 £
Adjusted trading profit	73,729	31,998
Less: capital allowances (W6)	(47,669)	(1,636)
Taxable trading income	26,060	30,362

2008/09
1 November 2006 – 5 April 2009

£26,060 × 5/11	11,845	

2009/10
1 November 2008 – 31 October 2009
1 November 2008 – 30 September 2009

		26,060

1 October 2009 – 31 October 2009

£30,362 × 1/12		2,530
		28,590

6   Capital allowances

	AIA £	Main pool £	Allowances £
p/e 30.9.09			
Additions qualifying for AIA			
11.08 Equipment	55,850		
AIA £50,000 × 11/12	(45,833)		45,833
Transfer balance to pool	10,017	10,017	
WDA @ 20% x 11/12		(1,836)	1,836
TWDV c/f		8,181	
Allowances			47,669
y/e 30.9.10			
WDA @ 20%		(1,636)	1,636
TWDV c/f		6,545	
Allowances			1,636

Advice on Maureen's VAT position

Deregistration

In order to voluntarily deregister for VAT you must satisfy HMRC that the value of your taxable supplies in the next twelve months will not exceed £65,000. You will then be deregistered with effect from the date of your request or a later date as agreed with HMRC.

On deregistering you are regarded as making a supply of all stocks and equipment in respect of which input tax has been claimed. However, the VAT on this deemed supply need only be paid to HMRC if it exceeds £1,000.

Once you have deregistered, you must no longer charge VAT on your sales. You will also be unable to recover the input tax on the costs incurred by your business. Instead, the VAT you pay on your costs will be allowable when computing your taxable profits.

You should monitor your sales on a monthly basis; if your sales in a twelve-month period exceed £67,000 you must notify HMRC within the 30 days following the end of the twelve-month period. You will be registered from the end of the month following the end of the twelve-month period.

Flat rate scheme

Rather than deregistering you may wish to consider operating the flat rate scheme. This would reduce the amount of administration as you would no longer need to record and claim input tax in respect of the costs incurred by your business.

Under the flat rate scheme you would continue to charge your customers VAT in the way that you do at the moment. You would then pay HMRC a fixed percentage of your VAT inclusive turnover each quarter rather than calculating output tax less input tax. This may be financially advantageous as compared with deregistering; I would be happy to prepare calculations for you if you wish.

12 Rowan Sorbus

> **Text references.** Chapters 11 to 13 for the CGT aspects in the question. Chapters 16 to 18 for IHT knowledge required.
>
> **Top tips.** When dealing with unquoted company shares, the related property rules for IHT are often tested. In this case, it was important to spot that the shares given to the charity were related property.

Marking scheme

		Marks
(a)	*Lifetime transfers*	
	Charity exemption	½
	PET to son – no lifetime tax	1
	Charge on death	½
	Related property rules/loss to donor	1
	Calculation of loss to donor	2
	Annual exemptions	½
	IHT calculation	1
	No BPR – explanation	1
	Death estate	
	Charge	½
	Domestica Limited shares	1
	Aria shares	1
	Property used by Domestica Limited	1
	Property used by Aria Limited	1
	Other assets	½
	IHT calculation	½

13

(b) *July 2008 gifts*

Charity – exempt	1
Gift to son – MV	½
Gain on gift	½
Gift relief	1
Entrepreneurs' relief	1
December 2009 sales	
Proceeds	½
Cost	2
IHT deduction	1
Annual exemption	½

Total $\frac{8}{21}$

(a) **Lifetime transfers**

10 July 2008

This was an exempt transfer to charity and there is no IHT implication.

20 July 2008

This transfer to his son was exempt to the extent of the annual exemptions for 2008/09 and 2007/08. The remainder of the transfer was a potentially exempt transfer (PET) because it was a transfer between individuals. There is no lifetime tax payable on a PET because it is treated as exempt during Rowan's lifetime.

The PET becomes chargeable on Rowan's death within seven years.

The value of the transfer needs to take account of the related property rules and the loss to donor principle. Only the shares owned by the charity will be counted under the related property rules, not those owned by his son.

The value of the transfer is:

	£
Before transfer:	
$\frac{40}{40+25} \times £2,100,000$ (value of 65% holding)	1,292,308
After transfer:	
$\frac{30}{30+25} \times £1,450,000$ (value of 55% holding)	(790,909)
Loss to donor	501,399
Less: AE 2008/09	(3,000)
AE 2007/08	(3,000)
PET now chargeable	495,399
Tax	
£312,000 × 0%	0
£183,399 × 40%	73,360
	73,360

No taper relief (death within three years).

Although Domestica Ltd is an unquoted trading company, there is no business property relief (BPR) available on the transfer because the shares were not owned by Rowan for two years before the transfer.

Death estate

There is a charge to IHT on Rowan's death estate as follows:

	£	£
Domestica Ltd shares		
$\dfrac{30}{30+25} \times £1,500,000$ (value of 55% holding)		818,182
Aria Ltd shares	100,000	
Less: BPR @ 100% (owned 2+ years)	(100,000)	0
Property used by Domestica Ltd (no BPR – not owned 2 years)		750,000
Property used by Aria Ltd	175,000	
Less: charge secured on property	(75,000)	
	100,000	
Less: BPR @ 50% (N)	(50,000)	50,000
Other assets		650,000
Chargeable estate		2,268,182
IHT @ 40% (nil band used by lifetime transfer)		907,273

Note. The property used by Aria Ltd attracts 50% BPR because it has been owned for at least two years and Aria Ltd is controlled by Rowan.

(b) **Gifts by Rowan in July 2008**

10 July 2008

This is a disposal by Rowan to a charity and therefore take place at no gain, no loss.

20 July 2008

This is a disposal between connected persons and so is deemed to be at market value. The gain is:

	£
MV of 10% holding in July 2008	150,000
Less: cost to Rowan	
10/65 × £650,000	(100,000)
Gain	50,000

Note. The market value used does not take account of any related property, which is an IHT concept only.

This gain can be deferred into the base cost of Rowan's son by gift relief. This is because the shares are in an unquoted trading company.

Entrepreneurs' relief is not available on the disposal despite Rowan owning at least 5% of the shares in a trading company for one year prior to disposal because he did not also work for the company.

Disposals by Rowan's son in December 2008

The disposal of the Domestica Ltd shares is matched with the share pool:

	£
Proceeds	1,500,000
Less: cost (W)	(918,182)
	581,818
Less: IHT paid on original gift	(73,360)
Gain	508,458
Less: annual exemption	(9,600)
Taxable gains	498,858

Again, entrepreneurs' relief is not available because Rowan's son has not worked for the company.

Working

Share pool

	Cost £
July 2008 acquisition	150,000
Less gift relief	(50,000)
	100,000
March 2009 acquisition	818,182
	918,182
December 2009 disposal	(918,182)
	–

13 Christopher

Text references. Basic IHT is in Chapters 16 and 17 with deeds of variation covered in Chapter 18. Basic CGT including part disposals are in Chapters 11 and 12.

Top tips. Do not confuse items that are exempt for one tax but not for another. The ISA would be tax free for income tax purposes but forms an asset in the death estate – so is subject to IHT.

Regarding Eleanor's part disposal, you were not asked to calculate the gain on the first disposal. However you did need to calculate how much of the original cost was used up by that first disposal.

Easy marks. Make sure you read the question and the question requirements carefully. Here you were told to ignore both gift relief and the annual exemption for Eleanor's CGT calculations. Do not waste time and effort on these.

Examiner's comments. This question was answered well. It covered the clearly well-practiced area of inheritance tax (IHT), with some trickier capital gains tax (CGT).

Most candidates coped well with the calculation of IHT on both lifetime gifts and the estate on death. The most common error was a failure to calculate correctly the nil rate band available for each gift/estate on death. Candidates appeared to forget to consider all chargeable gifts made in the previous seven years. Arguably the trickiest calculation – the quick succession relief – was spotted, and well attempted by the majority of candidates.

Part (b) produced the widest variation in answers. Some were extremely good, showing a sound appreciation of both the CGT and IHT implications of a particular course of action. This is an important skill for this paper. Several failed to read the question properly, and included gift relief, despite being specifically told this would not be claimed. The gift of the paintings gave the most problems. While many understood the issue and produced correct calculations a significant minority calculated the wrong gain – on the earlier, first part disposal, which was not required and therefore wasted time.

The question specifically asked you to recommend the most tax efficient solution, and it was pleasing to see most candidates did this. You should remember that as long as your conclusion is consistent with the points you have made, and figures you have calculated previously, the marks will be given.

Marks

(a)	Gifts into trust are chargeable lifetime transfers	½
	First gift: two annual exemptions (correct years)	½
	calculation of nil rate band remaining	½
	Second gift: two annual exemptions (correct years)	½
	correct gross-up calculation	1
	40% death rate	½
	Taper relief/rate (2 × ½)	1
	Less: lifetime tax paid	½
	Christopher's estate on death:	
	quoted shares– correct valuation	1
	– no BPR	½
	unquoted shares	½
	100% BPR	1
	SA	½
	cash/residence	½
	correct restriction of nil rate band	½
	tax at 40%	½
	Quick succession relief:	
	awareness	½
	correct percentage	½
	correct calculation basis	1
	Max	11
(b)	Gift of paintings:	
	part of set/part disposal rules	½
	cost disposed of previously/cost remaining	1
	CGT at 18%	½
	PET for IHT	½
	Availability of annual exemption	½
	no IHT/within nil band	½
	falls out of account after seven years	½
	Gift of cash	
	exempt for CGT purposes	½
	PET if made direct by Eleanor	½
	alter will so that gift passes directly from estate	½
	result is that IHT paid re estate is not affected	½
	Gift of shares	
	part of share pool	½
	disposal cost	½
	CGT at 18%	½
	PET but 100% BPR available	½
	Recommend gift of cash by varying will	1
		9
		20

(a)   IHT

Lifetime gifts

(i)   9/8/01 – CLT

	£
Gift	262,000
Less: AE 01/02	(3,000)
AE 00/01	(3,000)
	256,000

Below nil band (£312,000)

Therefore no tax due

(ii)   10/4/04 – CLT

	£	£
Gift		75,000
Less: AE 04/05		(3,000)
AE 03/04		(3,000)
		69,000
Less: nil band	312,000	
Less: chargeable transfers in previous 7 years	(256,000)	
		(56,000)
		13,000
Tax @ $^{20}/_{80}$		3,250
Gross chargeable transfer : £69,000 + £3,250		£72,250

Death tax

(i)   9/8/01 – more than seven years before death therefore no death tax

(ii)   10/4/04 – CLT

	£	£
GCT		72,250
Less: nil band	312,000	
Less: chargeable transfers in previous seven years	(256,000)	
		(56,000)
		16,250
Tax @ 40%		6,500
Less: taper relief @ 40%		(2,600)
[4.04 to 2.09 = 4 to 5 yrs]		3,900
Less: lifetime tax		(3,250)
Tax due		650

Death estate

	£	£
Residence		550,000
ISA		12,000
Cash		40,000
P Ltd shares	85,000	
Less: BPR @ 100%	(85,000)	0
B Plc shares (W1)		105,300
Chargeable estate		707,300
Tax £(707,300 – 239,750) @ 40% (W2)		187,020
Less: QSR (W3)		(3,429)
Tax due		183,591

Top tips. Always deal with the lifetime gifts first – lifetime tax (if relevant), then death tax on these gifts – and only then move onto the death estate. If you follow this method you will increase your chances of picking up all the available marks.

Workings

(1) *B Plc shares*

Lower of:

(i)   ¼ up rule: $\dfrac{708 - 700}{4} + 700 = 702p$

(ii)   average: $\dfrac{707 + 701}{2} = 704p$

$702p \times 15,000 = £105,300$

(2) *Remaining nil rate band on death estate*

	£
Nil rate band	312,000
Less: 10 April 2004 CLT	(72,250)
	239,750

The transfer on 9 August 2001 is more than seven years before death.

(3) *QSR*

QSR is available on the cash received from Christopher's uncle's estate. (Not on the shares as they are subject to BPR).

$$QSR = \text{Tax paid} \times \frac{\text{net transfer}}{\text{gross transfer}} \times \%$$

$$= £5,000 \times \frac{30,000}{35,000} \times 80\% \text{ (1 to 2 years)}$$

$$= \underline{£3,429}$$

(b)   Gifts to Sam in June 2009

(i)   Paintings

IHT

	£
Transfer of value	50,000
Less: AE (08/09 only available)	(3,000)
PET	47,000

No tax during lifetime

CGT

	£
Deemed proceeds (MV)	50,000
Less: cost (W)	(19,375)
Gain	30,625
Tax @ 18%	5,513

(ii)   Cash

IHT

	£
As above – PET	47,000

CGT

Cash is not a chargeable asset therefore no CGT

Eleanor can make a deed of variation to effectively change her father's will so that the cash goes directly to Sam. The cash will therefore not form part of her estate and will not be treated as a PET. The deed of variation must be made within two years of her father's death.

(iii)   G Ltd shares

IHT

	£
Transfer of value	50,000

Potential BPR at 100% provided Sam still owns the shares at Eleanor's death
PET so no tax during lifetime

CGT

	£
Deemed proceeds (MV)	50,000
Less: cost	(17,500)
Gain	32,500
Tax @ 18%	5,850

Advice

Option 2 with a deed of variation is best from a tax perspective as there are no IHT implications, as the cash is not treated as being Eleanor's. In addition there is no CGT to pay on the gift.

Working – painting base cost

	£
Original part disposal January 2003:	
Original cost (June 1996)	25,000
Less: Cost used:	
$25,000 \times \dfrac{9,000}{9,000 + 31,000}$	(5,625)
Cost for future disposal	19,375

Top tips. If the question asks for your advice…give it, even if you are not 100% sure that you are right!

---

14 Noland

Text references. Losses for capital gains tax are dealt with in Chapter 11. Inheritance tax is covered in Chapters 17 and 18. Stamp duty is covered in Chapter 19.

Top tips. In part (a) you were asked to compute the tax relief on the capital losses. You should then have realised that this amount was also an asset of the death estate and so affected the computation in part (b).

Easy marks. The calculation of inheritance tax on the death estate was straightforward. You should also have made sure you obtained the easy mark for the time limit for the variation.

Examiner's comments. Part (a) was done well by many candidates. Those who did not perform well were either not aware of the ability to carry back capital losses arising in the year of death or lacked precision in their application of the rules.

Part (b) required candidates to identify the immediate tax implications of a gift of shares. Answers to this part were relatively disappointing given the simplicity of the situation. It was particularly surprising to note how few candidates recognised that there would be no capital gain as the deemed proceeds would be equal to the donor's base cost. In addition, the word 'immediate' in the requirement meant that candidates should only have concerned themselves with what was going to happen now as opposed to what would happen in the future.

Part (c) was the easiest part of the question and rewarded those who got to the end of the question with sufficient time remaining. It was done well by many candidates. Common errors included the treatment of the chargeable lifetime transfer and the availability of business property relief in respect of the unquoted shares

Marking scheme

			Marks
(a)	Current year loss set against current year gains	1	
	Availability of carry back of losses on death	½	
	Three years (LIFO basis)	1	
	Calculation:		
	approach and layout	1	
	reduce to amount of annual exemption	½	
	rate of tax relief	½	
	Max		4
(b)	IHT on transfer of value – PET	1	
	CGT on disposal – no gain as no increase in value	1	
	Stamp duty exemption on gift	1	
	Use of variation for IHT	1	
	Statement for IHT and effect	1	
	Time limit	1	
	Max		5
(c)	Death estate:		
	quoted shares	½	
	house	½	
	shares in Kurb Ltd	½	
	chattels and cash	½	
	CGT refund	1	
	liabilities	½	
	Nil band available on death	1	
	IHT calculation	1	
	House:		
	identification of gift with reservation	½	
	reasoning	1	
	effect of gift with reservation of benefit	1	
	Shares:		
	no BPR with reason	1	
	Calculation of net gift of shares	1	
	Max		9
			18

(a) The potential tax relief available in respect of the capital losses realised in 2009/10

The capital losses must first be offset against the chargeable gains of £7,100 in 2009/10. This will not save any capital gains tax as the gains would have been relieved by the annual exemption.

The remaining capital losses of £10,700 (£17,800 – £7,100) may be offset against the chargeable gains of the previous three years on a last in, first out basis. The losses will reduce the chargeable gains of each year down to the level of the annual exemption. The personal representatives of Noland's estate will receive a refund of capital gains tax calculated as follows:

	Losses used £		Tax relief £
Net loss	10,700		
Less: used 2008/09 £(14,000 – 9,600)	(4,400)	× 18%	792
used 2007/08 £(14,000 – 9,600)	(4,400)	× 18%	792
used 2006/07 (balance)	(1,900)	× 18%	342
Loss ununused	0		
Total tax refund			1,926

(b) **Gift of the share portfolio to Avril**

Inheritance tax

The gift would be a potentially exempt transfer at market value. No inheritance tax would be due at the time of the gift. However, if Crusoe were to die within seven years of making the transfer, the transfer would become chargeable.

Capital gains tax

The gift would be a disposal by Crusoe deemed to be made at market value for the purposes of capital gains tax. No gain would arise as the deemed proceeds will equal Crusoe's base cost of probate value.

Stamp duty

There is an exemption from stamp duty on a transfer of shares for no consideration.

Strategy to avoid a possible tax liability in the future

Crusoe should make a written variation which states that Noland should be treated as making a will giving the shares to Avril.

The variation should contain a statement that it is to have effect for inheritance tax. The making of the variation would then not be a transfer of value for Crusoe and so would not affect his inheritance tax position if he dies within seven years. There is no additional inheritance payable as the estate is fully chargeable.

The deed of variation must be entered into by 1 October 2011, ie within two years of the date of Noland's death.

(c) **Death estate**

	£
Quoted shares	370,000
House – Gift with reservation (note 1)	310,000
Shares in Kurb Ltd (note 2)	38,400
Chattels and cash	22,300
Capital gains tax refund due	1,926
Less: liabilities due	(1,686)
Chargeable estate	740,940

	£	£
Nil rate band at death		312,000
Less: chargeable lifetime transfer	247,000	
less: annual exemption 2006/07	(3,000)	
annual exemption 2005/06 b/f	(3,000)	(241,000)
Available nil rate band		71,000
Inheritance tax on death estate		
£71,000 × 0%		0
£669,940 × 40%		267,976
£740,940		267,976

Inheritance tax payable by administrators (note 3)

$$\frac{£(740,940 - 310,000)}{£740,940} \times £267,976 \qquad 155,858$$

Value that can be transferred £(370,000 – 155,858)   214,142

Notes

1. The gift of the house was a potentially exempt transfer made more than seven years prior to 1 October 2009. However, as Noland has continued to live in the house and is not paying a full commercial rent, the gift is a gift with reservation of benefit. The house will therefore be included in Noland's death estate at its market value at the date of death.

2. Business property relief is not available in respect of the shares in Kurb Ltd as the shares were not owned by Noland for two years before his death.

3. The inheritance tax payable on the gift with reservation of benefit is payable by Crusoe personally as the person in possession of the property.

15 Stanley Beech

Text references. Incorporation relief is covered in Chapter 13. Remuneration packages are dealt with in Chapter 30.

Top tips. This question is actually two virtually separate questions carrying equal marks. You might have started with part (b) as this was slightly easier. Note that supporting calculations were only required in relation to the company car so don't waste time doing other ones.

Easy marks. The rules on dividend versus salary are a basic tax planning point and should have gained easy marks.

Marking scheme

				Marks
(a)	(i)	Split of consideration		
		Incorporation relief – conditions	1½	
		Amount of future cash payment:		
		Rationale – gains to equal annual exemption	1	
		Gains on transfer of business	1	
		Gains after reliefs:		
		Incorporation reliefs	1	
		Entrepreneurs' relief	1	
		Capital loss	1	
		Calculation of gains after reliefs	½	
		Solving to find value of the loan account	1	
		CGT base cost of shares:		
		Value of assets transferred for shares	½	
		Incorporation relief	1	
		Max		8
	(ii)	Benefit of using a loan account		
		Cash flow	1	
		Extract funds with no tax cost	½	
		Max		1
(b)		Advice on remuneration package		
		Dividend		
		Advice is incomplete – reason	1	
		CT position re dividend	½	
		CT position re bonus	½	
		Conclusion with reason	1	
		Interest free loan		
		Advice is incomplete – reason	1	
		Close company	½	
		Loan to a participator and reason	1	
		Tax due /when	1	
		Repayment position	½	

Company car		
The advice is incorrect – reason		1
Calculation		
Tax cost		1
Tax saving		1
	Max	9
		18

(a)   (i)   **Transfer of business to Landscape Ltd**

If Stanley transfers his entire business (ie all the assets, excluding cash) to Landscape Ltd (LL) there would be no capital gains tax because of the automatic availability of incorporation relief.

This would allow the gain arising on the transfer of any chargeable assets used in the business to be deferred until such time as Stanley sells the shares in LL. This occurs because the deferred gain reduces the base cost of the shares received on incorporation.

The full gain may be deferred to the extent that shares are received in exchange for the business. If any other form of consideration is received eg cash, loan notes or loan, a gain will arise in direct proportion to the amount of non-share consideration received.

Therefore if Stanley leaves some of the consideration outstanding on loan account a gain will arise in respect of that proportion of consideration. Entrepreneurs' relief can apply to this gain.

The maximum loan account balance that Stanley could receive without giving rise to a CGT liability would be £68,622. This is calculated as follows:

GAIN ON BUILDING:

	£
Proceeds (mv)	87,000
Less: cost	(46,000)
Gain before reliefs	41,000

GAIN ON GOODWILL:

	£
Proceeds (mv)	24,000
Less: cost	(nil)
Gain before reliefs	24,000

GAIN ON PLANT AND MACHINERY/CONSUMABLES

Plant & machinery would have had capital allowances claimed on them, and presumably any loss would have been taken through the capital allowances computation. There is therefore no capital loss.

The consumables are not chargeable assets and are therefore exempt from CGT.

The total gains before reliefs are therefore (£41,000 + £24,000) = £65,000.

It is easiest to calculate the amount of relief required to ensure no CGT arises by working backwards from the annual exemption:

	£
Annual exemption	9,600
Add: losses b/f	11,400
Gain after entrepreneurs' relief	21,000
Add: entrepreneurs' relief 4/5 × £21,000	16,800
Gain	37,800
Less: total gain	(65,000)
Incorporation relief required	27,200

The proportion of consideration that Stanley would need to receive in shares to arrive at this amount of incorporation relief would be:

$$\frac{X}{118,000} \times 65,000 = £27,200$$

X = MV of shares = £49,378

Therefore the balance of the consideration (£118,000 − 49,378) = £68,622 may be left on loan account.

Check:

	£
Gain before reliefs	65,000
Less: incorporation relief £65,000 × 49,378/118,000	(27,200)
	37,800
Less: entrepreneurs' relief (4/9 × £37,800)	(16,800)
	21,000
Less: losses	(11,400)
Less: AE	(9,600)
Taxable gain	Nil

The base cost of the shares would be:

	£
MV	49,378
Less: gain deferred	(27,200)
Cost c/f	22,178

(ii) **Benefit of taking payment in form of loan account**

The benefit of taking a loan account now is that the company does not have to provide cash up front. Also, it allows the gain to be calculated with no CGT exposure when the loan is eventually repaid.

(b) **Remuneration package advice**

(i) **Dividends v salary**

It is usually more tax efficient to receive dividends rather than a bonus.

However the advice given neglects to mention the fact that Landscape Ltd (LL) will be able to deduct the bonus from its trade profits as salaries and bonuses are treated as being paid wholly and exclusively for the purpose of the trade. This saves tax at 21%.

On the other hand, the dividends paid to Stanley are not tax deductible and therefore are a tax cost to LL at 21%.

Therefore although it is cheaper to pay dividends than salary, the position is not as clear cut as the previous advice suggests.

(ii) **Interest free loan**

It is true that from an employee's perspective loans under £5,000 are a tax-free benefit.

However once again the advice received does not mention the rules applying to close companies. As five or fewer participators control LL, it is therefore a close company. Consequently if the company makes beneficial loans to participators, it will be charged a penalty tax of 25% × the loan.

Therefore LL must pay 25% × £3,600 = £900 to HMRC in respect of the loan by the usual due date for corporation tax for non-large companies ie nine months one day after the end of the accounting period in which the loan is made (ie 1 January 2011).

This will be repayable by HMRC when Stanley repays the loan. The repayment will be due nine months one day after the end of the accounting period in which the loan is repaid.

(iii) **Company car**

Whilst it is true that the costs of providing a car are deductible for the company, the advice provided does not consider the difference in amounts taxable and deductible, nor does it consider the different tax rates involved for Stanley and the company.

If we compare the costs involved it will be seen that the advice provided is in fact incorrect.

	£	£
Cost for Stanley:		
Car benefit £3,420 @ 40%	1,368	
Cost for the company		
Class 1A: £3,420 @ 12.8%	438	
		1,806
Less: deductible for the company		
Lease rentals: £300 × 12 = £3,600 @ 21%	756	
Business fuel: £100 × 12 = £1,200 @ 21%	252	
Class 1A: £438 @ 21%	92	
		(1,100)
Tax cost of providing the car		706

16 Claus Rowen

Text references. Purchase of shares is covered in Chapter 23. Capital gains computations are in Chapter 11. Stamp duty is dealt with in Chapter 19. IHT is dealt with in Chapters 16 to 18.

Top tips. Remember that domicile is the key concept for overseas aspects of IHT but both residence/ordinary residence and domicile are relevant for CGT purposes.

Easy marks. The calculation of the extra income tax on the distribution and the gain on the capital were straightforward.

Marking scheme

		Marks
(a)	Sale of shares by Claus	
	Purchase of own shares	
	Identify and distinguish between the two possible treatments	1
	CGT treatment applies	1
	Reasons why:	
	Unquoted trading company	½
	Resident and ordinarily resident	½
	Owned for more than five years	½
	For benefit of company's trade with reason	1
	Reduction in holding criteria	1
	Not part of a scheme to avoid tax	½
	Availability of advance clearance	1
	Calculation	
	Gain	1
	Net of tax proceeds	½
	Max	8

(b) Gift to Tessa
    Stamp duty
        Not applicable, gift   ½
    CGT
        No CGT due   ½
        Reasons why:
            Not resident or ordinarily resident   ½
            Not temporarily non-resident   ½
            Asset acquired after becoming resident abroad   ½
    IHT
        IHT applies, UK domiciled & shares are UK property   ½
        Gift on 1 August 2009
            Transfer of value   1
            No BPR with reason   1
            Chargeable transfer (2 × annual exemption)   ½
            Taper relief available   ½
            Calculation of tax due   ½
            Reference to DTR   ½
        Gift on 1 June 2010
            Assumption re Tessa's continued ownership   1
            BPR   1
            Marriage and annual exemptions   1
        Advice   1
                                                                    Max   10
                                                                                 18

(a) **Tax treatment of proceeds**

Claus is selling his shares back to the company that issued them. This is known as a company repurchase of own shares.

The usual treatment for a shareholder when their shares are repurchased in this way is that the excess of proceeds over the amount subscribed for the shares is treated as a net income distribution (ie like a dividend).

	£
Proceeds (16,000/40,000) = 40% 16,000 × £38.60	617,600
Less: subscription cost: £16,000 @ £3.40	(54,400)
Net distribution	563,200
Gross income to include in tax return × 100/90	625,778
Tax @ 32.5%	203,378
Less: tax credit @ 10%	(62,578)
Income tax liability	140,800
Net cash: £(617,600 − 140,800)	476,800

The above is the case unless the shareholder satisfies a number of conditions which will allow the profit on sale back to the company to be taxed as a capital gain.

The conditions are as follows:

The company

(i)   must be an unquoted trading company

(ii) the repurchase must be taking place for the purpose of the trade

The shareholder

(i)   must be resident and ordinarily resident in the UK
(ii)   they must have owned the shares for at least five years
(iii)   their holding must be reduced by at least 25%
(iv)   after the repurchase they must own <30%

Generally the repurchase must not be part of a scheme designed to avoid tax. Clearance may be obtained to this effect, in advance of the repurchase, from HMRC.

Based on the facts provided, Claus will satisfy the above conditions and the capital treatment will apply. His net cash following the repurchase will be:

	£
Proceeds (as above)	617,600
Less: cost	(54,400)
Gain	563,200
CGT @ 18% (uses AE)	101,376
Net cash £(617,600 – 101,376)	516,224

This is £(516,224 – 476,800) = 39,424 more than if the income treatment were to apply. Entrepreneurs' relief does not apply because Claus resigned as a director more than one year before the disposal.

(b)   **Gifting shares**

When an individual makes a gift there are always two main taxes that must be considered. These are CGT and IHT.

There is also one further 'capital' tax that may be considered where assets are being transferred: Stamp Duty or Stamp Duty Land Tax (SDLT) depending on the asset transferred. As the assets here are shares, Stamp Duty may be in question but, as gifts are exempt from Stamp Duty (and SDLT), this tax does not need to be considered further. We therefore focus on CGT and IHT.

CGT

Maude is neither resident nor ordinarily resident in the UK and is therefore not subject to UK CGT under general rules.

She has been outside the UK for more than five complete tax years and therefore does not fall within the rules for temporary non-residents. In any case, the shares were acquired after she left the UK and the temporary non-resident CGT rules only apply to assets held pre-emigration.

There are therefore no CGT issues for Maude.

IHT

As Maude appears to have retained her UK domicile she will be subject to IHT on her worldwide assets. The shares are UK assets for IHT purposes as they are registered shares in a UK company.

Gifts of assets between individuals are Potentially Exempt Transfers (PETs). There are no tax consequences during the lifetime of the donor. However, if the donor dies within seven years of making the gift the PET will become chargeable and the donee will be required to pay any IHT due.

As we are told to assume that Maude will die on 31 December 2013 and therefore the gift will become chargeable regardless of whether it is made on 1 August 2009 or 1 June 2010.

The value of the gift will be as follows:

	£
Before the gift: 12,000/24,000 = 50% (Note)	
£38.60 × 12,000	463,200
After the gift: 8,000/24,000 = 33.33%	
£14.40 × 8,000	(115,200)
Transfer of value	348,000

Note. After the buy back of Claus's shares there will only be 24,000 shares in issue as the repurchased shares will be cancelled.

GIFT ON 1 AUGUST 2009

	£
Gift	348,000
BPR is not available as shares held < 2 years	
Less: 2 × annual exemptions	(6,000)
PET	342,000
Less: nil band	(312,000)
	30,000
Tax @ 40%	12,000
Less: taper relief (1.8.09 – 31.12.13 = 4 to 5 years): 40%	(4,800)
IHT due	7,200

Double tax relief should be available if there are any Canadian taxes due in respect of her death.

GIFT ON 1 JUNE 20010

	£
Gift	348,000
BPR @ 100% × £348,000 × $\frac{1,605}{1,647}$ (Note)	(339,126)
	8,874
Less: Marriage exemption	(5,000)
Less: – AE 10/11	(3,000)
– AE 09/10	(874)
PET	0

Therefore no IHT is due. This assumes that Maude's daughter retains the shares until her mother's death.

Clearly Maude should wait until June 2010 to make the gift as this produces no IHT charge.

Note. BPR is only available in respect of the underlying business assets of the company

ie $\dfrac{\text{All} - \text{investment \& surplus cash}}{\text{All}}$

The total market value of the company's assets is £1,647,000.

The value of the investments is £42,000 ie the quoted shares. We are not given details of any surplus cash.

BPR is therefore available on. $\dfrac{£1,647,000 \text{ less } £42,000}{£1,647,000}$

17 Paul and Sharon

Text references. Incorporation is dealt with in Chapters 13 and 30. Gift relief for CGT is also in Chapter 13. Share options are dealt with in Chapter 5 with NIC for employees in Chapter 4. Trusts are covered in Chapter 19.

Top tips. Incorporation is a topic which the examiner can use to test many aspects of the syllabus. Ensure you are happy with this topic.

There is a big difference between an approved and an unapproved share scheme. You were told this scheme was approved. So act accordingly and do not waste time and effort mentioning unapproved schemes.

Easy marks. The three parts were stand alone. You should attempt the part you feel most comfortable with first to gain the easy marks available.

For good marks don't just outline all you know about a subject eg incorporation relief but rather make it specific to the question facts.

Examiner's comments. This question produced the poorest answers on the paper.

[The part on the share scheme] was generally answered badly. On the whole, candidates were unclear as to the precise tax implications (IT and CGT) of approved and unapproved share options schemes, and answers were very confused, leading to a failure to pick up many marks.

Most candidates were able to state the main conditions for incorporation relief to apply, although several failed to advise Sharon as to whether or not it would be available to her, as specifically required. Most had a brave attempt at calculating the maximum cash she could take, picking up at least half marks, while a significant minority, who had clearly practised this, obtained the full three marks. Many candidates were able to identify the major disadvantages of incorporation relief, and suggest gift relief as a suitable alternative. However, several suggested rollover relief, which would not have been suitable in this scenario, as she was not planning to buy further assets. Candidates must consider what is appropriate in the given scenario, not just what is available generally.

Marking scheme

		Marks
(1)	Approved options CGT treatment	½
	Requirement to exercise after three years	½
	If condition not met, exercise treated as unapproved	½
	Taxed as employment income on exercise if before 25 June 2009	½
	Amount taxed is market value price paid on exercise	½
	Calculation: amount taxable	½
	income tax at 40%	½
	national insurance at 1%	½
	If exercise after 25 June no tax on exercise, capital gains treatment on sale	½
	Calculation: gain	½
	annual exemption	½
	capital gains tax at 18%	½
	Max	6
(2)	Transfer must be by a person	½
	Business must be transferred as a going concern	½
	Transfer must comprise all assets apart from cash	½
	Transfer wholly or partly in exchange for shares	½
	Application to Sharon	½
	Availability of annual exemption	½
	Entrepreneurs' relief	2
	Calculation of gain required/held over	½
	Formula for calculating gain to be rolled over	½
	Calculation of potential tax-free consideration	1
	Must put all assets into the company	½
	Double tax on property: sale/extraction of proceeds	½
	Deferral, not reduction in tax	½
	Gift relief: awareness	½
	Gain deferred set against base cost of new asset	½
	Potential for double tax charge	½
	Not all assets need to be transferred	½
	Max	10
(3)	IHT: creation: chargeable lifetime transfer	½
	annual exemptions	½
	nil rate band remaining	½
	tax at 20/80	½
	payment date	½
	gross chargeable amount	½
	additional tax if dies within seven years	½
	taper relief	½
	during: exit charge when assets leave trust	1
	principal charge every ten years	1

CGT:	creation:	chargeable disposal	½
		deemed market value/connected persons	½
		gain before taper relief deferred	½
		gift relief available	½
		chargeable lifetime transfer for IHT purposes	½
		deferral of liability only	½
		settlor interested trust implications	½
SDLT:	Gift: nil		2

Max 11

Format/Presentation

2

29

Report

To: Paul and Sharon Potter
From: A Adviser
Date: [date]
Subject: Share options, incorporation and trust planning

This report covers tax issues relating to:

(i)   Paul's share options
(ii)   Incorporation of Sharon's business
(iii)   Capital tax implications of setting up a trust

(1)   Paul's share options

There is no income tax charge on the exercise of approved share options so long as the exercise does not occur within three years of the date of grant. As your share options were granted on 25 June 2006 you will need to wait until 25 June 2009 to exercise the options without an income tax charge.

If you do not wait, the exercise will be treated as an exercise of unapproved options.

If you exercise the options immediately, there will therefore be an income tax charge on the difference between the market value at the date of exercise and the exercise price of £5,000, along with a National Insurance Contribution (NIC) charge of £125.

There would be no chargeable gain.

If you do wait until 25 June 2009 there will be no income tax or NIC charge. There will be a CGT charge of £522.

You will therefore save a total of £4,603 (5,000 + 125 – 522) by delaying the exercise until 25 June 2009.

Please see Appendix 1 for the calculation of the above figures.

(2)   Incorporation of Sharon's business

If you sell your business to a company you will make a disposal of all the business's assets. You can avoid an immediate charge to capital gains tax through incorporation relief.

This applies automatically when:

- There is a transfer of a going concern
- All assets (except cash) are transferred
- The transfer is by an individual to a company
- In return wholly or partly for share consideration from the company

If the above conditions are satisfied you would need to elect for the relief **not** to apply.

The full gain may be deferred where all of the consideration is received as shares. If any of the consideration is received in cash (or loan notes or left on a loan account) a proportion of the gain will remain chargeable.

Entrepreneurs' relief will apply to reduce this gain because Sharon has been in business for at least one year.

The maximum amount of cash that you could receive without triggering a gain is £25,920 (Appendix 2).

The disadvantages to incorporation relief are as follows.

- The base cost of the shares that you will be able to use when you eventually dispose of the shares will be reduced by the relief given to £31,360 (£94,080 – £62,720). Your gain would therefore be higher.
- You will have had to transfer every asset (except cash) even if you did not want to.
- The transfer of assets (such as property) may lead to a double tax charge in the future as corporation tax would be due from the company on the disposal of the asset and then when the proceeds are paid out to the shareholders there will be a further tax charge (eg income tax on dividends).

The disposal of the shares in the incorporated company will be eligible for entrepreneurs' relief if you hold at least 5% of the shares and you are a director or employee of the company for at least one year prior to any disposal.

As an alternative, you could consider gift relief. In this case you would need to gift the business's assets to the company and you would therefore be able to choose which assets to transfer and which to retain, eg the property.

Gift relief defers your gain by reducing the base cost of the asset for the recipient ie the company. The company would then have a lower base cost when it comes to sell the assets and therefore a higher gain.

Gift relief applies before entrepreneurs' relief so if the whole gain is deferred using gift relief, there will be no gain remaining on which entrepreneurs' relief can apply.

(3)   **Capital tax implications of the discretionary trust**

There will be both inheritance tax (IHT) and capital gains tax (CGT) implications when you set up the discretionary trust.

IHT

The creation of the trust will be a chargeable lifetime transfer for IHT purposes.

The transfer of value will be the market value of the property ie £160,000, which will be reduced by the annual exemptions of £3,000 each for 2008/09 and 2009/10.

As you made a gross chargeable transfer within the last seven years part of your nil rate band will be used, leaving you £112,000 which partially covers the gift to the trust. The balance will be taxed at 25% (20/80) assuming you pay the tax. You will therefore have an IHT liability of £13,500 (Appendix 3).

This is due for payment by the end of the month six months following the gift. So, if you make the gift in, say, July 2009 the tax will be due by 31 January 2010.

You should be aware that if assets are passed from the trust by the trustees to the children there will be an exit charge for IHT purposes. In addition, if the assets remain in the trust there will be a principal charge on every ten year anniversary of the trust. The maximum charge is 6%.

CGT

The creation of the trust will also be a deemed disposal at market value of the trust property for CGT purposes. The CGT payable is £16,200.

Gift relief is not available as the trust is a settlor interested trust, Paul's minor children being beneficiaries.

Once the trust is in place, if the trustees decide to sell the property while the children are still unmarried minors (under age 18), the gains will be taxed on Paul.

SDLT

No SDLT arises on the transfer since there is no consideration.

Appendix 1 – Share option exercise

Exercise immediately

Income tax

	£
MV at exercise: £6 × 5,000	30,000
Less: exercise price: £3.50 × 5,000	(17,500)
Chargeable as employment income	12,500
Tax @ 40%	5,000
Class 1 employees' NICs: 1% of £12,500	125

CGT

	£	£
Sale		
Proceeds		30,000
Less: cost	17,500	
Add: amount subject to IT	12,500	(30,000)
Chargeable gain		Nil

Delay until 25 June 2009

No income tax charge

CGT

	£
Proceeds: £6 × 5,000	30,000
Less: cost: £3.50 × 5,000	(17,500)
Gain	12,500
Less: AE	(9,600)
	2,900
Tax @ 18%	522

> **Top tips.** Make sure that you know the conditions for a scheme to be approved for tax purposes. If it is approved there are usually only CGT implications. Any other scheme will lead to income tax charges, which are usually higher than CGT.

Appendix 2 – Maximum cash consideration to take on incorporation

	£
Total consideration	120,000
Less: share consideration (W1)	(94,080)
Cash consideration	25,920

Workings

(1)   *Share consideration*

	£
We want relief of (W2) :	67,720
Gain before reliefs is:	80,000
Total consideration is:	120,000

Therefore share consideration must be:

$$\frac{62,720}{80,000} \times 120,000 \qquad\qquad £94,080$$

(2) *Relief to bring gain to nil* (hint: work backwards!)

		£
Total gain:		
Goodwill		40,000
Property		40,000
		80,000
Less: incorporation relief (bal)		(62,720)
Gain		17,280
Less: entrepreneurs' relief (4/9)		(7,680)
Chargeable gain		9,600
Less: AE		(9,600)
Taxable gain		Nil

Appendix 3 – Discretionary trust – capital tax issues

IHT

	£	£
Transfer of value		160,000
Less: 2 × annual exemptions		(6,000)
Chargeable		154,000
Less: nil rate band	312,000	
Less: May 2005 gift (in previous 7 years)	(212,000)	(100,000)
Taxable		54,000
Tax @ 20/80		13,500

CGT

	£
Deemed proceeds (MV)	160,000
Less: cost (8/07)	(70,000)
Chargeable gain (AE already used)	90,000
CGT @ 18%	16,200

Note. If Paul exercises his share options before 25 June 2009 his CGT annual exemption will be available to set against this gain.

18 Galileo

Text references. Inheritance tax is covered in Chapters 16 and 17. The overseas aspects of capital gains tax are in Chapter 14. Employment income is covered in Chapter 4.

Top tips. Do not get carried away doing unnecessary death estate calculations just because you have the information. You are asked for tax payable by Galileo on the inheritance of the shares. He will not have any tax to pay on the death estate as it will be paid by the executors.

Easy marks. Part (c) required to you state the benefit rules on relocation costs, interest free loans and job related employment. These should be well known and easy marks to obtain.

Examiner's comments. Part (a) required candidates to calculate the inheritance tax payable by the donee of a potentially exempt transfer following the death of the donor. This was done well by many candidates although a minority did not consider business property relief, which was an important element of the question. Those who did consider business property relief often failed to recognise the existence of excepted assets in the company. Candidates were also asked to explain why the tax could be paid in instalments and to state when the instalments were due. This was not handled particularly well; many candidates did not know the circumstances in which payment by instalments is available and the payment dates given often lacked precision.

Part (b) concerned the liability to capital gains tax of an individual coming to the UK. It was only for two marks but it illustrated continued confusion on the part of many as to the treatment of someone who is not resident or ordinarily resident. Such a person is not subject to UK capital gains tax on personal investment assets and the remittance or otherwise of the proceeds is irrelevant.

Part (c) involved the desire to assist an employee's relocation to the UK without giving rise to an income tax liability. This was done rather well with many candidates identifying the possibility of a tax free loan and relocation assistance.

Marks

(a)	(i)	Fall in value	1	
		Business property relief	1½	
		Annual exemptions	1½	
		Available nil band	1½	
		Inheritance tax at 40%	½	
		Taper relief	1	
		Tax due in respect of share in death estate	1	
		Max		7
	(ii)	Valid reason for payment by instalments being available	1	
		When due	1	
		Interest on instalments	1½	
		Implication of Galileo selling the shares	1	
		Max		3
(b)		Residence and ordinary residence position	1	
		Advice	1	
				2
(c)	(i)	Relocation costs		
		Tax free with maximum	1	
		Examples of qualifying costs (½ each, maximum 1)	1	
		Deadline	½	
		Interest-free loan		
		Maximum tax-free amount	1	
		Max		3
	(ii)	Provision of accommodation will be taxed	1	
		Reasons why not exempt	2	
		Max		2
				17

(a)   (i)   **Galileo – Inheritance tax payable**

The gift of shares to Galileo was a potentially exempt transfer. It has become chargeable due to Kepler's death within seven years of the gift.

	£
Value of Kepler's holding prior to the gift to Galileo (2,000 × £485)	970,000
Less: Value of Kepler's holding after the gift (1,400 × £310)	(434,000)
Loss to donor's estate	536,000
Business property (W1)	(367,843)
Less: Annual exemption 2004/05	(3,000)
Less: Annual exemption 2003/04 (W3)	(1,200)
Potentially exempt transfer	163,957

Lifetime transfers in previous seven years
1 February 2003   £298,000 – 3,000 – 3,000 = £292,000

IHT payable by Galileo

	£
£(312,000 – 292,000) = £20,000 × 0%	0
£(163,957 – 20,000) = £143,957 × 40%	57,583
	57,583
Less: taper relief (3 – 4 years) (20%)	(11,517)
IHT payable	46,066

The inheritance tax payable in respect of the shares in the death estate will be paid by the executors and borne by Herschel, the residuary legatee. None of the tax will be payable by Galileo.

Workings

1   Business property relief

$$£536,000 \times 100\% \times \frac{1,050,000}{1,530,000} \text{ (W2)} \qquad\qquad £367,843$$

2   Excepted assets and total assets

	Total assets £	Non-excepted assets £
Premises	900,000	900,000
Surplus land	480,000	–
Vehicles	100,000	100,000
Current assets	50,000	50,000
	1,530,000	1,050,000

3

	£
Annual exemption 2003/04	3,000
Less: gifts to nephews £900 × 2	(1,800)
Available to c/f to 2004/05	1,200

(ii)   **Payment by instalments**

The inheritance tax can be paid by instalments because it is due on a PET, Galileo still owns the shares and Messier Ltd is an unquoted company controlled by Kepler at the time of the gift.

The tax is due in ten equal annual instalments starting on 30 November 2008.

Interest will be charged on any instalments paid late; otherwise the instalments will be interest free because Messier Ltd is a trading company that does not deal in property or financial assets.

All of the outstanding inheritance tax will become payable if Galileo sells the shares in Messier Ltd.

Tutorial note Candidates were also given credit for stating that payment by instalments is available because the shares represent at least 10% of the company's share capital, are valued at £20,000 or more and the company remains unquoted.

(b)   **Minimising capital gains tax on the sale of the paintings**

Galileo will become resident and ordinarily resident from the date he arrives in the UK as he intends to stay for more than three years. Prior to that date he will be neither resident nor ordinarily resident such that he will not be subject to UK capital gains tax.

Galileo should sell the paintings before he leaves Astronomeria; this will avoid UK capital gains tax completely.

Tutorial note The gains would be taxable on the remittance basis if the paintings were sold after Galileo's arrival in the UK. However, this would not help Galileo to minimise the capital gains tax due as he needs to bring the sales proceeds into the UK in order to purchase a house.

(c)   (i)   **Relocation costs**

Direct assistance

Messier Ltd can bear the cost of certain qualifying relocation costs of Galileo up to a maximum of £8,000 without increasing his UK income tax liability. Qualifying costs include the legal, professional and other fees in relation to the purchase of a house, the costs of travelling to the UK and the cost of transporting his belongings. The costs must be incurred before the end of the tax year following the year of the relocation, ie by 5 April 2010.

Assistance in the form of a loan

Messier Ltd can provide Galileo with an interest-free loan of up to £5,000 without giving rise to any UK income tax.

(ii) **Tax-free accommodation**

It is not possible for Messier Ltd to provide Galileo with tax-free accommodation. The provision of accommodation by an employer to an employee will give rise to a taxable benefit unless it is:

- Necessary for the proper performance of the employee's duties, eg a caretaker; or
- For the better performance of the employee's duties and customary, eg a hotel manager; or
- part of arrangements arising out of threats to the employee's security, eg a government minister.

As a manager of Messier Ltd Galileo is unable to satisfy any of the above conditions.

19 Miller Plc

Text references. The calculation of corporation tax is covered in Chapters 21, 22 and 23. Trading losses are in Chapter 24. Groups are in Chapter 26. VAT is in Chapters 28 and 29.

Top tips. You could have attempted the VAT part of the question first if you were confident in that area. Just remember to put your answer in the correct order before you hand it in – you don't want to make the examiner hunt around to give you marks.

Easy marks. The calculations were straightforward. The examiner has said that he may test the computation of PCTCT so ensure you can do so quickly and efficiently, and then tie the figures into your answer.

			Marks
(a)	*Corporation tax calculation*		
	Trading profit (½ mark for each adjustment) Max	2½	
	Capital allowances	2	
	Trading loss b/f	½	
	Chargeable gain	1	
	Interest income	1	
	Property income	½	
	Foreign income	½	
	Deduct management expenses	1	
	Add back accrued donation/ no tax deduction for Gift Aid	1	
	CT limits	½	
	Tax at 28%	½	
			11
(b)	*Group relationships*		
	Associates	1	
	Loss group 1	1	
	Loss group 2	1	
	Gains group	1	4
	Use of group losses		
	Cannot surrender Bloom's loss b/f	½	
	Carry forward only in Bloom	½	
	Cannot carry forward if major change rules apply	½	
	Surrender Bloom's current year loss	½	
	Current year claim in Bloom	½	
	Carry forward in Bloom	½	
	Cannot surrender Weibrecht's capital loss	½	
	Carry forward against future gains	½	
	Election for deemed transfer of asset	½	
	Conclusion for use of losses	½	
	Calculation of loss relief	½	
	Max		5

(c)	*Advantages of VAT group*	
	Intra-group supplies exempt	½
	One VAT return	½
	Include companies making exempt supplies	½
	Group registration	
	Hillman Ltd excluded – holding	½
	Bloom Ltd repayment trader – implications	1
	Weibrecht exempt – implications	1
	Conclusion	1

		5
Format/Presentation		2
	Max	27

Report

To: Fred Kildow, Miller plc group finance director
From: Tax manager
Date: [date]
Subject: Tax issues for the Miller plc group

This report covers tax issues relating to:

(a) Miller plc's corporation tax liability for the period ended 31 March 2009
(b) Group issues
(c) VAT

(a) Miller plc's corporation tax liability for the period ended 31 March 2009

Miller plc's corporation tax liability for the eight month period from 1 August 2008 to 31 March 2009 is £94,008 (Appendix 1).

(b) (i) Group relationships

Miller Plc is associated with all the companies under its control ie Bode Ltd, Weinbrecht Ltd, and Bloom Ltd. The consequence of this is that the small companies limits' are divided by four.

Miller Plc is in a loss group with Bode Ltd, and Bloom Ltd because Miller Plc has a direct and indirect/effective interest of at least 75% in each company. This enables group relief to be claimed for trading and other losses.

There is a second loss group of Bode Ltd and Weinbrecht Ltd.

Miller Plc is in a gains group with Bode Ltd, Weinbrecht Ltd and Bloom Ltd because it has a direct holding of at least 75% and an indirect/effective interest of > 50%. This enables assets to be transferred around the group without crystallising chargeable gains.

(ii) Group losses

Bloom Ltd's brought forward loss

Bloom Ltd cannot surrender its brought forward trading loss.

The trading loss will instead be carried forward and must be set against the first available trading profits from the same trade.

If there has been a major change in the nature or conduct of Bloom Ltd's trade or if there is deemed to be a revival of trade after it has been negligible then the trading losses incurred before September 2008 (date of change of ownership of Bloom Ltd) cannot be carried forward against post acquisition profits.

Bloom Ltd's current year loss

Bloom Ltd can surrender its current year trading loss to Miller plc or Bode Ltd.

Alternatively Bloom Ltd could itself make a current year claim to set the loss against its own income and gains.

The loss should be used in the most effective way possible by offsetting it in the company with highest marginal rate of tax.

As Bloom Ltd will be taxed at 28% in 2011, any loss which will save tax at less than 28% this year, should be carried forward by Bloom Ltd.

Weinbrecht Ltd's capital loss

The capital loss itself cannot be surrendered.

The capital loss could be carried forward in Weinbrecht Ltd and set against any future gains.

Alternatively an election could be made to treat the asset as having been transferred to another group company prior to disposal so that the loss is deemed to have arisen in another group company.

The capital loss should be utilised against the capital gain in the company with the highest marginal rate of tax, ie Miller plc.

Conclusion

The optimum use of Bloom Ltd's losses would entail surrender of £110,000 to Bode Ltd and £380,000 to Miller plc. This would bring both companies' PCTCT to the small companies' rate level, so that each company would be paying tax at 21% (see Appendix 2).

The capital loss will reduce Miller plc's PCTCT to £455,000.

Trading losses of £160,000 (remainder of the current year loss of £110,000 plus the £50,000) will be carried forward within Bloom Ltd to the year ended 31 March 2011.

(c) **VAT group**

The following are benefits of a VAT group:

- No VAT is charged on intra-group supplies
- Only one VAT return is required, providing an administration saving as you could easily centralise this function
- Can exclude companies that only make exempt supplies

Hillman Ltd is not eligible to be included in the group registration as Miller plc does not hold at least 50% of the shares.

As an exporter to large businesses, Bloom Ltd's customers are likely to be VAT registered. Therefore 95% of the sales will be zero-rated. Bloom Ltd is thus a repayment trader. Bloom Ltd should be excluded from the VAT group otherwise the cash-flow advantage of a monthly VAT repayment will be lost.

Weinbrecht Ltd provides wholly exempt supplies. Including Weinbrecht Ltd in the group will make the whole group partially exempt. This may limit its recovery of input VAT if the total exempt input VAT of the group exceeds the *de minimis* limits.

The VAT group should include Miller plc and Bode Ltd. Weinbrecht Ltd should only be included if it does not reduce the total input VAT recoverable by the group.

Appendix 1 – Corporation tax computation for the period ended 31 March 2009

	£
Trading profit (W1)	281,068
Less: Trading losses brought forward	(95,000)
	186,068
Property business income	45,000
Foreign income	34,500
Chargeable gain (W3)	75,725
Interest income (W4)	6,000
	347,293
Less: general management expenses	(11,550)
Less: Gift Aid paid	–
PCTCT	335,743
Corporation tax (W5)	
£335,743 @ 28%	94,008

Workings

(1) *Trading profit*

	£
Tax adjusted profits	450,000
Loss on disposal of fixed asset	30,000
Gift aid accrued	10,000
Interest on overdue corporation tax	3,000
Client entertaining	37,750
UK rental income	(45,000)
Dividend from Bode Ltd	(13,500)
Dividend from Hillman Ltd	(27,000)
Dividend from Vogtli Inc	(34,500)
Interest received	(9,000)
Capital allowances (W2)	(120,682)
Taxable trading profit	281,068

(2) *Capital allowances*

	AIA £	FYA £	Main Pool £	Mercedes Car £	Allowances £
WDV b/f			450,000		
Additions					
Mercedes car				28,000	
Office furniture	61,250				
AIA (8/12 × £50,000)	(33,333)				33,333
Transfer to pool	27,917		27,917		
Disposal – Machine			(62,800)		
			415,117		
WDA @ 20% × 8/12			(55,349)		55,349
WDA £3,000 × 8/12				(2,000)	2,000
Additions qualifying for FYA					
Low emission car		30,000			
FYA @ 100%		(30,000)			30,000
					120,862
WDV c/f			359,768	26,000	

(3)   *Capital gain on disposal of Vogtli Inc*

Substantial shareholding exemption does not apply as Miller Plc's holding is < 10%.

	£
Proceeds	120,000
Less cost	(35,000)
Unindexed gain	85,000
Less Indexation allowance	(9,725)
Chargeable gain	75,275

(4)   *Interest income*

	£
Gross debenture interest from Bode Ltd	9,000
Interest charged on overdue corporation tax	(3,000)
	6,000

(5)   *Corporation tax rate*

Limits ÷ 4 associates

	£
PCTCT	335,743
FII (£27,000 × 100/90)	30,000
'Profits'	365,743
Upper limit (£1,500,000/4) = 375,000 × 8/12	250,000
Lower limit (£300,000/4) = 75,000 × 8/12	50,000

Full rate company

Appendix 2 – use of losses within the Miller plc group

	M Plc £	Bode Ltd £	Bloom Ltd £
Trading profit	320,000	125,000	–
Property business income	70,000		–
Interest income	10,000	60,000	20,000
Chargeable gain (100,000 – 45,000)	55,000		35,000
PCTCT pre loss-relief	455,000	185,000	55,000
CT rate (4 associates)	28%	29.75%	21%
Surrender order	2	1	–
Surrender until CT rate @ 21%	(380,000)	(110,000)	
Revised PCTCT	75,000	75,000	55,000
Revised CT rate	21%	21%	21%

20 Flop Ltd

Text references. CT computations in Chapters 21, 22 and 23 with payment of CT dealt with in Chapter 23. VAT penalties are covered in Chapter 28 and bad debts in Chapter 29. Ethics are in Chapter 30.

Top tips. Be methodical when calculating capital allowances. Ensure you adopt clear presentation.

Easy marks. Learn your administration rules for the different taxes – they are often tested in the exam. Make sure you do not confuse the rules for companies and those for individuals.

Examiner's comments. While candidates were broadly successful in identifying the main items to be disallowed in part (a), though candidates had little awareness of what legal and professional fees were allowable. The tendency was to disallow both the planning consent fees and the fees on attempting to secure a loan. The latter cost is specifically allowed by legislation.

The second element of part (a) asked candidates to state the dates for payment of tax and filling of the relevant tax returns. Far too many candidates confused corporation tax administration with personal tax administration, with the resulting loss of a significant number of marks. In addition, few candidates identified the fact that a company broadly has to be large for two years in succession before it is required to make quarterly instalment payments.

In many ways part (b), relating to value added tax (VAT) issues, was less straightforward yet many candidates scored solid marks here. The surcharge liability notice, and the implications for Fred Flop of being in the surcharge period was picked up by most candidates, as was the VAT treatment of bad debts.

Marking scheme

				Marks
(a)	(i)	Provision is general	½	
		General provisions – disallowed	½	
		Trading loan relationship costs – allowable	½	
		Trade costs – allowable	½	
		Costs of £5,700 capital – disallowed	½	
		Profit chargeable to corporation tax	½	
		Two associates	½	
		Calculation of CT	½	
		Computers are capital	½	
		Capital allowances on computers	½	
		Inclusion of bad debt	½	
		Revised PCTCT	½	
		Amendment of CT return	½	
		Money laundering	½	
		Max		6
	(ii)	Awareness of no quarterly payments	½	
		Reason: company was not 'large' in 2007	½	
		Due date nine months one day	½	
		Filing: twelve months from period of account	½	
		three months from date of notice	½	
		Take later	½	
		Fixed penalties	½	
		Tax geared penalties	½	
		Calculation of tax geared penalty	½	
		Interest periods: to late payment	½	
		Interest periods: to balancing payment	½	
		Payment date: large for second year	½	
		Quarterly payments apply	½	
		Dates of quarterly payments	1	
		Filing date	½	
		Penalty: fixed	½	
		Penalty: tax geared	½	
		Further penalty (submission beyond 30.6.10)	½	
		Interest from date of underpaid instalments	½	
		Max		7

(b) Default surcharge: awareness   ½
                    two or more within year   ½

Default surcharge: awareness	½
two or more within year	½
Issue of surcharge liability notice	½
Period runs from date of notice	½
Runs to anniversary of quarter in which default	½
Return and/or payment late	½
Further defaults extend surcharge period	½
Levy 2% surcharge if late payment	½
Progressive rates thereafter	½
Compliance for one year required	½
Extension as second return late	½
Extend again if June return is late	½
Calculation of £480	½
Exceeds de minimis level of £400	½
Submission date to avoid surcharge	½
Saving that would result	½
Period extended though no surcharge	½
Refund of VAT on bad debt	1
Conditions for refund (½ each)	1
Three-year time limit for claim	½
Calculation of VAT repayable	½
Net VAT repayment	½
	Max 9
	Max 22

(a) (i) **CT payable**

Year ended 31 March 2008

	£	£
Original PCTCT		741,800
Add: repairs provision (N1)	10,000	
professional fees (N2)	5,700	15,700
Revised PCTCT		757,500
CT @ 28% (W1) (assumed)		212,100

Year ended 31 March 2009

	£	£
Current PCTCT		815,000
Add: Computer equipment (N4)	50,000	
Less: bad debt (N3)	(50,000)	
CAs £50,000 × 20% (N4)	(10,000)	(10,000)
Revised PCTCT		805,000
CT @ 28% (W1)		225,400

Notes

1   If there is no supporting documentation for the provision it is likely that HMRC will treat it as a general provision, which is not allowable for tax purposes. If proof can be provided to confirm that this is a specific provision against a specific debt, it would be allowable.

2   So long as professional fees are incurred wholly and exclusively for the purpose of the trade, and do not relate to capital items they will be allowable. Consequently all the fees should be allowable except those incurred in respect of the planning consent (capital item).

3   VAT-exclusive bad debt amount is an allowable deduction for corporation tax purposes as the VAT is dealt with separately.

4   Capital expenditure is not an allowable expense for CT purposes. Capital allowances of 20% can be claimed for the year ended 31 March 2009.

5 An amendment to the corporation tax return for the year to 31 March 2008 should have been filed by 31 March 2010. Although this date has passed HMRC should be advised of the amendments.

6 A deliberate error should be reported under the money laundering regulations. If the error was innocent, the position is less clear and you should discuss it with your firm's money laundering officer.

Top tips. Always try to comment on **every** matter/issue/figure mentioned in the question. Do not ignore anything, even if it is something that you do not consider to be relevant/ taxable/deductible, as you will miss out on the allocated marks.

Workings

1 *CT limits*

Two associated companies therefore divide CT limits by 2:

	£	£
UL	1,500,000 ÷ 2	750,000
LL	300,000 ÷ 2	150,000

Therefore Flop Ltd is a large company for the first time in FY07 (y/e 31 March 2008) and also in FY08.

(ii) **Payment and filing dates**

Tax

FY07

Flop Ltd is a large company for corporation tax purposes for the first time in FY07 (it was not large in the previous year due to its level of profits).

Therefore its tax for the y/e 31 March 2008 would have been due 1 January 2009 (9 months 1 day following the chargeable accounting period). However, it did not pay its tax until 2 November 2009.

Therefore interest would have run from the due date to the date of payment (1.1.09 – 1.11.09) = 305 days late.

Interest due:

$$\frac{305}{365} \times 7.5\% \times £212,100 = £13,293.$$

Interest will continue to run at this rate on the underpayment of £88,600 (£212,100 – £123,500) until it is paid.

This interest is deductible for corporation tax purposes as a non-trading loan relationship.

FY08

Flop Ltd is a large company for corporation tax purposes again in FY08.

Therefore its tax for the y/e 31 March 2009 will be due via quarterly instalments of 25% of the current year's estimated CT liability.

The amounts due on each of these dates is:

£225,400 ÷ 4 = £56,350

The due dates are:

- 14 October 2008
- 14 January 2009
- 14 April 2009
- 14 July 2009

As it is now 10 May 2010, the company is late paying all four payments.

Interest runs from the due date on late paid instalments. The position is looked at cumulatively after the due date for each instalment. HMRC calculate the interest position after the company submit its corporation tax return.

Return

The company's returns are due on the later of:

(1)   Twelve months after the end of the period of account, and
(2)   Three months after the notice to complete a return has been issued.

For the y/e 31 March 2008, the due date will therefore be the later of:

(1)   31 March 2009, and
(2)   1 May 2009 ie 1 May 2009.

For the y/e 31 March 2009, the due date will therefore be the later of:

(1)   31 March 2010, and
(2)   27 October 2009 ie 31 March 2010.

If a return is filed up to three months late, a fixed penalty of £100 is imposed (or £500 for a third consecutive late return). If the return is over three months late, the fixed penalty is £200 (or £1,000 for a third consecutive late return).

If the return is filed more than six months late, an additional tax geared penalty is imposed of 10% of the unpaid tax. If the return is filed more than twelve months late, the penalty is 20% of the unpaid tax.

The company was over three months late in submitting the return for the y/e 31 March 2008 and will incur a £200 penalty. It was also more than six months late, so an additional penalty of £22,725 (£227,250 × 10%) can be levied.

If the company submits the return for the y/e 31 March 2009 before 30 June 2010, the penalty will be £100.

Late filing penalties can be mitigated if there is a reasonable excuse for the failure.

> **Top tips.** Do not ignore the tax **administration** rules as these are often examined as part of a question.

(b)   **VAT**

Filing a VAT return late leads to the issue of a Surcharge Liability Notice (SLN), as will the late payment of VAT. There is no separate system of interest for underpaid VAT.

When the 31 December 2009 return was submitted late an SLN would have been issued, running to 31 December 2010. No penalty would have arisen at that point as this was the first default.

When Flop Ltd defaults for the q/e 31 March 2010, which falls within the SLN period, there will be a surcharge of 2% of the outstanding tax, ie £480 (£24,000 × 2%). The SLN period will be extended until 31 March 2011.

If Flop Ltd is late in submitting its June 2010 return the surcharge will be 5% of the unpaid VAT (as it is the second default within the SLN period) ie £8,250 × 5% = £412.50, and the SLN period will be extended until 30 June 2011.

Only if Flop Ltd submits all its returns within the SLN period to 30 June 2011 on time, and pays all of its VAT on time, will the SLN be discharged.

Bad debt

Flop Ltd must write off the bad debt by making the appropriate entry in its 'refunds for bad debts' account.

If at least six months (but not more than three years and six months) have elapsed since the later of the date of supply or the due date for payment, the VAT may be reclaimed.

As the debt has been outstanding for just over twenty months, Flop Ltd may claim the following bad debt relief:

£50,000 × 17.5% = £8,750

21 Bargains Ltd

> **Text references.** CT basics in Chapters 21 to 23. Revenue and capital item treatment in Chapters 6 and 7. VAT is dealt with in Chapters 28 and 29. Employment benefits are covered in Chapter 4. Close companies are dealt with in Chapter 25.
>
> **Top tips.** The rules treating benefits to participators in close companies as distributions only apply when the normal employment income rules taxing benefits do not apply.

Marking scheme

			Marks
(a)	Accounting period	1	
	Pretrading expenditure deductable	1	
	Advertising – allowable	1	
	Refurbishment	2	
	VAT	1	
			6
(b)	Car benefit	1	
	Distribution treatment	1	
	Disallowable expenses	1	
	VAT treatment	1	
	Capital allowances	1	
	Additional expenses	1	
			6
(c)	Penalty tax	2	
	Del's tax	2	4
			16

(a) (i) The company's first accounting period will run from the start of trade on 1 April 2009 to its accounting date, 31 December 2009. Any deductible pre-trading expenditure will be treated as incurred on the first day of trading, and will therefore be deductible in this accounting period.

(ii) The pre-trading expenditure on advertising will be deductible for corporation tax purposes. The expenditure on refurbishment will also be deductible except to the extent that it is capital expenditure. Expenditure needed to make the premises fit for use will be capital expenditure *(Law Shipping Co Ltd v CIR 1923)*. Expenditure leading to significant improvements, such as the installation of a heating system where there was none before, will also be capital expenditure. Expenditure on routine repairs and redecoration, on the other hand, will be revenue expenditure.

The VAT incurred on both the advertising expenditure and the refurbishment expenditure will be recoverable, because it is VAT on services supplied not more than six months before registration.

(b) Rodney and Reggie will be taxed on earnings as follows.

160 (rounded down) − 135 = 25 ÷ 5 = 5

The benefit is $(15\% + 5\%) \times £10,575 \times \dfrac{9}{12} = £1,586$

There will be no employment income charge on Del, but the provision of a car to him will be treated as a distribution of £1,586 net. Del will be taxed as if he had received a dividend of this amount, giving him gross income of £1,586 × 100/90 = £1,762, a tax credit of £176 and no further tax liability unless he is a higher rate taxpayer. The actual cost of providing the car will be a disallowable expense for the company. The company will be treated as though it had paid a dividend of £1,586. Any motor expenses incurred by the company in respect of Del's car will be disallowable.

The VAT on the cars will not be recoverable because of the private use. Capital allowances will be available on the full cost (including VAT) of the cars provided for Rodney and Reggie, but not on the cost of the car provided for Del because its provision is treated as a distribution. The annual writing-down allowances will be 20% on a reducing balance basis. Because the first accounting period is only nine months long, the allowance in that period will be $2 \times £10,575 \times 20\% \times 9/12 = £3,172$. Any motor expenses incurred by the company in respect of servicing, insurance and general running of both Rodney and Reggie's cars will be tax deductible for the company.

(c)   On making the loan to Del, the company will become liable to account for an amount of tax of $£42,000 \times 25\% = £10,500$. This is, in general, due nine months after the end of the accounting period, so it is due by 1 October 2010. However, if the company becomes a large company the tax will be subject to the quarterly payments on account regime. This tax is recovered when the loan is repaid.

Del will only be taxed on the loan as income to the extent that it is written-off. He will then be treated as receiving a net dividend equal to the amount written-off.

Del will, however, be treated as receiving (and the company will be treated as paying) a dividend equal to the taxable benefit for interest-free loans. This will be the interest which Del would have had to pay at the official rate. The tax consequences will be the same as for the deemed distribution in respect of Del's car.

22 Lorna Mill Ltd

Text references. Chapters 21 to 23 cover the calculation of corporation tax liabilities. Close companies are covered in Chapter 25. Chargeable gains on takeovers are in Chapter 11 and leases are in Chapter 14. The tax implications of a sale of shares compared with a sale of assets can be found in Chapter 30.

Top tips. Do your calculations in an Appendix then feed the results into your written answer. Use headings and subheadings and keep paragraphs short and snappy to maximise your marks.

Easy marks. Once again the calculations and the presentation marks are the easy marks. Remember your proformas and presentation formats to get them.

Marking scheme

			Marks
(a)	**Calculations**		
	CT computation		
	Add back capital expenditure	½	
	Chargeable gains	½	
	FII	½	
	CT limits/rate	½	
	Tax calculation	1	
	Gain on leasehold property		
	Indexed gain	½	
	Cost × lease percentage	1	
	Frozen gain crystallised		
	Original gain	½	
	Rollover relief	1	
			6
(b)	**Explanations**		
	Corporation tax liability	½	
	Payment date	½	
	Cottage	2	
	Loan	2	
	Sale of leasehold building	2	
	Max		6

PRIVATE AND CONFIDENTIAL

[Our address]

[Your address]
[Date]

Dear Sirs

TAX POSITION YEAR ENDED 31 MARCH 2009 AND TAKEOVER IMPLICATIONS

This letter deals with the matters that will affect the Corporation Tax computation for the year ended 31 March 2009 and the tax and other implications of the proposed takeover by Evergreen plc.

(a) **Year ended 31 March 2009**

     The company must pay £75,268 corporation tax which is due on 1 January 2010 (see Appendix 1).

     The following matters were taken into account in arriving at this figure.

     (i)   *Country cottage to be lived in by Sam Bradley*

           The £11,000 relating to improvements will need to be added back to the adjusted trading profit. It is assumed that the remaining £9,000 is accepted as revenue expenditure.

           Sam Bradley is the sales director of the company. As such he will be assessed on the benefit of the provision of the cottage. This will be based on the annual value, and there will be an additional charge if the cottage cost (including improvements) more than £75,000.

     (ii) *Loan to John Harmer*

           As Lorna Mill Ltd is a close company, the loan to John Harmer attracts a 25% tax charge (a 'penalty tax'). The tax due to HMRC is £1,775 (25% × £7,100) and is due on the same day as the regular corporation tax liability ie 1 January 2010.

           When the loan is repaid the tax will also be repaid to the company. The repayment will be received nine months after the accounting period in which the loan is repaid. This penalty tax cannot be offset against the company's tax liability.

           If the loan is written off, the tax will be repaid, as above, and John will be treated as receiving a net distribution equal to the amount written off.

(iii) *Sale of leasehold building*

This gives rise to a chargeable gain of £20,366. Note that as the leasehold building is a wasting asset, its original purchase price is reduced when calculating the gain.

A further consequence will be that the gain arising on the sale of the freehold building in 1998 now crystallises as the gain was deferred into the acquisition of a replacement depreciating asset. This means that an additional gain of £47,600 is chargeable this year. Detailed calculations are contained in Appendix 2.

(b) **Considerations on proposed take-over**

(i) *Tax considerations*

Capital gains tax issues for disposal of shares

If the takeover is structured so that the shareholders of Lorna Mill Ltd sell their shares for cash, they will each crystallise a capital gain based on the excess of the cash received over the cost of their shares.

If shareholders choose to take the shares and loan stock package, no gain will arise. Instead, the original cost of the shares in Lorna Mill Ltd will be apportioned between the new securities acquired in the ratio of their respective market values at the date of the take-over.

The gain arising in respect of the shares received does not need to be calculated at the date of the takeover but instead will be deferred until the shares are sold.

The gain arising in respect of the QCB loan notes received will need to be calculated at the date of the takeover and frozen until the loan notes are redeemed. Any gain arising from the eventual redemption (ie disposal) of the QCB loan notes is exempt from CGT but at that date the frozen gain will become chargeable.

The shareholders who work for the company may wish to elect to disapply the paper for paper takeover rules so that entrepreneurs' relief can be claimed at the time of the takeover. The disposal of the shares in Lorna Mill Ltd will be eligible for the relief if the shareholders own 5% of the shares and are employees or directors of the company and have been so for the one year prior to the takeover.

Entrepreneurs' relief will reduce the effective rate of tax on gains to 10%.

Entrepreneurs' relief may not subsequently be available on the disposal of the shares in Evergreen plc if the shareholders do not satisfy these conditions. Any deferred gain would thus be chargeable at 18% rather than just 10% if the relief is entrepreneurs' claimed at the date of the takeover.

(ii) *Tax aspects of a sale of Lorna Mill Ltd's trade*

Gains will crystallise on the disposal of chargeable assets in the company which will then be subject to corporation tax.

From the shareholders' perspective, they will effectively suffer a double charge to CGT as the company will suffer corporation tax on the disposal of the assets and the shareholders will pay CGT on the disposal of their shares (as the proceeds will reflect the increase due to the sale of the assets at a profit).

Stock will be transferred at market value, giving rise to additional trading profit at the take-over date, although an election can be made to treat the stock as transferred at book value.

Any assets qualifying for capital allowances will also be transferred at market value, potentially giving rise to balancing charges.

Lorna Mill Ltd will be left with no trading assets so will become a close investment holding company. This means that it will pay corporation tax at 28% on its taxable income, irrespective of the size of that income.

The transfer of the trade is likely to be a transfer of a going concern and will therefore be outside the scope of VAT, assuming Evergreen plc is VAT registered.

If Lorna Mill Ltd ceases to make taxable supplies the company will have to notify HMRC within 30 days. It will then be deregistered.

(iii)   *Other considerations*

The shareholders must compare the consideration being offered with the potential income and capital streams from retaining the shares. They will of course want to maximise wealth now and in the future, so the total value of the package must be considered.

Will the employees and directors of Lorna Mill Ltd be able to retain their jobs if the company or trade is taken over? If so, what will their new terms of employment be, compared to their present position? As we have seen above, this could seriously affect the ability to claim entrepreneurs' relief in the future.

If Evergreen plc takes over the company (as opposed to the trade) it is likely to demand repayment of the loan made to John Harner. Will this cause difficulties to him?

By selling the trade, Lorna Mill Ltd (and hence the shareholders) will retain responsibility for any liabilities, especially any bank loans which may have personal guarantees to cover them. This may not be a desirable outcome.

As can be seen the takeover proposals have different advantages and disadvantages for different directors, shareholders and employees, and for the company. They may wish to consider taking independent advice about their own tax positions.

We trust that the above clarifies the points raised by you, but please contact us if we may be of further assistance.

Yours faithfully

Tax Manager

Appendix 1: Corporation tax computation – year ended 31 March 2009

	£
Trade profits (£255,000 + £11,000)	266,000
Chargeable gains (Appendix 2)	67,966
Profits chargeable to corporation tax	333,966
FII: £27,000 × $\frac{100}{90}$	30,000
'profits'	363,966
PCTCT × 28%	93,510
Less: marginal relief 7/400 × [1,500,000 – 363,966] × $\frac{333,966}{363,966}$	(18,242)
CT due 1 January 2010	75,268

Appendix 2: Chargeable gains

	£
Sale of leasehold	
Proceeds	125,000
Cost: £100,000 × $\frac{(\%20y9m)\ 74.169^*}{(\%30y)\ 87.330}$	(84,930)
Indexation: 0.232 × £84,930	(19,704)
Gain	20,366

*30yrs – 9 yrs 3m = 20 yrs 9m

%21 yrs:	74.635	
%20 yrs:	(72.770)	72.770
	$1.865 × \frac{9}{12}$ =	1.399
		74.169

Gain on freehold now crystallising	£
Proceeds	130,000
Cost	(40,000)
0.310 × £40,000	(12,400)
	77,600
Less: rollover relief (frozen gain now crystallising)	(47,600)
Gain chargeable at date of disposal ie proceeds not reinvested	
£130,000 − £100,000 =	30,000
Total gains £(20,366 + 47,600)	67,966

23 Trent plc

Text references. Chargeable gains for companies are in Chapter 21. Groups and the implications of transfers of a trade are dealt with in Chapter 26. You should also study Chapter 30 on tax planning. VAT is covered in Chapters 28 and 29.

Top tips. You must use the correct terminology in your answers. For example it would have been incorrect to discuss a mere change in the nature or conduct of trade – you must use the word 'major' to obtain the available mark.

Do not be afraid to submit your answer plan with your answer. It will show that you have taken the time to really think about the question and the examiner can give you credit for your ideas.

Easy marks. This was a complex question testing a number of issues that often crop up in the context of corporate restructuring, whether on a new acquisition or on the reorganisation of an existing group. The more you practise questions like this the easier the marks will be to obtain as you will be considering the same areas time and time again.

PRIVATE AND CONFIDENTIAL

[Our address]

[Your address]

[Date]

STRICTLY PRIVATE AND CONFIDENTIAL

Dear Sally

Purchase of Ivan Ltd

I am writing in reply to your letter of 17 July, asking for tax advice on the purchase of Ivan Ltd.

Use of Ivan Ltd's tax losses

Ivan Ltd's trading losses unrelieved at 31 August 2009 can only be carried forward against future profits from the same trade. However, if Trent plc makes a major change to the nature or conduct of Ivan Ltd's trade before 31 August 2012, then the carry forward of the losses will be denied. Any minor changes would be ignored.

In my opinion your proposals regarding Ivan Ltd's future will constitute a major change of trade and my advice would be to delay this until after 31 August 2012 if commercially possible.

Any trading losses incurred by Ivan Ltd after 31 August 2009 can be group relieved to Trent plc to reduce its own profits for the corresponding accounting period. Alternatively these losses could be set against any income or gains of Ivan Ltd for the period of the loss, and then the previous twelve months.

If you change the nature or conduct of the trade, then the post-acquisition losses could not be carried back to any accounting period before 31 August 2009, although it appears unlikely that there are any profits against which to obtain loss relief before 31 August 2009.

The capital losses at the date of acquisition (£2m) cannot be used to shelter any capital gains of assets owned by Trent plc, as these losses arose prior to the acquisition. They can only be set off against gains on assets owned by Ivan Ltd at the date of acquisition or purchased subsequently from a third party.

There is no question of the capital losses realised by Ivan Ltd being transferred to Trent plc.

Proposals to shelter gain on sale of old headquarters

As described above, Trent plc will not be able to utilise Ivan Ltd's capital loss of £2m as these losses cannot be transferred to Trent plc, and in any case they arose prior to acquisition of Ivan Ltd. A similar restriction applies where capital losses are realised after a company joins a group on assets held by the company on joining the group.

It may be possible to utilise some of the capital loss anticipated on the sale of Machinist House if the property is transferred to Trent plc prior to the sale. Although there is unlikely to be a large change in the value of the property in the next year so that it could be argued that the full loss in value arises prior to Ivan Ltd being acquired, the law allows the pre-acquisition loss to be computed on a time basis if it benefits the taxpayer.

Thus, with a proposed sale date of 31 August 2010, we can treat approximately £588,000 (Appendix 1) as a post-acquisition loss and, if realised by Trent plc, this can be set off against the gain on the sale of its headquarters.

As an alternative, the gain of £8m could be partly deferred by claiming rollover relief on the purchase of your new headquarters. Not all of the gain can be deferred however. Normally, the proceeds not used for the purchase of the new building of £4m (£13m – £9m) would remain chargeable, but in this case, not all of the new headquarters will be used in Trent's trade (as it will be subletting space). Thus only a proportion of the £9m will be allowed as qualifying cost, thus increasing the chargeable gain.

A further alternative is to delay the sale of Machinist House in order to increase the amount of post-acquisition loss which could be used by Trent plc. It is important to note, however, that the sale will need to be made in the same accounting period as the gain is realised on the headquarters. Any delay beyond this period would prevent the capital loss being used in this way.

Merger of trades of Ivan Ltd and Trent plc

The transfer of Ivan Ltd's trade to Trent plc would allow the trading losses of Ivan Ltd to be used in future (but only against profits of its trade).

No capital gains would arise on the transfer, as Ivan Ltd is at least 75% owned by Trent plc, and no balancing adjustments would arise on the transfer of assets qualifying for capital allowances - whichever way around the transfer was effected.

If Trent plc's trade was transferred to Ivan Ltd, then there would be no restriction against the losses being set against the profits of Trent's trade now transferred.

However if Ivan Ltd's trade is transferred to Trent plc, and it becomes dormant, its capital losses will be wasted.

For this reason (and the impact of setting off Ivan Ltd's losses brought forward as described above) I would recommend that Trent plc's trade is transferred to Ivan Ltd, so that the capital losses can be utilised by Ivan Ltd against gains on assets it already owns or buys after the transfer.

As stated above, in order to preserve Ivan Ltd's trade losses at the date of acquisition, you should ensure that you do not change the nature or conduct of its trade prior to September 2012.

VAT position on letting out part of the headquarters

In order to waive exemption on (or opt to tax) the new building, Trent plc needs to send a notice of election to HMRC which will be effective immediately. This notice must be sent within 30 days of making the election.

The advantage of Trent plc waiving the exemption is that it will be able to recover all of its input tax on any purchases or supplies received in relation to the building including the VAT charged on the purchase price.

If it did not opt to tax, then the rent charged would be an exempt supply, making Trent Ltd partially exempt. This would cause problems in recovering the full input VAT on the purchase price and on any repairs or expenses relating to the part let out. A further consequence of not opting to tax is that the 'capital goods scheme' would apply, leading to annual adjustments of the input tax recovery over the next ten years to reflect changes in the use of the building for making exempt supplies.

The main disadvantage of opting to tax is that Trent plc would have to charge VAT on the rent, which the insurance company would be unable to recover as it makes exempt supplies. This could make the rent uncompetitive with similar landlords who have not waived the exemption on their buildings and could jeopardise the arrangements.

Another disadvantage (albeit not of immediate concern), is that Trent plc would have to charge VAT on the eventual sale of the building, and if this is to an exempt supplier it would increase the 'cost' of the building to them, making it uncompetitive as discussed above.

I trust that the above clarifies the points raised in your letter, but should you have any further queries, please do not hesitate to contact me.

Yours sincerely

Tax Adviser

Appendix 1 – post acquisition loss on sale of Machinist House

	£
Anticipated proceeds	7,000,000
Less: cost	(12,000,000)
Loss	5,000,000
Time owned since purchased (28.2.02 to 31.8.10) =	8½ years
Post-acquisition period (1.9.09 to 31.8.10) =	1 year

$$\therefore \text{Post acquisition loss} = £5m \times \frac{1}{8\frac{1}{2}} = \underline{£588,235}$$

24 Irroy

Text references. Group relief of losses is covered in Chapter 26 and transfer pricing is dealt with in Chapter 20. Overseas aspects of CT is in Chapter 27 and overseas aspects of VAT is in Chapter 29.

Top tips. This question required a lot of writing for the answer, with minimal calculations. Answer plans are essential.

The two companies are associated with each other so don't forget to divide the small companies' limit by 2. Even through they are owned by a person rather than a company they are still associated for upper and lower limits purposes.

Easy marks. To pick up lots of marks (and to not confuse yourself or the examiner along the way) when considering two alternatives take it one at a time. Discuss the pros and cons of one alternative and then move onto the second. Where an answer keeps flicking from one alternative to another and then back it can be confusing and you may lose marks if the examiner cannot easily follow your answer.

Examiner's comments. A Corporation Tax (CT) question concerning groups. This question required candidates to suggest alternative group structures which would allow the companies to claim group relief, and also to explain the different CT and Value Added Tax (VAT) implications of an overseas subsidiary being treated as UK resident, or alternatively, overseas resident. It had a very high written component, as opposed to computational content, and was generally poorly done by the relatively few candidates who chose it.

In part (a) most candidates were able to recognise the problem with the current structure, and suggest at least one alternative, but still didn't include enough detail to gain more than half marks.

A surprising number of candidates slipped up in (a)(ii) by not recognising that the two companies were associated, therefore reducing the small companies' limits. This lost easy marks.

Part (b) was not well done. There were a lot of relevant points a candidate could have made in this question, some straightforward, some less so. The key was to adopt a structured, logical approach, but too often the answers adopted a haphazard, scattergun approach. When comparing two alternative situations (here, whether Green Ltd is UK resident or Irish resident), candidates must make it clear which scenario they are talking about when making their points. It is not enough to state a fact, then leave it to the marker to decide which of the alternatives it applies to. This will not gain marks.

Marks

(a)	(i)	Companies not part of a group	½	
		Inability to surrender losses	½	
		Ability to use losses in future	½	
		Shareholding requirements to make a group	½	
		Share for share: possibility	½	
		no immediate CGT consequences	½	
		commercial requirements	½	
		clearance procedure available	½	
		dormant company not an associate	½	
		Straight sale: consideration of CGT issues	½	
		availability of entrepreneurs' relief	½	
		availability of annual exemptions	½	
		Existing tax losses v future trading profit only	½	
		Max		5

	(ii)	Awareness of associated companies	½	
		No planning: Corporation tax at 28%	½	
		Marginal relief calculation	½	
		Planning: Restriction of group relief	½	
		Corporation tax at 21%	½	
		Calculation of tax saved	½	
				3

(b)	Residence:		
	incorporation not necessarily sufficient	½	
	central management/control	½	
	conduct meetings outside UK	½	
	if resident UK: taxed on worldwide income	½	
	. PE in ROI	½	
	consequences	½	
	if resident ROI: dividends/overseas income	½	
	still associated	½	
	no group relief	½	
	Double tax relief: relief for withholding tax	½	
	relief for underlying tax	½	
	10% plus holding	½	
	double tax: lower of	½	
	Transfer Pricing: identify issue	½	
	arm's length	½	
	applies in UK/exemption if SME	½	
	applies if Irish resident/exemption if SME	½	
	CFC issues: identify issue	½	
	dependent subsidiary	½	
	material difference in tax rates	½	
	conclusion: ROI low tax country	½	
	deemed distribution	½	
	requirement to self-report	½	
	£50,000 exemption	½	
	acceptable distribution policy		
	– identify exemption	½	
	– 90%/details	½	

VAT issues:	making taxable supplies in ROI	½
	UK zero rated	½
	VAT paid in ROI	½
	proof of supply required	½
	invoice to bear both VAT numbers	½
	alternative domestic treatment	½
	need for an ESL	½
	penalties	½

Max $\underline{14}$
$\underline{25}$

(a) (i) Aqua Ltd and Aria Ltd are both owned 75% by Irroy and 25% by Irwin.

Although both companies are under the control of Irroy they do not form a group for group relief purposes, and so it is not possible to claim group relief. To be part of a group, companies must be controlled by another company, not an individual. Had a group existed, Aria Ltd could have surrendered its trading loss to Aqua Ltd. This would have been set against Aqua's profits of the same accounting period.

Instead the losses of Aria Ltd can only be carried forward against future profits arising from the same trade which are not anticipated to arise before the year ended 31 March 2012 at the earliest.

The current structure could be amended by:

(1) Irroy and Irwin transferring their shareholdings in both companies to a third company in return for that company issuing shares to Irroy and Irwin in the same proportions. Aqua Ltd and Aria Ltd would each be wholly owned subsidiaries of the third company, so satisfying the conditions for group relief. The share exchange would be treated for capital gains purposes as a 'paper for paper' transaction, but it would be advisable to obtain advance clearance from HMRC.

(2) Irroy and Irwin transferring their shareholdings in one company, say Aria Ltd, to the other, say Aqua Ltd. Aria Ltd would then be a wholly owned subsidiary of Aqua Ltd, so again the conditions for group relief would be satisfied. As Irroy and Irwin are 75% and 25% shareholders in Aqua Ltd, their interests in Aria Ltd would be in the same proportions. Although the transfer would be a disposal for capital gains purposes it would appear unlikely that any gain would arise as Aria Ltd has made losses from the outset. If a gain did arise, entrepreneurs' relief would be available, and also Irroy's and Irwin's annual exemptions.

If a group structure is set up, only losses arising after that date can be relieved, using time apportionment if it occurs during an accounting period (unless some other method of apportionment would give a just and reasonable result).

(ii) (1) If no action is taken, there are two associated companies, as they are controlled by Irroy.

The corporation tax payable for the year to 31 March 2010 is:

	Aqua Ltd	Aria Ltd
	£	£
PCTCT (loss c/f 60,000 + 30,000 b/f = £90,000)	175,000	NIL
CT payable £175,000 × 28%	49,000	
Less MR 7/400 × (750,000 − 175,000)	(10,063)	
	38,937	NIL

(2) If an amended structure is implemented from 1 June 2009 there will still be two associated companies, assuming that if a holding company is interposed it does not trade and so can be disregarded for this purpose. Group relief can only be surrendered for the ten month period 1 June 2009 – 31 March 2010.

The corporation tax payable for the year to 31 March 2010 is:

	Aqua Ltd £	Aria Ltd £
Profits	175,000	
Less group relief 10/12 × 60,000	(50,000)	
PCTCT (loss c/f 60,000 − 50,000 + 30,000 b/f = £40,000)	125,000	NIL
CT payable £125,000 × 21%	26,250	NIL

The corporation tax saved by implementing the group structure is £38,937 − £26,250 = £12,687, although the losses carried forward in Aria Ltd are reduced by £50,000.

(b)   **Charge to corporation tax**

If Green Ltd had been incorporated in the UK it would have been resident in the UK. However Green Ltd is to be incorporated in the Republic of Ireland. It may still be treated as resident in the UK if its central management and control is exercised in the UK, such as through the holding of directors' meetings in the UK.

If Green Ltd is treated as UK resident, then it will be taxed in the UK on all of its worldwide profits, wherever arising. If any corporation tax were paid in the Republic of Ireland, then double tax relief would be available by allowing the Irish corporation tax as a credit against the UK corporation tax. Any dividends paid by Green Ltd to Aqua Ltd would be disregarded for UK corporation tax purposes.

If Green Ltd is not UK resident, then it will only be taxable in the UK on any income arising in the UK. If it pays any dividends to Aqua Ltd, then those dividends would be taxable on Aqua Ltd as foreign income. As Green Ltd will be a subsidiary of Aqua Ltd, Aqua will be entitled to double tax relief for any underlying foreign tax as well as for any withholding tax charged on the dividends paid.

As Green Ltd will be trading in the Republic of Ireland it is likely that the Irish authorities will consider it to be resident in the Republic of Ireland on the grounds that it has a permanent establishment there. It will then be liable to Irish corporation tax on its trading profits, and on any other income arising anywhere.

Since the rate of Irish corporation tax is lower than the rate of UK corporation tax it would seem to be preferable for Green Ltd to be treated as resident in the Republic of Ireland, and not in the UK. The net effect would be that all trading profits would be taxed at the Irish corporation tax rate of 12.5%, with this being topped up to Aqua Ltd's marginal rate of corporation tax only on those profits distributed to the UK.

It should be noted that Green Ltd will be treated as an associated company, so reducing the small companies' limits, regardless of residence.

Anti-avoidance legislation

Transfer pricing

Green Ltd will be selling water tanks supplied by Aqua Ltd. As the companies are under common control, it would be possible to manipulate the prices charged, so redirecting profits to the lower tax paying company. The transfer pricing rules are designed to prevent such manipulation. They can apply where there are transactions between companies under common control at non-arm's length prices, even if both companies are UK resident. However, the group is expected to continue to qualify as a small- and medium-sized enterprise, and the transfer pricing legislation does not generally apply to small- and medium-sized enterprises.

It may still apply if one party is not resident in the UK but is resident in a country which has a double tax treaty with the UK which does not contain a non-discrimination clause. This is not the case here. It may also apply to a medium sized enterprise if HMRC issues a transfer pricing notice in respect of a particular transaction or series of transactions.

Controlled foreign companies

The controlled foreign companies' legislation applies where a company which is controlled by a UK company is resident in a 'low tax country', ie one where the rate of tax is less than 75% of the UK rate. As the rate of Irish corporation tax is 12.5% compared to the UK small companies rate of 21%, this would appear to apply if Green Ltd is resident in the Republic of Ireland (12.5% ÷ 21% = 59.5%).

The consequence of the controlled foreign company legislation applying would be that Green Ltd's profits would be apportioned to Aqua Ltd, and subject to UK corporation tax at the full rate of corporation tax. Double tax relief would be given for any Irish tax paid on those profits.

The controlled foreign company legislation will not apply if Green Ltd's profits are less than £50,000, or if at least 90% of the profits are distributed to Aqua Ltd no later than eighteen months after the end of the accounting period.

VAT

Green Ltd will be making taxable supplies in the Republic of Ireland and will be required to register for VAT, unless its supplies fall below the taxable limits. Green Ltd will be required to charge Irish VAT at the rate of 21% on its supplies.

Aqua Ltd will be making supplies to another EU member state, to a customer registered for VAT in that member state. Provided it obtains Green Ltd's VAT number and quotes it on invoices issued, Green Ltd's supplies will be zero-rated in the UK. Depending on the volume of sales, Aqua Ltd may be required to complete a UK sales list.

As the supplies have been zero-rated, Green Ltd will be required to account for Irish VAT on those supplies at the Irish rate of 21%. It can, however, claim credit for the Irish VAT paid against the Irish VAT that it must charge on its supplies.

25 Dovedale Ltd

Text references. Capital allowances are covered in Chapter 7. CT is in Chapters 20 to 24 with group aspects dealt with in Chapter 26. Overseas aspects of CT is dealt with in Chapter 27. VAT groups are covered in Chapter 28, and Ethics in Chapter 30.

Top tips. Make sure you look at the marks available in each part of the question and allocate your time and effort accordingly.

Easy marks. You must show your workings clearly and explain why you have done what you did – marks for all of this. Keep calm, don't panic or rush – work through the question carefully to maximise marks.

				Marks
(a)	Gain on shares	½		
	Substantial shareholding exemption	½		
	Three conditions	1½		
	Possible degrouping charge	½		
	No gain, no loss transfers within six years	½		
			Max	3
(b)	Losses to be surrendered:			
	Calculation of group relief	1		
	Calculations of consortium relief	1½		
	Losses remaining:			
	Must be carried forward	½		
	No offset before year ending 31 March 2011	½		
	Change of ownership and trade	1		
	Capital allowances:			
	Claiming would increase unrelieved losses	½		
	Not claiming would increase next year's loss	½		
	Consortium relief available	½		
			Max	5

(c)	Trading profit and consortium relief		½	
	Chargeable gain:			
	Cost		1	
	Unindexed gain		½	
	Indexation		½	
	Rate of corporation tax		½	
	Corporation tax liability		½	
		Max		3
(d)	Conflict of interest		1	
	Resolution		1	
				2
(e)	Dovedale Ltd and Hira Ltd:			
	Control		½	
	Established in the UK with reason		1	
	Atapo Inc:			
	Control		½	
	Established in the UK		½	
	Fixed establishment in the UK with meaning		1	
		Max		3
(f)	May be CFC		½	
	Definition		½	
	Effect of being CFC		1	
	Exceptions not satisfied		1	
	Exempt activities		½	
	Motive test		½	
	Not CFC – not taxed in UK		½	
	Taxed on dividends received		½	
	Adjust for withholding tax and underlying tax		1	
	Double tax relief		1	
		Max		5
				21

(a) **Capital gains that may arise on the sale by Belgrove Ltd of shares in Hira Ltd**

Belgrove Ltd will realise a capital gain on the sale of the shares unless the substantial shareholding exemption applies. The exemption will be given automatically provided all of the following conditions are satisfied.

- Belgrove Ltd has owned at least 10% of Hira Ltd for a minimum of twelve months during the two years prior to the sale.
- Belgrove Ltd is a trading company or a member of a trading group during that twelve-month period and immediately after the sale.
- Hira Ltd is a trading company or the holding company of a trading group during that twelve-month period and immediately after the sale.

Hira Ltd will no longer be in a capital gains group with Belgrove Ltd after the sale. Accordingly, a capital gain, known as a degrouping charge, may arise in Hira Ltd. A degrouping charge will arise if, at the time it leaves the Belgrove Ltd group, Hira Ltd owns any capital assets which were transferred to it at no gain, no loss within the previous six years by a member of the Belgrove Ltd capital gains group.

(b) **The advantage of Hira Ltd not claiming any capital allowances**

In the year ending 31 March 2009 Hira Ltd expects to make a tax adjusted trading loss, before deduction of capital allowances, of £55,000 and to surrender the maximum amount possible of trading losses to Belgrove Ltd and Dovedale Ltd.

For the first nine months of the year from 1 April 2008 to 31 December 2008 Hira Ltd is in a loss relief group with Belgrove Ltd. The maximum surrender to Belgrove Ltd for this period is the lower of:

- the available loss of £41,250 (£55,000 × 9/12); and
- the profits chargeable to corporation tax of Belgrove of £28,500 (£38,000 × 9/12).

ie £28,500. This leaves losses of £12,750 (£41,250 – £28,500) unrelieved.

For the remaining three months from 1 January 2009 to 31 March 2009 Hira Ltd is a consortium company because at least 75% of its share capital is owned by companies, each of which own at least 5%. It can surrender £8,938 (£55,000 × 3/12 × 65%) to Dovedale Ltd and £4,812 (£55,000 × 3/12 × 35%) to Belgrove Ltd as both companies have sufficient taxable profits to offset the losses. Accordingly, there are no losses remaining from the three-month period.

The unrelieved losses from the first nine months must be carried forward as Hira Ltd has no income or gains in that year or the previous year. However, the losses cannot be carried forward beyond 1 January 2009 (the date of the change of ownership of Hira Ltd) if there is a major change in the nature or conduct of the trade of Hira Ltd. Even if the losses can be carried forward, the earliest year in which they can be relieved is the year ending 31 March 2011 as Hira Ltd is expected to make a trading loss in the year ending 31 March 2010.

Any capital allowances claimed by Hira Ltd in the year ending 31 March 2009 would increase the tax adjusted trading loss for that year and consequently the unrelieved losses arising in the first nine months.

If the capital allowances are not claimed, the whole of the tax written down value brought forward of £96,000 would be carried forward to the year ending 31 March 2010 thus increasing the capital allowances and the tax adjusted trading loss, for that year. By not claiming any capital allowances, Hira Ltd can effectively transfer a current period trading loss, which would be created by capital allowances, of £19,200 (20% × £96,000) from the year ending 31 March 2009 to the following year where it can be surrendered to the two consortium members.

(c) **Dovedale Ltd – Forecast corporation tax computation for the year ended 31 March 2009**

	£
Trading profit	875,000
Chargeable gain (W1)	15,647
	890,647
Less: Consortium relief (from (b))	(8,938)
Profits chargeable to corporation tax	881,709
Corporation tax liability	
£881,709 × 28% (W3)	246,879

Note. The two companies are not in a capital gains group as Dovedale Ltd owns less than 75% of Hira Ltd. Accordingly, Dovedale Ltd will realise a gain on the sale of the building.

Workings

W1 Chargeable gain on sale of office building

	£
Disposal proceeds	234,000
Less: Cost (W2)	(203,119)
	30,881
Less: Indexation	
(219.8 – 204.4)/204.4 = 0.075 × £203,119	(15,234)
Chargeable gain	15,647

W2 Base cost of office building

	£
Initial cost	210,000
Less: Rollover relief claimed	
Gain on factory £84,217	
Proceeds not invested £277,450 – £210,000 = £67,450	
Rollover relief claimed (£74,331 – £67,450)	(6,881)
	203,119

W3 Rate of corporation tax

Dovedale Ltd has one associate, Hira Ltd, for the year ending 31 March 2009. Accordingly, the upper limit will be £750,000 (£1,500,000 ÷ 2) and Dovedale Ltd will be taxed as a large company.

(d)   If you are asked to act in respect of a matter which affects two clients there may be a conflict of interests.

You need to consider carefully the advice that each client requires, and whether the advice given to one client would be detrimental to the other client. In that case it is likely that you should only act for one of the clients, and you would have to explain to the other that you could no longer act.

There may be instances where it is still possible to act for both clients if their interests do not conflict. This may be the case here, if both Dovedale Ltd and Belgrove Ltd are agreed on the terms of the sale. You should, however, advise each of them that you act for the other, and seek their consent to your acting for both. It may be advisable to suggest to one or both of them that they may like to take independent advice regarding the sale.

(e)   Dovedale Ltd and Hira Ltd can register as a group for the purposes of value added tax (VAT) because Dovedale Ltd controls Hira Ltd and both companies are established in the UK in that their head offices are in the UK.

Dovedale Ltd will also control Atapo Inc. However, Atapo Inc cannot be part of a group registration unless it is established in the UK or has a fixed establishment in the UK. It will be regarded as established in the UK if it is centrally managed and controlled in the UK or if its head office is in the UK. A fixed establishment is a place where the company has staff and equipment and where its business is carried on.

(f)   Atapo Inc appears to be a controlled foreign company (CFC) in that:

- it is resident outside of the UK in Morovia; and
- it is controlled by Dovedale Ltd, a UK resident company; and
- the rate of corporation tax in Morovia is less than three-quarters of that in the UK.

If Atapo Inc is a CFC its profits will be attributed to Dovedale Ltd and must be included in Dovedale Ltd's corporation tax return. The whole of the profits of Atapo Inc would be taxed at 28% with relief given for the Morovian tax suffered.

Atapo Inc will not be regarded as a CFC if it satisfies one of the exceptions. Three of the exceptions do not apply as Atapo Inc is not a quoted company, its profits exceed £50,000 and it does not intend to pay at least 90% of those profits to Dovedale Ltd. However, there are two further exceptions that it may be able to satisfy.

Atapo Inc will be regarded as carrying out exempt activities if:

(i)   it has a genuine physical presence in Morovia, as appears to be the case; and
(ii)   less than half of its gross trading receipts arise from transactions with Dovedale Ltd or other associated entities.

Alternatively, Atapo Inc may be able to satisfy the motive test. This test is satisfied if it can be argued that Atapo Inc was not formed in order to divert profits from the UK or reduce a UK tax liability.

If Atapo Inc is not a CFC it will not be taxed in the UK on its profits as it does not have a permanent establishment in the UK. However, Dovedale Ltd will be taxed on the dividends received from Atapo Inc.

The dividends received will be included in the corporation tax computation gross of underlying tax (the Morovian tax paid in respect of the profits distributed) and the tax withheld on the dividends paid. The underlying tax is included because Dovedale Ltd owns at least 10% of Atapo Inc.

The corporation tax at 28% on the gross dividend will then be reduced by double tax relief. The double tax relief will equal the underlying tax and the withholding tax on the dividend, as the total Morovian tax suffered is less than 28% of the gross dividend.

Note. If Atapo Inc is a CFC the tax payable by Dovedale Ltd on the profits apportioned to it will be reduced because it has received dividends from Atapo Inc.

26 Daniel Dare

Marking scheme

				Marks
(a)	(i)	Identification of group members	1	
		Identification of strategy	1	
		Calculation of corporation tax rate limits	1	
		Advice	1	
		Relevance of dividend received by Saturn Ltd	1	
		Tax saving	1	
		Submission date for group relief claim	1	
		Loss carryback	1½	
			Max	7

(ii)	Not in group relief group		1	
	Recognition of condition for consortium to exist/information required		2	
	Relief available if consortium exists		1½	
	Relief available if no consortium		1	
	Possible restriction on ability to carry forward loss		2	
		Max		6
(iii)	Value added tax/information required		2	
	No balancing charge		1	
	Capital gain		1	
	Rollover relief:			
	Assets to be acquired by Tethys Lt		1½	
	Amount of relief available		1	
	Relevant assets		1	
	Qualifying period		1	
		Max		7
(iv)	Stamp duty			2
	Appropriate style and presentation		1	
	Effectiveness of communication		1	
				2
(b)	Information needed – 1 mark each		3	
	Action to take			
	Threats and safeguards		2	
	Contact existing tax adviser		1	
		Max		5
				29

MEMORANDUM

To: Tax manager
From: Tax assistant
Date: 2 June 2009
Subject: Saturn Ltd group of companies

This memorandum considers a number of issues raised by Daniel Dare (DD), the managing directors of Saturn Ltd.

(a)   (i)   **Dione Ltd – value of tax loss**

- Any amount of the loss can be surrendered to the UK resident members of the 75% loss group, ie Saturn LT AND Rhea Ltd.

- The maximum tax saving will be obtained by offsetting the loss against profits between the limits for the small companies rate of corporation tax. The limits are divided by four as there are four associated companies (Titan Inc is included as overseas companies are associated for the purposes of determining the rate of corporation tax). Accordingly, for the year ending 30 June 2009 the limits are £75,000 and £375,000.

- The maximum tax saving will be achieved by surrendering the loss to Saturn Ltd. The first £10,000 of loss will relieve profits at the full rate of tax and the balance of the loss will save tax at 29.75%. Surrendering the loss to Rhea Ltd would only save tax at 28%.

- The dividend received by Saturn Ltd does not affect its corporation tax liability. Dividends received from UK resident companies are not subject to corporation tax and dividends received from a 51% subsidiary are not franked investment income.

- The corporation tax saved via the offset of the loss will be £55,458 ((£10,000 × 28%) + (£177,000 × 29.75%)).

- The claim must be submitted by 30 June 2011 (one year after the filing date of the corporation tax return).

Further information required:

- Income and gains of Dione Ltd for the year ended 30 June 2008
- The loss could be carried back for offset against the total profits of Dione Ltd for the year ended 30 June 2008. Whether or not this would be advantageous would depend on the company's total profits for that year. Although the maximum additional tax saving would be very small, there would be a cashflow benefit.

(ii) **Tethys Ltd – Use of trading loss**

- The two companies will not be in a group relief group as Saturn Ltd will not own 75% of Tethys Ltd.
- For a consortium to exist, 75% of the ordinary share capital of Tethys Ltd must be held by companies which each hold at least 5%. Accordingly, Tethys Ltd will be a consortium company if the balance of its share capital is owned by Clangers Ltd but not if it is owned by Edith Clanger.
- If Tethys Ltd qualifies as a consortium company: 65% of its trading losses in the period from 1 August 2009 to 31 December 2009 can be surrendered to Saturn Ltd, ie £21,667 (£80,000 × 5/12 × 65%).
- If Tethys Ltd does not qualify as a consortium company: none of its loss can be surrendered to Saturn Ltd.
- The acquisition of 65% of Tethys Ltd is a change in ownership of the company. If there is a major change in the nature or conduct of the trade of Tethys Ltd within three years of 1 August 2009, the loss arising prior to that date cannot be carried forward for relief in the future.

Further information required:

- Ownership of the balance of the share capital of Tethys Ltd.

(iii) **Tethys Ltd – Sale of the manufacturing premises**

Value added tax (VAT)

- The building is not a new building (ie it is more than three years old). Accordingly, the sale of the building is an exempt supply and VAT should not be charged unless Tethys Ltd has opted to tax the building in the past.

Taxable profits on sale

- There will be no balancing adjustment in respect of industrial building allowances as the building is to be sold on or after 21 March 2007.
- The capital gain arising on the sale of the building will be £97,760 (£240,000 – (£112,000 × 1.27)).

Rollover relief

- Tethys Ltd is not in a capital gains group with Saturn Ltd. Accordingly, rollover relief will only be available if Tethys Ltd, rather than any of the other Saturn Ltd group companies, acquires sufficient qualifying business assets.
- The amount of sales proceeds not spent in the qualifying period is chargeable, ie £40,000 (£240,000 – £200,000). The balance of the gain, £57,760 (£97,760 – £40,000), can be rolled over.
- Qualifying business assets include land and buildings and fixed plant and machinery. The assets must be brought into immediate use in the company's trade.
- The assets must be acquired in the four-year period beginning one year prior to the sale of the manufacturing premises.

Further information required:

- Whether or not Tethys has opted to tax the building in the past for the purposes of VAT.

(iv)   **Stamp duty and stamp duty land tax**

- The purchase of Tethys Ltd will give rise to a liability to *ad valorem* stamp duty of £1,175 (£235,000 × 0·5%). The stamp duty must be paid by Saturn Ltd within 30 days of the share transfer in order to avoid interest being charged. It is not an allowable expense for the purposes of corporation tax.

(b)   **Before agreeing to become tax advisers to the Saturn Ltd group**

Information needed:

- Proof of incorporation and primary business address and registered office.
- The structure, directors and shareholders of the company.
- The identities of those persons instructing the firm on behalf of the company and those persons that are authorised to do so.

Action to take:

- Consider whether becoming tax advisers to the Saturn Ltd group would create any threats to compliance with the fundamental principles of professional ethics, for example integrity and professional competence. Where such threats exist, we should not accept the appointment unless the threats can be reduced to an acceptable level via the implementation of safeguards
- Contact the existing tax adviser in order to ensure that there has been no action by the Saturn Ltd group that would, on ethical grounds, preclude us from accepting appointment.

27 Palm plc

Text references. Chapter 20 covers research and development and general computation of corporation tax. Chapter 24 covers corporate losses. Groups are covered in Chapter 26. Overseas aspects of corporation tax are dealt with in Chapter 27.

Top tips. Read the question carefully and make sure you use all the information given. For example, you were told that Palm plc has more than 40 wholly owned subsidiaries so that all group companies pay corporation tax at 28%. This made the calculations required in the question very easy once you had spotted the technical point being tested. You were also told to ignore indexation allowance which again simplified the required computation of the de-grouping charge.

Easy marks. Part (b) should have gained you easy marks as the question told you that making sales in North America would have no effect on input tax recovery. You then only need to think about why that was the case.

Examiner's comments. Part (a) was in two parts. Both parts required candidates to identify the implications of the proposed transactions and to apply their knowledge to the facts.

Part (i) concerned research and development and the use of brought forward losses. Whilst these issues were often successfully identified by candidates, the detail requested in the requirement was missing as was the effect of the issues on the amount of corporation tax payable. Some candidates thought, erroneously, that the restriction on the use of losses brought forward following the change in ownership and the major change in the nature of the trade related to group relief.

Part (ii) concerned the identification of a degrouping charge and the treatment of the profits of a controlled foreign company. Again, the issues were successfully identified by many candidates but there was a lack of precise knowledge of the rules and a tendency to describe the rules in general terms rather than to simply apply them to the facts.

Part (b) required candidates to understand the VAT implications of sales to domestic customers within and outside the European Union (standard rated and zero rated respectively). This was a straightforward test of important VAT rules but the majority of answers were poor and many confused the terms exempt and zero rated.

Marks

(a)   (i)   *Research and development*

Enhanced tax deduction	½	
130% for large company	1	
Effect on tax liability	1	
Conditions : ½ each max	1½	

Use of brought forward trading losses

Major change in nature and conduct of business (reasons)	2	
Within 3 years of change in ownership	1	
Losses cannot be c/f beyond date of change in ownership	1	
Tax effect of losses used/lost	2	
Max		8

(ii)   *De-grouping charge*

Identification of charge	½	
Leaving group within six years	1	
Tax effect	1½	

Controlled foreign company

Profits usually attributed to UK shareholders	½	
Acceptable distribution policy	½	

Dividend income

UK resident company taxable on worldwide income	1	
Gross dividend	1	
Effect of DTR	1½	
Max		7

(b)

Making standard rated supplies	1½	
Effect of making zero-rated supplies	1½	
		3
		18

(a)   **Nikau Ltd – Effect on corporation tax payable for the year ending 31 March 2010**

(i)   **Project Sabal**

Research and development expenditure

The expenditure incurred in respect of research and development will give rise to an enhanced deduction for the purposes of computing the taxable trading profits of Nikau Ltd. The enhanced deduction is 130% of the qualifying expenditure as Nikau Ltd is a large enterprise for this purpose.

The expenditure will reduce the profits chargeable to corporation tax of Nikau Ltd by £91,000 (£70,000 × 130%) and its corporation tax liability by £25,480 (£91,000 × 28%).

The budgeted expenditure will qualify for the enhanced deduction because it appears to satisfy the following conditions:

- it is likely to qualify as research and development expenditure within generally accepted accounting principles
- it exceeds £10,000 in Nikau Ltd's accounting period
- it relates to revenue expenditure as opposed to capital items
- it will result in an extension of trading activities for Nikau Ltd

Use of brought forward trading losses

The development of products for the North American market is likely to represent a major change in the nature and conduct of the trade of Nikau Ltd. This is because the company is developing new products and intends to sell them in a new market. It is a major change as sales to North America are expected to generate significant additional profits.

Because this change will occur within three years of the change in the ownership of Nikau Ltd on 1 November 2009, any trading losses arising prior to that date cannot be carried forward beyond that date. The profit for the year ending 31 March 2010 is apportioned on a time basis between the periods before and after the change as follows:

	1 April 2009 – 31 October 2009 £	1 November 2009 – 31 March 2010 £	Total £
Profits			
£(360,000 - 91,000) ×7/12: 5/12	156,917	112,083	269,000
Less: loss b/f (max)	(156,917)	(0)	(156,917)
Adjusted profit	0	112,083	112,083

The remainder of the loss of £(195,700 – 156,917) = £38,783 is lost, resulting in loss of tax relief of £(38,783 × 28%) =   £10,859

(ii) **Shares held in Date Inc and the related dividend income**

De-grouping charge

There will be a de-grouping charge in Nikau Ltd in the year ending 31 March 2010 in respect of the shares in Date Inc.

This is because Nikau Ltd has left the Facet Group within six years of the no gain, no loss transfer of the shares when it still owned the shares.

Nikau Ltd is treated as if it has sold the shares in Date Inc for their market value at the time of the no gain, no loss disposal. This gives rise to a gain of £(338,000 – 137,000) = £201,000.

This gain will mean additional corporation tax of £201,000 × 28% = £56,280.

Controlled foreign company

Date Inc is a controlled foreign company. The profits of such a company are normally attributed to its UK resident shareholders such that they are subject to UK corporation tax.

However, none of the profits of Date Inc will be attributed to Nikau Ltd because Date Inc distributes more than 90% (£115,000/£120,000 = 95.8%) of its chargeable profits to its shareholders.

Dividend income

Nikau Ltd is a UK resident company and is therefore subject to corporation tax on its worldwide income.

The dividend income will be grossed up in respect of the withholding tax. There is no underlying tax as there are no taxes on income or capital profits in Palladia.

The corporation tax of will be reduced by unilateral double tax relief equal to the withholding tax suffered:

	£
Corporation tax on gross dividend	11,142
£38,200 × 100/96 = £39,792 × 28%	
Less: DTR (overseas tax clearly less than UK tax)	
£39,792 × 4%	(1,592)
Corporation tax on dividend	9,550

(b) **Recoverability of input tax**

Sales by Nikau Ltd of its existing products are subject to UK VAT at 17.5% because it is selling to domestic customers who will not be registered for VAT. So Nikau Ltd can recover all of its input tax at the moment.

Sales to customers in North America will be zero rated because the goods are being exported from the EU. Zero rated supplies are classified as taxable for the purposes of VAT and therefore Nikau Ltd will continue to be able to recover all of its input tax.

28 Hutt plc

Marking scheme

		Marks
(a) Hutt plc trading losses		
Within Hutt plc		
Current year offset	½	
Available profits	1	
Application of the small companies rate limits	1	
Effective rate of tax/relief	1	
No carry back opportunity	½	
Group relief		
Direct ownership level	½	
Available relief	½	
Coronet Ltd:		
Available profits	½	
Effective rate of tax	1	
Rainbow Ltd:		
Effective rate of UK tax	½	
Tax position in Prismovia	1	
Effect of DTR	2	
Recommendation (combination claim)		
Identify correct objective	1	
Hutt plc – profits at 29.75%	½	
Rainbow Ltd – the balance	½	
Order of elections	1	
Group relief election – both companies/time limit	1	
Current year offset election/time limit	1	
	Max	13
(b) (i) The purchase price		
Trading losses:		
No current relief in Lucia Ltd	½	
No group relief with reason	1	
No carry forward with reasons	1½	
Conclusion	½	
Loan from BHC Bank		
Tax deduction per accounts treatment	1	
Total amount allowable in the period	½	
Amount relating to trading purpose	1	
Amount relating to non-trading purpose	2	
Uses of deficit (ie loss)	2	
Recommendation	½	
	Max	9

(ii)	**VAT issues**	
	Registration	
	Historic and future limits	1
	Registration and notification dates	1
	Calculation	
	Output tax	2½
	Input tax	1
	Disadvantage of group VAT registration – either of	
	Lucia Ltd in repayment position;	
	or administrative difficulties	1

Max   **6**

(iii)	**The office building**	
	Sale from Coronet Ltd to Lucia Ltd	
	Capital gain	
	CGT group	½
	Consequences	1
	Election re notional transfer – availability	1
	Stamp duty land tax	1
	VAT	
	If group registration	½
	If no group registration	1½
	Sale of building to Vac Ltd	
	Pre-entry asset	
	Identify	½
	Consequences	1
	Calculation of post-entry loss/tax saving	1
	Loss on sale – no IA	½
	Use of market value	½
	Both companies and time limit	1

Max   **9**

Format and style	
Appropriate style and presentation	1
Effectiveness of communication	1

    2

    39

(a)   **Hutt Plc trading losses**

There are three options available to Hutt Plc with regard to its trading losses. It may either (i) use the losses against its own profits, (ii) group relieve the losses, or (iii) use a combination of the two.

(i)   **Use within Hutt Plc**

Hutt Plc's profits for the year ended 31 March 2009 are:

	£	£
Trading profits		Nil
Capital Gain	144,000	
Less: losses b/f	(98,000)	
		46,000
Property income		65,000
Interest income		2,000
PCTCT		113,000

Hutt Plc has two associates and therefore the corporation tax (CT) limits must be divided by three to determine the CT rate payable.

Upper limit	1,500,000/3	500,000
Lower limit	300,000/3	100,000

As Hutt Plc's profits are between the two limits it is a marginal relief company and will pay CT at 28% less marginal relief. The marginal rate of tax (ie tax rate on profits above £100,000 and less than £500,000) is 29.75%.

The current year claim is an all or nothing claim and therefore if the losses are to be used in this year, £105,000 must be relieved. This will provide a tax saving of:

	£
£92,000 @ 21%	19,320
£13,000 @ 29.75%	3,868
Tax saved	23,188

It is not possible to make a claim to carry back losses to the previous year, to obtain tax relief in this case at the full rate for the year ended 31 March 2008, unless a current year claim has been made. As the losses available are completely used in the current year, a carry back claim cannot be made.

(ii) **Group relief**

As Hutt Plc owns at least 75% of Rainbow Ltd and Coronet Ltd, the three companies are in a group relief group for loss relief purposes. This means that losses may be relieved in the current period to these companies. The choice of which company to relieve the losses to will depend on the tax rate paid by that company.

Coronet Ltd has PCTCT of (£63,000 + 18,000) = £81,000. This is below the adjusted lower limit of £100,000 and Coronet Ltd therefore pays tax at 21% on its entire profits. There is thus no tax saving in surrendering losses to this company.

Rainbow Ltd has PCTCT of (£800,000 + 57,000 =) £857,000, which means that losses surrendered to it will provide tax relief at 28% ie £105,000 @ 28% = £29,400.

It should be noted that Rainbow Ltd's trading profits will likely also be taxed in Prismovia since their tax system is similar to the UK and it appears that Rainbow Ltd has a permanent establishment in that country. The UK would tax profits of a permanent establishment in another country in the UK (and allow their losses) and we must therefore assume that Prismovia will similarly tax Rainbow Ltd's UK profits in Prismovia.

To ensure that no foreign tax relief is wasted the maximum relief that should be surrendered to Rainbow would be:

	£
UK tax: £857,000 @ 28%	239,960
Overseas tax: £800,000 @ 26%	(208,000)
Maximum tax that can be relieved	31,960
Maximum loss relief claim (÷ 28%)	114,143

As the available loss is less than this amount, the full loss could potentially be set against Rainbow Ltd's profits.

(iii) Combination claim

Clearly it would be advantageous to be able to obtain relief in Hutt Plc at 29.75% and relief at 28% for the balance in Rainbow Ltd. This would provide relief as follows:

	£
£13,000 @ 29.75%	3,868
£92,000 @ 28%	25,760
Tax saved	29,628

Hutt Plc should therefore make a joint claim with Rainbow Ltd for group relief, surrendering £92,000 to Rainbow Ltd. This must be made within two years of the end of Rainbow Ltd's period of account ie by 31 March 2011.

Hutt Plc should then make a claim for current year relief of £13,000, again within two years of the end of the period in which the loss arose ie by 31 March 2011.

(b) **Report**

To: Hutt Plc Management
From: A Adviser
Date: [date]
Subject: Purchase of Lucia Ltd

This report covers tax issues relating to:

(i) The purchase price
(ii) VAT, and
(iii) The office building

(i) **The purchase price**

Valuation of Lucia Ltd's trading losses

Lucia Ltd's (LL) current owners have placed a value of £39,060 on the company's trading losses, which it currently cannot use as it has no other profits to set the losses against.

While it is true that once LL is purchased by Hutt Plc it will be part of the group for loss relief purposes (direct ownership of at least 75%), it will not be possible for Hutt Plc (or any of the other group companies) to claim any of LL's losses that arose in any part of the period prior to the acquisition. Only losses arising once the company joins the group may be group relieved.

In addition, LL will not be able to utilise the losses against its own income once it becomes profitable as HMRC are likely to argue that there has been a major change in the nature and conduct of trade following the change in ownership. As there will no longer be profits from the 'same' trade, LL will not be able to carry forward its losses against these profits and they will be lost.

Consequently there is no real value for the losses in considering the purchase price as they cannot be either group relieved or carried forward in LL.

Loan arrangement fees and interest

Both the loan arrangement fees and the interest due on the loan should be deductible when calculating Hutt Plc's PCTCT, and will broadly follow the accounts treatment (ie accruals basis). Whether the loan has been taken out for trade or non-trade purposes, however, will determine how the tax deduction will be given.

If it is for trade purposes then the deduction will be given directly from trade profits; conversely if the loan is for non-trade purposes it will be deducted according to the rules for non-trade loan relationships.

Of the total proposed loan of £190,000 it appears that only £15,000 (£190,000 – £130,000 – £45,000) will qualify as a trade purpose, as it will be used to fund the company's working capital. The rest of the funds will be treated as used for non trade purposes:

- acquiring shares in another company, even a subsidiary, is treated as an investment purpose; and
- Hutt Tower is let out and is not used in the trade, therefore the repairs will be for investment purposes.

This means that only $\frac{15,000}{190,000}$ × the amount charged in the accounts will be deductible against trade profits; the rest will be deducted from non-trade credits, ie the bank interest receivable.

CHARGED IN THE ACCOUNTS (1.7.09 – 31.3.10):

	£
Fee	1,400
Loan interest	
£190,000 × 7.25% × $^9/_{12}$	10,331
Total	11,731
Trading (× $\frac{15,000}{190,000}$)	926
Non trading (balance)	10,805

As there is only £2,000 of bank interest, this will result in a non-trade loan relationship loss (or deficit) of £8,805, which can be utilised as follows:

- set off against Hutt Plc's other current year profits
- carried back one year against non-trade credits (ie bank interest) only
- group relieved in the current period
- carried forward against non-trade profits.

The way in which the loss is used will, as always, depend on marginal tax rates and timing.

(ii) **VAT issues**

Registration

There are two tests to determine when a business must register for VAT:

(1) **Historic test**

Taxable supplies over the previous twelve months (looking back from the last day of the month) exceed £67,000. HMRC must be notified within 30 days and registration is required from the first day of the following month.

(2) **Future test**

Taxable supplies in the next month (looking forward from the first day of the month) exceed £67,000. HMRC must be notified within 30 days and registration is required from the first day of that month.

As the company's turnover for the nine-month period to 31 March 2010 will be £675,000 (accruing evenly), this means that the monthly turnover will be £75,000. Therefore, under the future test LL, looking forward from the first day of the nine-month period (1 July 2009), will need to notify HMRC by 30 July 2009 and will be registered from 1 July 2009.

VAT CALCULATION (1.7.09 – 31.3.10)

	£	£
All UK customers (Note 1): £110,000 × 17.5%	19,250	
EU customers (Note 2)		
VAT registered @ 0% (zero rated)	–	
non-VAT registered: £70,000 @ 17.5%	12,250	
Other non-UK customers @ 0% (zero rated) (Note 3)	–	
Dabet GmbH (Note 4): £17,000 @17.5%	2,975	
		34,475
UK businesses: £7,800 × 9 months	70,200	
Dabet GmbH (Note 4): £17,000 @17.5%	2,975	
		(73,175)
Repayment due from HMRC		(38,700)

Notes

1   It is irrelevant if UK customers are VAT registered – must still charge VAT (the VAT will be a real cost to non-VAT registered customers)

2   If EU customers are registered for VAT, standard rated supplies to them ('despatches') will be zero-rated. The EU customer will need to account for the VAT in their home country. Such supplies to non-registered EU customers will be charged at 17.5% as normal.

3   Standard-rated supplies ('exports') to other non-UK customers (ie those outside the EU) are always zero-rated. There is no requirement for the customer to be registered for VAT.

4   EU suppliers charge zero rate on their standard-rated supplies to other EU countries. It is necessary for the VAT on acquisitions from the EU to be included on the acquiring business's VAT return both as an input and an output amount in the same period.

Disadvantage of group registration

Where there is a group VAT registration, the representative member makes one VAT return for the whole group. This is usually done for administrative simplification.

However, the disadvantage to LL would mainly be a cash-flow issue. Since the majority of LL's supplies are zero-rated and it is due a repayment from HMRC it would be entitled to account for VAT on a monthly basis, thus receiving monthly repayments of VAT rather than quarterly. This would not be possible if the company was part of the VAT group.

Keeping a company outside of the group VAT registration would also add a layer of administrative complexity.

(iii) **The office building**

Tax implications of proposed sale

Corporation Tax

Once LL is acquired by Hutt Plc it will be part of the gains group (at least 75% direct ownership). Consequently any transfer of assets between two gains group companies will take place at no gain no loss, regardless of the amount paid for the asset. The base cost of the asset for the acquiring company is the original base cost plus any indexation up to the date of the intra-group transfer.

Stamp Duty Land Tax (SDLT)

There is an exemption for transfers of land that occur between companies which are under the same 75% ownership. Therefore no SDLT will be due.

VAT

If there is a VAT group, no VAT will need to be charged on the transfer of the asset.

Assuming the building has been owned for more than three years (ie it is not a 'new' commercial building), even if there are separate VAT registrations for each company there should be no VAT due as the supply will be exempt. This is the case unless Coronet Ltd had opted to tax the building (ie waived the exemption) in which case VAT would be due at 17.5%.

Capital loss offset

It has been proposed that LL will sell the building transferred by Coronet Ltd and utilise the capital losses arising on the sale of the factory to reduce the gain.

It should be noted that an actual transfer of the building is not required as an election may be made instead, within two years of the end of the period in which the disposal takes place ie by 31 March 2013, to treat the gain as having arisen in the transferee company.

Although this is usually sound tax planning, as LL owned the factory prior to joining the gains group the losses are treated as 'pre-entry' capital losses and their use is restricted.

There are two ways to determine how much of this pre-entry loss may be used.

Market value

A calculation is made as at the date that the company joins the gains group based on the market value at that date. That amount of the loss is 'ringfenced' and cannot be used against the loss arising on assets acquired post-entry.

	£
Proceeds (mv at entry)	80,000
Less: cost	(270,000)
Loss	190,000

Indexation cannot increase this loss. No IBAs have been claimed on the building (as its tax life (25 years) had expired by the time it was acquired by LL) and therefore the full capital loss is allowable.

As it is anticipated that the market value will not increase in the future the whole of the loss is a pre-entry loss and cannot be used.

Time basis

The alternative calculation is to calculate the loss at the date of sale and 'ringfence' the proportion of the loss that arose before the company joined the group based on the length of pre-entry ownership. The factory has been owned since 30 June 2005, the factory will be sold on 1 January 2010 and the company joined the group on 1 July 2009.

Therefore of the total period of ownership of 4.5 years, four years relates to the period before LL joined the group.

The pre-entry proportion of the loss that cannot be used is:

$$\frac{4}{4.5} \times £190,000 = £168,889$$

Only the balance of the loss (£190,000 – 168,889 =) £21,111 can be set against the gain on the building, saving tax of (28% × £21,111) £5,911.

It is therefore clearly more beneficial to go with the time basis calculation.

29 Tay Limited

Text references. Group aspects covered in Chapter 26. VAT penalties are dealt with in Chapter 28. Overseas aspects of groups is covered in Chapter 27. Capital allowances are in Chapter 7. Use of corporation tax losses are in Chapter 24.

Top tips. This required a highly written answer. Watch your time – don't overrun. A plan may help especially to ensure you don't forget some of your first thoughts as you get bogged down in writing your answer.

There are often more marks available than those stated in the requirements. You do not need to cover every single point in your solution, as we have in the model answer, to pass the question: you just need to get the main points.

In part (d) submission of an incorrect VAT return leads to a misdeclaration penalty. Penalties and VAT are very popular exam topics.

Easy marks. Write brief, to the point, concise comments to secure the marks. Don't waffle and only make your point once – no extra marks for saying the same thing twice.

Part (b) specifically asked for calculations as well as advice. Marks are awarded specifically for the numbers – make sure you do them.

In part (c) the examiner specifically asked you to ignore transfer pricing. So ignore it!

Examiner's comments. This question, which primarily concerned a UK company acquiring a UK subsidiary, and considering investment in a company overseas, produced a wide range of answers.

In part (a)(i) very few candidates were aware of the rules on capital allowances for intangible assets. A significant number confused intellectual property with industrial buildings (presumably due to the word 'property'!), and referred to the allowances available to these.

In calculating the corporation tax (CT) in (a)(ii), most candidates correctly reduced the small companies' rate limits as a result of having gained an associate. Most realised group relief would be available, but failed to calculate it correctly, as being from the date of acquisition to the end of the loss-making period only.

Virtually no candidates recognised the issue in (iii) which was regarding the possible restriction in carrying forward a trading loss following the change in ownership of the company, but, admittedly, this is a tricky area.

It was surprising in part (b) how few candidates recognised the problem of the pre-entry capital loss, most just discussing, often in considerable detail, the rules for offsetting losses against gains in a gains group, and thereby missing out on several marks.

In part (c) most candidates seemed to be aware of the issues, but didn't always make it clear in their answer which alternative (purchase of shares or assets) they were dealing with. Subheadings are useful here. You cannot leave it to the marker to guess whether a particular point you are making relates to a share purchase or an asset purchase. Several marks were undoubtedly lost unnecessarily in this way.

Knowledge of the VAT issues in part (d) was, in the main, very sketchy. Several candidates used words such as 'surcharge' and 'misdeclaration', but without appearing to understand the context in which they used them. This is textbook stuff, and should be learned accurately.

				Marks
(a)	(i)	Allowances usually equal to amortisation	½	
		Alternative 4% allowance where no depreciation	½	
		Time limit for election	½	
		Election irrevocable	½	
				2
	(ii)	Deduction for IP allowance	½	
		Group relieve only post-acquisition loss	½	
		'Lower of' calculation (2 × ½)	1	
		Corporation tax at 28%	½	
		Marginal relief calculation	½	
				3
	(iii)	Change of ownership and nature of trade	½	
		Three-year time limit	½	
		Losses blocked at date of acquisition	½	
		Quantify losses/tax at risk (2 × ½)	1	
		Advice and recommendation	½	
		Max		2
(b)		Awareness of pre-entry losses	½	
		Formula basis: Statement/explanation	1	
		Calculation of allowable loss	½	
		Pre-entry proportion	½	
		Alternative election: treatment and effect	½	
		calculation of pre-entry loss	½	
		Recommend making the election	½	
		Use of pre-entry loss – possibilities	½	
		Max		3
(c)		Acquisition of shares:		
		associated company	½	
		limits reduced, possibly increased tax	½	
		profits taxed in Portugal	½	
		remitted profits taxed as overseas income	½	
		double tax relief for withholding tax	½	
		double tax relief for underlying tax	½	
		requirement for 10% plus holding	½	
		relief is lower of UK/Portuguese tax	½	
		losses cannot be relieved against UK profits	½	
		Acquisition of assets		
		permanent establishment, so no extra associate	½	
		taxed in UK as extension of trade	½	
		permanent establishment: taxed in Portugal	½	
		DTR available	½	
		capital allowances can be claimed	½	
		loss offset automatically as part of UK company	½	
		Max		6

(d) Default surcharge: issue surcharge notice ½
runs to anniversary ½
further defaults extend period ½
further late payments will incur a penalty ½
2% initially rising to 15% ½

Error:
notify in writing ½
penalty ½
Percentage of PLR ½
Careless ½
Reduction of disclosure ½
Likely treatment ½
in writing/ASAP ½
Default interest: chargeable even with voluntary disclosure ½
basis period ½
Ethical issues 1

Max 5
21

(a) (i) **Tax allowances**

Intellectual property is an intangible asset. The writing-down allowances on intangible assets are usually equal to the depreciation charge in the accounts. If there is no depreciation charge in the accounts an alternative is available.

Tay Limited will be entitled to claim capital allowances for the intellectual property it purchased.

The allowance will be 4% of the cost ie 4% × £250,000 = £10,000 pa for 25 years.

The irrevocable election for the capital allowances must be within two years of the end of the accounting period.

(ii) **Corporation Tax y/e 31 March 2009**

	£
Trade profit	250,000
Less: Allowance	(10,000)
PCTCT	240,000
Less: group relief (W1)	(40,000)
Revised PCTCT	200,000
Tax @ 28%	56,000
Less: Marginal relief (W2)	
7/400 × (750,000 − 200,000)	(9,625)
CT due	46,375

Workings

(1) *Group relief*

Trade losses may be shared between the two companies but only for the corresponding accounting periods since Trent joined the group ie for the period 1.9.08 to 31.12.08.

Loss available for group relief is therefore the lower of:

Profit of Tay Ltd £240,000 × $^4/_{12}$ = £80,000
Loss of Trent Ltd £120,000 × $^4/_{12}$ = £40,000 ie £40,000

(2) *CT limits*

£1,500,000/2	£750,000
£300,000/2	£150,000

Therefore Tay Limited is a marginal relief company

(iii) **Transferring work to Trent Limited**

The problem with transferring orders to Trent Limited is that HMRC may argue that there has been a 'major change in the nature or conduct' of Trent Limited's trade which would result in the corporation tax losses not being able to be carried forward in Trent Limited to use against profits from the orders.

This treatment is applied if, within **three** years of a change in ownership, there is a major change in the trade.

A change in customers could be a fundamental change for these purposes and it is therefore essential that Trent Limited maintains its original suppliers, pricing policies etc to avoid a successful attack by HMRC.

If there is a major change in the trade within three years then losses of £380,000 (£300,000 + $^8/_{12}$ × £120,000) will be wasted, along with potential tax reductions of £106,400 (£380,000 × 28%). The charges should be delayed until 1 September 2011 if possible.

(b) **Capital gains implications for sale of buildings**

The two companies are in a gains group for corporation tax purposes. This means that assets may be transferred around the group at no gain/ no loss in order to take advantage of lower tax rates or capital losses available elsewhere in the group.

The issue for Trent Limited and Tay Limited is that Trent Limited had the unrealised loss when it was acquired by Tay Limited and therefore the pre-entry element of the loss will not be available for use against Tay Limited's gain.

The available loss would be limited to the amount of loss that has arisen since the group was formed. This can be done on a time basis or based on the market value when Tay Limited joined the group.

On the time basis, the available loss would be calculated as follows:

	£
Proceeds	250,000
Less: cost	(400,000)
Loss	(150,000)

Time since joined group: 1.9.08 – 1.9.09 = 1 yr

	£
Total ownership: 9.98 – 9.09 = 11yrs	
$^1/_{11}$ × (150,000)	(13,636)

On the market value basis, the available loss would be calculated as follows:

	£
Proceeds	250,000
Less: MV when joined group	(300,000)
Loss	(50,000)

The company would clearly choose the market value basis to obtain a larger loss. Assuming Tay Limited's asset is transferred to Trent Limited prior to sale, or an election is made to treat the gain as having been made in Trent Limited, the remaining gain would be taxed at Trent Limited's marginal rate (21%), as follows:

	£
Gain	75,000
Less: capital loss	(50,000)
Chargeable gain	25,000
Tax @ 21%	5,250

The balance of the loss (£100,000) can only be used in Trent Limited against gains arising on sales of its own assets.

(c) **Acquiring shares or assets of Tagus LDA**

If Tay Limited acquires the shares of Tagus LDA it would be acquiring a overseas subsidiary company; if it acquires the assets and continues the business in Portugal it would be acquiring a overseas permanent establishment.

The corporation tax (CT) issues that Tay Limited should consider are therefore:

CT issue	Overseas subsidiary	Overseas permanent establishment (ie branch)
Associates	There will be another associate for CT purposes. CT limits will need to be divided by three.	Not an associate.
Losses	Losses made by EU subsidiaries may be relieved against the profits of UK group companies, but only where all possibilities for the losses to be relieved at any time against profits in the subsidiary's own country have been exhausted.	Not in a group relief group but in any case, overseas losses will be set against UK profits.
Capital gains group	Will not be part of the UK gains group.	Overseas gains will be included in UK company's trade profits
Profit	Will not be taxed in the UK unless dividends paid to UK owner.	Will be included as part of the UK company's profits.
DTR	Lower of UK tax (average rate) and overseas tax, which includes both withholding and underlying tax (as owns > 10%).	Lower of UK tax (average rate) and overseas tax (27.5%).
P&M	Will continue with Portuguese method.	FYAs/AIA available (where applicable), then WDAs at 20%.
Interest deduction	No trade deduction for loan interest incurred in connection with purchase.	Interest paid will be deductible so long as money borrowed wholly and exclusively for the trade.
Sale of shares/ assets	Substantial shareholding exemption may apply if sell shares after at least 12 months.	Gain on assets sold; base cost will be market value when acquired by UK company

Top tips. It is perfectly acceptable to use a table, like the one above, where you are comparing or contrasting two areas. It may even help you to brainstorm the issues

(d)   **Incorrect VAT return**

As the error of £55,000 is greater than:

- £10,000; and
- 1% of net VAT turnover for the return period (1% of £142,500 being £1,425).

The error cannot be corrected on the next return.

The error should be notified to HMRC on form VAT 652 or by letter.

A penalty for error may be imposed and interest will be charged.

Any penalty will be based on the Potential Lost Revenue (PLR) to HMRC as a result of the error, in this case £55,000.

The maximum penalty is 100% of PLR if the error is deliberate and concealed reducing to 30% if careless. In this case if it is deemed to be a genuine error (careless) the maximum penalty would be £16,500.

This penalty can be reduced further if the error is disclosed. If disclosure is unprompted it can be reduced to nil; if prompted it can be reduced to 15% of PLR which is £8,250.

It is likely in this instance, if the error is notified to HMRC quickly, the penalty could be reduced to nil.

As part of the tax liability for the quarter to 31 March 2009 is paid late, HMRC may issue a surcharge liability notice. Therefore if an VAT is paid late, or return made late in the next four quarters a surcharge will apply, starting at 2% × unpaid tax.

You should advise Trent Ltd that it should notify its error to HMRC at the earliest opportunity. If Trent Ltd agrees you need take no further action, assuming the under declaration was a genuine error. If Trent Ltd refused to notify the error, then you would be obliged to refuse to act for the company as this would be the concealment of a tax irregularity. You should also report the matter to your firm's money laundering officer.

30 Andrew

Text references. CGT on leases is in Chapter 14. Accrued income scheme is in Chapter 3. EIS is in Chapters 1 and 2 with EIS CGT deferral relief in Chapter 13. Pensions are looked at in Chapter 2. Types of finance are dealt with in Chapter 31.

Top tips. The question in part (a)(i) asked for a **chargeable gain** – this is before deducting the annual exemption.

The examiner prefers to see questions with several parts presented with the parts in the correct order; you don't need to have done the earlier parts to do the later parts but make sure you answer all parts and put them in the correct order when you're done.

Easy marks. Show all your workings to achieve maximum marks. Plus if you've made a mistake you can gain some marks for your workings.

When answering a question asking for general rules such as part (b)(i) keep points short and snappy. Make a new point on a new line. This lets the marker see your points clearly set out and allocate marks accordingly.

Along a similar line if you can answer using a table (such as in (b)(ii) here) then do so – again great presentation and it all helps gain easy marks.

Examiner's comments. This was a mixed question, largely discursive, on a variety of investment and finance issues for both an individual and companies.

In part (a)(i), many candidates produced a correct calculation of the chargeable gain on assignment of a short lease. Note that a 'chargeable gain' is after deducting taper relief, but before deducting the annual exemption. Failure to appreciate this led to a failure to gain all marks, or time being wasted.

Surprisingly few candidates knew that government stock was exempt from CGT, with most calculating an unnecessary gain. Virtually no-one mentioned the accrued income scheme, although those who appreciated that there were income tax implications in respect of the interest did gain marks.

Part (b) was generally well done, with many candidates showing a good, detailed knowledge of the conditions for and impact of EIS relief. However many then spoiled this somewhat by going on to discuss VCTs in equal detail.

				Marks
(a)	(i)	Restriction of cost	1	
				1
	(ii)	Exempt from CGT	½	
		IT under accrued income scheme	½	
		Nominal value >£5,000	½	
		Basis of IT charge	½	
		Income accrued on a daily basis to 14 March	½	
		Taxed at 40%	½	
				3

(b)	(i)	Identification of EIS relief		½
		Qualifying individual:		
		not employee		½
		not director at time of issue		½
		No material (≥30%) interest		½
		Timing requirements		½
		Relevant date definition		½
		Currently connected		½
		Investment by fourth individual advisable		½
		Eligible shares		
		New and fully paid-up		½
		Not redeemable for three years		½
		No preferential rights to dividends		½
		Qualifying company		
		Unquoted		½
		Not controlled by another company		½
		Qualifying trade, wholly/mainly in UK (2 × ½)		1
		Time limits/% reinvestment (2 × ½)		1
		Income tax:		
		Tax reduction		½
		20%		½
		£500,000 limit		½
		≤50% of investment pre-6 Oct carried back		½
		Capital gains tax:		
		EIS shares exempt		½
		Capital losses allowable, reduced by relief		½
		Deferral relief for any gains		½
		Set loss against income		½
		Timing requirements		½
		income tax relief not essential		½
		Application to Andrew		½
		Relief withdrawn if:		
		Shares sold within three-year period		½
		Value received from company		½
		Individual or company ceases to qualify		½
		Repayment of loans possible issue		½
			Max	12
	(ii)	*Equity:*		
		Costs of issuing share capital are not tax deductible		½
		Costs of making distributions are not tax deductible		½
		Distributions themselves not tax deductible		½
		Loan finance/debt:		
		Interest on loan to finance business is allowable		½
		Capital costs not deductible as trading expense		½
		Incidental costs of raising loan finance are allowable		½
			Max	2
(c)		Current contributions		½
		Relief for contributions		1
		Maximum		½
		Annual allowance		½
		Lifetime allowance		½
				3
			Total	21

(a) (i) **Assignment of lease**

	£
Proceeds	90,000
Less cost (W)	(46,895)
	43,105

Working

Cost $\times \dfrac{\%36\text{yrs}}{\%47\text{yrs}}$

	£
$£50,000 \times \dfrac{92.761}{98.902}$	46,895

(ii) **Disposal of government stock**

Government stock is exempt from CGT.

It is, however, a security for the purposes of the accrued income scheme, if it has a nominal value in excess of £5,000.

When he sells the stock he will be taxed on the income that had accrued up to the date that he sold it, as this will form part of the sale proceeds he receives.

Interest accrued from 21.10.08 – 14.3.09	
145/182 × £350	£279
£279 × 40%	£112

(b) (i) **Investment in Scalar Ltd**

If Andrew invests in Scalar Ltd (S Ltd), which appears to be an Enterprise Investment Scheme (EIS) company, he will be entitled to the following reliefs:

EIS income tax relief

A tax reduction of 20% × his investment (maximum £500,000).

May carry back up to 50% × investment (maximum £50,000) to obtain relief in the prior year, where made before 6 October.

This can reduce his tax liability to nil but not create a repayment.

EIS CGT exemption

Any shares attracting the above income tax relief will be exempt from CGT if they are sold after a minimum holding period of three years.

Loss relief

If an investor sells EIS shares at a loss, that loss may be used as a normal capital loss or it may be used against income.

EIS CGT deferral relief

If an individual disposes of any asset at a gain he can defer the gain (along with its original taper relief) where he purchases EIS shares in the period twelve months before to three years after the disposal.

Unlike the above two reliefs, there is no maximum amount that can be deferred. The investor may choose the optimum amount of relief in order to preserve the annual exemption, losses and entrepreneurs' relief.

Conditions

There are a number of conditions that must be satisfied both by the company and Andrew in order for the income tax relief and CGT exemption to be available:

S Ltd

Must be an unquoted (AIM is included for these purposes) trading company performing qualifying activities.

Prohibited activities include land, financial, legal, accountancy and property-back trades.

The company must have gross assets of ≤ £7 million before and ≤ £8 million after the share issue.

80% of the funds raised must be used by the company (or a 90% subsidiary) in the first twelve months and the balance in the following twelve months.

The trade must take place wholly or mainly in the UK.

The shares issued must be new, ordinary shares. They must be fully paid-up and not redeemable.

The above conditions must continue to be satisfied for at least three years from the share issue.

Andrew (& other investors)

Must subscribe for the shares (ie cannot simply purchase them from the stock market) wholly in cash.

Must not be 'connected' with the company ie cannot be an employee or own more than 30% of the shares/ voting rights/ rights to assets on a winding-up, along with their 'associates' (eg spouse or child but not brother or sister).

Note that if there were only three investors they would all have >30% of the shares and so the relief would not be available.

This rule applies for the period of one year before and three years after the share issue.

If the investor receives 'value' from the company in this period the relief can be adjusted/ withdrawn.

The interest received from the company in respect of the proposed loans could be considered to be 'value' if it is not at a commercial rate.

It would be advisable for the company to issue the shares and then obtain the loans from the investors to avoid the loan interest being treated as a return of value.

Conclusion

If there are four investors who subscribe for the shares prior to making loans to the company and all the above conditions are satisfied, the immediate relief available to each will be: £112,500 @ 20% = £22,500 tax reduction.

(ii) **Equity and loan finance tax implications**

	Equity finance	**Loan finance**
Legal costs	Not tax deductible	Tax deductible
Return to investors	Dividends – not deductible for tax purposes	Interest paid will be part of a trading or non-trading loan relationship (depending on reason for raising money) – deductible in both cases

(c) Even though Andrew and his employer contribute to his occupational pension he may still contribute to a personal pension.

His current contributions are:

	£
Andrew: 6% × £300,000	18,000
Employer: 8% × £300,000	24,000
Occupational pension	42,000

He is not taxed on the employer contributions ie they are not treated as salary or a taxable benefit.

He will obtain tax relief at his marginal rate (40%) for his own contributions as they will reduce the amount of employment income he will need to report on his tax return:

	£
Earnings	300,000
Less: contributions	(18,000)
Employment income	282,000

The maximum tax-relievable that he may contribute to a pension in the year is the greater of:

(i)   £3,600; and
(ii) the amount of his earnings

ie £300,000.

However, there is a 40% charge if he contributes more than the annual allowance, which is £235,000 (2008/09).

To avoid any charge Andrew may therefore contribute:

	£
Annual allowance	235,000
Less: total occupational pension contributions	(42,000)
Available contributions	193,000

If he makes this contribution it will be paid net of basic rate tax ie 80% × £193,000 = £154,400. In this way he receives basic rate tax relief automatically.

As he is a higher rate taxpayer he will also obtain higher rate relief by extending his basic rate band by the gross contribution. This amount will be taxed at the basic rate of tax rather than the higher rates. He will therefore obtain 20% (40% − 20%) relief in this way.

In terms of limits for the future, Andrew should be aware that there is a lifetime allowance that applies to the amount of contributions he can make over his lifetime. This is currently £1,650,000.

31 Bluetone Ltd

Text references. IHT aspects of question covered in Chapters 16 to 18. CGT gift relief is in Chapter 13 and the CGT computation is in Chapters 11 and 12. Purchase of own shares is dealt with in Chapter 23.

Top tips. You may need to use two different values for the same asset in a question: one for CGT (usually the market value), the other for IHT (the loss to donor or diminution in value). They are frequently tested in the same question; do not confuse the two!

Easy marks. Ensure you show all of your workings, eg for the share valuations and how you calculated the average IHT rate. Never do a working in your head/on your calculator without writing it down on your answer script. There are marks available for workings.

			Marks
(a)	Wedding gift	½	
	Chargeable lifetime transfer	½	
	Shares in Expanse plc	1	
	Shares in Bluetone Ltd/units in Word-Growth	1	
	BPR not available	1	
	Building society deposits/life policy	1	
	Income tax/funeral expenses	1	
	House	1	
	IHT liability/IHT due by Melody	1	
	Due date/instalments	1½	
	Max		8

(b)   *CGT:*

Gift relief	2
Deemed consideration	1
Cost/Indexation	1
Entrepreneurs' relief	1
Annual exemption/CGT	1

IHT:

Value transferred		2	
BPR		1	
	Max		8

(c)

Capital gain		1	
Entrepreneurs' relief		1	
Additional income tax liability on distribution		2	
Conclusion		1	
	Max		4
			20

(a)   *Melody's IHT liability*

The lifetime gifts made by her father within seven years of his death will affect Melody's IHT liability as they will use up part of the available nil rate band. The amount of the lifetime gifts are:

	£
PET	30,000
Less: Marriage exemption	(5,000)
Annual exemption (04/05)	(3,000)
Annual exemption (03/04)	(3,000)
	19,000

	£
Chargeable lifetime transfer	
Gift	184,000
Less: Annual exemption (05/06)	(3,000)
	181,000

The available nil rate band on death is therefore £(312,000 − 19,000 − 181,000) = £112,000:

Death estate	£	£
Personal		
Bluetone Ltd Shares (Note 1) £11 × 50,000		550,000
Expanse plc shares		
Lower of		

$$\frac{1}{4} \text{ up} \quad \frac{320 - 312}{4} + 312 = 314$$

and

$$\text{mid-bargain} \quad \frac{324 + 282}{2} = 303$$

	£	£
ie 303p × 42,000		127,260
World-Growth units (80p × 26,000)		20,800
Building society deposits (29,000 + 3,000) (Note 2)		32,000
Life policy (proceeds)		61,000
		791,060
Less: income tax	6,600	
Gambling debts (Note 3)	Nil	
Funeral expenses	3,460	(10,060)
		781,000
Realty		
House	125,000	
Less: secured debt	(42,000)	83,000
Chargeable estate		864,000

Notes

1. No BPR is available as Melody's father did not own the Bluetone Ltd shares for at least two years prior to his death.

2. No IHT exemption is available for an ISA, only for IT and CGT.

3. Gambling debts are not deductible.

IHT on estate

£(864,000 – 112,000) = £752,000 × 40% = £300,800

Melody's IHT

$$\frac{550,000}{864,000} \times £300,800 = \underline{£191,481}$$

£191,481 is all due for payment on 31 August 2009 (or the delivery of the IHT account, if earlier).

Melody can elect to pay the tax in ten equal annual interest-free instalments of £19,148. The first instalment is due on 31 August 2009.

(b) *CGT on Liam's gift to his son*

	£
Deemed proceeds (£9 × 30,000)	270,000
Less: cost	(30,000)
Gain	240,000

Gain immediately chargeable to CGT (excess proceeds):

£(75,000 – 30,000) = £45,000

	£
Gain after gift relief	45,000
Less: entrepreneurs' relief (4/9 × £45,000)	(20,000)
	25,000
Less: annual exemption	(9,600)
	15,400
Tax @ 18%	2,772

Gift relief £(240,000 – 45,000) = £195,000. This deferred gain also reduces the son's base cost.

IHT on Liam's gift

The value of the lifetime transfer will be:

		£
Before:	50,000 × £15 (part of 50% holding with Opal (related property))	750,000
After:	20,000 × £12.50 (part of 35% holding with Opal)	(250,000)
		500,000
Less:	Proceeds paid	(75,000)
Gift		425,000

BPR will be available at 100% as these are unquoted trading company shares. However, the relief will be withdrawn if Liam dies within seven years and his son does not own the shares as business property at the date of Liam's death (unless the shares have been sold and replaced with other business property).

(c) *Noel*

If repurchase treated as distribution:

£(550,000 – 50,000) = £500,000 net

	£
Grossed up 100/90 × £500,000 =	555,556
Tax @ 32.5%	180,556
Less: credit	(55,556)
Tax to pay	125,000

If treated as CGT disposal:

	£
Proceeds	550,000
Less: cost	(50,000)
Unindexed gain	500,000
Less: entrepreneurs' relief (4/9 × £500,000)	(222,222)
Less: Annual exemption	(9,600)
Taxable gain	268,178
Tax @ 18%	£48,272

Therefore it is better to use the CGT route (which is mandatory if the relevant conditions are satisfied in any case). Neither option has any effect for Bluetone Ltd.

32 Graeme

Text references. Basic CGT is covered in Chapter 11. Shares and securities are dealt with in Chapter 12. CGT reliefs are in Chapter 13 and the overseas aspects dealt with in Chapter 14. IHT on lifetime gifts is covered in Chapter 16. Furnished holiday lettings are covered in Chapter 3.

Top tips. You need to calculate the value of the shares when first disposed of because we use this to apportion the cost and indexed cost on reorganisation.

Read the question requirements carefully. The question says ignore the CGT annual exemption – so ignore it. Similarly the question told you not to discuss the IT treatment of the cottage – don't discuss it.

Rollover relief does not apply to overseas assets.

Easy marks. You can lose marks by confusing CGT and IHT. It is best to write your answer to each tax separately. So cover all your IHT points and then all CGT (or the other way around if you find this easier). It helps to reduce your confusion.

Examiner's comments. This question had a heavy emphasis on CGT. Candidates had to calculate gains on disposals of shares following a reorganisation of share capital, and advise on both CGT and IHT implications of gifting further shares, and on the CGT and income tax (IT) implications of replacing a UK holiday cottage with a villa abroad.

Share for share exchanges was examined in part (a) which produced some very confused answers. Many candidates were clearly not familiar with this topic.

Part (b) was answered better, but again highlighted the confusion which exists in a significant number of candidates between CGT and IHT. The fact that the question specifically instructed candidates to ignore the CGT annual exemption did not prevent a good number from mentioning it.

Part (c) was generally poorly answered. This was largely due to a failure to read the question. It specifically said that you were not required to discuss the IT treatment of the country cottage, yet many candidates' answers did little else. In many cases they included a detailed description of the furnished holiday letting rules, which were not required, and therefore could not be awarded marks.

A reasonable number were aware of the availability of rollover relief for furnished holiday lettings, but few realised that this is only available where the replacement asset is in the UK, so the holiday villa abroad would not qualify.

Marks

(a)	Rights issue: shares, cost		½
	Reorganisation:	correct basis of apportionment	1
		number/value of 'T' shares	½
		'T' share costs	½
		number/value of 'D' shares	½
		'D' share costs	½
	'T' shares:	disposal cost	½
	'D' shares:	disposal cost	½
		Max	**4**
(b)	Transfers to Catherine:	no gain/no loss disposal	½
		spouse inherits tax history	½
		exempt from IHT	½
	Transfers to Barry:	connected persons	½
		proceeds (MV)	½
		cost	½
		availability of gift relief	½
		unquoted trading company	½
	Effect of deferring gain:	Barry's base cost reduced	½
		jointly written claim	½
		time limit for claim	½
	Inheritance tax:	100% business property relief	½
		if held by Barry from gift until Graeme's death	½
		PET for IHT purposes	½
		annual exemption up to × 2	½
		taper relief 3 to 7 years	½
			8

(c) *Sale of existing property*
Capital gains

	business asset while FHL for rollover relief	½
	qualifying asset for rollover relief	½
	proportion of gain while FHL	½
	need to acquire further qualifying asset within qualifying period	½
	overseas villa not a qualifying asset	½

Acquisition of overseas property

Residence:	UK residents therefore taxed on worldwide income		½
	significant periods of absence will not per se change residence status		½
	criteria for becoming non-resident (2 × ½)		1
Income tax:	Overseas income		½
	DTR:	availability	½
		lower of UK/foreign tax	½
	villa:	does not qualify as FHL	½
		reason/situated outside UK	½
	not relevant income for pension purposes		½
	trading loss offset facility not available		½
Capital gains:	does not qualify as a business asset		½
		Max	**8**
			20

(a)   **Thistle Dubh Ltd shares pool**

		Number	Cost £
December 1987	Acquisition	10,000	36,000
March 1993	Rights issue 1:2 @ £10	5,000	50,000
		15,000	86,000
October 2008	Reorganisation:	30,000 T shares	
		45,000 D shares	

		Value	Cost £
May 2009	Sale of T shares		
	30,000 T shares @ 300p	90,000	21,500
	45,000 D shares @ 600p	270,000	64,500
		360,000	86,000

The shares are unquoted so the cost is apportioned in the ratio of the values at the time of the first disposal.

Chargeable gains computation

		£
May 2009	12,000 T shares proceeds 12,000 × 300p	36,000
	Cost 12,000/30,000 × 21,500	(8,600)
	Gain	27,400
October 2009	45,000 D shares proceeds	85,000
	Cost	(64,500)
	Gain	20,500

(b)   Graeme now holds 18,000 T shares with a cost of £12,900.

(i)   If Graeme gifts the shares to Catherine she will acquire them with the same cost as Graeme, as transfers between spouses are made on a no gain no loss basis. There will be no capital gain.

The gift is an exempt transfer for inheritance tax purposes.

(ii)   If Graeme gifts the shares to Barry there will be a disposal for capital gains tax purposes. The chargeable gain would be 18,000 × 384p = 69,120 − 12,900 = £56,220.

Graeme and Barry could make a joint gift relief claim to defer the gain on the gift since the shares are unquoted shares in a trading company. There would be no chargeable gain but Barry's base cost would be £12,900. Thus any gain would be deferred until Barry sells the shares.

The gift is a potentially exempt transfer for IHT purposes and will be exempt if Graeme survives seven years. If Graeme has made no other gifts, however, his annual exemption for the current year and the previous year would first be set against the gift.

If Graeme should die within seven years of the gift 100% BPR will be available provided Barry still holds the shares (or previously died still holding them) and they are still unquoted. Should business property relief not be available and inheritance tax be due on the gift, then the tax will be tapered if death occurs between three and seven years after the gift.

> **Top tips.** Try and consider the CGT and IHT issues separately to avoid confusion. You can then put the 'pieces' back together in your answer. An answer plan would help with a question like this.

(c)   If Graeme and Catherine sell their UK country cottage a capital gain will arise.

The cottage will qualify as a business asset for rollover relief purposes for any period during which it qualifies as furnished holiday lettings. Thus, had Graeme and Catherine decided to acquire a new business property in the UK any gain attributable to the use as furnished holiday lettings could be rolled over against the acquisition, but rollover relief is not available against the purchase of the villa abroad.

The foreign villa will be a chargeable asset for capital gains tax purposes and if it should be sold whilst Graeme and Catherine are still UK resident any gain would be chargeable. If they should become non-resident and subsequently sell the property the gain would not be chargeable to UK capital gains tax unless they resumed UK residence.

If the property is let while Graeme and Catherine are UK resident they will be liable to UK income tax on any profit. The profit will be based on the rental income less any expenses of letting, but relief cannot be claimed for any proportion of expenses incurred which relate to periods during which Graeme and Catherine are using the property. If foreign tax is payable, then relief for this will be given against any UK tax due.

If Graeme and Catherine become non-resident then they will not be liable in the UK on the rental profits. They will have to take care as they will be categorised as UK resident if they are in the UK for six months in any year or for more than three months pa averaged over a four-year period.

Properties abroad do not qualify as furnished holiday lettings so Graeme and Catherine will not qualify for any of the tax reliefs which apply to such properties in the UK, such as offset of losses against income or rollover relief.

33 Reisling Ltd

Text references. Hive downs are covered in Chapter 26. Chapter 29 deals with overseas aspects of VAT. Tax planning in Chapter 30.

Top tips. The question helpfully set out the scenario for you. An answer plan is essential. You should be able to come up with the tax issues by brainstorming the different taxes. The non-tax issues are common sense.

Easy marks. Stick to the basics, stating fundamental points such as 'Reisling Ltd and Plonk Ltd will be in a gains group (direct ownership ≥75%)' to pick up easy marks. Don't struggle to get the difficult marks.

Marking scheme

			Marks
(a)	**Transfer of assets to Plonk Ltd**		
	Gains group	1	
	No gain/no loss transfer	1	
	Disposal of winery	1	
	Cannot transfer capital losses	1	
	CAs continue	1	
	Trading losses can be carried forward	1	
	VAT – TOGC	1	
	Corporation tax – associate affects tax rate	1	
	SDLT	1	
			9
(b)	**Sale of Plonk Ltd to Chardonnay Ltd**		
	No chargeable gain	1	
	VAT	1	
	Stamp duty	1	
	Anti avoidance		
	Degrouping charge	2	
	Major change in nature and conduct of trade	1	
			6

(c) **Other considerations**

Redundancy payments deductible for employer	1
Statutory redundancy tax free for staff	1
Contractual termination payments taxable	1
Ex gratia payments £30,000 exemption	1
Tell customers/suppliers	1
Rollover relief may be available	1
Ethical issues	2

8

(d) **Exports**

Non EU – zero-rated	2
EU – zero-rated to registered customers	1
– standard-rated to non-registered customers	1

4

Format/presentation

2

29

Notes for meeting

Date: [date]

Subject: Chardonnay Ltd's proposed acquisition of Reisling Ltd's wine making business

These notes cover tax issues relating to:

(a) The transfer of Reisling Ltd's wine production trade to Plonk Ltd

(b) The sale of Plonk Ltd to Chardonnay Ltd

(c) Other considerations

(a) **The transfer of Reisling Ltd's wine production trade to Plonk Ltd**

Chargeable gains

Reisling Ltd and Plonk Ltd will be in a gains group (direct ownership ≥75%). Consequently the transfer of the assets will take place at no gain/no loss.

The only asset not transferred, ie the winery, will be sold to a third party for £50,000. Subject to the amount of indexation allowance, this will crystallise a chargeable gain in Reisling Ltd, which will be available to offset against the £42,000 capital losses brought forward in that company.

Capital losses

The unrelieved capital losses will remain with Reisling Ltd.

Capital allowances

The assets will be automatically transferred at their tax written-down value for capital allowance purposes.

Trading losses

The trade is treated as continuing so Plonk Ltd will inherit the tax affairs of Reisling Ltd in relation to carried forward trading losses and will be available to set against future profits of the same trade.

The amount of loss available to transfer is £(290,000 + 60,000) unless any part of the current year's loss is relieved against Reisling Ltd's other income.

VAT

The transfer of the business as a going concern will be outside the scope of VAT.

Corporation tax

For year ended 31 December 2009 Reisling Ltd will have had an associated company for part of the year. This will impact on the small companies' limits for corporation tax and potentially the tax rate payable by the company.

Stamp duty land tax

Stamp duty land tax relief may be available for the intra-group transfer of land and buildings.

(b) **Sale of Plonk Ltd to Riesling Ltd**

Chargeable gains

No chargeable gain will arise on the sale of the shares to Riesling Ltd as the shares are being sold at their cost of £475,000 (ie the market value at the date of issue). The substantial shareholding exemption is not available as the shares have not been held for at least twelve months.

VAT

A sale of shares is exempt from VAT.

Stamp Duty

A sale of shares attracts stamp duty at 0.5%.

Anti avoidance

Riesling Ltd must ensure that the improvements it makes to the trade in order to make it profitable again does not constitute a major change in the nature or conduct of trade, or the trading loss being carried forward will be extinguished.

The gains deferred by the no gain/no loss treatment on the transfer of the assets from Reisling Ltd to Plonk Ltd will crystallise in Plonk Ltd in the accounting period that it leaves the group, as this occurs within six years of the transfer of assets.

It is unlikely that the parties would agree that the charge should accrue to the other group member ie Reisling Ltd.

(c) **Other considerations**

As a result of the reorganisation it is likely that Reisling Ltd will have to make some staff redundant. The redundancy costs are an allowable expense for corporation tax purposes for the company.

The staff will receive statutory redundancy pay free of tax.

Management may have service contracts. Termination may trigger termination payments which, due to being contractual, will be fully taxable. Any *ex gratia* payments will be exempt up to £30,000 (although any statutory redundancy pay will use part of this exemption).

Existing trade customers and suppliers need to be told of the proposals.

If the chargeable gains arising on the disposal of the winery cannot be relieved against capital losses, the gain may be rolled over if reinvested into a qualifying assets within three years of the disposal.

The directors are all shareholders of Riesling Ltd and will need to consider the effects of the proposed sale on their investment as well as on their roles as directors. Some of the directors may hope to become directors of Plonk Ltd or Chardonnay Ltd, whilst some may prefer to remain with Riesling Ltd.

As the interests of the different directors may conflict they may like to take independent advice.

(d) **Exports**

The VAT treatment of exports depends on whether the export is to an EU member state or to a non-EU country.

If the export is to a non-EU country, the export is zero-rated.

If the export is to an EU member state, the treatment depends on whether the customer is VAT registered:

- If he is VAT registered and provides Riesling Ltd with his VAT registration number, then the export is zero-rated.

- If he is not VAT registered, or if he does not provide his VAT registration number, the export should be standard-rated.

34 Vikram Bridge

> **Text references.** Capital gains tax disposals are covered in Chapter 11. IHT is dealt with in Chapters 16 to 18. Shares for employees and termination payments are covered in Chapter 5. Income tax computation is in Chapter 1.
>
> **Top tips.** Look out for gifts with reservation of benefit for IHT where someone gifts an asset but continues to enjoy a benefit from it such as living in a house without paying a market rent.
>
> **Easy marks.** The calculation of the gain and remaining basic rate band were standard computations.

Marking scheme

				Marks
(a)	(i)	Taxable capital gain on the sale of the house		
		Computation of capital gain		
		Gain	½	
		Annual exemption	½	
		Effect of gift to Alice	1	
		Capital gains tax payable	<u>1</u>	
				3
	(ii)	Treatment of payments on redundancy	1½	
		Salary	½	
		Relocation costs	1	
		Dividends	½	
		PA	<u>½</u>	
				4
(b)		Inheritance tax due in respect of the house		
		Gift more than seven years prior to death	½	
		Gift with reservation rules apply	½	
		Consequences	<u>1</u>	
				2
(c)		Shares in Dreamz Technology Ltd		
		Identify two possible treatments	½	
		Treatment if no share incentive plan	1	
		Exemption under share incentive plan	1	
		Withdrawal from plan within three years	½	
		Withdrawal from plan within three to five years	<u>½</u>	
			Max	3
(d)		Amount of income tax on dividend income		
		Tax position whilst working for Bart Industries Ltd		
		No tax payable on dividends	1	
		Computation	1	
		Tax position while working for Dreamz Technology Ltd	1½	
		Date of payment of income tax on dividend income		
		Due date with reason	1½	
		Computation	<u>2½</u>	
			Max	<u>6</u>
				<u>18</u>

(a) (i) **CGT on sale of Wales house**

2009/10

	£
Proceeds	195,000
Less: cost 9/01	(145,000)
Less: enhancement	(18,000)
Gain	32,000
Less: AE (£9,600 – £1,200)	(8,400)
Taxable gain	23,600
CGT due: £23,600 @ 18%	4,248

No PPR relief is available, as Vikram Bridge (VB) has never lived in the property as his main residence.

The CGT position would be the same if VB transferred the property to Alice as the disposal would be deemed to take place at market value. The transfer would only be at no gain, no loss if they were married.

(ii)

	£
B Ltd termination payment – all exempt (W2)	Nil
DT Ltd salary 6/12 × £40,500	20,250
Relocation costs: £9,400 – £8,000 (exempt)	1,400
Dividends: £7,800 × 100/90	8,667
Net income	30,317
Less: PA	(6,035)
Taxable income	24,282

Termination payments

- The PILON of £4,700 is taxable in 2008/09 as it is a contractual payment.

- Statutory redundancy is exempt from income tax.

- The £14,500 payment is also exempt as it comes within the £30,000 exemption available for *ex gratia* (ie compensatory) payments.

(b) **IHT on VB's mother's death**

When VB's mother originally made the gift it would have been a PET for IHT purposes. As she survived more than seven years the PET is completely exempt.

However, as his mother continued to live in the property until her death it will be treated as part of her estate for IHT purposes.

Therefore it will be necessary to include £140,000 in her death estate in respect of the property.

(c) **Income tax treatment of DT Ltd shares**

If an employee receives free shares from their employer, under general principles, they will be taxable on the market value of those shares. Therefore VB would include the £2,750 value of the shares in his employment income in 2010/11. There would also be an NIC charge if the shares were readily convertible assets (ie traded on a recognised investment exchange).

However, if the shares are awarded as part of an approved Share Incentive Plan (SIP) there will be no taxable benefit when the shares are awarded so long as the value of the shares is less than £3,000. These 'free' shares are free from income tax (and NIC where applicable) so long as they remain within the SIP for a five year period, at which point they may be removed with no tax consequences.

If the shares are removed from the plan within three years there will be an income tax charge on their value when removed. If they are removed within three to five years, tax will be charged on the lower of the market value when removed and the original value.

(d) **Taxation of dividend income**

As VB's income will now take him into the higher band of taxation, there will be a tax charge on the dividend income.

Previously, he was a basic rate taxpayer:

	£
Employment income:	
£4,700 × 12/2	28,200
Dividend income (as above)	8,667
Total income	36,867
Less: PA	(6,035)
Taxable income	30,832

The dividends would have been taxed at 10%, but as they come with a 10% tax credit, there was no further liability.

In 2011/12 and following years his position is as follows:

	£
DT Ltd salary	42,500
Dividends	8,667
Total income	51,167
Less: PA	(6,035)
Taxable income	45,132

The whole of the dividend income therefore now falls into the higher rate tax band. It will be taxed at 32.5% and come with the 10% tax credit. The effective tax rate on the net dividend is 25%, which means that (25% × £7,800) = £1,950 additional higher rate tax will be due on the dividends.

Payment date

The additional tax on the dividends will need to be paid via self-assessment by 31 January following the end of the tax year ie by 31 January 2013. The tax due on the DT Ltd salary will be paid via PAYE as normal.

It is also possible that payments on account will need to be made if the tax collected at source on the total income is less than 80% of the total liability, or, conversely the amount not collected at source (on the dividends) exceeds 20% of the total liability.

The total liability will be:

	£
Taxable income (as above)	45,132
£34,800 @ 20%	6,960
£(36,465 − 34,800) = £1,665 @ 40%	666
£8,667 @ 32.5%	2,817
Total tax liability	10,443
20% × £10,443	2,089
Tax not collected at source (on dividends) (2,817 − 867)	1,950

Therefore POAs are not required.

35 Stuart and Rebecca

Marking scheme

			Marks
1	Acquisition cost	½	
	Principal private residence:		
	correct treatment of each period (× 7)	3½	
	PPR exempt gain: exempt fraction	½	
	Letting exemption:		
	awareness	½	
	calculation of let period gain	½	
	identification of other limits (½ × 2)	1	
	lowest of three	½	
	Offset of capital losses	½	
	restricted to preserve annual exemption	½	
	Annual exemption	½	
	Correct order of offset of exemptions and reliefs	½	
		Max	8
2	Holding required to get BPR for listed company	½	
	Rate of BPR that applies	½	
	Omikron small shareholding, no BPR	1	
	Omega: related property shareholdings	½	
	calculation of shares required	½	
	hold for more than two years	½	
	Reasoned conclusion	½	
		Max	3

3	Stuart: exempt estate to spouse	½
	Rebecca: Omega shares valuation/lower of two methods	1
	estate: value of shares	½
	deduction of BPR	1
	other assets: investments	½
	cash deposits	½
	cash (insurance policy)	½
	residence	½
	nil rate band	½
	IHT at 40%	½
		6

4	Transfer of nil rate bands	1
	No point gifting Omega shares as BPR is available	1
	No PETs, re Stuart	½
	Reason/reference to taper relief 3–7 years	½
	Lifetime gift/PET nil rate band re Rebecca	½
	Still should not be Omega shares/BPR	½
	Make use of annual exemptions	½
	Availability of two annual exemptions each	½
	Calculation of immediate tax saving	½
	Small exempt gifts	½
	Expenditure out of normal income – identify relief	½
	Usual standard of living/pattern of giving (2 × ½)	1
	Use of insurance	½
	Max	**7**
	Format/ presentation	**2**
		26

PRIVATE AND CONFIDENTIAL

[Our address]

[Your address]

[Date]

Dear Stuart

TAX POSITION AND ESTATE PLANNING

This letter deals with the capital gains tax implications of your recent property sale and your current and potential inheritance tax liabilities.

1   **Capital gains tax on property disposal 2009/10**

The capital gain arising on the disposal of the Plymouth house is £16,532.

This is after taking account of principal private residence relief of £141,318, based on an exempt period of 90 months out of a total ownership period of 151 months, and lettings relief of £40,000.

The calculation of the above figures can be found in Appendix 1.

2   **Proposed investment**

As you are considering making an investment in a quoted company you will only be able to obtain business property relief for inheritance tax purposes if you, together with Rebecca, control the company, ie over 50% of the shares.

You could buy approximately 1 million shares in Omikron plc. This would be in the region of a 2% holding, so no business property relief would be available.

Alternatively you could buy approximately 194,000 shares in Omega plc with the proceeds, at a cost of 216p. Currently you and Rebecca jointly hold 4.8 million shares. Provided you achieve a slightly lower price or invest slightly more so that you purchase 200,001 shares, you and Rebecca will have a controlling holding. Provided you then survive for at least two years you will achieve 50% business property relief on your Omega plc shares.

3   **Inheritance tax on Rebecca's estate 1 March 2012**

If, following your death, Rebecca were to die on 1 March 2012, and no IHT planning is implemented, the IHT liability would be £2,522,820 (Appendix 2).

4   **Lifetime IHT planning**

As your will leaves all of your estate to Rebecca you have not taken advantage of your nil rate band. However on Rebecca's death her nil rate band will be increased by the proportion of nil rate band unused at your death. She will therefore have an additional 100% of nil rate band available on her death. This will be based on the value of the nil rate band at that time.

The Omega plc shares should be left to Rebecca so that the 50% BPR would be available on her death or earlier gift of the whole shareholding.

Rebecca should consider making lifetime gifts in the hope that she will survive for seven years, so that they become completely exempt. If she survived more than three but less than seven years, and IHT was payable on the lifetime gifts, then the IHT payable would be tapered.

Both of you should make lifetime gifts utilising your annual exemptions. You may also be able to establish a regular pattern of giving to use the exemption for normal expenditure out of income. Your wealth would appear to be such that it would be simple to demonstrate that capital was not being eroded by this strategy.

It could be possible to give away the life policy before death at a lower value than the death benefit. It would then be excluded from the death estate and escape any IHT liability.

Top tips. Do not ignore easy planning points such as use of exemptions. These are easy marks – don't lose them.

Appendix 1 – disposal of Plymouth property

	£
Sale proceeds	422,100
Less cost May 1997	(185,000)
	237,100
Less PPR exemption $\dfrac{90}{90+61} \times £237,100$ (W)	(141,318)
	95,782

Less letting exemption, lowest of:
(i)   PPR relief given: £141,318

(ii)   Gain in let period: $\dfrac{27}{90+61} \times £237,100 = £42,395$

(iii) Maximum: £40,000	(40,000)
Gain	55,782
Less capital losses brought forward	(29,650)
	26,132
Less annual exemption	(9,600)
Taxable gain	16,532

Working

Periods of occupation		*Exempt Months*	*Non-exempt Months*
1 May 1997 – 28 Feb 1998	Occupied	10	
1 March 1998 – 31 Dec 2001	Unoccupied – absence for any reason	36	
	Unoccupied		10
1 Jan 2002 – 31 Mar 2004	Let		27
1 Apr 2004 – 30 Nov 2004	Occupied	8	
1 Dec 2004 – 30 Nov 2006	Unoccupied		24
1 Dec 2006 – 30 Nov 2009	Last 36 months	36	
		90	61

Top tips. Get into the habit of listing out the periods of occupation and non-occupation of a private residence to help determine the correct proportion of the gain that is exempt. This will show the examiner your understanding of the PPR rules.

Appendix 2 – Rebecca's IHT liability with no IHT planning

	£	£
London property		900,000
Cash deposits (including £200,000 from life policy)		530,000
Quoted investments		250,000
Shares in Omega plc 5,001,000 × 210p (1/4 up is lower)	10,502,100	
Less BPR @ 50%	(5,251,050)	
		5,251,050
		6,931,050
Less nil rate band (£312,000 + 100% × £312,000)		(624,000)
Taxable at 40%		6,307,050
IHT liability		2,522,820

36 Spica

Text references. Purchase of own shares is covered in Chapter 23. Overseas aspects of corporate tax is in Chapter 27.

Top tips. In part (a)(ii) you only needed the points in relation to Spica, not the company. You knew the company conditions were met from the information in the question. Stating the company conditions would waste time and score no marks.

Easy marks. The purchase of own shares calculations are straightforward as it is always the same method in such situations. A well prepared student could score full marks on these.

Examiner's comments. Part (a) was in two parts. The first part was a relatively straightforward test of the tax treatment of a purchase of own shares whilst the second part tested the conditions that needed to be satisfied for capital treatment to apply.

The first part was done well by the majority of candidates. The only common error was the general failure to recognise that, under the income distribution route, the distribution is the amount received less the amount originally subscribed for the shares (as opposed to the cost to the shareholder). A minority of candidates did not pick up easy marks by failing to include the personal allowance and/or the annual exemption or by using incorrect rates of tax.

Performance in the second part was not as good with many candidates simply listing all of the conditions they could think of as opposed to thinking and identifying the particular conditions that were relevant in these particular circumstances. This meant that time was wasted and that irrelevant conditions were provided at the expense of some that would have earned marks.

Part (b) was more difficult and was not done particularly well. The question required candidates to explain the maximum rate of tax that would be suffered on profits generated by non-UK resident companies, depending on whether or not they were distributed to the shareholder and whether or not a double tax treaty existed. A methodical approach was important here as there were a number of different situations to consider. However, many candidates addressed the issues in a fairly general manner and did not consider each of the possible situations.

				Marks
(a)	(i)	Income treatment		
		Calculation of distribution	1	
		Gross up by 100/90	½	
		Personal allowance	½	
		Income tax liability	1	
		Income tax credit	½	
		Capital treatment		
		Capital gain	1	
		Entrepreneurs' relief	1	
		Annual exemption	1	
		Capital gains tax liability	1	
		Conclusion	½	
		Max		7
	(ii)	Trading company	1	
		Spica UK resident and ordinarily resident	1	
		Benefit of company's trade	2	
		Five year ownership period	1	
		Max		4
(b)		Undistributed profits		
		Profits taxed in country of residency	1	
		Overall maximum rate	1	
		Distributed profits with treaty		
		Gross up with reason	1	
		Double tax relief is lower of UK and overseas tax	1	
		Onshore processing	2	
		Distributed profits with no treaty		
		Unilateral relief	1	
		Overall maximum rate	1	
		Max		6
				17

(a) **Spica**

(i) **The most beneficial tax treatment of the payment received**

The payment received by Spica will be treated as either an income distribution or as capital.

Income treatment

	£
Payment received (8,000 × £8)	64,000
Less: original subscription price (8,000 × £1.90)	(15,200)
Distribution	48,800
Taxable dividend income (£48,800 × 100/90)	54,222
Less: personal allowance	(6,035)
Taxable income	48,187

Income tax

£		
34,800 × 10%		3,480
13,387 × 32.5%		4,351
48,187		
		7,831
Less: income tax credit (£48,187 × 10%)		(4,819)
Income tax payable		3,012

Tutorial note

A capital loss of £800 [8,000 × (£2.00 – £1.90)] will also arise. Spica cannot claim to offset this capital loss against income as she did not subscribe for the shares.

Capital treatment

	£
Sales proceeds (8,000 × £8)	64,000
Less: cost (8,000 × £2)	(16,000)
	48,000
Less: entrepreneurs' relief (4/9 × £48,000)	(21,333)
Taxable gains	26,667
Less: remainder of the annual exemption (£9,600 – £3,800)	(5,800)
	20,867
£20,867 × 18%	3,756

The income treatment gives rise to the lower tax liability.

(ii) **Ensuring capital treatment**

For the capital treatment to apply, a number of conditions need to be satisfied such that the following points need to be confirmed.

- The business of Acrux Ltd consists wholly or mainly of the carrying on of a trade as opposed to the making of investments. This also affects the entitlement to entrepreneurs' relief.

- Spica is UK resident and ordinarily resident despite living in both the UK and Solaris.

- The transaction is being carried out for the purpose of the company's trade and is not part of a scheme intended to avoid tax. This is likely to be the case as HMRC accept that a management disagreement over the running of the company has an adverse effect on the running of the business.

In addition, Spica must have owned the shares for at least five years. This will be the case on 1 October 2008.

If the conditions for the capital treatment are met then it is mandatory. Therefore as Spica would prefer the income treatment she should ensure the transaction takes place before 1 October 2008 so that the criteria for the capital treatment are not satisfied.

(b) **Rate of tax on profits of non-UK resident investee companies**

Undistributed profits

The companies will be subject to tax in the countries in which they are resident; this is because of their residency status or because they have a permanent establishment in that country. Undistributed profits will not be taxed in the UK.

The rate of tax on undistributed profits will therefore be the rate of tax in the country of residency of the respective companies

Distributed profits with double tax treaty

The dividends received by Acrux Ltd from each of the overseas companies will be grossed up in respect of underlying tax (the overseas corporation tax paid on the distributed profits) because Acrux Ltd will own at least 10% of the overseas companies. The gross amount will then be included in Acrux Ltd's profits chargeable to corporation tax.

The treaty will provide double tax relief in the UK for the overseas tax suffered in respect of each dividend up to a maximum of the UK tax on the grossed up overseas dividend. As a result of the double tax relief, the overall rate of tax suffered will be the higher of the UK rate paid by Acrux Ltd and the overseas tax rate borne by the overseas company.

Where the rate of overseas tax in respect of a particular dividend exceeds the rate of corporation tax in the UK, excess foreign tax will arise. This can be relieved, via onshore pooling, against the UK tax due on those dividends where the rate of tax in the UK exceeds the rate overseas. This will reduce the overall rate of tax suffered on the total overseas profits of the overseas companies as a whole.

Distributed profits with no double tax treaty

Where there is no double tax treaty, unilateral double tax relief will be available in the UK. This relief will operate in the same way as double tax relief under a double tax treaty such that the overall rate of tax on each dividend will be the higher of the UK rate paid by Acrux Ltd and the overseas rate borne by the overseas company. Relief via onshore pooling will also be available.

37 Gargarin

Text references. The rules on EIS relief and related CGT deferral are in Chapters 2 and 13. The capital goods scheme is in Chapter 29.

Top tips. Only attempt this question if you have learnt the rules and conditions for EIS relief. It will not be possible to score well if the precise rules are not known.

Easy marks. Part (a) should be relatively straightforward if you had learnt the EIS rules.

Examiner's comments. Part (a) of the question was in two parts. The first part required candidates to identify the tax incentives available to potential investors and the second part asked for the answers to questions that potential investors may raise.

In the first part, although most candidates had a good knowledge of the income tax deduction available to investors, many of them did not identify the possibility of investors deferring capital gains. A minority of candidates included information regarding the conditions that needed to be satisfied by the company despite a specific instruction in the question not to do so.

When it came to addressing the possible questions from investors, candidates did well on the implications of a future sale of the shares. However, when addressing the maximum investment by a potential shareholder, candidates resorted to making general comments in relation to the maximum investment of £500,000, when they should have applied the specific rules to the facts of the question. This would have led them to the need to restrict any investment to no more than 30% of the company, i.e. £315,000.

Although this part of the question was answered well, many candidates would have done better if they had written less and spent some time relating their knowledge to the particular situation in the question.

Part (b) concerned the recovery of VAT input tax in respect of a building acquired by a partially exempt company. It was not answered well with many candidates failing to identify the need to apply the capital goods scheme to the situation.

Marks

(a)	(i)	Income tax		
		Reduction in income tax	1	
		Carry back	2	
		Capital gains tax		
		Deferral	1	
		Any asset	½	
		Time period	1	
		Max		5
	(ii)	Maximum investment	1½	
		Borrowing to finance the purchase	1	
		Sale of the shares		
		Importance of three-year period	1	
		Withdrawal of income tax relief	1	
		Treatment of gain arising	1	
		Treatment of loss arising		
		Allowable	1	
		Affect on loss of income tax relief	½	
		Relief of loss against income	1	
		Gain deferred at time of subscription	1	
		Max		7
(b)		Recoverable input tax in the year ending 31 March 2009	1	
		Additional recoverable input tax		
		Capital goods scheme applies	1	
		Explanatory rationale	1	
		Input tax recoverable in future Years	2	
		Input tax recoverable following sale	2	
		Max		5
				17

(a)   (i)   **The tax incentives immediately available**

Income tax

- The investor's income tax liability for 2008/09 will be reduced by 20% of the amount subscribed for the shares.

- Up to half of the amount invested can be treated as if paid in 2007/08 rather than 2008/09. This is subject to a maximum carryback of £50,000

This ability to carryback relief to the previous year is useful where the investor's income in 2007/08 is insufficient to absorb all of the relief available.

Tutorial note. There would be no change to the income tax liability of 2007/08 where an amount is treated as if paid in that year. This ensures that such a claim does not affect payments on account under the self assessment system. Instead, the tax refund due is calculated by reference to 2007/08 but is deducted from the next payment of tax due from the taxpayer or is repaid to the taxpayer.

Capital gains tax deferral

- For every £1 invested in Vostok Ltd, an investor can defer £1 of capital gain and thus, potentially, 40 pence of capital gains tax.

- The gain deferred can be in respect of the disposal of any asset.

- The shares must be subscribed for within the four year period starting one year prior to the date on which the disposal giving rise to the gain took place.

(ii)   **Answers to questions from potential investors**

Maximum investment

- For the relief to be available, a shareholder (together with spouse and children) cannot own more than 30% of the company. Accordingly, the maximum investment by a single subscriber will be £315,000 (15,000 × £21).

Borrowing to finance the purchase

- There would normally be tax relief for the interest paid on a loan taken out to acquire shares in a close company such as Vostok Ltd. However, this relief is not available when the shares qualify for relief under the enterprise investment scheme.

Implications of a subscriber selling the shares in Vostok Ltd

- The income tax relief will be withdrawn if the shares in Vostok Ltd are sold within three years of subscription.
- Any profit arising on the sale of the shares in Vostok Ltd on which income tax relief has been given will be exempt from capital gains tax provided the shares have been held for three years.
- Any capital loss arising on the sale of the shares will be allowable regardless of how long the shares have been held. However, the loss will be reduced by the amount of income tax relief obtained in respect of the investment. The loss may be used to reduce the investor's taxable income, and hence his income tax liability, for the tax year of loss and/or the preceding tax year.
- Any gain deferred at the time of subscription will become chargeable in the year in which the shares in Vostok Ltd are sold.

(b)   **Recoverable input tax in respect of new premises**

Vostok Ltd will recover £47,880 (£446,500 × 7/47 × 72%) in the year ending 31 March 2009.

The capital goods scheme will apply to the purchase of the building because it is to cost more than £250,000. Under the scheme, the total amount of input tax recovered reflects the use of the building over the period of ownership, up to a maximum of ten years, rather than merely the year of purchase.

Further input tax will be recovered in future years as the percentage of exempt supplies falls. (If the percentage of exempt supplies were to rise, Vostok Ltd would have to repay input tax to HMRC.)

The additional recoverable input tax will be computed by reference to the percentage of taxable supplies in each year including the year of sale. For example, if the percentage of taxable supplies in a particular subsequent year were to be 80%, the additional recoverable input tax would be computed as follows.

£446,500 × 7/47 × 1/10 × (80% − 72%) = £532

Further input tax will be recovered in the year of sale as if Vostok Ltd's supplies in the remaining years of the ten-year period are fully chargeable to VAT. For example, if the building is sold in year seven, the additional recoverable amount for the remaining three years will be calculated as follows.

£446,500 × 7/47 × 1/10 × (100% − 72%) × 3 = £5,586

38 Karen Wade

Text references. VAT is in Chapter 28 and 29. Employment income is in Chapter 4. Trading income and NIC for the self employed is covered in Chapter 6 with capital allowances in Chapter 7. Investment issues are in Chapter 31. Pensions are in Chapter 2.

Top tips. You must quickly and efficiently calculate the turnover for VAT for part (1) so that you can comment on the registration position. All figures should be contained in a separate Appendix – you can work on the figures first and then place the Appendix at the end of your answer. This makes your work look more professional.

Easy marks. You should be able to write about and apply the VAT registration test rules as they are an essential planning issue for new business start ups.

			Marks
(a)	Taxable supplies	½	
	Historic test	½	
	Future test	½	
	Turnover thresholds	1	
	Date by which to notify HMRC	½	
	Registration date	½	
	VAT liability	1	
	Output VAT	½	
	Motor car	½	
	Fuel scale charge	½	
	Input VAT	½	
	Blocked input VAT	½	
	Quarterly returns	½	
	Max		6
(b)	*Change of use of vans*		
	No consequences for Karen	½	
	Costs deductible for trade purposes	½	
	Taxable benefit for nephew for private use	½	
	Scale charges	½	
	No benefit if only used for commuting	½	
	Max		2
	Trading income assessment		
	Profit adjustments (½ mark for each item correctly adjusted)	Max 2	
	Capital allowances	Max 3	
	Wages allowed	½	
	Private use of car	½	
	AIA	½	
	Max		6
	Income tax and NIC		
	Calculation of income tax	4	
	Class 2 NIC	1	
	Class 4 NIC	1½	
	Max		6
(c)	*Investment strategy*		
	Surplus £10,000		
	Consideration (½ mark for each relevant item)	Max 2	
	Required information (½ mark for each relevant item)	1	
	Max		3
	Quoted shares v property		
	Liquidity	1½	
	Risk	1½	
	Capital vs income growth	1½	
	Taxation	1½	
			6

Pension

£3,600 or 100% × income	½
Annual allowance	½
Paid net	½
Tax recovered from HMRC	½
Extend basic rate band	½
Tax relief	½
Contribute from capital (no tax relief)	½
Income and gains grow tax free in the pension	½
Lifetime allowance	½

Max 4

Format/Presentation 2

35

Report

To: Karen Wade
From: Tax Manager
Date: [date]
Subject: Tax issues for 2009/10 tax year

This report covers tax issues relating to:

(i) VAT registration and liability
(ii) Income tax and NIC issues
(iii) Investment strategy

(a) **VAT registration and liability**

Registration

You will be liable to register for VAT if the value of your taxable supplies (standard- and zero-rated) exceed the statutory limits. All of your supplies are standard-rated and therefore taxable.

You liable to register:

(i) at the end of any (relevant) month if the value of taxable supplies, in the twelve months then ended, has exceeded £67,000, or

(ii) at any time if there are reasonable grounds for believing that taxable supplies in the next 30 days will exceed £67,000.

Sales of capital assets are ignored when considering the registration limits.

You will not become liable under (ii) as your maximum turnover for a month is £7,451 (see Appendix 1).

However, your taxable supplies exceed the limits under (i) by the end of June 2010 (Appendix 1).

You must notify HMRC within 30 days of the end of the relevant month, ie by 30 July 2010.

You will be registered from the end of the month following the relevant month, ie from 1 August 2010.

There is no requirement to register under (i) above if HMRC are satisfied that the taxable supplies in the twelve months beginning 1 July 2010 will not exceed £65,000.

It is anticipated that these will be £67,062 (Appendix 1) (more if the catering contract continues); therefore there will be a liability for you to register.

VAT liability

You will have no VAT liability in the seven months to 31 July 2010 as you will not be registered.

From 1 August 2010 you will prepare quarterly returns of output tax (ie VAT on your taxable supplies) and input tax (ie VAT reclaimable from HMRC on goods and services purchased by you).

(1)   Output VAT

The output tax (amounts owed to HMRC) on sales for the each month from August to December 2010 (assuming VAT will be added to current prices) will be £1,304 (£7,451 × 17.5%).

Output tax on sales for each month from 31 January 2011 assuming the catering contract ceases will be £652 (£3,726 × 17.5%).

Note. Business customers will be able to reclaim the VAT you charge. Private customers cannot, and you will need to check carefully whether adding output tax to your current charges will lose business. You may need to adjust prices to absorb part of the increase.

VAT on private use of motor car

No output tax is due on the private use of your car as no input tax was recoverable on the purchase of the car.

Output tax is payable, however, on the fuel provided for your private motoring. The VAT element of this is estimated by using the VAT scale charges and is dependent upon the CO_2 emissions of the car.

(2)   Input VAT

You can reclaim any input tax suffered on most of the supplies you receive.

Certain input tax is never reclaimable. This includes input tax on:

- motor cars and accessories supplied with them (unless wholly used for business purposes), and
- entertaining (except of employees).

Accounting for VAT

The quarterly returns must be completed and sent to HMRC, together with any tax, within one month of the end of the quarter.

(b)   **Income tax and NIC issues**

Consequences of the change of use of the van from 1 July 2010

Consequences for Karen

There are no income tax consequences for you as you do not use the van for private use.

All costs of running the van remain allowable against your trading income as they are incurred wholly and exclusively for the purposes of the business.

Consequences for your nephew

Your nephew has earnings in excess of £8,500 pa. He will therefore be assessed on the use of the van at weekends as a taxable benefit, using a scale rate of £3,000 per annum.

Note that ordinary commuting in the van is not treated as private use, however any other private use of the van (ie at weekends) gives rise to the benefit charge. You could, therefore, allow him to use the van for travel to and from work, but prohibit any other private use.

If you pay for his private fuel he will also have a further benefit of £500.

Trading income assessment – 2009/10

Adjusted trading profit of year ended 31 December 2009

Your trading income assessment for 2009/10 will be the taxable profits of the year ended 31 December 2009 on the 'current year basis', ie £3,833 (Appendix 2).

In coming to this figure I have allowed the wages paid to your nephew and son on the assumption that these are reasonable for the work performed.

I have also estimated the private use of your car based on the private and business mileage driven ie

$$\frac{2,500}{2,500+12,500} = \frac{1}{6}.$$

All of your expenditure eligible to go into the capital allowances main pool has been fully relieved due to the availability of an annual investment allowance of £50,000 for all businesses.

Income tax and NIC – 2009/10

Your income tax for 2009/10 is £2,469, which is due under self-assessment.

Both dividends received from shares in an ISA and Premium Bond prizes are exempt from income tax.

As your accounting profit exceeds the small earning limit of £4,825, you will need to pay Class 2 NICs of £120. These are payable monthly by direct debit or by quarterly demand.

Your earnings for Class 4 NIC purposes are the taxable trading profits ie £13,233. You will therefore be required to pay Class 4 contributions of £624, also by self assessment.

All figures above are shown in Appendix 3.

(c) **Investment strategy**

(i) **Investing the surplus £10,000**

The following personal circumstances will all impact on your investment strategy:

- You are 42 years old and single
- Your son is going to university shortly and you may need to contribute towards his fees and maintenance
- You have £10,000 of surplus income per annum
- You currently have a significant investment in quoted shares – assuming a yield of, say, 4%, the shares are worth approximately £563,400 (£22,536 ÷ 4%)
- You would like to reduce your exposure to risk by investing in property

In order to properly advise on an appropriate investment strategy, the following information is required regarding your plans for the future:

- Will you need to realise significant sums at short notice?
- When do you plan to retire?
- How do you intend to replace your earned income?

(ii) **Investment in quoted shares compared with commercial property**

When comparing investments, there are four factors to consider: liquidity, risk, capital growth versus income and, of course, taxation.

Liquidity

The main difference between investing in quoted shares and commercial property is their relative liquidity. Quoted shares can be realised for cash at very short notice. Commercial property, on the other hand, cannot be realised until a buyer has been found and title has been investigated. This disadvantage could be reduced by investing through a Real Estate Investment Trust (REIT) where the investor holds shares in the investment company.

Risk

Quoted shares are medium/high risk depending on the companies concerned. Commercial property may be regarded as medium risk. Again, the risk would be reduced by investing in a REIT.

Capital growth vs income

Both investments should be regarded as likely to generate capital growth in the long-term. In the shorter-term, depending on the companies concerned and the nature of the properties, there is also the possibility of investment income.

Taxation

Dividend income from share investments has an effective rate of taxation for a higher rate taxpayer like yourself of 25% of the dividend received. For example, a net dividend of £10,000 will give you a tax liability of £2,500. Income from property, whether directly held or via a REIT, is taxed as non savings income at the higher rate of 40%. So, income of £10,000 will give you a higher rate tax liability of £4,000. From a purely tax perspective, an investment in shares is more tax efficient.

This also applies if you are a basic rate tax payer on any part of the income (as may be the case if the new contract is not renewed). To the extent that they fall in the basic rate band no additional tax is payable on dividends, whereas basic rate income tax would be due on property income at 20%.

(iii) Investing in a personal pension scheme

Each tax year you can obtain tax relief on the greater of £3,600 and 100% of your relevant earnings (trading income).

- The amount you contribute will be deemed to be net of 20% income tax. The tax deducted at source will be recovered by the pension fund from HMRC.

- As you are in the future likely to be a higher rate taxpayer, you will be able to extend the basic rate band by the gross contribution so that more income is taxed at the basic rather than higher rates. This will provide a minimum tax saving of an additional 20%.

- You can also contribute additional amounts from capital, although these will not attract initial tax relief. These will not count towards the annual allowance, which is currently £235,000.

- Income and gains within the fund are tax free

- Funds can usually only be withdrawn when you reach retirement age (50 up to 5 April 2010 and 55 thereafter).

- The pension fund will be tested against the lifetime allowance when funds are vested to provide a pension and/or lump sum. Tax is payable if the fund exceeds the lifetime allowance (currently £1.65 million).

Appendix 1 – VAT taxable turnover

(1) Taxable turnover

Assuming turnover accrues evenly over a year and at the same rate.

	£
Normal monthly turnover = £44,710 ÷ 12	3,726
Additional turnover from 1 January 2010	3,725
	7,451

Year ended	Less earliest month £	Add next month £	Cumulative turnover for 12 months £
31 December 2009			44,710
31 January 2010	(3,726)	7,451	48,435
28 February 2010	(3,726)	7,451	52,160
31 March 2010	(3,726)	7,451	55,885
30 April 2010	(3,726)	7,451	59,610
31 May 2010	(3,726)	7,451	63,335
30 June 2010	(3,726)	7,451	67,060

(2) Taxable turnover in the twelve months after 30 June 2010

		£
July 2010 – December 2010	(6 × £7,451)	44,706
January 2011 – June 2011	(6 × £3,726)	22,356
		67,062

Appendix 2

Taxable trading profits

	£
Net profit per accounts	11,300
Wages – self (drawings)	12,000
Depreciation	
Equipment	1,300
Car	700
Van	500
Loss on sale of car	200
Motor expenses – Karen's car – Private use disallowable ($^{1}/_{6} \times$ £800)	133
	26,133
Less Capital allowances (W)	(12,900)
Trading income assessment	13,233

Working: Capital allowances – twelve months ended 31 December 2009

	AIA £	Main Pool £	Car (1) £	Car (2) £	Allowances £
WDV b/f		12,000	7,000		
Additions qualifying for AIA					
1.09 Van	5,000				
2.09 Office equipment	2,000				
9.09 Refrigerator	800				
10.09 Coffee machine	300				
11.09 Computer/printer	1,300				
	9,400				
AIA	(9,400)				9,400
Additions not qualifying for AIA					
8.09 Car				9,600	
Disposals					
8.09 Car			(7,600)		
BC			(600) $\times ^{5}/_{6}$		(500)
WDA @ 20%		(2,400)			2,400
WDA @ 20%				(1,920) $\times ^{5}/_{6}$	1,600
WDVs c/f		9,600		7,680	
Allowances					12,900

Appendix 3

Income tax and NIC liabilities 2009/10

Income tax

	Non-savings Income £	Savings income £	Dividend Income £	Total £
Trading income	13,233			
NS + I interest		4,015		
Dividend £22,536 × 100/90			25,040	
Net income	13,233	4,015	25,040	42,288
Less: personal allowance	(6,035)			(6,035)
Taxable income	7,198	4,015	25,040	36,253

Tax	£
£7,198 × 20%	1,440
£4,015 × 20%	803
£23,587 × 10%	2,359
£450 × 10% (extended band) (N)	45
£1,003 × 32½%	326
Tax liability	4,973
Less: tax credit on dividends	
£25,040 × 10%	(2,504)
Tax payable	2,469

Note. Basic rate band extended by gross gift aid donation (£360 × $^{100}/_{80}$) = £450.

NIC

Class 2: 52 × £2.30 = £120

Class 4: 8% × £(13,233 – 5,435) = £624

39 Alasdair

Text references. Extracting value from a company is covered in Chapter 30. Liquidation is mentioned in Chapter 30 and also in Chapter 23. Property income and other investment income is covered in Chapter 3. Basic IHT is dealt with in Chapters 16 and 17 with basic CGT in Chapter 11 and rollover relief in Chapter 13. VAT aspects are dealt with in Chapters 28 and 29. Stamp duty is in Chapter 19. IBAs are in Chapter 7. Investment products are covered in Chapter 31.

Top tips. In part (b) look at each of the three investments suggested one by one outlining both the tax consequences and financial risks as asked by the question.

Easy marks. Try and set out your answer in a logical way. Where a question asks for two of more taxes to be considered (as was asked in part (b)(ii) by the examiner) look at each tax separately. This helps to reduce the possibility of you getting confused and losing marks.

BPR only applies to IHT. It is a popular topic with lots of (easy) marks awarded to the student who knows something about it.

Examiner's comments. This question, involving primarily the IT, CGT, and IHT implications of different investments, was not well done by the relatively few candidates who attempted it.

Part (a) concerned the practical issue of stripping out the value of a company prior to liquidation by means of a dividend, or leaving the cash in the company, and facing a higher CGT charge on the deemed disposal of the shares on liquidation. It was clearly a scenario with which candidates were unfamiliar. Although the dividend option was dealt with reasonably in some cases, a very small number made references to the CGT implications of liquidation.

In part (b) many candidates' answers again suffered from a haphazard, unstructured approach. Those who thought logically, and described the fundamental rules regarding the taxation of property (eg taxable rental income, tax relief for expenses, relief for losses etc), and shares (eg taxation of dividends) scored reasonably.

Most candidates were aware of the existence of reliefs available under CGT and IHT in (b)(ii), although again the details of these, in particular BPR, were sketchy.

Marks

(a) *Dividend:*
- Personal allowance — ½
- Recognition of remaining basic rate band — ½
- Gross up of dividend — ½
- Tax at 10% — ½
- Tax at 32·5% — ½
- Less tax credit — ½
- Net cash after tax — ½

Liquidation:
- Tax treatment of liquidation (CGT) — ½
- Deduction of liquidator's costs — ½
- Disposal cost — ½
- Annual exemption — ½
- Extra tax payable (18%) — ½
- Net cash after tax and expenses — ½

Summary/recommendation — ½

7

(b) (i) *Income tax: direct investment*
- investment income as property income — ½
- normal trading rules re deduction of expenses — ½
- interest allowed on borrowing to purchase — ½
- use of losses — ½
- commercial property: possibly claim plant allowances — ½
- residential property: wear & tear allowance (furnished) — ½
- normal tax rates (20/40%) — ½

Income Tax: collective investment
- distributions taxed at 10/32.5% with tax credit — ½
- no relief for interest or other expenses — ½
- REIT – taxed as property income — ½

CGT:
- normal rules apply — ½
- not normally a business asset — ½
- collective investment may be ISA'd — ½

VAT position on purchase
- new, commercial/residential — ½
- second hand, commercial — ½

Stamp Duty Land Tax/Stamp Duty — ½

Investment risks/benefits: direct investment
- high risk other than long-term — ½
- substantial initial costs — ½
- significant ongoing running costs — ½
- illiquid investment (particularly commercial property) — ½
- cyclical market — ½
- residential property historically good inflation hedge — ½

Investment risks/benefits: collective investment
- reduced risks via diversification through large portfolio — ½
- more liquid investment — ½

Max 9

Note. Additional half marks up to the maximum will be given for other
relevant points.

(ii)	Availability of BPR	1
	Rate of BPR	½
	Two-year ownership condition	½
	Availability of rollover relief	1
	Operation of rollover relief	½
	Requirement for replacement asset	½
	Availability of entrepreneurs' relief	½
	Max	4
		20

(a) Extracting cash from Beezer Ltd

Taking a dividend will result in net proceeds of £91,987 (W1), compared with net proceeds of £96,208 (W2) if the company is liquidated. Alasdair should therefore liquidate the company so that he receives an additional £4,221 of net cash.

Workings

(1) *Dividend payment – income tax computation*

	£
Gross dividend £120,000 × 100/90	133,333
Income tax	
£(34,800 – (32,000 – 6,035)) = £8,835 @ 10%	884
133,333 – 8,835 = £124,498 @ 32.5%	40,462
	41,346
Less tax credit	(13,333)
Additional income tax payable	28,013

Net proceeds £120,000 – £28,013 = £91,987

(2) **Liquidation – capital gains tax computation**

	£
Proceeds (£120,000 – £5,000)	115,000
Cost	(1,000)
	114,000
Chargeable gain	
Less annual exemption	(9,600)
Taxable gain	104,400

	£
Capital gains tax	
£104,400 @ 18%	18,792

Net proceeds £115,000 – £18,792 = £96,208

(b) (i) (1) Buy to let residential property

For income tax purposes Alasdair will be liable to income tax on the letting profit. This will be the excess of rents receivable over letting costs, such as agents' fees, repairs and maintenance and mortgage interest. Capital allowances are not generally available in respect of residential property (except for furnished holiday lettings), apart from on plant and machinery used to maintain the lettings. Wear and tear allowance at the rate of 10% of rents is available for property which is let furnished. If a loss should arise it will be carried forward and set against future rental profits from any UK properties (residential or commercial) as soon as they arise. Losses may arise if Alasdair finds it difficult to let the property.

When Alasdair sells the property he will be liable to capital gains tax on any increase in value of the property during his period of ownership.

VAT is not charged on the letting of residential property.

Financially Alasdair will be exposed to fluctuations in the property market. Property is illiquid, and it may not be possible to sell the property at short notice. Property should be viewed as a long-term investment. There are also substantial costs associated with buying and selling, such as stamp duty land tax (at 0%, 1%, 3% or 4%), estate agents' and solicitors' fees.

(2) **Commercial property**

As for residential property, Alasdair will be liable to income tax on the letting profit. Capital allowances are generally available on plant and machinery and fixtures in the building. Industrial buildings allowance is available on certain commercial buildings such as factories, but not on buildings such as office and shops. Again losses may be carried forward against future rental profits.

When Alasdair sells the property he will be liable to capital gains tax on any increase in value of the property during his period of ownership. If the property is used for the purposes of a trade in which Alasdair is involved he will be entitled to entrepreneurs' relief.

If the property is less than three years old on acquisition or the option to tax has previously been exercised, VAT will be charged on the purchase of the building. If Alasdair also opts to tax, he may reclaim the VAT on the purchase price but must charge VAT on the rental income and on the subsequent sale of the building.

As for residential property, investment in commercial property must be regarded as long term. The commercial property market is even more exposed to external factors, and during a downturn a sale may take a significant time. Again there are significant costs associated with buying and selling commercial property.

(3) **Shares in a property investment company/unit trust**

For income tax purposes Alasdair will be liable to income tax only if dividends are paid to him. Additional tax will only be payable if he is a higher rate taxpayer. If Alasdair should have to borrow to purchase the shares or units, no tax relief is available for the interest paid.

The disposal of shares or units will be a chargeable disposal for capital gains tax purposes. Alasdair will be liable to CGT on any gain.

Income and capital gains can be sheltered from tax if the investment is made through an individual savings account.

There are no VAT consequences on buying or selling shares or units, but stamp duty at the rate of 0.5% is payable on the purchase of shares. Purchasing units in a unit trust may incur an initial management charge, which is reflected in the difference between the buying and selling prices of units.

Shares and units are risky investments as they are dependent on the company's performance. However the risk is spread over the portfolio of properties owned by the company or trust, which is less risky than having a single investment. The investment is subject to fluctuations both in the stock market and in the property market due to the underlying investment. Provided the shares or units are quoted they are comparatively liquid as it should be possible to dispose of the shares or units at short notice.

Alasdair might also consider investing in a Real Estate Investment Trust (REIT). Any distributions received will be taxed as property income, not as company dividends and basic rate tax (20%) will be deducted at source from the distribution paid.

(ii) If Alasdair acquires the warehouse and leases it to Gallus & Co he will be entitled to business property relief for inheritance tax purposes at the rate of 50%. The relief is given by reducing the value of the property by 50% on a transfer of value.

Normally business property relief is only available once the property has been held for two years. Relief may be available earlier if the warehouse can be regarded as replacement property.

For capital gains tax purposes the warehouse will be occupied by a partnership which is carrying on a trade or profession. It will therefore qualify for entrepreneurs' relief, though this will be restricted if rental income is received from Gallus & Co. If market value rent is charged no entrepreneurs' relief will be available. It would not still qualify for entrepreneurs' relief if occupied by a third party.

Furthermore if the warehouse is used by Gallus & Co it would qualify for capital gains tax rollover relief, provided Alasdair reinvested the proceeds in a replacement business asset. It would not be necessary for the replacement asset to be used by Gallus & Co, Alasdair could, for example, set up a business as a sole trader and use the replacement asset in that business.

40 Adam Snook

Text references. Chapter 12 covers shares and securities. Chapter 11 deals with calculating CGT for an individual. Employment income is covered in Chapter 4. Financial management is covered in Chapter 31. Trading income and national insurance contributions for the self-employed are dealt with in Chapter 6. Value added tax is covered in Chapters 28 and 29. Inheritance tax on lifetime gifts is covered in Chapter 16.

Top tips. You needed to be very organised in your approach to this question. There were quite a lot of calculations in part (a) so you must set them out in a logical manner. Then you needed to work through the specific points asked in parts (b) and (c). Remember that you need to attempt every part of the question to succeed in the exam.

Easy marks. The calculation of taxable income and the remaining basic rate band was straightforward. The inheritance tax explanation was also relatively easy for the 4 marks obtainable.

Examiner's comments. In part (a) (i) candidates had to calculate the external finance required by the new business. It was necessary to calculate the capital gains arising on the sale of shares and loan stock acquired as a result of a paper for paper transaction. Whilst many candidates were aware that particular rules applied in this situation (and many described them, unnecessarily, in great detail) only a well prepared minority were able to calculate the gains correctly.

Part (a)(ii) required candidates to identify a strategy to increase the after tax proceeds from the sale of the loan stock and to suggest a form of external finance more appropriate than a bank overdraft. The first task was not done well as many candidates were of the opinion, incorrectly, that the sale of the loan stock would not give rise to a tax liability and therefore the position could not be improved. The second task was done well.

Part (b) required candidates to address various issues relating to the new business. Candidates performed well when calculating the taxable income. The rest of the question was not done particularly well. Candidates were happy to outline the national insurance position of unincorporated traders in general but, unfortunately, were less willing to apply their knowledge to the taxpayer's particular situation. When addressing the income tax relief available in respect of the purchase of the theatre, many candidates were under the misapprehension that a theatre is an industrial building. The VAT implications of renting out the building were not well understood.

The final part of the question concerning the potential inheritance tax liability in respect of a lifetime gift was done well.

Marking scheme

				Marks
(a)	(i)	External finance required	1	
		Calculation of gains:		
		Division of original cost	1	
		Frozen gain on loan stock	1	
		Gain on sale of shares	1	
		No gain on QCB	½	
		Crystallisation of gain on loan stock on sale	½	
		Annual exemption	½	
		CGT on gains	1	
		Assumptions ½ mark each	1	
		Max		6

(ii)	Proposal to increase after tax sales strategy:		
	Identification	1	
	Tax saved	1	
	More appropriate forms of finance:		
	Bank overdraft inappropriate	1	
	Longer term finance	1	
	Max		3

(b) *Income tax liability*

Taxable income:		
Salary	1	
Car benefit	1½	
Trading income	1	
Personal allowance	½	
Income tax liability	½	
National insurance contributions		
Class 2	1	
Class 4	1	
Income tax on theatre		
No capital allowances on purchase	1	
Two possible treatments of renovations	2	
Value added tax		
Partial exemption	1½	
Recoverable input tax	1½	
De minimis limits	1	
Effect of opting to tax	1½	
Factors affecting decision	2	
Max		14

(c)	Transfer of value - PET	1	
	No IHT effect if aunt survives 7 years	½	
	Maximum possible liability	1	
	Taper relief if survives between 3 to 7 years	1	
	Use of annual exemptions	½	
	Nil rate band	½	
	Max		4

Appropriate style and presentation	1	
Effectiveness of communication	1	
		2
		29

(a) (i) External finance required

	£	£
Total cost of project		310,000
Sale proceeds of shares	104,370	
Sale proceeds of loan stock	29,900	
	134,270	
Less: CGT on sales (working 1)	(6,323)	
		(127,947)
External finance required		182,053

Workings

1   *Capital gains tax on sales*

		£
Gain on shares (working 2)		36,114
Gain on loan stock (working 3)		8,616
		44,730
Less: annual exemption		(9,600)
Taxable gains		35,130

Tax

	£
£35,130 × 18%	6,323

2   *Gain on sale of shares*

There is no gain on the shares on the takeover in November 2009. The original cost of the shares in Brill plc will be apportioned between the shares and the loan stock in Snapper plc (working 5). A gain will arise on the sale of the shares as follows:

	£
Proceeds	104,370
Less: cost (working 5)	(68,256)
Gain	36,114

3   *Gain on sale of loan stock*

No gain arises on the sale of the loan stock because it is a qualifying corporate bond (QCB).

However, the frozen gain of £8,616 (working 4) calculated on the takeover will become chargeable.

4   *Frozen gain on loan stock*

A gain will be calculated on the takeover in November 2009 in respect of the takeover of Brill plc by Snapper plc in respect of the loan stock as follows:

	£
Market value at takeover	28,400
Less: cost (working 5)	(19,784)
Gain	8,616

5   *Division of original cost of Brill plc shares*

	MV at takeover	Cost
	£	£
Shares	97,980	68,256
Loan stock	28,400	19,784
Totals	126,380	88,040

Assumptions

- AS has made no other disposals for the purposes of capital gains tax in 2009/10.
- AS has no capital losses brought forward.

(ii)   **Proposal to increase the after tax proceeds from the sale of the loan stock**

AS should delay the sale of the loan stock until after 5 April 2010. The gain made at the time of the takeover would then crystallise in 2010/11 and would be covered by the annual exemption for that year. The net proceeds would be increased by the capital gains tax saved of £1,551 (£8,616 × 18%).

More appropriate forms of external finance

A bank overdraft is not the most appropriate form of long term business finance. This is because the bank can demand repayment of the overdraft at any time and the rates of interest charged are fairly high.

AS should seek long term finance for his long term business needs, for example a bank loan secured on the theatre, and use the bank overdraft to finance the working capital required on a day-to-day basis.

(b) Related matters

(i) *Income tax liability in 2009/10*

AS has an income tax liability of £3,987 (see Working 1) which all falls within the basic rate band.

(ii) *National insurance contributions in 2009/10*

The profit for the period ending 31 March 2010 is expected to be £1,200 (£400 × 3).

No class 2 contributions will be due as the profit is less than the small earnings exception limit of £4,825.

No class 4 contributions will be due as the profit is less than the lower profits limit of £5,435.

(iii) *Purchase and renovation of the theatre*

The theatre is a capital purchase that does not qualify for capital allowances as it is a building but not an industrial building. Accordingly, the cost of purchasing the theatre will not give rise to a tax deduction for the purpose of computing AS's taxable trading income.

The tax treatment of the renovation costs may be summarised as follows:

- The costs will be disallowed if the renovations are necessary before the theatre can be used for business purposes. This is because they will be regarded as further capital costs of acquiring appropriate premises.

- Some of the costs may be allowable if the condition of the theatre is such that it can be used in its present state and the renovations are more in the nature of cosmetic improvements.

(iv) *VAT position*

The grant of a right to occupy the theatre in exchange for rent is an exempt supply. Accordingly, as all of AS's activities will be regarded as one for VAT purposes, AS will become partially exempt once he begins to rent out the theatre.

AS will be able to recover the input tax that is directly attributable to his standard rated supplies, ie those in connection with the supply of children's parties. He will also be able to recover a proportion of the input tax on his overheads; the proportion being that of his total supplies that are standard rated.

The remainder of his input tax will only be recoverable if it is no more than £625 per month on average and no more than 50% of his total input tax.

If AS were to opt to tax the theatre, the right to occupy the theatre in exchange for rent would then be a standard rated supply. AS could then recover all of his input tax, regardless of the amount attributable to the rent, but would have to charge VAT on the rent and on any future sale of the building.

The decision as to whether or not to opt to tax the theatre will depend on:

- the amount of input tax at stake; and
- whether or not those who rent the theatre are in a position to recover any VAT charged.

Workings

1   *Income tax computation for 2009/10*

		£
Taxable income:		
Salary		
April to December 2009		
9/12 × £25,200		18,900
January to March 2010		
3 × £1,050		3,150
Car benefit (working 2)		2,720
Trading income		
First year of trading – actual basis		
January to March 2010		
3 × £400		1,200
Net income		25,970
Less: personal allowance		(6,035)
Taxable income		19,935
Income tax liability £19,935 @ 20%		3,987

2   *Car benefit*

Percentage to be used

175 – 135 = 40 ÷ 5 = 8 + 15 + 3 (diesel) = 26%

26% × £13,950 × 9/12 (available April to December 2009)   £2,720

(c)   **Inheritance tax payable by Adam**

The gift by AS's aunt was a potentially exempt transfer.

The transfer will have no effect for inheritance tax if she survives until 1 June 2016 (seven years after the date of the transfer).

The maximum possible liability, on the assumption that there are no annual exemptions or nil band available, is £35,216 (£88,040 × 40%). This will only arise if AS's aunt dies before 1 June 2012.

The maximum liability will be reduced by taper relief of 20% for every full year after 31 May 2012 for which AS's aunt survives.

If the annual exemptions for 2008/09 and/or 2009/10 is/are available, these will reduce amount of the potentially exempt transfer by a maximum of £3,000 for each available exemption.

The IHT liability will also be lower to the extent that the aunt has not used up the whole of her nil rate band of £312,000 with chargeable transfers in the seven years prior to the potentially exempt transfer.

Mock exams

ACCA Professional Paper P6 – Options Module

Advanced Taxation (UK)

Mock Examination 1

Question Paper	
Time allowed	**Reading and planning: 15 minutes** **Writing: 3 hours**
This paper is divided into two sections	
Section A	**BOTH questions are compulsory questions and MUST be attempted**
Section B	**TWO questions ONLY to be attempted**

During reading and planning time only the question paper may be annotated

DO NOT OPEN THIS PAPER UNTIL YOU ARE READY TO START UNDER EXAMINATION CONDITIONS

SECTION A: BOTH questions are compulsory and MUST be attempted

Question 1

Stephan Antrobus is 48 years old and married to Jeanette. The couple have two children, Don and Stella, aged 25 and 21 years respectively. Stephan and Jeanette have lived in the country of Meriva since 1983. On 11 June 2007 the family moved to the UK to be near Stephan's father, Pierre, who was very ill. Stephan and Jeanette are UK resident, but not ordinarily resident in the tax years 2007/08 and 2008/09. They are both domiciled in the country of Meriva.

On 12 March 2009 Pierre Antrobus died. He was UK domiciled, having lived in the UK for the whole of his life. For the purposes of inheritance tax, his death estate consisted of UK assets, valued at £980,000 after deduction of all available reliefs, and a house in the country of Artica valued at £87,000. The executors of Pierre's estate have paid Artican inheritance tax of £1,600 and legal fees of £5,800 in respect of the sale of the Artican house. Pierre left the whole of his estate to Stephan.

Pierre had made two gifts during his lifetime:

(i)   21 August 2005: He gave Stephan 115 acres of farm land situated in the UK. The market value of the land was £274,000, although its agricultural value was only £142,000. Pierre had acquired the land on 22 May 1997 and granted an agricultural tenancy on that date. Stephan continues to own the land as at today's date and it is still subject to the agricultural tenancy.

(ii)   23 November 2007: He gave Stephan 8,000 shares valued at £212,000 in Timer Ltd, a UK resident trading company. Gift relief was claimed in respect of this gift. Pierre had acquired 18,000 shares in Timer Ltd on 10 April 1998 for £62,600.

You may assume that Stephan is a higher rate taxpayer for the tax years 2007/08 and 2008/09. In 2008/09 he made the following disposals of assets:

(i)   On 9 November 2008 he sold the 8,000 shares in Timer Ltd for £247,000.

(ii)   On 10 December 2008 he sold 2,000 shares in Lazula Inc, a company resident in Meriva, for £9,300. Stephan had purchased 4,500 shares in the company on 10 December 2005 for £28,250.

(iii)   On 31 January 2009 he transferred shares with a market value of £92,000 in Rangle plc, a UK quoted company, to a UK resident discretionary trust for the benefit of Don and Stella. Stephan had purchased these shares on 3 January 2008 for £77,500.

Stephan has not made any other transfers of value for the purposes of UK inheritance tax. He owns the family house in the UK as well as shares in UK and Merivan companies and commercial rental property in the country of Meriva.

Jeanette has not made any transfers of value for the purposes of UK inheritance tax. Her only significant asset is the family home in the country of Meriva.

Stephan and his family expect to return to their home in the country of Meriva in November 2009 once Pierre's affairs have been settled. There is no double taxation agreement between the UK and Meriva.

Required

(a)   Calculate the inheritance tax (IHT) payable as a result of the death of Pierre Antrobus. Explain the availability or otherwise of agricultural property relief and business property relief on the two lifetime gifts made by Pierre.   **(7 marks)**

(b)   Calculate Stephan Antrobus's capital gains tax liability for the tax year 2008/09 on the assumption that all available reliefs are claimed and that he claims the remittance basis.   **(6 marks)**

(c)   (i)   Explain the inheritance tax (IHT) implications and benefits of Stephan Antrobus varying the terms of his father's will such that part of Pierre Antrobus's estate is left to Don and Stella. State the date by which a deed of variation would need to be made in order for it to be valid;   **(3 marks)**

(ii)   Identify any further planning opportunities available to Stephan Antrobus in order to minimise the UK inheritance tax (IHT) due when he dies. He does not wish to make any lifetime gifts other than to his wife, Jeanette. **(5 marks)**

(d)   Although you have acted for Pierre Antrobus for many years you have not previously acted for Stephan. Explain what steps you should take. Would it make any difference to your answer if you discovered that the income from the farmland had been omitted from Stephan's tax return for 2007/08? **(4 marks)**

(Total = 25 marks)

Note. You should assume that the rates and allowances for the tax year 2008/09 apply throughout this question.

Question 2

The Court Partnership consisted of three partners, Colin, Brian and Alice, who shared the profits of the business equally. On 28 February 2009 the partners sold the business to Sandals Ltd, in exchange for shares in Sandals Ltd, with each former partner owning one third of the new company.

The recent, tax adjusted, trading profits of the Court Partnership have been as follows:

	£
Year ended 30 September 2008	89,354
1 October 2008 to 29 February 2009	60,276

Colin, who was 65 on 5 January 2009, retired when the business was sold to Sandals Ltd. He is now suggesting that if the sale of the partnership, and his retirement, had been delayed until 30 April 2009, his total tax liability would have been reduced. Colin's only other income is gross pension income of £7,600 per year, which he began receiving in the tax year 2007/08. Colin did not receive any salary or dividends from Sandals Ltd. It is estimated that the partnership's tax adjusted trading profits for the period from 1 March 2009 to 30 April 2009 would have been £18,600. Colin has overlap profits of £8,340 brought forward from when the partnership began trading.

Brian and Alice, who are brother and sister, each inherited a half interest worth £68,000 in a property, 'Bank Cottage', in May 2006. In June 2006 it was badly damaged by fire. In September 2006 the insurance company made a payment of £83,500 each to Brian and Alice. In November 2006 Brian and Alice each spent £60,000 of the insurance proceeds on restoring the property. Each half share of 'Bank Cottage' was worth £140,500 following the restoration work. In November 2008, Brian and Alice sold 'Bank Cottage' and each received proceeds of £157,500.

Brian is 34 years old. He is the managing director of Sandals Ltd on a salary of £70,000 per year and taxable benefits of £6,800 pa. He expects to receive dividends from UK companies of £2,250 and bank interest of £720 in the tax year 2009/10. Brian intends to set up a personal pension plan in September 2009. He has not made any pension contributions in the past and proposes to use part of the proceeds from the sale of 'Bank Cottage' to make the maximum possible tax allowable contribution.

Sandals Ltd manufactures industrial leatherwork tools. On 1 October 2009, Sandals Ltd will subscribe for the whole of the ordinary share capital of Brogues Inc, a company newly incorporated in the country of Tannin. It is intended that Brogues Inc will purchase partly finished tools from Sandals Ltd and customise them in Tannin. It is anticipated that Brogues Inc's annual profits chargeable to corporation tax will be approximately £115,000.

Brian and Alice will be the directors of Brogues Inc, although Brian will not be involved in the company's business on a day-to-day basis. Alice intends to spend one or two weeks each month in the country of Tannin looking after the company's affairs. The remainder of her time will be spent in the UK. Alice is also a director of Sandals Ltd and has employment contracts with both Sandals Ltd and Brogues Inc and her duties for Brogues Inc will be carried out wholly in Tannin. She will be liable to pay tax in Tannin in respect of the employment income arising from Brogues Ltd. Brogues Inc will pay for Alice's flights to and from Tannin and for her husband and baby to visit her there twice a year. Alice is currently UK resident and ordinarily resident.

The system of income tax and corporation tax in the country of Tannin is broadly similar to that in the UK although the rate of corporation tax is 38% regardless of the level of profits. There is no double tax treaty between the UK and Tannin. Brogues Inc will only be treated as resident in Tannin for Tannin tax purposes if its central control and management are exercised there. If Brogues Inc is not resident in Tannin, it will only be subject to Tannin tax if it has a permanent establishment in that country. Tannin is not a member of the European Union.

Required

(a) (i) Calculate Colin's taxable trading profits for the tax years 2008/09 and 2009/10 for both of the alternative retirement dates (28 February 2009 and 30 April 2009). **(3 marks)**

   (ii) Analyse the effect of delaying the sale of the business of the Court Partnership to Sandals Ltd until 30 April 2009 on Colin's income tax position.

   You are not required to prepare detailed calculations of his income tax liability. **(3 marks)**

(b) Calculate the chargeable gains arising on the receipt of the insurance proceeds in September 2006 and the sale of 'Bank Cottage' in November 2008. You should assume that any elections necessary to minimise the gain on the receipt of the insurance proceeds have been submitted. **(4 marks)**

(c) Calculate and explain the amount of income tax relief that Brian will obtain in respect of the pension contributions he proposes to make in the tax year 2009/10 and contrast this with how his position could be improved by delaying some of the contributions that he could have made in 2009/10 until 2010/11. You should include relevant supporting calculations and quantify the additional tax savings arising as a result of your advice.

   You should assume that Brian's income will not change in 2010/11. **(10 marks)**

(d) Draft a report as at today's date advising Brogues Inc on its proposed activities. The report should cover the following issues:

   (i) The rate at which the profits of Brogues Inc will be taxed. This section of the report should explain:

   – the company's residency position in UK tax law and what Brian and Alice would have to do in order for the company to be regarded as resident in the UK under UK tax law;

   – the meaning of the term 'permanent establishment';

   – the rate at which the profits of Brogues Inc will be taxed on the assumption that it is resident in the UK and either does or does not have a permanent establishment in Tannin. **(7 marks)**

   (ii) The UK value added tax (VAT) implications for Sandals Ltd of selling tools to and purchasing tools from Brogues Inc; **(2 marks)**

   (iii) The extent to which Alice will be subject to income tax in the UK on her earnings in respect of duties performed for Brogues Inc and the travel costs paid for by that company. **(4 marks)**

Appropriateness of format and presentation of the report and the effectiveness with which its advice is communicated. **(2 marks)**

Note.

You should assume that the income tax rates and allowances for the tax year 2008/09 and the corporation tax rates and allowances for the Financial Year 2008 apply throughout this question. **(Total = 35 marks)**

SECTION B: TWO questions ONLY to be attempted

Question 3

Robert and Imogen, currently aged 54 and 45 respectively, were married on 1 December 1998. Robert is a higher rate taxpayer who has realised taxable capital gains in 2009/10 in excess of his capital gains tax annual exemption.

Robert moved into Imogen's house in London on the day they were married. Robert's own house in Cambridge, where he had lived since acquiring it for £153,600 on 1 May 1997, has been empty since that date although he and Imogen have used it when visiting friends. Robert has been offered £344,950 for the Cambridge house and has decided that it is time to sell it. The house has a large garden such that Robert is also considering an offer for the house and a part only of the garden. He would then sell the remainder of the garden at a later date as a building plot. His total sales proceeds will be higher if he sells the property in this way.

Imogen received the following income from quoted investments in 2008/09:

	£
Dividends in respect of quoted trading company shares	1,845
Dividends paid by a Real Estate Investment Trust out of tax exempt property income	630

On 1 August 2008, Imogen was granted a 25 year lease of a commercial investment property. She paid the landlord a premium of £8,500 and also pays rent of £2,250 per month. On 1 September 2008 Imogen granted a ten year sub-lease of the property. She received a premium of £16,900 and receives rent of £2,250 per month.

Imogen began working for Sparks plc, a quoted company, on 1 July 2008 having had a two year break from her career. She earns an annual salary of £39,750 and was paid a bonus of £5,500 in October 2008 for agreeing to come and work for the company. On 1 September 2008 Imogen was provided with a fully expensed company car, including the provision of private petrol, which had a list price when new of £24,400 and a CO_2 emissions rate of 177 grams per kilometre. Imogen is required to pay Sparks plc £25 per month in respect of the private use of the car. In July and August 2008 Imogen used her own car whilst on company business. She drove 650 business miles during this two month period and was paid 30 pence per mile. Imogen had PAYE of £6,650 deducted from her gross salary in the tax year 2008/09.

After working for Sparks plc for a full year, Imogen becomes entitled to the following additional benefits:

- The opportunity to purchase a large number of shares in Sparks plc on 1 August 2009 for £4.30 per share. It is anticipated that the share price on that day will be at least £8.50 per share. The company will make an interest-free loan to Imogen equal to the cost of the shares to be repaid in two years.
- Exclusive free use of the company sailing boat for one week in July 2009. The sailing boat was purchased by Sparks plc in January 2006 for use by its senior employees and costs the company £1,250 a week in respect of its crew and other running expenses.

Required:

(a) (i) Calculate Robert's capital gains tax liability for the tax year 2009/10 on the assumption that the Cambridge house together with its entire garden is sold on 30 April 2009 for £344,950. Comment on the relevance to your calculations of the size of the garden; **(5 marks)**

(ii) Advise Robert of the capital gains tax implications of the alternative of selling the Cambridge house and garden by means of two separate disposals as proposed. Calculations are not required for this part of the question. **(3 marks)**

(b) (i) Calculate Imogen's income tax payable for the tax year 2008/09; **(8 marks)**

(ii) Explain the income tax implications for Imogen for the tax year 2009/10 of the additional benefits offered by Sparks plc. **(4 marks)**

Note. You should assume that the rates and allowances for the tax year 2008/09 apply throughout this question.

(Total = 20 marks)

Question 4

The Adze Ltd group consists of Adze Ltd, a close company, which owns 100% of the ordinary share capital of each of Chisel Ltd, Mallet Ltd and Brace Ltd. The group was formed in December 2004. All four companies began trading on 1 January 2005, are UK resident and prepare accounts to 30 June each year. Adze Ltd and Mallet Ltd make standard rated supplies and are registered separately for the purposes of value added tax (VAT). Chisel Ltd and Brace Ltd make exempt supplies only. The Adze Ltd group is classified as a large group for the purposes of capital allowances.

On 1 May 2009, Adze Ltd paid a premium of £253,800, inclusive of VAT, to acquire the 20 year lease of a warehouse for use in its trade. The warehouse is not an industrial building for the purposes of capital allowances. Adze Ltd will pay rent of £22,560 per annum, inclusive of VAT, for the warehouse.

The budgeted results for the trades carried on by the Adze Ltd group for the year ending 30 June 2010 are as follows:

	Adze	Chisel	Mallet	Brace
	£	£	£	£
Tax adjusted trading profit/(loss)	226,000	(46,000)	74,000	1,050,000

Chisel Ltd will also have trading losses brought forward as at 1 July 2009 of £68,000.

It is proposed that the Adze Ltd group will be restructured on 30 June 2009 when the trades and assets of Chisel Ltd, Mallet Ltd and Brace Ltd will be sold to Adze Ltd. Adze Ltd will then operate all four trades and the three subsidiary companies will become dormant. This restructuring is being carried out for commercial reasons although the directors will not proceed with it if it is going to give rise to significant tax costs.

The assets owned by the three subsidiaries consist of plant and machinery and goodwill in addition to net current assets.

Required

(a) Advise Adze Ltd of the corporation tax and value added tax (VAT) implications of the payments made to the owner of the warehouse in respect of the lease; **(3 marks)**

(b) Explain the corporation tax and value added tax (VAT) implications of the following aspects of the proposed restructuring of the Adze Ltd group.

    (i) The immediate tax implications of the restructuring. **(5 marks)**

    (ii) Any increase or decrease in the group's budgeted corporation tax liability for the year ending 30 June 2010 due to the restructuring on the assumption that trading losses will be used as efficiently as possible. **(6 marks)**

    (iii) The effect of the restructuring on the group's ability to recover directly and non-directly attributable input tax. **(6 marks)**

    You are required to prepare calculations in respect of part (ii) only of this part of this question.

Note. You should assume that the corporation tax rates and allowances for the Financial Year 2008 apply throughout this question.

(Total = 20 marks)

Question 5

(a) Grinder Ltd was incorporated and began trading in October 2004. It is a close company with no associated companies. It has always prepared accounts to 31 December and will continue to do so in the future.

It has been decided that Grinder Ltd will sell its business as a going concern to Millstone Ltd, an unconnected company, on 31 July 2009. Its premises and goodwill will be sold for £2,270,000 and £310,000 respectively and its machinery and equipment for £203,000. The premises, which do not constitute an industrial building, were acquired on 1 October 2004 for £1,850,000 and the goodwill has been generated internally by the company. The machinery and equipment cost £320,000; no one item will be sold for more than its original cost.

The tax adjusted trading profit of Grinder Ltd in 2009, before taking account of both capital allowances and the sale of the business assets, is expected to be £92,000. The balance on the plant and machinery pool for the purposes of capital allowances as at 31 December 2008 was £225,500. Machinery costing £40,000 was purchased on 1 March 2009.

On 1 August 2009, the proceeds from the sale of the business will be invested in either an office building or a portfolio of UK quoted company shares, as follows:

Office building

The office building would be acquired for £3,250,000; the vendor is not registered for value added tax (VAT). Grinder Ltd would borrow the additional funds required from a UK bank. The building is let to a number of commercial tenants who are not connected with Grinder Ltd and will pay rent, in total, of £55,000 per calendar quarter, in advance, commencing on 1 August 2009. The company's expenditure for the period from 1 August 2009 to 31 December 2009 is expected to be:

	£
Loan interest payable to UK bank	18,000
Building maintenance costs	9,250

Share portfolio

Shares would be purchased for the amount of the proceeds from the sale of the business with no need for further loan finance. It is estimated that the share portfolio would generate dividends of £33,000 and capital gains, after indexation allowance, of £15,000 in the period from 1 August 2009 to 31 December 2009.

All figures are stated exclusive of value added tax (VAT).

Required

(i) Taking account of the proposed sale of the business on 31 July 2009, state with reasons the date(s) on which Grinder Ltd must submit its corporation tax return(s) for the year ending 31 December 2009. **(2 marks)**

(ii) Explain whether or not Grinder Ltd will become a close investment-holding company as a result of acquiring either the office building or the share portfolio and state the relevance of becoming such a company. **(2 marks)**

(iii) Calculate the corporation tax liability of Grinder Ltd for the year ending 31 December 2009 based on its anticipated results under each of the investment strategies, on the assumption that all beneficial elections are made. **(8 marks)**

Notes:

- You should assume that the corporation tax rates and allowances for the financial year 2008 will continue to apply for the foreseeable future.

- You should ignore value added tax (VAT).

- Relevant retail price index figures are:

October 2004	188.6
July 2009	224.0

(b)   The directors of Grinder Ltd are aware that some of the company's shareholders want to realise the value in their shares immediately. Accordingly, instead of investing in the office building or the share portfolio they are considering two alternative strategies whereby, following the sale of the company's business, a payment will be made to the company's shareholders.

(i)   Liquidate the company. The payment by the liquidator would be £131 per share.

(ii)   The payment of a dividend of £130 per share following which a liquidator will be appointed. The payment by the liquidator to the shareholders would then be £1 per share.

The company originally issued 20,000 £1 ordinary shares at par value to 16 members of the Pepper family. Following a number of gifts and inheritances there are now 36 shareholders, all of whom are family members. The directors have asked you to attend a meeting to set out the tax implications of these two alternative strategies for each of the two main groups of shareholders: adults with shareholdings of more than 500 shares and children with shareholdings of 200 shares or less.

Required

Prepare notes explaining:

–   the amount chargeable to tax; and

–   the rates of tax that will apply

in respect of each of the two strategies for each of the two groups of shareholders ready for your meeting with the directors of Grinder Ltd. You should assume that none of the shareholders will have any capital losses either in the tax year 2009/10 or brought forward as at 5 April 2009.   **(8 marks)**

Note. You should assume that the rates and allowances for the tax year 2008/09 will continue to apply for the foreseeable future.

(Total = 20 marks)

Answers

A plan of attack

What's the worst thing you could be doing right now if this was the actual exam paper? Sharpening your pencil? Wondering how to celebrate the end of the exam in about three hours time? Panicking, flapping and generally getting in a right old state?

Well, they're all pretty bad, so turn back to the paper and let's sort out a **plan of attack**!

First things first

You have fifteen minutes reading time. Make sure you spend it wisely, looking through the paper in detail working out which optional questions to do and the order in which to attack the questions. You've got **two options**. Option 1 is the option recommended by BPP.

Option 1 (if you're thinking 'Help!')

If you're a bit worried about the paper, do the questions in the order of how well you think you can answer them. If you find the questions in Section B less daunting than the compulsory questions in Section A start with Section B. Remember you only need to do two of the three questions in Section B; you may find it easier if you start by deciding which question you will not do and put a line through it.

- **Question 3** is a good choice because it deals with quite basic income tax and capital gains tax computations.
- **Question 4** is a question dealing with a group of companies. If you feel confident with this area you could have selected this question first.
- **Question 5** deals with some more advanced aspects of companies such as close investment-holding companies and liquidations. However, the requirements are set out very clearly so you will probably be able to work out whether this is good question for you to choose.

Ensure that you do not spend longer than your allocated time on Section B. When you've spent the allocated time on **two** of the three questions in Section B turn to the longer questions in Section A. Read these questions through thoroughly before you launch into them. Once you start make sure you allocate your time to the parts within the questions according to the marks available and that, where possible, you attempt the easy marks first.

Lastly, what you mustn't forget is that you have to **answer both questions in Section A and TWO in Section B**. Do not miss out more than one question in Section B and do not waste time answering three questions in Section B or you will seriously affect your chance of passing the exam.

Option 2 (if you're thinking 'It's a doddle')

It never pays to be overconfident but if you're not quaking in your shoes about the exam then **turn straight to the compulsory questions** in Section A.

Once you've done these questions, move to Section B.

- The question you attempt first really depends on what you are most confident at.
- You then have to select one of the two remaining questions. If you are undecided look at the requirements. It maybe easier to obtain more marks if these are broken down into several smaller parts.

No matter how many times we remind you....

Always, always **allocate your time** according to the marks for the question in total and then according to the parts of the question. And **always, always follow the requirements** exactly. Question 5 part (a)(i), for example, asks you to state the dates on which Grinder Ltd must submit its corporation tax return. This is two easy marks. Make sure you get them.

You've got spare time at the end of the exam.....?

If you have allocated your time properly then you **shouldn't have time on your hands** at the end of the exam. But if you find yourself with five or ten minutes to spare, check over your work to make sure that there are no silly arithmetical errors.

Forget about it!

And don't worry if you found the paper difficult. More than likely other candidates will too. If this were the real thing you would need to **forget** the exam the minute you leave the exam hall and **think about the next one**. Or, if it's the last one, **celebrate**!

Question 1

Marking scheme

				Marks
(a)	*Farm land*			
	Calculation of PET		1	
	IHT liability		½	
	Availability of APR/BPR		2	
	Timer Ltd			
	Calculation of PET		½	
	IHT liability		1	
	Availability of BPR		½	
	Death estate			
	Value of estate		1½	
	IHT due		1½	
		Max		7
(b)	*Timer Ltd*			
	Gift relief on gift to Stephan		1½	
	Stephan's gain		1½	
	Lazula Inc		2	
	Rangle plc		1½	
	CGT due		1	
		Max		6
(c)	(i)	IHT on Pierre's estate	½	
		Comprised in Stephan's estate	½	
		Gift by PET	½	
		Variation		
		IHT on Pierre's estate unaffected	½	
		Passing directly to Don and Stella	½	
		Not a PET by Stephan	½	
		Date	½	
		Max		3
	(ii)	*IHT charge*		
		UK assets only chargeable	1	
		Calculation of available nil rate band	1	
		Acquire foreign assets	1	
		Gifts to Jeanette		
		Spouse exemption	1	
		Use of Jeanette's nil band	1	
		Max		5

(d)	Client identification	1
	Previous accountant	1
	Disclose omission	1
	Money laundering report	1

$$\frac{4}{25}$$

(a) **IHT payable as a result of the death of Pierre Antrobus**

Lifetime transfers

21 August 2005: Gift of farmland – a PET which becomes chargeable

	£
Value transferred	274,000
Less APR	(142,000)
Less annual exemptions 2005/06 and 2004/05	(6,000)
PET	126,000
IHT chargeable on death £126,000 × 0%	0

APR is available on the agricultural value only, and is not withdrawn as Stephan still held the property as agricultural property at the date of Pierre's death.

BPR is not available as Pierre does not farm the land himself.

23 November 2007: Gift of shares in Timer Ltd – a PET which becomes chargeable

	£
Value transferred	212,000
Less annual exemptions 2007/08 and 2006/07	(6,000)
	206,000
IHT chargeable on death	
£(312,000 - 126,000) = 186,000 × 0%	0
£(206,000 – 186,000) = 20,000 × 40%	8,000
	8,000

BPR is not available since Stephan had disposed of the shares before the date of Pierre's death.

Death estate

	£	£
UK assets		980,000
House in Arctica	87,000	
Less legal fees £5,800, restricted to 5%	(4,350)	
		82,650
		1,062,650
IHT payable @ 40% (no nil rate band remaining)		425,060
Less DTR (clearly less than £82,650 × 40%)		(1,600)
		423,460

(b) **Stephan Antrobus CGT Liability 2008/09**

	£
Summary:	
Timer Ltd (W1)	211,178
Rangle Ltd (W4)	0
Lazula Inc (W3)	(3,256)
Net Chargeable gains	207,922
No annual exemption available because remittance basis claimed	
CGT £207,922 × 18%	37,426

Workings

1

	£
9 November 2008 8,000 shares in Timer Ltd	
Proceeds	247,000
Less: Cost (W2)	(27,822)
IHT on PET becoming chargeable	(8,000)
Gain	211,178

2

	£
Gift Holdover relief will have been claimed on the gift of shares by	
Pierre to Stephan:	
Deemed proceeds 23.11.07	212,000
Less cost 8,000/18,000 × £62,600	(27,822)
Gain held over	184,178

Base cost for Stephan:	
	£
Deemed proceeds 23.11.07	212,000
Less Gain held over	(184,178)
Base cost	27,822

3 10 December 2008 2,000 shares in Lazula Inc

	£
Proceeds	9,300
Less cost 2,000/4,500 × £28,250	(12,556)
Loss	(3,256)

Stephen can make an election to treat this non–UK loss as an allowable loss. It will be set against his UK gains since these are the only gains arising in the tax year.

4 31 January 2009 shares in Rangle plc

	£
Proceeds	92,000
Less cost	(77,500)
Gain	14,500

As the gift to the trust is a transfer which is immediately chargeable to IHT, gift relief is available so no gain is immediately chargeable.

(c) (i) Under the terms of his will Pierre's estate passed in its entirety to Stephan. The estate was subject to IHT at 40%.

Unless Stephan gives away the UK assets that he has inherited at least seven years before he dies, then they will be comprised in his estate on his death, and will then be liable to IHT.

If Stephan does not need the capital and income, he could give the UK assets to Don and Stella. If he does this by means of a lifetime gift it would be a PET which would be liable to IHT should he die within seven years.

Stephan could instead make a deed of variation under which the UK assets from Pierre's estate would pass directly to Don and Stella. Provided the deed is made within two years from the date of death (ie by 12 March 2011) the deed is treated as if it rewrote the will so that the assets are treated as passing directly to Don and Stella on Pierre's death. The deed must contain a statement to this effect. This will not incur any additional IHT since the estate was in any event taxable, but there is no potential liability should Stephan die within seven years.

(ii) Since Stephan is not domiciled in the UK then only his UK assets are treated as comprised in his estate for IHT purposes. He has already made a chargeable lifetime transfer on the transfer of the shares in Rangle plc to the discretionary trust, the chargeable transfer being £86,000 (£92,000 less the annual exemptions of £3,000 each for 2008/09 and 2007/08). He therefore only has £226,000 of his nil rate band remaining if he should die before 31 January 2016.

Stephan should therefore consider rearranging his affairs so that he holds foreign assets rather than UK assets so that they are not within the scope of UK IHT. Where this involves selling assets which are standing at a gain then the sale should be delayed until Stephan is not UK resident so as to avoid incurring a CGT liability.

To the extent that he then still holds UK assets he should consider gifting then to his wife Jeanette. Any gifts to Jeanette are exempt from IHT – the £55,000 restriction for transfers to non-domiciled spouses does not apply here as both Stephan and Jeanette are not domiciled in the UK. If Jeanette's UK assets do not exceed £312,000 in value they will be covered by her nil rate band on death.

(d) On commencing to act for Stephan proof of identity must be obtained under the money laundering regulations. This could comprise a passport, driving licence, HMRC notice of coding, and proof of address. A copy of the documents should be kept for at least five years after the end of the appointment.

If Stephan has previously used the services of another accountant, the previous accountant should be requested to confirm that there is no professional or other reason why you should not act for Stephan. The existing accountant is bound by confidentiality and Stephen must give permission for the accountant to disclose information.

If he refuses permission, the existing accountant should inform you and you must then inform Stephen that you are unable to accept the appointment.

If you discover that income has been omitted from returns previously filed by Stephan you will need to consider your position carefully. You must advise Stephan that he should immediately make full disclosure of the omissions to HMRC, and if he refuses to do so you should not act. Even if he agrees to make the disclosure you need to consider the money laundering rules. If you suspect that money laundering has taken place, a money laundering report should be made.

Question 2

Text references. Basis periods are covered in Chapter 6, partnerships in Chapter 9 and pensions in Chapter 2. Compensation for damaged to assets is in Chapter 14. Overseas aspects of income tax are in Chapter 10 and overseas aspects of corporation tax in Chapter 27.

Top tips. Part (a)(i) was a straightforward exercise in computing trading profits on a cessation. In part (a)(ii) you just had to think how the profits had to be taxed; you did not have to do the sums.

Easy marks. Part (c) asked for you to quantify the tax savings from deferring pension contributions, an easy computation if you realised that you did not need to repeat the sums for 2008/09 if no higher rate tax was payable.

Marking scheme

					Marks
(a)	(i)	Cessation on 28 February 2009		1½	
		Cessation on 30 April 2009		2	
			Max		3
	(ii)	Additional two months of profits		1	
		Income tax rates in the two years		1	
		Personal age allowance			
		Identification of issue		½	
		Abatement		1	
		Conclusions		½	
			Max		3
(b)		Chargeable gain on insurance proceeds		2	
		Base cost c/f		1	
		Chargeable gain on sale		2	
			Max		4

(c)		
Maximum contributions payable		1½
Contributions made net of basic rate income tax		½
Basic rate income tax relief		½
Income tax relief from extending basic rate band		3
Advice to improve the position		
Identifying advantage of delaying some contributions with reason		1½
Calculation of optimum amount of contributions to defer		1
Calculation of additional income tax saved		
2009/10 liability unchanged		1
Calculation of potential saving		2
	Max	10

(d)	(i)	*Residency*		
		Incorporation	1	
		Central management and control	1	
		Action required – location of board meetings	1	
		Permanent establishment		
		Meaning	1	
		UK resident with no permanent establishment in Tannin		
		Conclusion – taxed at 20%	1	
		UK resident with permanent establishment in Tannin		
		Taxed in both countries with DTR in UK	1	
		DTR is the lower of UK tax and Tannin tax	1	
		Conclusion – taxed at 38%	1	
		Max		7
	(ii)	Exports – zero-rated and evidence	1	
		Imports – account for VAT and claim as input tax	1	
				2
	(iii)	Alice remains UK resident and ordinarily resident	½	
		Income from Brogues Inc taxed in the UK	1	
		Income from Brogues Inc taxed in Tannin	½	
		Double tax relief – lower of UK tax and Tannin tax	½	
		Alice's travel costs with reason	1	
		Alice's family's travel costs with reason	1	
		Max		4
		Format and style		
		Appropriate style and presentation	1	
		Effectiveness of communication	1	
				2
				35

(a) (i) Colin's taxable trading profits 2008/09 and 2009/10

	2008/09	2009/10
Cessation 28 February 2009		
Basis period	1.10.07 – 28.02.09	
	£	
Profits 1/3 × £(89,354 + 60,276)	49,877	
Less overlap profits	(8,340)	
	41,537	0
Cessation 30 April 2009		
Basis period	1.10.07 – 30.09.08	1.10.08 – 30.4.09
	£	£
Profits 1/3 × £89,354	29,785	
1/3 × £(60,276 + 18,600)		26,292
Less overlap profits		(8,340)
	29,785	17,952

(ii) The effect of delaying the sale of the business until 30 April 2009 is to:

- Shift £11,752 of profits from 2008/09 to 2009/10, and
- Earn an additional £6,200 of profits in taxable in 2009/10.

By shifting profits from 2008/09 to 2009/10 Colin ensures that his profits are taxed at the basic rate of income tax, whereas for a cessation in 2008/09 some of the profits would have been taxed at the higher rate in 2008/09.

Colin is entitled to the age related personal allowance in both 2008/09 and 2009/10. However this is clawed back once total income exceeds £21,800, with there being no age related personal allowance remaining once income exceeds £27,790 (£21,800 + 2 × (9,030 − 6,035)). Colin will therefore not be entitled to any age related personal allowance in 2008/09 irrespective of the date of cessation. In 2009/10 he would be entitled to the full age related personal allowance if cessation was on 28 February 2009, but only some if cessation was on 30 April 2009 because his net income would be £(17,952 + 7,600) = £25,552.

(b) **Bank Cottage chargeable gains for each of Brian and Alice**

September 2006 insurance proceeds; part disposal

	£	£
Capital sum not used in restoration £(83,500 − 60,000)		23,500
Less: part of original cost		
£68,000 × $\dfrac{23,500}{23,500 + 140,500}$	9,744	
part of restoration cost		
£60,000 × $\dfrac{23,500}{23,500 + 140,500}$	8,598	(18,342)
Gain		5,158

Base cost of half share of restored cottage

	£	£
Original cost		68,000
Restoration expenditure		60,000
		128,000
Less: costs used in part disposal	18,342	
restoration expenditure rolled over	60,000	(78,342)
Base cost		49,658

November 2008 sale

	£
Proceeds	157,500
Less: base cost	(49,658)
Gain	107,842

(c) **Brian pension contributions**

Brian's maximum tax relievable gross personal pension contribution for 2009/10 is equal to his employment income of £70,000 + £6,800 = £76,800. This would be paid net of 20% basic rate tax to the pension provider, the net payment being £61,440.

Higher rate tax relief is given by extending Brian's basic rate band by the gross contribution.

Brian's taxable income for 2009/10 is:

	Non-savings income	Savings income	Dividend income	Total
	£	£	£	
Salary	70,000			
Benefits	6,800			
Employment income	76,800			
Dividends £2,250 × 100/90			2,500	
Bank interest £720 × 100/80		900		
Net income	76,800	900	2,500	80,200
Less personal allowance	(6,035)			
Taxable income	70,765	900	2,500	74,165

Brian's income tax payable with the pension contribution is:

	£
Non savings income	
£70,765 × 20%	14,153
Savings income	
£900 × 20%	180
Dividend income	
£2,500 × 10%	250
	14,583

Brian's income tax payable without the pension contribution is:

	£
Non savings income	
£34,800 × 20%	6,960
£35,965 × 40%	14,386
70,765	
Savings income	
£900 × 40%	360
Dividend income	
£2,500 × 32.5%	813
	22,519

The tax saving from paying the pension contribution is £(22,519 – 14,583) = £7,936 + (£76,800 × 20%) = £23,296, and average rate of £23,296/76,800 × 100 = 30.33%.

Brian has only achieved higher rate tax relief on £(35,965 + 900 + 2,500) = £39,365 of his pension contribution out of total contributions of £76,800. He should consider deferring the payment of £76,800 - £39,365 = £37,435 of the contributions to 2010/11. (These figures are stated gross.) As Brian's income is not expected to change he will then obtain higher rate tax relief on the total contributions paid.

Brian's income tax liability for 2009/10 would be £14,583 as computed above, and for 2010/11 will be £15,311 as follows:

	£
Non savings income	
£34,800 × 20%	6,960
£35,965 × 20% (extended band)	7,193
£70,765	
Savings income	
£900 × 20%	180
Dividend income	
£570 × 10%	57
£1,930 × 32.5%	627
	15,017

This achieves an additional higher rate tax saving of £(22,519 – 15,017) = £7,502, leading to total tax relief on the pension of £7,502 + £23,296 = £30,798, and average rate of £30,798/76,800 × 100 = 40.1%.

(d)   **Report to the directors of Brogues inc**

To   The directors of Brogues Inc
From   AN Accountant
Date   7 June 2009
Re   The proposed Activities of Brogues Inc

(i)   Rate of tax on the profits of Brogues Inc

Residence

Under UK law a company which is incorporated in the UK is resident in the UK for tax purposes. Brogues Inc is not incorporated in the UK, so will be regarded as UK resident if its central management and control are exercised in the UK. Central management and control are usually treated as exercised where the board of directors meets, so that for Brogues Inc to be resident in the UK under UK law Alice and Brian must hold the board meetings in the UK.

Permanent establishment

A permanent establishment is a fixed place of business through which the business of the enterprise is wholly or partly carried on. It includes a branch, office, factory or workshop, but does not include use of storage facilities, maintenance of a stock of goods and delivery of them or a fixed place of business used solely for purchasing goods. If the company regularly concludes contracts in Tannin this may also result in it being treated as having a permanent establishment there.

Rate of tax

If Brogues Inc is resident in the UK and does not have a permanent establishment in Tannin, then its profits will be liable to UK corporation tax at the rate of 21% so long as its profits do not exceed the small companies limit of £150,000 (as there are two companies in the group).

If Brogues Inc is resident in the UK and does have a permanent establishment in Tannin, then its profits will be liable to UK corporation tax at the rate of 21% so long as its profits do not exceed the small companies limit of £150,000. However the profits of the permanent establishment will be subject to corporation tax in Tannin at the rate of 38%. Double tax relief can be obtained against UK corporation tax by deducting the Tannin corporation tax paid from the UK corporation tax payable, but the amount that can be deducted cannot exceed the UK corporation tax liability. Since the rate of corporation tax in Tannin is 38% the double tax relief will clearly be restricted by reference to the UK tax payable, so that the effective rate of tax on the profits of the permanent establishment would be 38%.

(ii)   **The VAT effects of selling tools between Sandals Ltd and Brogues Inc**

If Sandals buys tools from Brogues Inc it must account for the output VAT due on the goods at the point of entry into the UK, but can recover this as input VAT payable on its next VAT return.

The export of tools by Sandals Ltd to Brogues Inc is zero rated. Sandals Ltd must retain evidence of the export such as copy invoices and consignment notes.

(iii)   **Income tax on Alice's earnings from Brogues Inc and travel costs**

As Alice is not going to Tannin to work for a period spanning a complete tax year she will remain UK resident and ordinarily resident. She will therefore be taxed in the UK on her earnings from Brogues Inc.

As the income arises in Tannin she is subject to tax in Tannin on those earnings. However she will be able to claim unilateral double tax relief in the UK for the Tannin tax suffered. The relief is limited to the lower of the UK tax and the Tannin tax.

Although Alice's travel costs are allowable provided the journey is wholly and exclusively for the purposes performing her duties in Tannin, the costs of her husband and baby travelling on visits to Tannin are not allowable as Alice is not outside the UK for a continuous period of 60 days or more.

Question 3

Marking scheme

				Marks
(a)	(i)	Gain	1	
		PPR exemption	2	
		Capital gains tax payable	1	
		Size of garden	1	
				5
	(ii)	Additional proceeds will increase gains	½	
		Sale of house and part of garden		
		Allowable cost	½	
		PPR	½	
		Subsequent sale of remainder of garden		
		Allowable cost	½	
		No PPR relief with reason	1	
				3
(b)	(i)	Salary	½	
		Bonus	½	
		Car and fuel benefit		
		Percentage	½	
		Time apportion	½	
		Contribution	½	
		Fuel	½	
		Claim in respect of business mileage	½	
		Property income		
		Rent receivable	½	
		Premium received	1	
		Relief for premium paid	1½	
		Relief for rent payable	½	
		Dividend income		
		Quoted shares	½	
		Real Estate Investment Trust	½	
		Personal allowance	½	
		Calculation of income tax liability	1½	
		Income tax credits	1	
		Max		8

(ii)	P11D employee	½
	Benefits taxed at 40%	½
	Shares – Taxable benefit	½
	Loan	
	£5,000 *de minimis*	½
	Calculation of benefit	½
	Application of rules to 2009/10	½
	Sailing boat	
	Annual benefit	½
	Apportionment	½
	Running costs	½

Max   4

20

(a)   (i)   **Robert CGT liability 2009/10**

	£
Proceeds	344,950
Less cost	(153,600)
	191,350
Less Principal private residence relief (W) 55/144 × £191,350	(73,085)
Gain before taper relief	118,265
CGT payable £118,265 × 18%	21,288

The calculation has been prepared on the basis that the whole property is eligible for the principal private residence exemption. The exemption covers the house and garden of up to ½ hectare. If the garden is larger than ½ hectare exemption will be available if the garden is required for the reasonable enjoyment of the house, and so will depend on the size and nature of the house. If the garden exceeds the permitted area then the gain attributable to the excess land is not eligible for relief.

Working

	Exempt months	Chargeable months
1.5.97 – 30.11.98 actual occupation	19	
1.12.98 – 30.4.06 absence		89
1.5.06 – 30.4.09 last 3 years	36	
Total 144 months	55	89

(ii)   **Implications of two disposals**

If the property is sold by one disposal then, subject to the garden not exceeding the permitted area, principal private residence exemption will be given.

If the property is sold by means of two separate disposals, house first, then the sale of the house is a part disposal. The original cost attributable to the first disposal will be calculated using the formula A/(A + B), where A is the proceeds of the part sold and B is the market value of the part retained. The principal private residence exemption is available on this disposal.

On the subsequent disposal of the garden the remainder of the cost is allowable. There will not, however, be any principal private residence exemption on the disposal.

Thus although splitting the proposal will increase the sale proceeds this must be balanced against the reduction in the principal private residence exemption.

(b)   (i)   **Imogen income tax payable 2008/09**

	Non savings income £	Dividend income £	Total £
Salary £39,750 × 9/12	29,813		
Bonus	5,500		
Car benefit (W1)	3,099		
Fuel benefit (W1)	2,267		
Mileage deduction 650 × (40 − 30)p	(65)		
Employment income	40,614		
Income from property (W2)	9,840		
REIT dividend £630 × 100/78	808		
Dividends £1,845 × 100/90		2,050	
Net income	51,262	2,050	53,312
Less personal allowance	(6,035)		
Taxable income	45,227	2,050	47,277

Non savings income

£34,800 × 20%	6,960
£10,427 × 40%	4,171
45,227	

Dividend income

£2,050 × 32.5%	666
	11,797
Less: tax credit on dividend	
£2,050 × 10%	(205)
tax withheld on REIT	
£808 × 22%	(178)
PAYE	(6,650)
Income tax payable	4,764

Workings

1   Car benefit

	£
177g/km: 15 + (175 − 135)/5 = 23%	
£24,400 × 23% × 7/12	3,274
Less contribution £25 × 7	(175)
	3,099
Fuel benefit £16,900 × 23% × 7/12	2,267

2

	£	£
Lease premium received		16,900
Less £16,900 × (10 − 1) × 2%		(3,042)
		13,858
Less deduction for premium paid		
Premium	8,500	
Less £8,500 × (25 − 1) × 2%	(4,080)	
	4,420	
Deduction 10/25 × £4,420		(1,768)
		12,090
Rent receivable 7 × £2,250		15,750
Less rent payable 8 × £2,250		(18,000)
Taxable property income		9,840

(ii) **Income tax implications of additional benefits**

Imogen is a P11D employee and will be charged to income tax at her marginal rate of 40% on benefits provided by Sparks plc.

The purchase of shares at an undervalue will lead to taxable employment income. The undervalue is £(8.50 – 4.30) = £4.20 per share.

The company is making a beneficial loan to Imogen of the purchase price of the shares. Unless the loan is for less than £5,000 there will be taxable employment income of the amount of the loan times the official interest rate. If the loan is only outstanding for part of the year the charge is scaled down proportionately (ie 8/12 for 2009/10).

The use of the yacht for one week will lead to a charge of:

- 20% of the cost of the yacht × 1/52, plus
- Running costs for one week of £1,250.

Question 4

Text references. Corporation tax losses are covered in Chapter 24 and groups in Chapter 26. VAT is in Chapters 28 and 29.

Top tips. Where a trader makes exempt supplies you should be looking out for complications arising from partial exemption.

Easy marks. The computations of corporation tax in (b)(ii) were very straightforward. You just had to watch how you dealt with losses and what rate of corporation tax you used.

Marking scheme

				Marks
(a)	Recoverability of input tax		1	
	Corporation tax			
	Premium		2	
	Rent		½	
		Max		3
(b)	(i)	Capital gains – no gain/no loss	1	
		IFA – no gain/no loss	1	
		Trading losses of Chisel Ltd	1	
		Capital allowances	1	
		VAT on transfer of trades	1	
		Deregistration	1	
			Max	5
	(ii)	Following the restructuring		
		Income	1	
		Use of current period trading losses	½	
		Corporation tax liability	1	
		Under the existing group structure		
		Income	1	
		Group relief with reason	1	
		Rates of corporation tax	½	
		Corporation tax liabilities	1	
		Conclusion	1	
			Max	6

(iii)	Under the existing group structure	1	
	Following the restructuring		
	Partially exempt person	1	
	Attributable input tax	1	
	Non-attributable input tax	1	
	De minimis limits	1½	
	Conclusion	1	
	Max		6
			20

(a) **CT and VAT implications of the payments for the lease of the warehouse**

Adze Ltd is registered for VAT and makes standard rated supplies. It will therefore be able to claim the VAT on the premium and rentals as deductible input tax.

The VAT on the premium is £253,800 × 7/47 = £37,800, and the net premium is £216,000.

The VAT on the annual rent is £22,560 × 7/47 = £3,360 and the net rent is £19,200.

Adze Ltd will be able to claim a deduction in its computation of taxable trading income for the rent paid and for a proportion of the lease premium paid. The deduction will be:

	£
Premium paid	216,000
Less £216,000 × (20 – 1) × 2%	(82,080)
	133,920
Annual deduction £133,920/20	6,696
Annual rent payable	19,200
Annual deduction	25,896

The deduction for the year to 30 June 2009 will be 2/12 × £25,896 = £4,316 as the lease was acquired two months before the year end.

(b) (i) **Immediate impact of restructuring**

As the Adze Ltd group is both a 75% group and a capital gains group the immediate corporation tax implications of the restructuring are:

- Any assets which are chargeable assets for capital gains purposes will be transferred at no gain/no loss

- Any goodwill will be transferred at no gain/no loss under the intangible fixed asset rules

- The trading losses of Chisel Ltd will be transferred to Adze Ltd under the succession to trade rules as both companies are substantially in the same ownership. The losses can only be set against future profits arising from the same trade

- There will be no balancing charges/allowances on the transfer of plant and machinery for the same reason

The transfers of the trades will be treated as transfers of going concerns for VAT purposes and no VAT will be chargeable.

Mallet Ltd will cease to make taxable supplies following the transfer and must notify HMRC within 30 days.

Impact on corporation tax liability

If the restructuring does not take place the corporation tax liability of the group will be as follows:

	Adze	Chisel	Mallet	Brace
	£	£	£	£
Trading profits	226,000	0	74,000	1,050,000
Less group relief	(46,000)			
PCTCT	180,000	0	74,000	1,050,000
CT payable				
@ 21%			15,540	
@ 28%	50,400			294,000
Less £(375,000 − 180,000) × 7/400	(3,413)			
Total £356,437	46,897	0	15,540	294,000

Note the trading losses of £68,000 brought forward by Chisel Ltd at 1 July 2009 are carried forward against future profits.

Group relief will be claimed by Adze Ltd as it is a marginal company, whilst Mallet Ltd is a small company and Brace Ltd is a large company. (The small company lower and upper limits are divided by 4 and are £75,000 and £375,000 respectively.)

If the restructuring does take place then Adze will be carrying on four separate trades and the profits from each will be computed separately. A claim may be made to set the loss from the Chisel trade against other income of the same accounting period, although the loss brought forward of £68,000 must be carried forward against future profits of the Chisel trade.

The corporation tax liability of Adze Ltd will be:

	£
The Adze trade	226,000
The Mallet trade	74,000
The Brace trade	1,050,000
	1,350,000
Less loss of Chisel trade	(46,000)
PCTCT	1,304,000
CT @ 28%	365,120
Less £(1,500,000 − 1,304,000) × 7/400	(3,430)
Corporation tax payable	361,690

The proposed restructuring would increase the corporation tax payable from £356,437 to £361,690, an increase of £5,253.

(iii) **VAT implications**

If the restructuring does not take place then Adze Ltd and Mallet Ltd, which are companies making standard rated supplies, will recover all their input tax. Chisel Ltd and Brace Ltd make exempt supplies, cannot register for VAT and cannot recover any input tax.

If the restructuring takes place then Adze Ltd will make both standard rated and exempt supplies, and so will be partially exempt. It will be able to recover any input tax which is directly related to its taxable supplies.

Input tax which cannot be attributed directly to either standard rated supplies or exempt supplies is apportioned between them in the ratio of taxable to exempt supplies. The proportion attributable to taxable supplies is expressed as a percentage and rounded up to the next whole number. The input tax apportioned to taxable supplies is recoverable.

Input tax directly related to exempt supplies and non-attributable input tax apportioned to exempt supplies is not recoverable unless it falls below the de minimis limits.

If the input tax related to exempt supplies is less than £625 per month on average and is less than 50% of the total input tax, then it may be recovered in full.

Whether the restructuring will lead to a greater ability to recover input tax for the group as a whole will depend on the ratios of taxable and exempt supplies and the amount of non-attributable input tax. Given the level of Brace Ltd's profits it seems likely that the partial exemption de minimis limits will be exceeded.

Question 5

Text references. Accounting periods are covered in Chapter 20 and close investment-holding companies in Chapter 25. Liquidations are in Chapter 23.

Top tips. In part (b) you were asked to prepare notes with specific reference to two specific groups of shareholders. This allowed you to focus on higher rate taxpayers and non-taxpayers.

Easy marks. The corporation tax computations in (a)(iii) were straightforward once you had spotted that there were two accounting periods.

Marking scheme

				Marks
(a)	(i)	Two accounting periods with reason	1	
		Statement of submission date rule	1	
		Date	½	
		Max		2
	(ii)	Office building – status with reason	1	
		Share portfolio – status and implication	1	
				2
	(iii)	AP ending 31 July 2009		
		Tax adjusted trading profit	1½	
		Chargeable gain	1	
		Corporation tax liability	2	
		AP ending 31 December 2009 – Office building		
		Profits chargeable to corporation tax	1½	
		Corporation tax liability	½	
		AP ending 31 December 2009 – Share portfolio	½	
		Profits chargeable to corporation tax	½	
		Corporation tax liability	½	
				8
(b)		Liquidation		
		Capital gain arises	½	
		Cost of shares	1	
		Unquoted trading company	½	
		Entrepreneurs' relief	½	
		Spouse transfers	½	
		Annual exemption	½	
		Tax rates	½	
		Comparison of adults with children with effective rates	2	
		Dividend followed by liquidation		
		Gross up by 100/90	½	
		Tax rates	½	
		Tax credit	½	
		Comparison of adults with children with effective rates	1½	
		Liquidation – no gain/possible capital loss	1	
		Max		8
				20

(a)   (i)   **CT returns**

As Grinder Ltd ceased trading on 31 July 2009 two accounting periods fall within the period of account of 12 months to 31 December 2009. They are the period 1 January 2009 to 31 July 2009 and 1 August 2009 to 31 December 2009.

The corporation tax return must be filed by the later of 12 months after the end of the accounting period and 12 months after the end of the period of account within which the accounting period ends. Both returns must therefore be filed by 31 December 2010.

(ii)   **Close investment company**

If a company holds land or shares as investments then it will be regarded as an investment company. Grinder Ltd is a close company and so holding a portfolio of quoted shares will make it a close investment-holding company.

If Grinder Ltd acquires property for letting on a commercial basis it will not be regarded as a close investment-holding company. Therefore investing in the office building will not make Grinder Ltd a close investment-holding company.

If a company is a close investment-holding company then it pays corporation tax at the full rate of 28% regardless of the level of its profits.

(iii)   **Corporation tax computation year to 31 December 2009**

Accounting period of 7 months to 31 July 2009

	£
Trading profits	92,000
Less capital allowances on plant and machinery (W1)	(62,500)
Add profit on disposal of goodwill (W2)	310,000
Taxable trading profits	339,500
Chargeable gain (W3)	72,200
PCTCT	411,700
Corporation tax payable	
£411,700 × 28% (W4)	115,276
Less marginal relief £(875,000 – 411,700) × 7/400	(8,108)
	107,168

Accounting period of 5 months to 31 December 2009

Investment in property

	£
Rental income 5 × £55,000/3	91,667
Less maintenance costs	(9,250)
Income from property	82,417
Less Deficit on non-trading loan relationships (W5)	(18,000)
PCTCT	64,417
Corporation tax payable	
£64,417 × 21% (W4)	13,528

Investment in shares

	£
Chargeable gains/PCTCT	15,000
Corporation tax payable	
£15,000 × 28%	4,200

Summary:

	Property	Shares
	£	£
1.1.09 – 31.7.09	107,168	107,168
1.8.09 – 31.12.09	13,528	4,200
Total	120,696	111,368

Workings

1   Plant and machinery

	£
Tax WDV b/f at 1.1.09	225,500
Acquisitions	40,000
Disposals	(203,000)
Balancing allowance	62,500

2   The goodwill falls under the rules for intangible fixed assets. The profit on disposal is included in taxable trading profits.

The profit is £310,000 (there is no cost).

3   Chargeable gain on disposal of premises

	£
Proceeds	2,270,000
Less cost	(1,850,000)
Less indexation allowance	
$\dfrac{224.0 - 188.6}{188.6} = 0.188 \times £1,850,000$	(347,800)
Gain	72,200

4   The small companies limits are scaled down as the accounting periods are less than twelve months long

	1.1.09 – 31.7.09	1.8.09 – 31.12.09
Lower limit: £300,000 × 7/12: × 5/12	£175,000	£125,000
Upper limit: £1,500,000 × 7/12: × 5/12	£875,000	£625,000
	Marginal	
If property investment		Small
If share portfolio		Full rate

5   Relief for the non-trading loan deficit will be claimed against other income of the same accounting period to obtain relief as soon as possible.

(b)   (i)   **Liquidation only**

If Grinder Ltd is liquidated there will be a chargeable disposal by each shareholder, with the proceeds being equal to the payment by the liquidator, ie £131 per share.

To calculate the capital gain the cost of the shareholding is deducted from the proceeds. The cost will be determined as follows:

- If the shares have been held since incorporation; £1 per share.
- If the shares were acquired by gift and gift relief was not claimed; the market value at the date of the gift.
- If the shares were acquired by gift and gift relief was claimed; the cost is the same as the donor's cost
- If the shares were acquired by inheritance; the market value at the date of death.
- If the shares were acquired from a spouse or civil partner other than by inheritance, the cost will be that of the donor spouse or civil partner.

The gain is the excess of the proceeds over cost. Grinder Ltd is an unquoted trading company. If any of the shareholders have more than 1,000 shares (5%) and are employees or officers of Grinder Ltd for the one year prior to liquidation, the gain can be reduced by entrepreneurs' relief. This will reduce the gain by 4/9. It appears this is unlikely to be the case for the majority of the shareholders.

If the shares were acquired from a spouse or civil partner other than by inheritance, then the period of ownership by the donor spouse or civil partner is treated as a period of ownership by the donee spouse or civil partner.

The annual exemption (£9,600) is deducted from the gain to the extent that it is not already used, and capital gains tax charged on the chargeable gain. The rate of CGT is 18%.

A child with a holding of 200 shares who has held them since incorporation will realise a gain of 200 × £(131 − 1) = £26,000. If the child had acquired the shares by gift within the last year and gift relief had been claimed the gain after the annual exemption would be £16,400.

An adult with a holding of 500 shares who has held them since incorporation will realise a gain of 500 × £(131 − 1) = £65,000.

(ii) **A dividend followed by liquidation**

Any dividend paid will be taxable income in the hands of the recipient. The net dividend will be £130 per share, which equates to a taxable gross amount of £144 with a tax credit of £14.

The income tax position is:

- If the gross dividend is covered by the personal allowance or other reliefs no tax is payable, but the tax credit is not repayable.
- If the gross dividend falls within the basic rate band, income tax is payable at the rate of 10%, but this is covered by the tax credit.
- If the gross dividend falls within the higher rate band, income tax is payable at the rate of 32.5%. The 10% tax credit can be set against this liability, leaving tax payable at the net rate of 22.5%. This equates to 25% of the net dividend.

For a child with 200 shares the dividend will be 200 × £130 = £26,000 net, which equates to £28,889 gross. Unless the child has significant other income this is likely to fall within the basic rate band and there will be no additional liability.

For an adult with 500 shares the dividend will be 500 × £130 = £65,000 net, which equates to £72,222 and it is likely that all or part of this will fall within the higher rate band. If it all falls within the higher rate band the higher rate tax liability will be £72,222 × 22.5% = £16,250

The liquidation will result in a chargeable disposal by each shareholder, with the proceeds being equal to the payment by the liquidator, ie £1 per share.

From the proceeds can be deducted the cost of the shareholding. The cost will be determined as before. Shareholders who have held their shares since incorporation will therefore have nil chargeable gain, but shareholders whose base cost exceeds £1 per share will realise a capital loss unless they acquired the shares when they were valued at less than £1 each.

A capital loss must be set against other gains of the same year and before the annual exemption. Any loss remaining unrelieved may be carried forward against capital gains in future years.

ACCA Professional Paper P6 – Options Module

Advanced Taxation (UK)

Mock Examination 2

Question Paper	
Time allowed	**Reading and planning: 15 minutes** **Writing: 3 hours**
This paper is divided into two sections	
Section A	**BOTH questions are compulsory questions and MUST be attempted**
Section B	**TWO questions ONLY to be attempted**

During reading and planning time only the question paper may be annotated

DO NOT OPEN THIS PAPER UNTIL YOU ARE READY TO START UNDER EXAMINATION CONDITIONS

SECTION A: BOTH questions are compulsory and MUST be attempted

Question 1

Your manager has had a meeting with Joan Thompson, owner of Spark Ltd, an electrical retail company, and has sent you a copy of the following memorandum.

To   The files
From   Tax manager
Date   12 May 2010
Subject Spark Ltd group

Spark Ltd

Spark Ltd acquired a freehold property (The Hutch) from Burn Ltd for £180,000 on 19 April 2009. The property's market value at that date was £200,000. It was immediately used for the company's trade.

Char Ltd

Last year it was decided that Char Ltd should cease investing in commercial property (as had been the case until then) and should invest instead in quoted shares in unrelated companies and in government securities. In consequence Char Ltd has carried out a number of capital transactions:

1 March 2009: – sold its leasehold interest in Watt Hall for £656,000.

               – purchased shares in Blowemup plc for £300,000, and £440,000 5% Funding Stock 2015 for £300,000.

1 June 2009:   – sold the freehold in its only remaining property, Place House, for £185,000.
               – purchased shares in Ultracool plc for £240,000.

Fizzle Ltd

Due to poor trading conditions Fizzle Ltd sold its biggest trade freehold property, Electric House, for £800,000 on 16 May 2009. Another freehold building, Rumble House, was purchased on 22 December 2009 for £200,000, and was immediately brought into use for the company's trade.

No more purchases or sales of properties held for the use of any trade are anticipated in the foreseeable future.

Results for the year ended 31 March 2009 and 2010

Before taking into account the above transactions, the results for the group were as follows:

	Year ended 31 March 2009 £'000	Year ended 31 March 2010 £'000
Spark Ltd:		
Trading profits/(losses)	172.5	(120)
Burn Ltd:		
Trading profits	25	55
Char Ltd:		
Property business income	97.5	10
Interest income	–	22
Dividend received (including tax credit)	–	30
Fizzle Ltd:		
Trading (losses)/profits	(260)	97.5

Burn Ltd has trading losses brought forward at 1 April 2008 of £75,000. In the year ended 31 March 2008 no company in the group had a corporation tax liability in excess of the small companies' rate.

An extract from an email from your manager is set out below.

Please prepare notes for my next meeting with Joan Thompson incorporating the following:

1 Discuss the available reliefs that are available to keep the corporation tax liabilities of the group to a minimum for the two years shown.

Mention any other matters you consider relevant.

Give your reasons for accepting or rejecting any possible reliefs.

2 In the light of your conclusions, calculate the corporation tax payable by each company for the years ended 31 March 2009 and 2010.

You can ignore the effect of capital allowances.

When you come to calculate the gain on the sale of the leasehold property you will need the following percentages from the lease percentage table:

16 years: 64.116%
25 years: 81.100%

Tax manager

You have extracted the following further information from client files.

- Burn Ltd, Char Ltd and Fizzle Ltd are 100% subsidiaries of Spark Ltd.
- All Spark Ltd group companies make up accounts to 31 March each year.
- Burn Ltd is a property dealing and development company which holds no property by way of investment. It was incorporated in June 2001 and had acquired The Hutch for £180,000 on 1 June 2008.
- Char Ltd is an investment company that was incorporated in September 1992. It had purchased Watt Hall on 1 March 2000 for £400,000 when the lease had exactly 25 years to run, and had purchased Place House on 25 April 1999 for £120,000.
- Fizzle Ltd was incorporated on 1 April 2007 and trades as a retail grocer in the north of England. Electric House had been transferred to it from Spark Ltd for its open market value of £850,000 on 1 May 2008. Spark Ltd had purchased Electric House for £325,000 in November 2001.

Required

Prepare the notes requested by your manager. Marks are available as follows.

(a) Discussing the available reliefs to reduce to a minimum the corporation tax liabilities of the group for the two years shown. **(16 marks)**

(b) Discussing any other relevant matters. **(4 marks)**

(c) Reasons for accepting or rejecting any possible reliefs. **(5 marks)**

(d) Computing the corporation tax payable by each company for the years ended 31 March 2008 and 2009. **(5 marks)**

You should assume the following indexed rises.

April 1999 to June 2009   56.6%
March 2000 to March 2009   50.6%
November 2001 to May 2008   36.0%
May 2008 to May 2009   2.2%

You may assume that the rates and allowances for the tax year 2008/09 and Financial Year 2008 continue to apply for the foreseeable future.

(Total = 30 marks)

Question 2

Your manager has had a meeting with Tim Topper, son of your recently deceased client, Leo Topper, and has sent you a copy of the following meeting notes via email.

To	The files
From	Tax manager
Date	1 November 2009
Subject	Leo Topper

Tim Topper (TT) provided the following information following his father, Leo's, death.

Leo Topper (LT)

- Died suddenly aged 54 on 15 June 2009.

- Was managing director of VDV Ltd, a company transferring films from VHS to DVD, earning over £200,000 a year. TT has now been appointed managing director of VDV Ltd.

- Had also carried on a sole trader film making business since July 2001, which he sold shortly before his death. Details are at Appendix A.

LT's estate

- Apart from a legacy of £100,000 to charity, all his assets were left to TT, his only son, who is also his executor.
- Values of assets held at death are at Appendix B.

Tim Topper (TT)

- Sold 17 of the 47 antiques from Leo's estate (Appendix B) and added the remaining 30 items to his own collection. The 17 items were sold for £72,000, one item being sold for £6,750, the other 14 for under £6,000 each.

- Also sold three items from his own collection for £4,500 each.

VDV Ltd

- TT will ask the company accountant to provide this office with a copy of the profit and loss account for the year ended 31 December 2009.

- Plans to purchase 90% of the issued share capital of MD Ltd, a company with unrelieved trading and capital losses brought forward and currently trading at a loss.

- VDV Ltd joined the annual accounting scheme for VAT in 2002 when its turnover was lower than at present. It has made monthly interim payments of £9,000 for the year ended 31 December 2009 on the due dates.

Tax manager

Appendix A – Film making business

	£
Freehold property purchased on 1 July 2001 – cost	110,000
Adjusted profit for year ended 30 June 2002	24,000
(Profits increased steadily until 2007)	
Adjusted profit for year ended 30 June 2008	52,000
Adjusted profit for period ended 31 May 2009	46,000
Freehold property disposed of on 1 June 2009 – proceeds	300,000

Appendix B – LT's death estate – probate values

	£
50,000 shares in VDV Ltd (25% of issued share capital)	500,000
10,000 shares in Film plc, a listed company (0.01% of issued share capital)	25,000
Bank account containing proceeds of sale of property used in business	300,000
Shares in an ISA	17,000
Antiques (each item under £6,000)	175,000
Freehold cottage – LT's principal private residence	437,500
Private motor car	23,500
Loan owing to Westland Bank	(150,000)

An extract from the email from your manager is set out below.

Please prepare a letter from me to Tim Topper, setting out the following:

1   Calculations to show how much IHT is due on LT's estate. TT will also need to know his administrative responsibilities.

2   Explanations of LT's income and capital gains tax liabilities in the two years before his death.

3   The criteria to be considered in deciding on the tax treatment of TT's disposals of the antiques.

4   The projected VAT and corporation tax liabilities for VDV Ltd for the year ended 31 December 2009. TT is also concerned about the tax consequences and opportunities arising to VDV Ltd following the purchase of the shares of MD Ltd.

You have extracted the following further information from client files.

- LT's only lifetime gift was a cash transfer in May 2002 to a discretionary trust. The trustees paid IHT of £49,000. The gross chargeable amount of the gift was £485,000.
- VDV Ltd operates from a factory bought new in 2000 for £300,000 excluding land. Capital allowances on plant have been calculated to be £15,900.
- VDV Ltd is VAT registered. All its sales are standard-rated.

VDV Ltd's company accountant sends a copy of the projected profit and loss account for the year ended 31 December 2009 which shows the following information.

VDV Ltd
Profit and loss account – year ended 31 December 2009

	Notes	£	£
Sales	(1)		1,420,000
Cost of sales (videos and DVDs)			(800,000)
			620,000
Wages		210,000	
Electricity		16,000	
Entertaining of clients		7,000	
Depreciation of equipment	(2)	57,000	
			(290,000)
Operating profit			330,000
Rental income	(3)		30,000
Profit for the year			360,000

Notes to the accounts

(1)   All figures are shown exclusive of VAT unless non-reclaimable.

(2)   Rental income is in respect of an unused office and comprises the following.

	£	£
Rent receivable – including £3,000 owing at 31 December 2009		42,000
Business rates	5,000	
Management costs	1,800	
New air-conditioning unit (May 2008)	5,200	
		(12,000)
Net rental income		30,000

Required

Prepare the letter for Tim in respect of his various tax queries. The letter should be in four sections, addressing the four sets of issues set out below, and should, where appropriate, include supporting calculations.

(a)   Inheritance tax on Leo Topper's estate

Advise Tim how much IHT will be due Leo's death.

You should state the due dates of payment and submission of the IHT account and the person liable. Ignore any other taxes owing at death.   **(8 marks)**

(b)   Leo's income tax and CGT position

Show Leo's income tax liability arising in respect of the final year of the film making business.

Explain, with supporting calculations, the tax arising from the disposal by Leo of the freehold property used in the film making business, assuming Leo has made no other disposal in 2009/10.

Advise how these liabilities would impact your answer to (a) above.   **(5 marks)**

(c)   Disposals of antiques

State the criteria to be considered in deciding on the tax treatment of Tim's disposals of antiques.

For both of the two possible tax treatments identify the taxes which could be payable by Tim.   **(6 marks)**

(d)   VDV Ltd

State the VAT payable by VDV Ltd in respect of the year ended 31 December 2009 along with the due date of payment and submission of the return, and comment briefly on the VAT position for the following year. Ignore VAT on the rental activities.   **(4 marks)**

Compute the corporation tax payable by VDV Ltd for the year ended 31 December 2009.   **(3 marks)**

State the taxation consequences and opportunities arising to VDV Ltd following the purchase of the shares of MD Ltd.   **(6 marks)**

Appropriateness of the format and presentation of the notes and the effectiveness with which the information is communicated.   **(2 marks)**

You may assume that the rates and allowances for the tax year 2008/09 and Financial Year 2008 continue to apply for the foreseeable future.

                                                                        (Total = 34 marks)

SECTION B: TWO questions ONLY to be attempted

Question 3

For the purposes of this question you should assume that today's date is 1 March 2008.

Nui Neu is to commence in business on 6 April 2008 running a retail shop. She is unsure whether to run the new business as a sole trader or as a limited company.

The following information has been extracted from client files and from meetings with Nui.

Nui:

- Is not married.
- Has no other sources of income for 2008/09.
- Has a personal pension.

If she runs the retail shop as a sole trader:

- The tax adjusted trading profit for the year ended 5 April 2009 is expected to be £30,000.
- Nui will withdraw £25,000 of this profit as drawings.

If she runs the retail shop through a limited company:

- The company will make up accounts to 5 April.
- The company's trading profit for the year ended 5 April 2009 is also expected to be £30,000.
- This figure is before taking account of director's remuneration and employer's Class 1 national insurance contributions.
- Nui will personally withdraw £25,000 of the company's profits.

Nui's proposed extraction of profits from the company:

- This might be as gross director's remuneration of £25,000.
- Alternatively Nui might take net dividends of £25,000.

Required

(a)   Explain to Nui the income tax, national insurance and corporation tax implications if she runs her business:

   (i)   as a sole trader
   (ii)   as a limited company and she withdraws gross director's remuneration of £25,000, and
   (iii)   as a limited company and withdraws net dividends of £25,000.

   You should provide calculations in support of your explanations, stating the net spendable income available to Nui for each option.

   You should assume that the corporation tax rates and limits for the Financial Year 2009 are the same as those for the Financial Year 2008.   **(14 marks)**

(b)   Based on your calculations, advise Nui whether it will be beneficial to run her business as a sole trader or whether she should run it as a limited company. In your conclusion, suggest one other simple remuneration planning strategy that will increase Nui's net spendable income.   **(4 marks)**

(Total = 18 marks)

Question 4

Jimmy Generous is a wealthy individual aged 57, in good health and married to Jane, aged 54 and also in good health. The couple have two children, Jack, aged 34 and Jill, aged 37, who both have children of their own. You should assume that today's date is 4 June 2009.

The following information has been extracted from client files and from meetings with the shareholders.

Jimmy:

- Currently owns 60% of the issued chare capital of JG Limited, a UK resident trading company (see below).
- Works as a part-time director of JG Limited.
- Receives gross annual salary of £22,500.
- Contributed £3,750 to JG Limited's registered occupational pension scheme.
- Received £45,000 net dividend income from JG Limited.
- Received £8,000 net building society interest.
- Subscribed £20,000 for 20,000 £1 ordinary shares in Pail Ltd, a small unquoted trading company.
- Paid £1,000 of interest on a loan of £20,000 that he took out to pay for the shares in Pail Ltd.
- Has no other income or outgoings in 2008/09.

JG Ltd:

- Set up by Jimmy in 1983.
- Remaining shares are held 20% by his daughter Jill and 20% by unconnected third parties.
- The company has been very successful in recent years.

Lifetime gifts:

- Jimmy agreed that he would pay any Inheritance Tax arising on these gifts.

- *4 June 2001* £303,000 cash gift to a discretionary trust created for the benefit of his grandchildren.

- *4 March 2003* 20% of the shares in JG Limited to his daughter Jill. At this time the JG Limited shares were valued as follows:

Shareholding	Value
	£
20%	100,000
60%	450,000
80%	600,000
100%	800,000

- *4 June 2007* A further £100,000 cash gift to the discretionary trust created on 4 June 2001.

Required

(a) Discuss the tax reliefs available for the purchase of shares in Pail Ltd and for the interest on the share purchase loan. **(4 marks)**

(b) Assuming that he obtains the most beneficial relief under part (a) calculate Jimmy's 2008/09 income tax and national insurance contribution liabilities. **(7 marks)**

(c) Explain the Inheritance Tax implications arising from the gifts made between 4 June 2001 and 4 June 2007. Your answer should include a calculation of any Inheritance Tax payable and an explanation of any exceptions or reliefs available. You are not required to consider the implications for the trustees of the discretionary trust.

You should assume that the rates and allowances for 2008/09 apply throughout this part of the question. **(7 marks)**

(Total = 18 marks)

Question 5

Your client, Mr Royle, is considering acquiring the business of a local company.

The following information has been extracted from client files and from meetings with Mr Royle.

Mr Royle

- Made redundant by his employer last year.
- Received a large cash payment.
- Will use this cash to buy the business.
- Considering either buying the assets of the company or buying the whole of the shares in the company.

The company

- Has previously been profitable.
- Owns various items of machinery and a factory.
- Has made losses in the last two years due to the ill-health of the managing director.

Managing director

- Is also the majority shareholder.

Mr Royle is confident that he can turn the business around and make it profitable again.

Required

Write a letter to Mr Royle outlining the advantages and disadvantages of buying:

(a)	the assets of the business; or	**(8 marks)**
(b)	the shares in the company.	**(10 marks)**
	Your answer should consider all relevant taxes.	**(Total = 18 marks)**

Answers

DO NOT TURN THIS PAGE UNTIL YOU HAVE
COMPLETED THE MOCK EXAM

A plan of attack

What's the worst thing you could be doing right now if this was the actual exam paper? Sharpening your pencil? Wondering how to celebrate the end of the exam in about three hours time? Panicking, flapping and generally getting in a right old state?

Well, they're all pretty bad, so turn back to the paper and let's sort out a **plan of attack**!

First things first

You have fifteen minutes reading time. Make sure you spend it wisely, looking through the paper in detail working out which optional questions to do and the order in which to attack the questions. You've got **two options**. Option 1 is the option recommended by BPP.

Option 1 (if you're thinking 'Help!')

If you're a bit worried about the paper, do the questions in the order of how well you think you can answer them. If you find the questions in Section B less daunting than the compulsory questions in Section A start with Section B. Remember you only need to do two of the three questions in Section B; you may find it easier if you start by deciding which question you will not do and put a line through it.

- **Question 3** compares trading as a sole trader or through a company. It was reasonably straightforward but involved a lot of computations for the marks.
- **Question 4** tests EIS relief, income tax and capital gains tax and inheritance tax on lifetime gifts. You needed to be able to make a good attempt on all parts.
- **Question 5** compares buying a trade via assets or shares. A good question if you know the technical aspects because it did not involve lengthy computations.

Do not spend longer than the allocated time on Section B. When you've spent the allocated time on **two** of the three questions in Section B turn to the longer questions in Section A. Read these questions through thoroughly before you launch into them. Once you start make sure you allocate your time to the parts within the questions according to the marks available and that, where possible, you attempt the easy marks first.

Lastly, what you mustn't forget is that you have to **answer both questions in Section A and TWO in Section B**. Do not miss out more than one question in Section B and do not waste time answering three questions in Section B or you will seriously affect your chance of passing the exam.

Option 2 (if you're thinking 'It's a doddle')

It never pays to be overconfident but if you're not quaking in your shoes about the exam then **turn straight to the compulsory questions** in Section A.

Once you've done these questions, move to Section B.

- The question you attempt first really depends on what you are most confident at.
- You then have to select one of the two remaining questions. If you are undecided look at the requirements. It maybe easier to obtain more marks if these are broken down into several smaller parts.

No matter how many times we remind you....

Always, always **allocate your time** according to the marks for the question in total and then according to the parts of the question. And **always, always follow the requirements** exactly. Question 3 part (a), for example, asks you to prepare calculations of the net spendable income for Nui, so you must calculate this, not just the tax liabilities.

You've got spare time at the end of the exam.....?

If you have allocated your time properly then you **shouldn't have time on your hands** at the end of the exam. But if you find yourself with five or ten minutes to spare, check over your work to make sure that there are no silly arithmetical errors.

Forget about it!

And don't worry if you found the paper difficult. More than likely other candidates will too. If this were the real thing you would need to **forget** the exam the minute you leave the exam hall and **think about the next one**. Or, if it's the last one, **celebrate**!

Question 1

Text references. The calculation of PCTCT and the corporation tax computation are in Chapters 20 to 22. Losses are in Chapter 24. Gains are covered in Chapter 21. Corporate groups are in Chapter 26. VAT is in Chapters 28 and 29.

Top tips. The key here is to deal with the property transactions and establish the PCTCT for each company for each year. Burn Ltd's loss brought forward should be dealt with first, before considering Fizzle's loss and making an initial conclusion on the best available relief. Finally, consider Spark's loss bearing in mind the use of Fizzle's loss.

Easy marks. This is a tough question and there are no easy marks as such. You really need to think about the loss relief rules and how they apply within a group and be methodical when writing your answer.

Marking scheme

				Marks
(a)	Burn Ltd's brought forward losses		1	
	Options for Fizzle Ltd's loss	Max	4	
	Conclusion		1	
	Options for Spark Ltd's loss	Max	4	
	Conclusion		1	
	Spark Ltd purchase of The Hutch		1	
	Spark Ltd transfer of Electric House		1	
	Burn Ltd's transfer of The Hutch		1	
	Char Ltd sale of Watt Hall lease		1	
	Char Ltd sale of Place House		1	
	Fizzle Ltd sale of Electric House		2	
	No rollover available due to proceeds not reinvested		1	
		Max		16
(b)	*Other matters*			
	Claim requirements		1	
	Order of relief		1	
	Availability of rollover relief		1	
	VAT aspects		1	
				4
(c)	Rejecting/accepting loss relief claims			5
(d)	*Corporation tax computations*			
	Spark Ltd		1½	
	Burn Ltd		1	
	Char Ltd		1½	
	Fizzle Ltd		1½	
		Max		5
				30

Notes for meeting

(a) **Available reliefs to reduce Spark Ltd group's corporation tax liability**

Burn Ltd's trading losses brought forward

- Must use these before any other available losses.

- Leaves no profit for y/e 31.3.09 and remaining loss of £30,000 (£75,000 – £(25,000 + 20,000 (W2)) to carry forward.

- Burn Ltd's profit y/e 31.3.10 of £55,000 (no profit arises on the transfer of The Hutch as the transfer takes place at no gain/ no loss) is reduced by the loss carried forward of £30,000 to £25,000. There is no other option for dealing with loss.

Fizzle Ltd's loss £260,000 for y/e 31.3.09

- Can be used in the following ways:

  (i)   Group relief to Spark Ltd: save tax @ 29.75% until profits reach £75,000, then 21% thereafter. Maximum loss used £172,500.

  (ii) Group relief to Burn Ltd: not an option as Burn will have used its loss b/fwd already.

  (iii) Group relief to Char Ltd: has profits of £97,500 and a gain of approximately £179,800 (W2), a total of £277,300. Loss will save tax @ 29.75% until profits reach £75,000 (ie on £202,300) then @ 21% on remainder. Max loss to use: £260,000.

  (iv) Combination of (i) & (iii)

        ie use loss to bring Spark Ltd profits down to £75,000, by using £97,500 of loss, then group relief to Char Ltd remaining loss of £162,500. This has advantage of saving tax @ 29.75% on entire loss in current year.

  (v)   Bring Char Ltd profits to £75,000 first, then group relief remaining loss to Spark Ltd – same effect as in (iv) above, leaving Spark Ltd with profit of £114,800 (W3).

  (vi) Carry back loss (no current year profits) in Fizzle Ltd to year ended 31.3.08. Relief obtained earlier than (i)-(v) above but maximum relief 20%. Interest will be paid on any corporation tax repaid. Rejected due to low rate of relief and insufficient profits to absorb loss.

  (vii) Carry loss forward against Fizzle Ltd's trading profit for year 31.3.10 – save tax at 29.75% on £97,500 (no relief available against gain of £348,300 in that year). Rejected as it delays relief.

On balance options (iv) and (v) offer best combination of earliest relief and highest tax savings. Of these, option (v) will be best in view of treatment of Spark Ltd's loss (see below).

Spark Ltd's loss of £120,000 for y/e 31.3.10

- Can be used in the following ways:

  (i)   Carry back to y/e 31.3.09 (no profits in y/e 31.3.10). Saves tax @ 29.75% until profits reach £75,000, saving 21% thereafter. This will interact with option (v) above. Spark would have remaining profits of £114,800 (W3), so that 29.75% tax is saved on losses up to £39,800 (£114,800 – £75,000), leaving £75,000 losses attracting relief at 21%, and £5,200 losses to be relieved elsewhere.

  (ii) Group relief to Burn Ltd:

        Burn Ltd has profits of £25,000 remaining in y/e 31.3.10 (see above). Relief would only be 21% and is therefore rejected as better relief could be obtained elsewhere.

  (iii) Group relief to Char Ltd

        Char Ltd is now a close investment holding company (probably since 1.3.09 when it ceased to invest wholly or mainly in land and building) and will pay tax on its profits at the full rate of 28%. For y/e 31.3.10, it could utilise loss of £32,000 to save tax @ 28%. This is rejected to minimise tax liabilities.

(iv)   Group relief to Fizzle Ltd

Fizzle Ltd has profits of £445,800 (£97,500 + £348,300 (W2)) and so relief would be initially at 28%. This would apply for losses of up to £70,800 (£445,800 - £375,000). Thereafter, relief would be at 29.75%.

(v)   Carry forward the loss against Spark Ltd's future trading profits This is rejected as there is no indication of the level of those profits, while also delaying possible relief.

Conclusion

- Take option (v) for Fizzle Ltd's loss for y/e 31.3.09 discussed above.

- Group relief £80,200 of Spark Ltd's loss to Fizzle Ltd to save tax at 28/29.75%, then carry back the remaining loss of £39,800 against Spark Ltd's profit for y/e 31.3.09 to bring that profit down to £75,000, saving tax @ 29.75% with the bonus of interest on repaid corporation tax. This gives the best combination of early relief and maximum tax saving.

Other matters

- Group relief requires a written claim within two years of the end of the claimant company's accounting period. Carry back of losses requires a written claim within two years of the end of loss-making period.

- Some of the capital gains may be rolled over if reinvestment into qualifying assets is made within three years of the relevant disposals. There is still time left to do this and it would obviously change the planning discussed above. Note that reinvestment could be undertaken by any of the group companies as long as the asset is used for business purposes, which seems to exclude Char Ltd.

- Technically the group relief claim should be made before the carry back claim to restrict the loss to be carried back. But in practice HMRC will accept a simultaneous claim.

- Sale of commercial buildings under three years old is a standard-rated supply. Any other sale is exempt unless any of the companies has waived exemption in which case 17½% VAT would have to be added to the sale price. If a group registration exists, the transfer of property between group companies within the registration will be outside the scope of VAT.

(b)   **Corporation tax computation**

Spark Ltd
y/e 31.3.09

	£
Trading profit	172,500
s.393A loss c/back	(39,800)
Group relief (W3)	(57,700)
PCTCT	75,000
Tax @ 21% =	15,750

y/e 31.3.10
CT = Nil

Burn Ltd

y/e 31.3.09

CT = Nil

y/e 31.3.10

Trading profit = £25,000 (see part (a))

Tax @ 21% = £5,250

Char Ltd

	£
y/e 31.3.09	
Property business income	97,500
Gains	179,800
	277,300
Group relief (W3)	(202,300)
PCTCT	75,000
Tax @ 21% =	£15,750
y/e 31.3.10	
Property business income	10,000
Interest income	22,000
PCTCT	32,000

	£
Tax @ 28% (CIC)	8,960

Fizzle Ltd

y/e 31.3.09

CT = <u>Nil</u>

	£
y/e 31.3.10	
Trading profit	97,500
Gains (W2)	348,300
	445,800
Group relief	(80,200)
PCTCT	365,600
Tax @ 28%	102,368
Less: marginal relief	
$7/400 \times £[375,000 - 365,600]$	(165)
CT payable	102,203

Workings

(1) *Group structure*

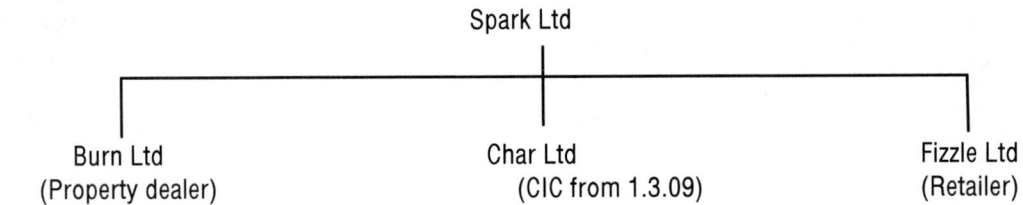

FY 08 and FY 09

$$UL = \frac{1,500}{4} = 375,000$$

$$LL = \frac{300}{4} = 75,000$$

(2) *Property transactions*

Spark Ltd

y/e 31.3.10

- Purchased building 'The Hutch' from Burn Ltd 19.4.09 – deemed cost £200,000 (see below).

y/e 31.3.09

- Transfer of building 'Electric House' to Fizzle Ltd (1.5.08) (no gain/no loss rules automatically apply)

Burn Ltd:

Sale of 'The Hutch' to Spark Ltd

- The Hutch was held as trading stock and is treated as appropriated to fixed assets immediately before the transfer at its market value of £200,000. This leads to additional trading profit of £20,000. The transfer to Spark Ltd is a no gain/no loss transfer.

Char Ltd

- Investment company – no rollover relief

y/e 31.3.09

Sale of lease on Watt Hall

	£
Proceeds	656,000
Cost	
$400,000 \times \dfrac{64.116\,(\%16)}{81.100\,(\%25)}$	(316,232)
	339,768
Indexation	
$50.6\% \times £316,232$	(160,013)
Gain	179,755

(say £179,800)

Question 2

Text references. Chapters 16 to 18 deal with IHT. Trading income is in Chapter 6 with IBAs in Chapter 7. The basic rules for gains are in Chapter 11. VAT is in Chapter 28. Corporation tax is in Chapters 20 to 22 with groups in Chapter 26.

Top tips. It is unlikely that you will get so many computations in one question in the exam. Use this question to make sure that you can perform straightforward calculations quickly and efficiently using standard proformas, feeding your results into your written answer.

Easy marks. Set up your letter to obtain the easy presentation mark. For part (b) be sure to discuss how your answer impacts part (a).

Marking scheme

			Marks
(a)	Lifetime gift		
	Valuation of death estate	½	
	Availability of BPR	3	
	Debt	½	
	Exempt legacy	½	
	Nil band	½	
	Tax rate	½	
	Tax due date	1	
	Person liable	½	
	Return due date	1	
			8

(b) *Income tax*

Cessation rules	1	
Overlap (opening year rules)	1	
Higher rate taxpayer	½	
CGT		
Gain	½	
Annual exemption	½	
CGT @ 18%	½	
Impact on IHT liability	1	
		5

(c) ½ mark for each criterion and explanation (max) 3

Taxation if capital disposal		
CGT	½	
Chattels rules	1	
Taxation if trading income		
Income tax	½	
NIC	½	
VAT	1	
Max		6

(d) *VAT*

Supplies	½	
Video tapes	½	
Electricity	½	
Wages	½	
Entertaining	½	
VAT due – annual accounting	1	
y/e 31 December 2009	1	
Max		4

Corporation tax

Adjustment of profits	1	
IBAs	1	
Property business income	1	
CAs on property business equipment	1	
Corporation tax	1	
Max		3

Implications for purchase of shares

Associates	1	
CT groups and implications	2	
Current year losses	1	
Brought forward losses	2	
Capital losses	1	
Group VAT registration	1	
Max		6
Format/ presentation		2
		34

[Our address]

[Your address]

[Date]

Dear Tim

TAX ISSUES

This letter deals with the tax position for your father and his estate, as well as tax issues arising for VDV Ltd.

(a)   **Inheritance tax on your father's estate**

The IHT arising on your father's estate on death will be £291,200 (see Appendix 1).

You will note that Business Property Relief (BPR) is not available for the quoted company shares, as your father did not have a controlling interest in the company. Nor is BPR available for the cash proceeds received from the sale of his business. The relief is only available if the business had been owned at the date of death and there was no binding contract for sale.

The tax must be paid by you, as the Executor of the estate, by 31 December 2009 to avoid interest running from this date until the actual date of payment. You have until 30 June 2010 to submit the IHT account.

You will need to declare the lifetime gift to the discretionary trust on the IHT return, but any additional IHT that may be due is the responsibility of the trustees.

(b)   **Your father's income tax and CGT position**

Your father's earnings from his directorship with VDV Ltd make him a higher rate tax payer.

His income tax liability for the year of his death is £11,200 and his CGT liability is £17,272.

See Appendix 2 for our calculation of these figures.

These may both be deducted from your father's estate, so reducing the IHT liability by £11,389 ((£11,200 + £17,272) @ 40%)

(c)   **Your disposals of antique furniture**

HMRC look at several criteria to decide whether proceeds from the disposals should be treated as capital proceeds (and therefore assessed to capital gains tax) or trading receipts (assessed to income tax).

The criteria relevant to you are as follows.

Factors to consider	Indicative of a capital gain or trading income?
Profit motive	The profit motive is not clear. You inherited the items, some of which you did not wish to add to your own personal collection. As you did not purchase them with the intention of selling them at a profit this could be treated as not trading. However, you also sold three of your own items for a profit. A profit motive would indicate trade.
Subject matter	Antiques are normally acquired for personal pleasure or for their investment potential, which is not indicative of trading.
Length of ownership	You did not own the antiques for long as the disposal was shortly after you acquired/inherited them. If assets are only held for a short period, this suggests a trading profit. However, they were bought by your father and inherited (not bought) by you.
Frequency of transactions	Isolated transactions would be treated as a capital gain. However, more than one similar transaction (as in this case) could be indicative of trading.
Supplementary work	No supplementary work is carried out. This suggests a capital disposal, not a trading activity.
Reason for sale	As an unwanted legacy, the disposal appears to be a result of a personal choice between items. This does not suggest a trading activity.

Overall, it is likely that these transactions will be treated as capital disposals. This is mainly because:

*   You are not personally involved in the antiques trade, and
*   The acquisition of the personal assets was a result of a legacy (not a purchase by you with a view to profit).

If the sales are treated as capital disposals:

- CGT will be due if the proceeds exceed the probate value (MV at date of death)
- Chattels costing and sold for under £6,000 are exempt. Chattels sold for ≥ £6,000 would be chargeable but a restriction (5/3rds rule) would apply.

If instead they are treated as trading income:

- The excess of proceeds over probate value will be liable to income tax. No chargeable gains arise on the disposal of the assets as they are treated as trading stock.
- If the profit exceeds the lower limits, Class 2 and Class 4 National Insurance contributions would be payable.
- As the turnover exceeds £67,000, the business might need to register for, and charge, VAT.

(d) (i) **VDV Ltd VAT payable – y/e 31 December 2009 (ignoring VAT on rental activity)**

The projected VAT due for the year ended 31 December 2009 is £105,700 (Appendix 3).

As VDV Ltd is registered under the annual accounting system, the due dates for payment are as follows:

	£
Interim monthly payments	
30 April 2009 to 31 December 2009 (inclusive) (9 × £9,000 (given))	81,000
Final payment – 28 February 2010	24,700
	105,700

The VAT return must be submitted by 28 February 2010.

VAT position for year ended 31 December 2010

VDV Ltd's taxable turnover (£1,420,000) currently exceeds the limit for joining the annual accounting scheme (£1,350,000) but falls below the limit where withdrawal from the scheme is required (£1,600,000).

As a result VDV Ltd can remain within the scheme and will pay nine monthly interim payments of £10,570 (£105,700 ÷ 10) starting on 30 April 2009.

(ii) **Corporation tax – y/e 31 December 2009**

The projected corporation tax payable by VDV Ltd for the year ended 31 December 2009 is £92,414 (see Appendix 3).

(ii) **Purchase of an 85% interest in the shares of MD Ltd**

Taxation consequences

Associated companies

VDV Ltd will have an associated company. The limits for determining the rate of corporation tax payable by each company must be halved.

This could increase the rate of tax payable by VDV Ltd. (MD Ltd is currently loss-making and therefore unlikely to be paying corporation tax.)

Group definition – Capital gains group and group relief group

As MD Ltd will be a 75% subsidiary, both companies form a group for capital gains and group relief purposes.

Opportunities for use of trading and capital losses

Current year trading losses in MD Ltd

Group relief claims are possible between the companies in any direction, but for current year trading losses only. Brought forward trading losses cannot be group relieved.

Brought forward trading losses in MD Ltd

MD Ltd's brought forward trading losses can only be carried forward and utilised in that company. However, it is important to remember that where there is a major change in the nature or conduct of trade in the following three years, the use of these losses is denied.

Therefore care should be taken to avoid a major change in the nature or conduct of trade of MD Ltd.

Capital losses in MD Ltd

Capital losses brought forward in MD Ltd cannot be group relieved/transferred to VDV Ltd. They can only be utilised by MD Ltd against future capital gains.

Furthermore, the use of these 'pre-entry capital losses' is restricted in the future. These losses cannot be matched against gains realised on assets transferred to MD Ltd intra-group at nil gain/nil loss.

Other opportunities

Capital gains privileges available

- Intra-group transfers at nil gain/nil loss possible.
- Group rollover relief claims possible.
- Minimisation of group corporation tax by electing for gains to crystallise in the company paying the lowest marginal rate of tax, and use of post-acquisition capital losses as soon as possible.

Group VAT registration possible

Both companies can form a VAT group and submit one group VAT return, which saves on administration and allows companies to ignore accounting for VAT on any inter-group transactions.

If you have any further queries or would like to discuss the above further, please do not hesitate to contact me.

Yours sincerely

Tax manager

Appendix 1 – Inheritance tax liabilities

Gift to discretionary trust – May 2002

	£
Gross chargeable amount (given)	485,000

Uses nil rate band

Note. You were asked to calculate the IHT due on LT's estate, not the additional IHT (if any) due from the trustees of the discretionary trust.

Death estate

	£	£
VDV Ltd shares	500,000	
Less BPR (100%)	(500,000)	
		Nil
Film plc shares		25,000
Bank account		300,000
Shares in an ISA		17,000
Antiques		175,000
Cottage		437,500
Motor car		23,500
		978,000
Less debts – loan to bank		(150,000)
		828,000
Less exempt legacies – charity		(100,000)
Gross chargeable estate		728,000
IHT on estate at death (£728,000 × 40%)		291,200

(No nil rate band available).

Appendix 2 – income tax and CGT liabilities 2008/09

Trading income

	£
2008/09 year of cessation	
1 July 2007 – 31 May 2008	46,000
Less overlap profits (W)	(18,000)
	28,000
Tax @ 40% (higher rate taxpayer)	£11,200

Disposal of freehold property

	£
Sale proceeds (June 2008)	300,000
Cost (July 2000)	(110,000)
Gain	190,000
Less entrepreneurs' relief (4/9 × £190,000)	(84,444)
Less annual exemption	(9,600)
Taxable gain	95,956
CGT £95,956 × 18%	£17,272

Working

Overlap profits

		£
2000/01	Opening year – actual profits	
	1 July 2000 – 5 April 2001	
	($^9/_{12}$ × £24,000)	18,000
2001/02	Second year – 12 months ending in the tax year	
	y/e 30 June 2001	24,000
Overlap profits	(1 July 2000 – 5 April 2001)	18,000

Appendix 3 – VDV Ltd tax liabilities year ended 31 December 2009

VAT payable

	£
VAT on outputs	
Standard-rated supplies (£1,420,000 × 17½%)	248,500
VAT on inputs	
Purchases of videos and DVDs (£800,000 × 17½%)	(140,000)
Wages (Note 1)	Nil
Electricity (£16,000 × 17½%)	(2,800)
Entertaining customers (Note 2)	Nil
Depreciation (Note 3)	Nil
VAT payable for the year	105,700

Notes

1   Wages are outside the scope of VAT.

2   VAT incurred in respect of entertaining customers is not recoverable.

3   Depreciation is not a supply of goods or services for VAT purposes. VAT incurred on the purchase of equipment would have been recovered at the date the equipment was acquired.

Corporation tax payable

	£
Trading profit (W1)	369,100
Property business income (W3)	30,000
PCTCT	399,100

Corporation tax (W5)

	£
£399,100 × 28%	111,748
Less Marginal relief $^7/_{400}$ × (£1,500,000 – £399,100)	(19,266)
Corporation tax payable	92,482

Workings

(1) *Trading profit*

	£
Operating profit per accounts	330,000
Add Entertaining clients	7,000
Depreciation	57,000
	394,000
Less Capital allowances	
Plant and machinery (given)	(15,900)
Industrial building (W2)	(9,000)
Adjusted trading profit	369,100

(2) *Industrial buildings allowances*

A writing-down allowance (WDA) of 3% is available on the cost of the factory (excluding land) within its tax life.

WDA = £300,000 × 3%	£9,000

(3) *Property business income*

	£
Rental income per accounts (amounts receivable)	42,000
Less Allowable deductions	
Business rates	(5,000)
Management costs	(1,800)
Capital allowances (W4)	(5,200)
Property business income	30,000

(4) *Capital allowances – rental property*

	£
Air-conditioning unit	5,200
AIA	(5,200)
WDV c/f	–

(5) *Corporation tax rates*

FY 2008 and FY 2009

	£
PCTCT = Profits (as no dividends received)	399,100
Small companies – upper limit	1,500,000
– lower limit	300,000
	Marginal relief

Question 3

Marking scheme

		Marks	
(a)	**Sole trader**		
	Income tax liability	1	
	Class 2 NIC	1	
	Class 4 NIC	1	
	Net spendable income	1	
	Director's remuneration		
	Income tax liability	1	
	Employee's Class 1 NIC	1	
	Employer's Class 1 NIC	1	
	No corporation tax liability	1	
	Net spendable income	1	
	Dividends		
	No income tax payable	1	
	No employee's Class 1 NIC liability	1	
	Corporation tax liability	2	
	Net spendable income	1	
			14
(b)	Conclusion	2	
	Mix of dividends and salary	2	
			4
			18

(a) **Income tax, national insurance and corporation tax liabilities**

    (i) **Sole trader**

        If Nui operates the shop as a sole trader any drawings taken are irrelevant as a sole trader is taxed on the entire profits of the business. The whole of the £30,000 profits is therefore taxable on Nui as non-savings income. As a sole trader Nui will need to pay both Class 2 and Class 4 national insurance contributions.

        Her net spendable income would be £23,122 (see Appendix 1).

    (ii) **Company – salary £25,000**

        If Nui sets up a company to run the shop any salary paid to Nui will be taxable on her as non-savings income and there will also be Class 1 primary (Nui) and secondary (the company) NIC contributions due. The salary and secondary Class 1 NIC (but not the primary Class 1 NIC) are deductible expenses for the company for corporation tax purposes.

        Her net spendable income in this case would be £21,027 (see Appendix 1).

(iii) **Company – dividends £25,000**

If Nui sets up a company to run the shop and receives dividends she will be taxable on the gross dividend (ie net dividend × 100/90). As Nui is a basic rate taxpayer (she has no other taxable income) the dividends are taxed at 10% and come with a 10% tax credit, so there is no further income tax liability.

There are no NICs either for Nui or the company on the dividends. Her liability is therefore £nil. However, dividends are not deductible for the company and therefore the full profit is taxable in the hands of the company.

Her net spendable income in this case would be £23,700 (see Appendix 1).

(b) **Conclusion**

Based on the above calculations, it appears that running the business through a company, with Nui taking dividends, appears to be most beneficial as it results in more profits after tax and NIC and gives Nui more net cash in her hands.

However, Nui may wish to consider taking a combination of salary and dividends to further increase her net spendable income. A salary of £6,035 would use the personal allowance and would only be subject to a small amount of NIC. The balance of the profit could then be paid out as a dividend. The salary would also reduce the company's taxable profits.

Nui's net spendable income would therefore be £24,841 (see Appendix 2), which would give Nui an additional £1,141 (£24,841 – £23,700) of spendable income.

Appendix 1

	Non- savings
Sole trader:	
Income tax	£
Trading profit (N)	30,000
Less: Personal allowance	(6,035)
Taxable income	23,965
Tax	
£23,965 @ 20%	£4,793
Income tax payable	
National insurance contributions	£
Class 2 £2.30 × 52	120
Class 4 (£30,000 – £5,435) @ 8%	1,965
	2,085
Net spendable income	£
Profit	30,000
Less: Income tax and NIC (£4,793 + £2,085)	(6,878)
Net income	23,122

Company – salary £25,000	Non-savings
Income tax for Nui	£
Employment income	25,000
Less: Personal allowance	(6,035)
Taxable income	18,965
Tax	
£18,965 @ 20%	£3,793
Income tax payable	
NIC	
Class 1 primary (£25,000 – £5,435) @ 11%	£2,152

	£
Corporation tax	
Trading income	30,000
Less: salary	(25,000)
Less: employer's Class 1 NICs on salary (£25,000 – £5,435) @ 12.8%	(2,504)
PCTCT	2,496
Tax @ 21%	524

	£
Net spendable income:	
Profit	30,000
Less: Income tax and NIC (£3,793 + £2,152)	(5,945)
Employer's NIC	(2,504)
Corporation tax	(524)
Net income	21,027

Company – dividends £25,000

	Dividend/ Total income £
Income tax for Nui	
Dividend income × 100/90	27,778
Less: Personal allowance	(6,035)
Taxable income	21,743
Tax	
£21,743 @ 10%	2,174
Less: tax credit £21,743 @ 10%	(2,174)
Income tax	0

NIC – none

Trading income/PCTCT	£30,000
Tax @ 21%	£6,300

No employer's NIC

	£
Net spendable income:	
Profit	30,000
Less: Income tax and NIC	0
Employer's NIC	0
Corporation tax	(6,300)
Net income	23,700

Appendix 2

Company – salary £6,035, dividends £18,965

	Non-savings £	Dividends £
Income tax for Nui		
Employment income	6,035	
Dividend income × 100/90		21,072
Less: Personal allowance	(6,035)	
Taxable income	Nil	21,072

	£
Tax	
£21,072 @ 10%	2,107
Less: tax credit £21,972 @ 10%	(2,107)
Income tax	0

NIC

Class 1 Primary (£6,035 – £5,435) @ 11%	66

	£
Corporation tax	
Trading income	30,000
Less: salary	(6,035)
Less: employer's Class 1 NICs on salary (£6,035 – £5,435) @ 12.8%	(77)
PCTCT	23,888
Tax @ 21%	5,016

Net spendable income:	£
Profit	30,000
Less: Income tax and NIC	(66)
Employer's NIC	(77)
Corporation tax	(5,016)
Net income	24,841

Question 4

Text references. EIS is covered in Chapters 1 and 2, with the IT computation also in Chapter 1. NIC is in Chapter 4. IHT on lifetime gifts is dealt with in Chapter 16.

Top tips. Make a good effort at all parts of a multi-tax question like this one. Parts (a) and (b) are on income tax and national insurance and do not affect part (c) on capital taxes.

Easy marks. The income tax computation was very straightforward and the examiner made the IHT computations easier by using up the nil rate band with the first chargeable lifetime transfer.

Examiner's comments. (Part (a) has been amended).

Part (b) was reasonably well attempted by most candidates although a sizeable minority continue to make basic errors such as grossing up dividends at 20%. Also many muddled the relief for the contributions to the occupational pension scheme with the way relief is given for contributions paid into personal pension schemes. This sort of confusion really needs to be eliminated by the time of the examination.

Part (c) was again reasonably attempted by most candidates. Some, however, muddled chargeable lifetime transfers (CLTs) with potentially exempt transfers (PETs). Some thought that transfers to discretionary trusts were PETs while those to individuals were CLTs. Perhaps unsurprisingly, candidates making this kind of fundamental error scored very poorly with this question part. Other common errors included the omission of annual exemptions, the incorrect application of the loss to the donor principle and the failure to identify (and properly explain) the availability of business property relief where appropriate.

(c) *4 June 2001*

CLT	1
AEs	½
IHT	½
4 March 2003 – Jill	
Valuation	1½
BPR	1
4 June 2007	
Grossing	½
IHT	1
Death	1
	$\underline{7}$
	$\underline{18}$

(a) Jimmy may be able to obtain EIS income tax relief on the shares subscribed for. The relief is given as a tax reduction and is the lower of 20% × £20,000 = £4,000 and Jimmy's income tax liability.

For EIS relief to be available the following conditions must be satisfied:

(i) The shares must be subscribed for in cash

(ii) Jimmy must not be connected with Pail Ltd, ie broadly he must not own more than 30% (including holdings of associates ie spouse or child, but not a brother or sister) of the issued share capital

(iii) Pail Ltd must be unquoted and the funds raised must be used in carrying out a qualifying trade. At least 80% of the money raised by the EIS share issue must be so used within twelve months of the issue, and the remainder within a further twelve months (ie within twenty-four months).

(iv) The gross assets of the company must not exceed £7m prior to nor £8m after the investment.

If the shares are disposed of within three years the relief will be withdrawn.

If EIS relief is available, no relief is given for the interest paid on the share purchase loan. If EIS relief is not given, interest relief will be due if Pail Ltd is a close trading company and Jimmy holds a more than 5% interest in the share capital or works full time as a manager or director of the company.

(b) **Jimmy Generous – Income Tax 2008/09**

	Non-savings income £	Savings income £	Dividend income £	Total £
Salary	22,500			
Less: Pension	(3,750)			
Employment income	18,750			
BSI £8,000 × $^{100}/_{80}$		10,000		
Dividends £45,000 × $^{100}/_{90}$			50,000	
Net income	18,750	10,000	50,000	78,750
Less: Personal allowance	(6,035)			
Taxable income	12,715	10,000	50,000	72,715

Tax

	£
£12,715 × 20%	2,543
£10,000 × 20%	2,000
£12,085 × 10%	1,208
£37,915 × 32½%	12,322
	18,073
Less: EIS relief (£20,000 @ 20%)	(4,000)
Income tax liability	14,073

Jimmy Generous – Class 1 NICs 2008/09

$£(22,500 - 5,435) \times 11\%$ £1,877

Note. No deduction for pension contribution.

(c)   **Inheritance tax**

4 June 2001

Chargeable lifetime transfer

	£
Gift	303,000
Less: AE 2001/02	(3,000)
AE 2000/01 b/f	(3,000)
CLT	297,000

This is within the nil rate band of £312,000 (2008/09 rates used as standard in examination questions) so no lifetime IHT payable.

4 March 2003

Potentially exempt transfer

Note. On 4 June 2009 we are told Jimmy owned 60% of shares. Thus when he gives his daughter a 20% holding in March 2003 this means that prior to the gift he held 80% of the shares.

	£
Before 80% holding	600,000
After 60% holding	(450,000)
Loss to donor	150,000
Less: 100% BPR	(150,000)
PET	0

The value of the transfer is the loss to the donor, using the value of Jimmy's shareholding before and after the gift. BPR at 100% is available as this is a gift of unquoted trading company shares owed for at least two years. No IHT will be payable if Jimmy survives until 4 March 2010 or dies before that time and Jill still owns the shares (or certain replacement business property).

4 June 2007

Chargeable lifetime transfer

	£
Gift	100,000
Less: AE 2007/08	(3,000)
AE 2006/07 b/f	(3,000)
CLT	94,000

Nil rate band of $£(312,000 - 297,000) = £15,000$ available as reduced by transfer in previous seven years.

£15,000 @ 0%

$£79,000 \times {}^{20}/_{80} = £19,750$

The transfer must be grossed-up to find the loss to donor as Jimmy agrees to pay the IHT due (stated in question).

If Jimmy dies before 4 June 2014, additional tax may become payable by the trustees, subject to taper relief.

Question 5

Marking scheme

			Marks
(a)	Choose which assets	1	
	Capital allowances and IBAs	1	
	Consideration	1	
	No liabilities	1	
	No use of losses	1	
	VAT charge	1	
	TOGC relief	1	
	CGT base cost	1	
	SDLT	1	
	Max		8
(b)	Business carries on	1	
	Liabilities transferred	1	
	Capital allowances and IBAs	1	
	Losses used	1	
	Restriction on losses	2	
	Close company issues	2	
	CGT base cost	1	
	Stamp duty	1	
			10
			18

[Our address]

Mr J Royle

[Address]

[Date]

Dear Mr Royle

Purchase of business

Thank you for your enquiry about your proposed purchase. I will outline the advantages of either buying the assets of the business or shares in the company.

Purchase of assets

(a)   You will be able to choose which assets you wish to acquire, rather than the whole of the assets of the company.

(b)   You will be entitled to claim capital allowances on plant and machinery. Industrial buildings allowance may also be available on the factory.

(c)   It may be possible to maximise the use of capital allowances by allocating consideration to assets which attract more capital allowances, eg plant and machinery.

(d)   The liabilities of the company will not be passed to you.

(e)   One disadvantage is that you will not be able to utilise the existing losses of the company.

(f)   VAT may be chargeable on the assets acquired by you. If you cannot fully recover all the VAT paid on acquiring the assets, this may be unattractive.

There is a relief which provides that VAT is not chargeable on the transfer of a business as a going concern, but this may not be available if you only purchase some of the assets.

(g)   The base cost of each asset for CGT purposes will be the price paid for it.

(h)   Stamp duty land tax will be payable on any land and buildings, including the factory. The rate of tax depends on the price paid, but would be nil if it were less than £150,000, or 1% if between £150,000 and £250,000.

Purchase of shares

(a)   The business of the company will continue uninterrupted.

(b)   You will be taking over the liabilities of the company as well as the assets, albeit within the company not personally.

(c)   Capital allowances and industrial buildings allowance will be unaffected by the purchase.

(d)   It may be possible for the losses incurred by the company to be carried forward and used against profits in future years.

However, where there is a change in ownership of a company and a major change in the nature of the conduct of the company's trade occurs within three years, trading losses cannot be carried forward. This also applies where there is a change in ownership after the scale of activities has become small or negligible before it revives.

(e)   The company will be 'close' for corporation tax purposes as it is currently, and will continue to be, controlled by five or fewer participators or any number of directors.

If loans are made by the company to participators this will usually result in a penalty tax charge of 25% being due to HMRC. Any amounts written-off will be taxable on the participator as a distribution. Distributions are not deductible for corporation tax purposes.

Benefits provided to non-employee participators will also be taxed as distributions from the company.

(f)   The capital gains base cost of the assets in the company will be unaffected by the sale. Any gains on subsequent disposals will be taxable in the company. The base cost of the shares will be the price paid.

(h)   Stamp duty will be payable on the price of the shares purchased at the rate of 0.5%.

I hope this is helpful. I suggest we meet to discuss your proposed purchase further.

Yours sincerely,

Certified Accountant

ACCA Professional Paper P6 – Options Module

Advanced Taxation (UK)

Mock Examination 3 (December 2008 paper)

Question Paper	
Time allowed	**Reading and planning: 15 minutes** **Writing: 3 hours**
This paper is divided into two sections	
Section A	**BOTH questions are compulsory questions and MUST be attempted**
Section B	**TWO questions ONLY to be attempted**

During reading and planning time only the question paper may be annotated

DO NOT OPEN THIS PAPER UNTIL YOU ARE READY TO START UNDER EXAMINATION CONDITIONS

SECTION A: BOTH questions are compulsory and MUST be attempted

Question 1

You have received the following memorandum from your manager.

To	Tax senior
From	Tax manager
Date	27 November 2009
Subject	Maria Copenhagen and Nucleus Resources

I spoke to Maria Copenhagen this morning. We arranged to meet on Thursday 3 December to discuss the following matters.

Nucleus Resources

Maria is planning a major expansion of her business, Nucleus Resources. I attach a schedule, prepared by Maria, showing the budgeted income and expenditure of the business for a full year. Maria wants to know how much additional after tax income the expansion of the business will create depending on whether she employs the two additional employees or uses a sub-contractor, Quantum Ltd.

Quoted shares

In October 2007 Niels, Maria's husband, received a gift of shares with a value of £170,000 from his uncle. The shares are quoted on the Heisenbergia Stock Exchange. The uncle died in November 2009 and Maria wants to know whether there will be any UK inheritance tax in respect of the gift. The uncle had been living in the country of Heisenbergia since moving there from the UK in 1989 and had made substantial gifts to other close relatives in 2006 and 2007. Inheritance tax of £30,600 has been charged in Heisenbergia in respect of the gift to Niels.

According to Maria, Niels is considering transferring the shares to a trust for the benefit of their two sons.

Please prepare the following:

(a) In respect of Nucleus Resources:

Calculations of the additional annual after tax income that would be generated by the expansion of the business under the two alternatives ie the recruitment of the additional employees and the use of the sub-contractor. You should check to see if Maria is currently a higher rate taxpayer. If she is, you can simply deduct tax and national insurance at the marginal rates from the additional profits.

Don't worry about the precise timing of the capital allowances in respect of the car, just spread their effect equally. Also, watch out for the VAT implications of the expansion; there is bound to be an effect on the recoverability of input tax due to the business being partially exempt.

(b) In respect of the quoted shares:

(i) A list of the issues to be considered in order to determine whether or not the gift from the uncle is within the scope of UK inheritance tax and the treatment of any inheritance tax suffered in the country of Heisenbergia.

(ii) A brief outline of the tax implications of transferring the shares to the trust and the taxation of the trust income paid to the beneficiaries. The shares are currently worth £210,000.

(iii) Notes on the extent to which it is professionally acceptable for me to discuss issues relating to the shares with Maria.

I want to be able to use the calculations and notes in my meeting with Maria (or in a subsequent meeting with Niels) and I may not have much time to study them beforehand so please make sure that they are clear, concise and that I can find my way around them easily.

Thank you

Tax manager.

The schedule prepared by Maria is set out below.

Nucleus Resources – Estimated income and expenditure for a full year

Notes

1.   The figures in the 'expansion' column relate to the expansion only and will be in addition to the existing business.

2.   Nucleus Resources is registered for VAT.

3.   All amounts are stated exclusive of VAT.

4.   Materials and overheads are subject to VAT at 17.5%. The expenditure cannot be attributed to particular supplies.

		Existing business £	Expansion £
Turnover:	Standard rated	40,000	190,000
	Exempt	90,000	–
Expenditure:	Materials and overheads	37,000	See
	Wages	35,000	below

Costs relating to the expansion

In order to expand the business I will either recruit two additional employees or sub-contract the work to Quantum Ltd, an unconnected company. Details of the expenditure relating to these two possibilities are set out below.

Employees

Employee 1 would be paid a salary of £55,000. He would also be provided with a petrol driven car with a list price when new of £12,800 (including VAT) and a CO_2 emission rate of 143 grams per kilometre. It can be assumed that the car will be sold in five years time for £2,000. Employee 2 would be paid a salary of £40,000 and would not be provided with a car.

There would also be additional materials and overheads, net of VAT at 17.5%, of £20,000.

Quantum Ltd

Quantum Ltd would charge an annual fee of £140,000 plus VAT.

There would be no additional materials or overheads.

Niels and Maria Copenhagen are both clients of your firm. The following information has been obtained from their files.

Niels Copenhagen

–   Resident, ordinarily resident and domiciled in the UK.

–   Niels has not made any previous transfers for the purposes of inheritance tax.

–   Married to Maria. They have two children; Hans (11 years old) and Erik (8 years old).

Maria Copenhagen

– Resident, ordinarily resident and domiciled in the UK.

– Trades as 'Nucleus Resources', an unincorporated business.

Required

Prepare the meeting notes requested by your manager. The following marks are available.

(a) Calculations of the annual additional after tax income generated by the expansion of Maria's business under each of the two alternatives. **(14 marks)**

(b) (i) The issues to be considered in order to determine whether or not the gift from the uncle is within the scope of UK inheritance tax and the treatment of any inheritance tax suffered in the country of Heisenbergia. **(6 marks)**

(ii) The tax implications of transferring the shares to the trust and the taxation of any trust income paid to the beneficiaries, Hans and Erik. **(7 marks)**

(iii) The extent to which it is professionally acceptable to discuss issues relating to the shares with Maria. **(4 marks)**

Appropriateness of the format and presentation of the notes and the effectiveness with which the information is communicated. **(2 marks)**

(Total = 33 marks)

Assume that the tax rules and rates for 2008/09 continue to apply in subsequent years.

Question 2

An extract from an e-mail from your manager is set out below.

I attach a schedule I received this morning from Max Constant, the new managing director of the Particle Ltd group of companies. With Max in charge this client has recently become a lot more lively! This e-mail will make more sense when you have read Max's schedule so I suggest you read that first.

Report

Please prepare a report to the management of Particle Ltd addressing the three areas of advice requested by Max. The report should also cover the following additional points.

Sale of Kaon Ltd – the value added tax (VAT) implications of selling the trade and assets of the business.

Muon Inc – any tax problems in connection with the loan.

Payment of corporation tax – the advantage of group payment arrangements.

Further information

The information in Max's schedule is pretty clear but you will see that there are two question marks in connection with the assets of Kaon Ltd. I've spoken to him about this and to check on a couple of other things and I set out below some additional information that you will need.

– All of the companies are UK resident with the exception of Muon Inc, which is resident in the country of Newtonia. Newtonia is not in the European Union (EU) and there is no double tax treaty between Newtonia and the UK.

– Shortly after its acquisition, Muon Inc approached a number of financial institutions for a loan. However, the interest rates demanded were so high that Particle Ltd has made the loan to Muon Inc instead. Particle Ltd is charging 4% interest on the loan. By the way, Muon Inc is not a controlled foreign company.

– The goodwill of Kaon Ltd has been created within the company since its formation on 1 May 2002.

– Kaon Ltd purchased its premises (Atom House) from Baryon Ltd on 1 March 2003 for its market value at that time of £490,000. Baryon Ltd purchased Atom House on 1 July 1999 for £272,000. Three months later, on 1 October 1999, Baryon Ltd sold another building (Bohr Square) for £309,400 making a capital gain of £89,000 and claimed rollover relief in respect of the purchase of Atom House. No option to tax for VAT purposes has been made in respect of Atom House.

Max has a reasonable knowledge of the UK tax system so keep the narrative in the report brief. As always, assume that all beneficial claims will be made and include a reference to them in the report.

A final thought; watch out for the impact of the sale of the business on the rate of corporation tax payable by Kaon Ltd.

Tax manager

The schedule from Max Constant is set out below.

Particle Ltd Group – Situation as at 1 December 2009

Background information

– Particle Ltd owns 100% of its five subsidiaries. All six companies are trading companies preparing accounts to 31 March.

– Their approximate annual taxable profits are included in the group structure below.

– None of the companies receive any franked investment income and there are no unused trading losses within the group.

– Baryon Ltd has a capital loss of £37,100 brought forward in respect of a disposal on 1 May 2004.

– Particle Ltd, Baryon Ltd and Kaon Ltd have a group VAT registration.

Group structure

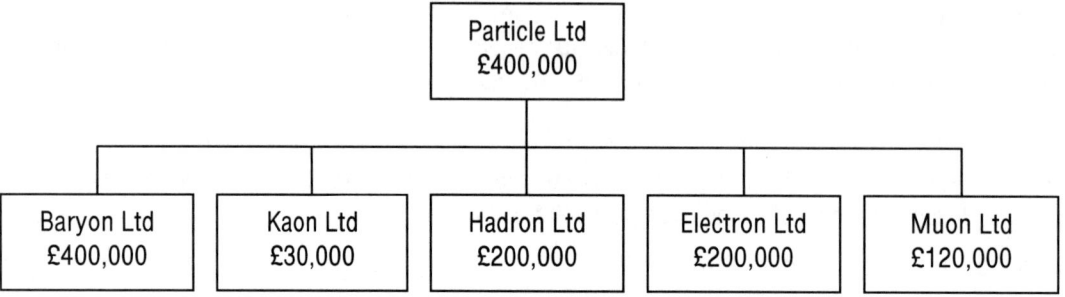

Notes

1. Baryon Ltd has been a subsidiary since 1995.

2. Kaon Ltd was incorporated by Particle Ltd on 1 May 2002. This company is to be sold – see below.

3. Hadron Ltd, Electron Ltd and Muon Inc were all purchased on 1 August 2009 from three unrelated individual vendors.

The sale of Kaon Ltd

The sale will take place on 31 January 2010. We have received offers from two separate purchasers.

Offer 1 – Sale of shares

We have been offered £650,000 for the whole of the company's share capital.

Offer 2 – Sale of trade and assets of the business

We have been offered £770,000 for the company's trade and assets as follows:

	Offer	Cost	Tax written down value
	£	£	£
Office premises (Atom House)	604,000	490,000?	N/A
Machinery and equipment	46,000	80,000	65,000
Goodwill	120,000	Nil	?
	770,000		

This will leave Kaon Ltd with net current liabilities of £25,000, which it will pay out of the sale proceeds of the business.

Advice required

(a)   Sale of Kaon Ltd – the after tax proceeds in respect of each of the two offers.

(b)   Muon Inc – the possibility of avoiding any VAT problems on the future sale of components by Baryon Ltd to Muon Inc by bringing Muon Inc into the Particle Ltd VAT group with Baryon Ltd.

(c)   Payment of corporation tax – whether the recent corporate acquisitions will change the dates on which the group companies are required to pay corporation tax.

Required

(a)   Prepare the report requested by your manager. The report should include explanations together with supporting calculations. The following marks are available for the three areas of the report.

(i)   The sale of Kaon Ltd – after tax proceeds and VAT.

Note: Marks for (i) are allocated as follows: sale of the share capital – 2 marks, sale of the trade and assets of the business – 12 marks.   **(14 marks)**

(ii)   Muon Inc – VAT and issues in connection with the loan.   **(5 marks)**

(iii)   Payment of corporation tax – payment dates and group payment arrangements.   **(7 marks)**

Appropriateness of the format and presentation of the report and the effectiveness with which the information is communicated.   **(3 marks)**

Note: The following indexation factors should be used.

July 1999 to March 2003 0.090

July 1999 to January 2010 0.378

May 2002 to January 2010 0.306

March 2003 to January 2010 0.265

(Total = 29 marks)

Assume that the tax rules and rates for 2008/09 and Financial Year 2008 continue to apply in subsequent years.

SECTION B: TWO questions ONLY to be attempted

Question 3

Ernest intends to sell a capital asset on 1 February 2010 and wishes to maximise his after tax sales proceeds. He is also seeking advice on his inheritance tax position and on his will.

The following information has been obtained from a telephone conversation with Ernest and from client files.

Ernest:

- Is 54 years old and unmarried.
- Lives with Georgina, who is 48 years old, and her adult daughter, Eileen.
- Earns a salary of £130,000 per year.
- Has as yet made no disposals of capital assets in the tax year 2009/10.
- Intends to sell either an oil painting or 7,700 shares in Neutron Ltd on 1 February 2010.

Oil painting:

- Ernest inherited the painting on the death of his uncle on 1 May 2005 when it was worth £23,800.
- Ernest's uncle purchased the painting on 1 July 1991 for £19,500.
- The painting is expected to be worth £47,000 on 1 February 2010.

Shares in Neutron Ltd:

- Qualified for income tax relief under the enterprise investment scheme (EIS) although Ernest did not claim any relief.

- 1 April 2002   Ernest subscribed for 18,600 shares at £8.90 per share.

- 1 March 2004   Ernest received a 1 for 4 bonus issue.

- 1 July 2007   Ernest purchased his full entitlement under a 1 for 10 rights issue at £4.20 per share.

- The shares are expected to be worth £5 each on 1 February 2010.

Neutron Ltd:

- Has an issued share capital of two million £1 ordinary shares.
- Is not quoted on any stock exchange.
- Manufactures and distributes radiation measuring equipment.

Inheritance tax planning and wills:

- Neither Ernest nor Georgina have made any lifetime gifts.
- In his will, Ernest has left the whole of his estate to Georgina.
- In her will, Georgina has left the whole of her estate to Eileen.
- Ernest and Georgina wish to minimise their total inheritance tax liability.
- They are willing to make lifetime gifts to each other but not to Eileen or any other person or organisation.

Current market values of assets owned:

	Ernest £	Georgina £
Family home	620,000	–
Antiques and works of art	400,000	60,000
Investment property	380,000	–
Shares in Neutron Ltd	127,875	–

Required

(a) Prepare calculations of the after tax sales proceeds that would be realised on the proposed sale of the painting and on the proposed sale of the shares on 1 February 2010.

Note: you should assume that Ernest will make any necessary beneficial claims or elections. **(7 marks)**

(b) Prepare brief notes explaining the inheritance tax liabilities that will arise on the deaths of Ernest and Georgina if no action is taken to reduce such liabilities; identify any actions that could be taken in order to reduce these liabilities and explain the inheritance tax and capital gains tax implications of these actions.

Note: you are not required to prepare calculations for part (b) of this question. **(12 marks)**

(Total = 19 marks)

Assume that the tax rules and rates for 2008/09 continue to apply in subsequent years.

Question 4

James is about to be made redundant by Quark Ltd. He is seeking advice on the taxation of his redundancy payment and on the sale of shares acquired via an approved share incentive plan. He intends to form Proton Ltd, which is expected to be treated as a personal service company, and wants to know how much better or worse off he will be as compared to the job he is about to lose.

The following information has been obtained from a meeting with James.

James – Income, national insurance and capital gains tax position:

- James is paid a salary of £70,000 per year by Quark Ltd.

- He is not contracted out of the State Second Pension.

- He has no income other than that from Quark Ltd and Proton Ltd in the tax year 2009/10.

- He withdrew shares from the Quark Ltd approved share incentive plan on 1 September 2009.

- His disposal of the shares in Quark Ltd is his only disposal for the purposes of capital gains tax in the tax year 2009/10.

Withdrawal and sale of shares from the Quark Ltd approved share incentive plan:

- James has been awarded free shares on 1 June every year since 2005.
- James withdrew all of the shares in the plan on 1 September 2009 and immediately sold them.

Redundancy and future plans:

- Quark Ltd will make James redundant on 31 January 2010.
- The company will make a redundancy payment to James of £38,500.
- In accordance with its usual policy, the company will also pay James £17,500 in lieu of notice.
- James will form a new company, Proton Ltd.

Proton Ltd – Activities:

- Proton Ltd will provide services to Quark Ltd and to other companies.

- The services will be carried out by James personally.

- All of Proton Ltd's income will be in respect of relevant engagements and therefore subject to the personal service company (IR35) legislation.

Proton Ltd – Estimated income and outgoings for a full year:

	£
Gross fee income	80,000
Salary paid to James	48,000
Administrative expenses	3,000
Travel expenses reimbursed to James	1,500
Dividends paid to James	18,000

Notes:

1. Where applicable, the above amounts are stated excluding value added tax (VAT).

2. The travel expenses are those which will be necessarily incurred by James in performing the work for Quark Ltd and the other customers of Proton Ltd.

Required

(a) Identify the income tax, national insurance contribution and capital gains tax implications, if any, of the withdrawal and subsequent sale of the shares in Quark Ltd, the redundancy payment and the payment in lieu of notice. **(6 marks)**

(b) (i)   Prepare calculations to determine the effect on James's annual income, after deduction of all taxes, of working for Proton Ltd rather than Quark Ltd. **(8 marks)**

    (ii) Calculate the effect on James's annual income, after deduction of all taxes, if the income of Proton Ltd were not regarded as being in respect of relevant engagements. **(2 marks)**

(c) Give three examples of specific contractual arrangements that would assist in arguing that the relationships between Proton Ltd and its customers do not amount to relevant engagements such that they would no longer be covered by the personal service company (IR35) legislation. **(3 marks)**

(Total = 19 marks)

Assume that the tax rules and rates for 2008/09 continue to apply in subsequent years.

Question 5

Boson has been living overseas and is about to return to the UK. He requires advice on his capital gains tax position and on whether to retain an overseas investment property or to sell it and invest the funds in the UK.

The following information has been obtained from telephone conversations with Boson.

Boson's current position:

–   He is UK domiciled.
–   He had lived in the UK all of his life until he moved to the country of Higgsia on 1 January 2005.
–   He sold shares in Meson plc whilst living in Higgsia.
–   He purchased a house in Higgsia but retained his principal private residence in the UK.

Boson's future:

–   Boson plans to return permanently to his home in the UK on 20 January 2010.

–   He has signed an employment contract with Graviton Ltd, which commences on 15 April 2010.

–   He is considering selling the house in Higgsia and investing the after tax proceeds in a portfolio of quoted shares in UK companies or, alternatively, retaining the house and renting it out.

Sales of shares in Meson plc:

–   Meson plc is a UK resident quoted company.
–   Boson inherited 19,500 shares on 1 August 1998 when they were worth £2 each.
–   Boson sold 10,000 shares on 1 May 2005 for £11 each.
–   Boson sold the remaining shares on 1 November 2009 for £15 each.

House in the country of Higgsia:

–   Purchased by Boson on 1 May 2005 for £105,000.
–   Could be rented out for £11,000 per year after deduction of allowable expenses.
–   Is currently worth and could be sold for £200,000.

The tax system in the country of Higgsia:

- Non-residents of Higgsia are charged income tax at 30% on income arising in the country of Higgsia.
- No capital gains tax.
- No double tax treaty with the UK.

Employment contract with Graviton Ltd:

- Boson will be paid an annual salary of £33,560.

Portfolio of quoted shares:

- The portfolio would be expected to generate annual dividends at the rate of approximately 4.3% of the capital invested.

Required

(a) Advise Boson, by reference to his residence and ordinary residence position, as to whether the sales of the shares in Meson plc on 1 May 2005 and 1 November 2009 and the possible sale of the house in the country of Higgsia will be subject to capital gains tax. State what he should do in order to ensure that any gains arising are not subject to capital gains tax.

Note: you are not required to prepare calculations for part (a) of this question. **(9 marks)**

(b) (i) Calculate Boson's annual rental income after deduction of all taxes in respect of the house in Higgsia. **(4 marks)**

(ii) On the assumption that the house in Higgsia is sold for £200,000, with no capital gains tax payable, calculate the annual after tax income generated if the whole amount is invested in the portfolio of quoted shares. **(3 marks)**

(iii) Calculate the maximum by which the rate of return on the portfolio of quoted shares could fall before the after tax income generated would cease to exceed the return from renting out the house in Higgsia. **(3 marks)**

(Total = 19 marks)

Assume that the tax rules and rates for 2008/09 continue to apply in subsequent years.

Mock Exam 3 (December 2008 paper): questions

Answers

DO NOT TURN THIS PAGE UNTIL YOU HAVE
COMPLETED THE MOCK EXAM

A plan of attack

What's the worst thing you could be doing right now if this was the actual exam paper? Sharpening your pencil? Wondering how to celebrate the end of the exam in about three hours time? Panicking, flapping and generally getting in a right old state?

Well, they're all pretty bad, so turn back to the paper and let's sort out a **plan of attack**!

First things first

You have fifteen minutes reading time. Make sure you spend it wisely, looking through the paper in detail working out which optional questions to do and the order in which to attack the questions. You've got **two options**. Option 1 is the option recommended by BPP.

Option 1 (if you're thinking 'Help!')

If you're a bit worried about the paper, do the questions in the order of how well you think you can answer them. If you find the questions in Section B less daunting than the compulsory questions in Section A start with Section B. Remember you only need to do two of the three questions in Section B; you may find it easier if you start by deciding which question you will not do and put a line through it.

- **Question 3** had two parts Part (a) contained some reasonably simple capital gains calculations. Part (b) dealt with IHT planning for an unmarried couple and you could have scored good marks with some fairly simple suggestions.

- **Question 4** required some quite detailed knowledge of share incentive schemes and personal service companies. It was probably obvious to you whether you had the required knowledge or not.

- **Question 5** dealt with overseas aspects of tax for an individual. There were some relatively easy marks to be gained for outlining the rules on capital gains. The computations were slightly tricky.

Do not spend longer than the allocated time on Section B. When you've spent the allocated time on **two** of the three questions in Section B turn to the longer questions in Section A. Read these questions through thoroughly before you launch into them. Once you start make sure you allocate your time to the parts within the questions according to the marks available and that, where possible, you attempt the easy marks first.

Lastly, what you mustn't forget is that you have to **answer both questions in Section A and TWO in Section B**. Do not miss out more than one question in Section B and do not waste time answering three questions in Section B or you will seriously affect your chance of passing the exam.

Option 2 (if you're thinking 'It's a doddle')

It never pays to be overconfident but if you're not quaking in your shoes about the exam then **turn straight to the compulsory questions** in Section A.

Once you've done these questions, move to Section B.

- The question you attempt first really depends on what you are most confident at.
- You then have to select one of the two remaining questions. If you are undecided look at the requirements. It maybe easier to obtain more marks if these are broken down into several smaller parts.

No matter how many times we remind you....

Always, always **allocate your time** according to the marks for the question in total and then according to the parts of the question. And **always, always follow the requirements** exactly.

You've got spare time at the end of the exam.....?

If you have allocated your time properly then you **shouldn't have time on your hands** at the end of the exam. But if you find yourself with five or ten minutes to spare, check over your work to make sure that there are no silly arithmetical errors.

Forget about it!

And don't worry if you found the paper difficult. More than likely other candidates will too. If this were the real thing you would need to **forget** the exam the minute you leave the exam hall and **think about the next one**. Or, if it's the last one, **celebrate**!

Question 1

Marking scheme

				Marks
(a)	VAT position			
	Existing business	3		
	Expand with employees	2		
	Expand with Quantum Ltd	2		
	Employ additional staff			
	Turnover	½		
	Irrecoverable VAT	1		
	Salaries and Class 1 NIC	1½		
	Car			
	Cost	1		
	Class 1A NIC	1½		
	Additional overheads	½		
	Income after tax	1		
	Use Quantum Ltd			
	Turnover	½		
	Irrecoverable VAT	1		
	Annual fee	½		
	Income after tax	½		
		Max		14
(b)	(i)	Relevance of domicile	1	
		Relevance of location of shares	1	
		Uncle's domicile in 1989	2	
		Acquisition of domicile of choice in Heisenbergia	1	
		Location of shares	1	
		Double tax relief	1	
		Max		6
	(ii)	Inheritance tax		
		Chargeable lifetime transfer	1	
		Annual exemptions	½	
		Business property relief	½	
		Covered by nil rate band	1	
		Capital gains tax		
		Gain by reference to market value	1	
		Gift relief available	1	
		Income tax		
		Payable by Niels, with reasons	2	
		Tax credit for tax paid by trustees	½	
		Stamp duty	1	
		Max		7

(iii)	Two separate clients		1	
	Statement of general rule		1	
	Transfer of shares to trust		1½	
	Inheritance tax on gift from uncle		2	
		Max		4
(c)	Appropriate style and presentation		1	
	Effectiveness of communication		1	
	Logical structure		½	
		Max		2
				33

Notes for meeting with Maria Copenhagen

(a) **After tax income generated by expansion of Nucleus Resources**

Maria is a higher rate taxpayer, as the current net income from the business exceeds £40,835 (£6,035 + £34,800). Accordingly, the additional net income generated by the expansion will be subject to tax at a total of 41% (income tax at 40% and Class 4 national insurance contributions at 1%).

Employ additional employees

	£
Additional turnover	190,000
Add: VAT now recoverable (W1, W2)	4,468
Additional income	194,468
Salaries £(55,000 + 40,000)	95,000
Class 1 NICs on salaries (W3)	10,769
Car (W4)	2,422
Additional overheads	20,000
Additional expenditure	128,191
Net additional income	
£(194,468 – 128,191)	66,277
Less: income tax and NICs	
41% x £66,277	(27,174)
Additional income after tax	39,103

Workings

1   *Existing business – irrecoverable VAT*

$$\frac{\text{Taxable turnover excluding VAT}}{\text{Total turnover excluding VAT}} = \frac{40}{40 + 90} \times 100 = 31\% \text{ (rounded up)}$$

	£
Total input tax £37,000 x 17.5%	6,475
Less: attribute to taxable supplies	
31% x £6,475	(2,007)
VAT attributable to exempt supplies	4,468

This is irrecoverable because it is more than 50% of the total input tax. However, it will be recoverable if the business expands using employees (W2).

2   *Expanded business using employees*

$$\frac{\text{Taxable turnover excluding VAT}}{\text{Total turnover excluding VAT}} = \frac{40 + 190}{40 + 190 + 90} \times 100 = 72\% \text{ (rounded up)}$$

	£
Total input tax £(37,000 + 20,000) x 17.5%	9,975
Less: attributable to taxable supplies	
72% x £9,975	(7,182)
VAT attributable to exempt supplies	2,793

This is below the de minimis limit of:

- £625 per month (£7,500 per year) and
- 50% of the total input tax

As a result, all the input tax is recoverable, resulting in additional VAT recoverable of £4,468 (W1).

Tutorial note

This answer assumes that the additional overheads and materials are unattributable (following the statement in the question that such expenditure cannot be attributed to particular supplies). It is arguable that additional amount relates *only* to the expansion which consists entirely of taxable supplies and therefore the partial exemption fraction only applies to the original unattributable supplies. The examiner would have accepted either approach in the examination.

3   *NIC on salaries*

	£
Total salaries	95,000
Less: lower limit £5,435 x 2	(10,870)
	84,130
x 12.8%	10,769

4   *Car*

	£
$\dfrac{£ (12,800 - 2,000)}{5}$	2,160
Class 1A NICs	
$\dfrac{(140 - 135)}{5} = 1\% + 15\% = 16\%$	
16% x £12,800 x 12.8%	262
Annual cost of car	2,422

Use Quantum Ltd

	£
Additional turnover	190,000
Add: VAT now recoverable (W)	4,468
Additional income	194,468
Additional expenditure – fee to Quantum Ltd	140,000
Net additional income	
£(194,468 – 140,000)	54,468
Less: income tax and NICs	
41% x £54,468	(22,332)
Additional income after tax	32,136

Working

Expanded business using Quantum Ltd

$$\frac{\text{Taxable turnover excluding VAT}}{\text{Total turnover excluding VAT}} = \frac{40 + 190}{40 + 190 + 90} \times 100 = 72\% \text{ (rounded up)}$$

	£
Total input tax £37,000 x 17.5%	6,475
Less: attributable to taxable supplies	
72% x £6,475	(4,662)
VAT attributable to exempt supplies	1,813

This is below the de minimis limit of:

- £625 per month (£7,500 per year) and
- 50% of the total input tax

As a result, all the input tax is recoverable, resulting in additional VAT recoverable of £4,468 (see above).

Tutorial note

The approach taken in this answer is that, as the VAT on the £140,000 invoice paid to the supplier relates to the expansion of taxable supplies, the whole of the VAT is attributable to taxable supplies. Therefore the partial exemption fraction only applies to the original unattributable supplies. The ACCA examiner's answer takes the approach that the VAT relating to the invoice is also unattributable. In the examination, the examiner would have accepted either approach.

(b)   (i)   **Inheritance tax consequences of transfer of quoted shares to Niels**

The inheritance tax position depends on the domicile of the uncle and the location of the quoted shares:

- If the uncle was domiciled in the UK when he made the gift in October 2007, the value of the shares at the time of the gift be subject to inheritance tax wherever the shares are situated.

- If the uncle was domiciled in Heisenbergia, the gift only be subject to UK inheritance tax if the shares are UK-situated assets.

Uncle's domicile

- If the uncle was not UK domiciled in 1989 it seems very unlikely from what we know that he would have acquired a UK domicile whilst living in Heisenbergia.

- However, if the uncle was UK domiciled at the time he left the UK in 1989, he will continue to be UK domiciled unless he acquired a domicile of choice in Heisenbergia.

- In order to have acquired a domicile of choice in Heisenbergia, the uncle would have had to have severed his ties with the UK and exhibited a clear intention of making Heisenbergia his permanent home.

Location of the quoted shares

- The shares are UK assets if the company is incorporated in the UK or the shares are registered in the UK.

Inheritance tax suffered in Heisenbergia

- Any UK inheritance tax due in respect of the gift can be reduced by double tax relief in respect of the inheritance tax charged in Heisenbergia up to the amount of the UK inheritance tax.

(ii)   **Creation of trust for children**

Inheritance tax

- The gift of shares to the trust would be a transfer of value for inheritance tax.

- The transfer of value would probably not attract business property relief because this only applies to quoted shares if the donor has control of the company (unlikely).

- Annual exemptions of £3,000 for the tax year of the transfer and the preceding year would apply.

- The remaining value not covered by the exempt transfers would be a chargeable lifetime transfer.

- No lifetime inheritance tax would be payable because the chargeable lifetime transfer would fall within the nil rate band of Niels (£312,000).

Stamp duty

- There will be no stamp duty on the transfer of the shares to the trustees because it is a transfer with no consideration.

Income tax

- If either of the minor beneficiaries of the trust receives income from the trust, the income will be taxed on Niels as his income, unless the amount received is £100 or less. This is because the trust is being set up by Niels for his children.

- If income is deemed to be Niels', a tax credit will be given in respect of the tax paid on that income by the trustees.

(iii)   **Ethical issues**

- Maria and Niels are separate clients and must be treated as such from the point of view of confidentiality.

- We must not disclose information relating to Niels to anyone, including Maria, unless we have permission from Niels (or such disclosure is required by law or professional duty). Accordingly, we should check to see if we have written permission from Niels to discuss his affairs with his wife.

- Unless we have permission from Niels, we should not discuss the situation relating to the proposed transfer of shares to the trust. This is because we cannot explain the situation to Maria without referring to Niels' tax position, for example, the fact that he has not made previous transfers of value.

- Maria's question concerning inheritance tax on the gift from the uncle is different because it can be answered without making any reference to the tax affairs of Niels. It is, arguably, a general question on the workings of inheritance tax. There would be no breach of confidentiality if we discussed this matter with Maria.

- However, we know that it is not a general question and we should still consider the potential problems that could arise in discussing matters with Maria that relate to the personal affairs of Niels without first obtaining permission from Niels.

Question 2

Text references. Chargeable gains for companies are covered in Chapter 21. Calculation of corporation tax and payment of tax are in Chapter 22. Transfer pricing is dealt with in Chapter 20. VAT is covered in Chapters 28 and 29 and transfer of a going concern in Chapter 30.

Top tips. Remember to set out your report in the appropriate style and present it neatly. Plan your answer before starting to write it in order to produce a logical structure. Use workings and reference them correctly

Easy marks. If you spotted that the substantial shareholding exemption applied on a sale of Kaon Ltd shares, the calculation of the after-tax proceeds should have gained you easy marks.

Marks

(a)	(i)	Sale of share capital		
		Availability of substantial shareholding exemption	1	
		Reason for availability	1	
		After tax proceeds	½	
		Sale of business		
		Atom House		
		Cost of Atom House		
		Use of original cost to Bayron Ltd	½	
		Rollover relief	1½	
		IA to March 2003	1	
		Gain on sale by Kaon Ltd	½	
		Transfer of part of gain to Bayron Ltd	1	
		Claim required	1	
		Machinery and equipment	1	
		Goodwill	1	
		Rate of corporation tax	1½	
		Payment of net liabilities	1	
		After tax proceeds	½	
		Explanatory notes – 1 mark each – maximum 3 marks	3	
		VAT	2	
		Max		14
	(ii)	VAT group	1	
		Zero rated	1	
		Transfer pricing		
		Identification of issue	1	
		Why rules apply	2	
		Effect	1	
		Max		5
	(iii)	Year ended 31 March 2009	1½	
		Year ended 31 March 2010	1½	
		Year ended 31 March 2011		
		Reason for instalment basis	1	
		Due dates	1	
		Interest and need to estimate liabilities	1½	
		Group payment		
		Operation	1	
		Why possibly beneficial	1	
		Max		7
	(iv)	Appropriate style and presentation	1	
		Effectiveness of communication	1½	
		Logical structure	½	
				3
				29

(a)

Report

To: **The management of Particle Ltd**

From: **Tax advisers**

Date: **1 December 2009**

Subject: **Particle Ltd Group – Various group issues**

(i)   **Sale of Kaon Ltd**

Sale of share capital

A sale by Particle Ltd of the share capital of Kaon Ltd will not result in a tax liability due to the availability of the substantial shareholdings exemption. This exemption is available because Particle Ltd is selling shares in a trading company of which it has held at least 10% of the share capital for a continuous twelve month period in the two years prior to the disposal.

Accordingly, the after tax proceeds resulting from the sale will be £650,000.

Tutorial note

A degrouping charge will not apply in respect of Atom House, as Kaon Ltd is leaving the group more than six years after the no gain, no loss transfer.

Sale of trade and assets of business

	£
Sale proceeds	770,000
Less: corporation tax (W1)	(101,920)
repayment of liabilities	(25,000)
Net after tax proceeds	643,080

The sale of the business of Kaon Ltd will be outside the scope of VAT provided that the following conditions are satisfied:

- the purchaser intends to use the assets to carry on the same kind of business as Kaon Ltd, the business being sold as a going concern.

- the purchaser is registered for VAT or will become registerable as a result of the purchase.

Workings

1   *Corporation tax*

	£
Gain on sale of Atholl House (W2)	263,001
Balancing allowance on machinery	
£(46,000 – 65,000)	(19,000)
Profit on sale of goodwill	
£(120,000 – nil)	120,000
Amount subject to corporation tax	364,001
Corporation tax @ 28% (W5)	101,920

2   *Gain on Atholl House*

	£
Proceeds	604,000
Less: cost (W3)	(240,236)
Unindexed gain	363,764
Less: indexation allowance (3.03 to 1.10)	
0.265 x £240,236	(63,663)
Indexed gain	300,101

In order to use the loss of £37,100 in Baryon Ltd, Kaon Ltd and Baryon Ltd can make an election (by 31 March 2012) as members of a capital gains group, that part of Atom House is treated as being transferred to Baryon Ltd immediately before disposal, to the extent of the loss. The net gain will then be £(300,101 – 37,100) = £263,001.

3   *Cost of Atholl House to Kaon Ltd*

	£
Original cost to Baryon Ltd	272,000
Less: rollover relief (W4)	(51,600)
Revised cost	220,400
Add: indexation allowance (7.99 to 3.03)	
0.090 x £220,400	19,836
Deemed proceeds for no gain, no loss	240,236

4   *Rollover relief in respect of Atholl House*

	£
Gain on sale of Bohr Square	89,000
Less: immediately chargeable	
£(309,400 – 272,000)	(37,400)
Rollover relief	51,600

5   *Rate of corporation tax*

In the year ended 31 March 2010, there are six associated companies in the group. The limits are therefore:

£1,500,000/6	£250,000
£300,000/6	£50,000

Kaon Ltd will therefore pay corporation tax at the full rate (28%).

(ii)   **Muon Ltd**

VAT

It will not be possible for Muon Inc to join the Particle Ltd group registration unless it has an established place of business in the UK. This is not a problem, however, as there will be no VAT on the sales of components to Muon Inc because exports to countries outside the European Union (EU) are zero rated.

Interest on the loan from Particle Ltd.

The profit or loss arising on transactions between Particle Ltd and Muon Inc must be determined as if the two companies are independent of each other under the transfer pricing rules because Particle Ltd controls Muon Inc. This rule applies regardless of the size of Particle Ltd because Muon Inc is resident in a country that does not have a double tax treaty with the UK.

Accordingly, the taxable profit of Particle Ltd must be increased in order to reflect a market rate of interest on the loan.

Particle Ltd should include this adjustment in its corporation tax return and not in its financial statements.

(iii)   **Payment of corporation tax**

In the year ended 31 March 2009 there were three companies in the group. Accordingly, the limits would have been divided by three to determine the rate of corporation tax. The taxable profit of each of the three companies was less than £500,000 (£1,500,000/3) such that no company will have to pay tax at the full rate. Therefore, the tax is due on 1 January 2010, nine months and one day after the end of the accounting period.

In the year ended 31 March 2010, some of the companies in the group will pay tax at the full rate because of the additional associated companies and the resulting lower limits. However, this will not affect the date on which corporation tax is payable since it is the first year in which full rate tax is payable. Corporation tax will therefore be payable on 1 January 2011.

In the year ended 31 March 2011, there will be five companies in the group. Those companies with taxable profits in excess of £300,000 (£1,500,000/5) will have to pay their corporation tax liability in four equal instalments (if they paid tax at the full rate in the year ending 31 March 2010). The instalments will be due on 14 October 2010, 14 January 2011, 14 April 2011 and 14 July 2011.

Once the final liability is known, interest will be charged by HMRC on any amounts paid late and will be paid (at a lower rate) to the company on any amounts paid early or overpaid. Interest paid is allowable for tax purposes and interest received is taxable.

Alternatively, if more than one company in the group is liable to pay tax by instalments, group payment arrangements may be made for the instalments to be paid by one company (the nominated company) and allocated amongst the group. This enables overpayments and underpayments to be offset and so mitigates the differential between interest payable and interest receivable.

Question 3

> **Text references.** Calculation of capital gains tax is covered in Chapter 11. Shares are dealt with in Chapter 12. Share loss relief is covered in Chapter 8. Inheritance tax is dealt with in Chapters 17 to 19.
>
> **Top tips.** You must make sure you follow any notes the examiner gives you. In part (a), the examiner told you to assume that Ernest will make any necessary beneficial claims or elections (so you should look out for what might be available). In part (b), the examiner stated that you were not required to prepare calculations so you should assume that no marks were allocated for calculations.
>
> **Easy marks.** There were easy marks for the computation of the gain on the painting and the loss on the shares, even if you did not spot the loss relief for unquoted shares.

Marking scheme

		Marks
(a)	Sale of painting	
	Capital gain	1
	Annual exemption	½
	Capital gains tax payable	½
	After tax sales proceeds	½
	Sale of shares	
	Cost of shares sold	2
	Capital loss	½
	Tax savings in respect of losses	1½
	After tax sales proceeds	½
		7
(b)	Current position	
	Business property relief on the shares in Neutron Ltd	1
	Ernest dies before Georgina	
	Tax on Ernest's death estate	1
	Tax on Georgina's death estate	1
	Identification of problem	1
	Quick succession relief	½
	Georgina dies before Ernest	
	Tax on Georgina's death estate	½
	Tax on Ernest's death estate	½
	Identification of problem	1
	Advice	
	Marry	
	Transfer of assets	1
	Election to transfer nil rate band	1
	Sensitivity	½

Gift assets to Georgina		
Inheritance tax implications	1	
Should not gift shares in Neutron Ltd	½	
Potential inheritance tax implications	1	
Capital gains tax implications	2	
Change will and leave assets to Eileen	1	
Potential inheritance tax savings	½	
	Max	12
		19

(a) After tax sales proceeds

Sale of painting

	£
Proceeds	47,000
Less: cost (probate value)	(23,800)
Gain	23,200
Less: annual exemption	(9,600)
Taxable gain	13,600
CGT @ 18%	2,448
Net proceeds £(47,000 − 2,448)	44,552

Sale of shares

	£
Proceeds £5 x 7,700	38,500
Less: cost (W)	(52,780)
Allowable loss	14,280
Income tax refund £14,280 x 40% (N)	5,712
Net proceeds £(38,500 + 5,712)	44,212

Note

Share loss relief against general income is available for capital losses on unquoted shares which satisfy the conditions of the EIS. However, it is not necessary for EIS income tax relief to have been claimed on the shares. Relief will be at 40% because Ernest has a salary of £130,000 per year and so is a higher rate taxpayer.

Working
Share pool

	No. of shares	Cost
		£
1.4.02 Acquisition	18,600	165,540
1.3.04 Bonus 1:4	4,650	–
	23,250	165,540
1.7.07 Rights 1:10 @ £4.20	2,325	9,765
	25,575	175,305
1.2.10 Disposal	(7,700)	(52,780)
c/f	17,875	122,525

(b)   **Planning for inheritance tax**

Current position

- The shares in Neutron Ltd will be fully relieved via business property relief (BPR) and therefore will not give rise to any inheritance tax either on Ernest's death or in the case of their subsequent gift (on death or by lifetime gift) by whoever inherits them.

    Tutorial note

    The minimum two years ownership period does not apply to inherited assets if they qualified for business property relief at the time of the original death.

If Ernest dies before Georgina

- Ernest's estate, as reduced by the nil band of £312,000, will be taxed at 40%.

- When Georgina dies, her estate (including those assets inherited from Ernest), as reduced by her nil band of £312,000, will be taxed at 40%.

- Problem: some of Ernest's assets will be taxed twice, once on his death and again on the death of Georgina. Quick succession relief will mitigate the double taxation if the deaths occur within five years of each other but only to a limited extent.

If Georgina dies before Ernest

- Georgina's estate of £60,000 will be covered by the nil rate band such that there will be no inheritance tax liability.

- When Ernest dies, his estate, as reduced by his nil band of £312,000, will be taxed at 40% (as above).

- Problem: Georgina is wasting most of her nil rate band due to an insufficiency of assets and, since Ernest and Georgina are not married, it is not possible to claim to transfer her unused nil rate band on the death of Ernest.

Advice to Ernest

- Ernest and Georgina should consider marrying

    If Ernest and Georgina were married, assets could be transferred between them with no inheritance tax (exempt transfers) and no capital gains tax (no gain/ no loss disposals) to equalise their estates so that they each have about £312,000 of assets to use their nil rate bands. Alternatively, if Georgina were to die first and her nil rate band was not completely utilised, it would be possible for Ernest's executors to claim the unused amount to set against Ernest's death estate.

    Obviously this matter would need to be dealt with sensitively, since Ernest and/or Georgina might have strong reasons why they do not wish to marry.

- Ernest should give assets worth up to £252,000 to Georgina.

    If Ernest and Georgina do not wish to marry, then Ernest should consider equalising estates by giving assets worth £252,0000 to Georgina. This gift will be a potentially exempt transfer but will become a chargeable transfer if Ernest dies within seven years. The gift should not be made out of the Neutron Ltd shares because of the availability of the 100% business property relief.

    The gift will improve Ernest's inheritance tax position because the value of the assets given will be frozen at the time of the gift and the gift will be reduced by two annual exemptions.

    On Georgina's death, £312,000 of her estate, ie £252,000 more than before, will not give rise to any inheritance tax as it will be covered by her nil rate band.

    Accordingly, there will be no inheritance tax liability in respect of the value of the gift if Ernest survives the gift by seven years.

    However, the gift will be a disposal at market value for the purposes of capital gains tax. Since assets available to be gifted will not qualify for gift relief, this could result in an immediate charge to capital gains tax. More information is required about the acquisition of the assets and the potential gains or losses on disposal.

- Ernest should change his will and leave some assets directly to Eileen

    Again, if Ernest and Georgina do not wish to marry, the assets gifted in the will to Eileen should be those in excess of the nil rate band. These assets will then be subject to inheritance tax once only rather than potentially twice (on the deaths of both Ernest and Georgina) saving inheritance tax up to a maximum of 40%.

Question 4

Text references. Share Incentive Plans and payments on redundancy are covered in Chapter 5. Personal service companies are dealt with in Chapter 4.

Top tips. Look carefully at the marking scheme as it will give you an idea of what the question involves. For example, part (b)(i) was worth 8 marks so you should have expected to undertake a fairly complex computation. The key point to note was that you needed to work out the deemed employment income payment under the IR35 legislation and the income tax and national insurance contributions on this payment.

Easy marks. You should have been able to state three specific contractual arrangements which would assist in arguing that the IR35 legislation did not apply as these are also relevant in deciding whether an individual is employed or self employed.

Marking scheme

				Marks
(a)	Shares in Quark Ltd			
	Income tax where shares in plan for less than three years	1		
	Income tax where shares in plan for three years or more	1½		
	Also subject to NIC	½		
	Capital gains tax on sale	1		
	Redundancy payment			
	Statutory redundancy	1		
	£30,000 exemption	1½		
	Payment in lieu of notice	1		
	Max		6	
(b) (i)	Effect of fall in salary net of all taxes	2½		
	Dividend income	½		
	No tax on dividend income	1		
	Tax and NIC on deemed employment income	1		
	Deemed employment income			
	Income net of 5% deduction	1		
	Travel expenses, salary (½ each)	1		
	Employer's NIC on salary	1		
	Employer's NIC on deemed payment	1		
	Max		8	
(ii)	Income tax and NIC no longer payable	1		
	Income tax on dividends	1		
			2	
(c)	One mark for each contractual arrangement	3		
			3	
			19	

(a)   **Taxation of shares in Quark Ltd and redundancy payment**

Shares in Quark Ltd

Withdrawal of shares

- If the shares have been within the plan for less than three years, income tax and national insurance contributions will be charged on their market value at the time of withdrawal.

- If the shares have been within the plan for between three and five years, income tax and national insurance contributions will be charged on the lower of their value at the time they were awarded to James and their value at the time of withdrawal.

Tutorial note

There is no need to consider the situation where the shares have been in the plan for five years or more as the first award was less than five years prior to the date on which they will be withdrawn as the first award was made in 2005. The exemption for redundancy also does not apply because James withdrew all of the shares in the plan in September 2009 but was not made redundant until January 2010.

Sale of shares

- The shares will have a base cost for the purposes of capital gains tax equal to their market value at the time of their withdrawal from the plan. Accordingly, no capital gain will have arisen on their immediate sale.

Redundancy payment

- Any amount of statutory redundancy included within the payment is exempt from income tax.

- The first £30,000 of the balance of the payment, as reduced by any amount of tax-free statutory redundancy, will be exempt from income tax provided it relates solely to redundancy and is not simply a terminal bonus. The remainder of the payment will be taxable as specific employment income.

  Tutorial note

  Thus a total maximum of £30,000 statutory and ex gratia redundancy pay is exempt from income tax.

- The payment in lieu of notice will be subject to income tax as general earnings because it is a payment to which the employee is contractually entitled.

(b)   (i)   **Effect on James' annual income if works for Proton Ltd instead of Quark Ltd**

	£
Reduction in salary £(70,000 – 48,000)	(22,000)
Add: income tax on salary £22,000 x 40% not payable	8,800
NICs on salary £22,000 x 1% not payable	220
additional dividend receiveable	18,000
Less: tax on dividend (N)	–
tax on deemed employment income (W)	(7,465)
NICs on deemed employment income	(187)
Net decrease in James' annual income	(2,632)

Working

		£
Income £80,000 x 95%		76,000
Less:	travel expenses	(1,500)
	salary	(48,000)
	employer's NIC on actual salary	
	£(48,000 – 5,435) x 12.8%	(5,448)
		21,052

Less: employer's NIC on deemed payment	
$\dfrac{12.8}{112.8}$ x £21,052	(2,389)
Deemed employment income	18,663

Income tax on deemed employment income	
£18,663 x 40%	7,465
NICs on deemed employment income	
£18,663 x 1%	187

James will be a higher rate tax payer and will pay the additional rate NICs because his salary will cover the personal allowance, basic rate band and main rate of NICs.

Note

Because James is treated as receiving deemed employment income from the company, the dividend received from the company is not also subject to income tax.

(ii) **Effect on James' annual income if Proton Ltd not subject to IR35**

		£
Anticipated fall in annual income (as in part (i))		(2,632)
Add:	income tax no longer payable on deemed employment income (as in part (i))	7,465
	NICs no longer payable on deemed employment income (as in part (i))	187
Less:	income tax on dividend	
	£18,000 x $\dfrac{100}{90}$ x (32.5 – 10)%	(4,500)
Net increase in James' income		520

Tutorial note

As the whole of the dividend is taxable at the higher rate it would have been equally valid to calculate the tax due on the dividend as simply the net dividend x 25% ie £18,000 x 25% = £4,500.

(c) **Specific contractual arrangements for IR35 argument**

Any THREE of the following:

- Any necessary equipment or tools should be provided by Proton Ltd rather than its customers.
- The degree of the customer's control over when and how the work is carried out by James should be kept to a minimum.
- Proton Ltd should bear a degree of financial risk, for example by quoting fixed contract prices and bearing the cost of rectifying unsatisfactory work.
- Payments should be made under the contracts by reference to the work done rather than periods of time such as a daily or monthly rate.
- Payments should be made under the contracts in respect of the work carried out. The contracts should not include any provisions whereby payments will be made in respect of illness or holidays.
- Each contract should only come to an end when the work is completed or the contract has been breached in some way and there should be no obligation for further work to be provided.

Tutorial note

The relationships between Proton Ltd and its customers will each have to be considered separately. A contract may be regarded as a relevant engagement if it would have been an employer/employee relationship had it been between the customer and James.

Question 5

Text references. Overseas aspects of capital gains tax are covered in Chapter 14. Overseas aspects of income are dealt with in Chapter 10. Personal financial management is discussed in Chapter 31. Calculation of tax at the marginal rate is covered in Chapter 1.

Top tips. In part (a), it was important to apply the general rules about the charge to capital gains tax for non-residents to the specific assets.

Easy marks. The calculation of DTR in part (b)(i) was relatively straightforward because the examiner had stated that the taxpayer had an amount of UK income which used up most of his basic rate band.

Marking scheme

				Marks
(a)	Position whilst living in Higgsia			
		Not subject to UK capital gains tax with reason	2	
		Circumstances giving rise to temporary non-resident status	2	
		Implications of temporary non resident status	2	
	Position on returning to the UK			
		Subject to capital gains tax with reason	1½	
	Sales of shares		1½	
	Potential sale of house		2	
		Max		9
(b)	(i)	Higgsian income tax	½	
		UK income tax		
		Remainder of basic rate band		
		Salary	½	
		Personal allowance	½	
		Excess over basic rate band	½	
		Tax at appropriate rates	½	
		Double tax relief	1	
		Income after deduction of all taxes	½	
				4
	(ii)	Taxable dividend income	1	
		Tax at appropriate rates	1	
		Tax credits	½	
		Income after deduction of all taxes	½	
				3
	(iii)	Maximum fall dividend income	1½	
		Minimum yield required	1	
		Maximum fall in rate of return	½	
				3
				19

(a)   **Boson – capital gains tax position**

Liability to capital gains tax

Boson will have been non-resident and non-ordinarily resident in the UK whilst living in Higgsia as he has been abroad for more than three years. Accordingly, under general principles, he would not be subject to capital gains tax on disposals made during that period.

However, there are special rules which apply to an individual who is a temporary non-resident. Boson will be treated as a temporary non-resident if he returns to the UK on or before 5 April 2010. This is because he will have been absent for less than five complete tax years and he was UK resident for four of the seven years prior to leaving the UK. If he returns after 5 April 2010, these special rules will not apply because he will then have been absent for five complete tax years (2005/6 to 2009/10 inclusive).

If Boson returns as planned on 20 January 2010, as a temporary non-resident, any capital gains he made during the non-resident period on assets owned at the time he left the UK will be subject to capital gains tax in the year of return (2009/10). Gains on assets purchased in the non-resident period do not come within the temporary non-residence rules.

Boson will become UK resident and ordinarily resident from the date he returns to the UK as he is returning permanently. He will then be subject to capital gains tax on his worldwide assets.

Sale of the shares in Meson plc on 1 May 2005 and 1 November 2009

Boson owned the shares at the time he left the UK. Accordingly, Boson should delay his return to the UK until after 5 April 2010 in order to avoid the temporary non-residence rules. The disposals will then not be subject to capital gains tax.

Sale of the house in Higgsia

Boson purchased the house after leaving the UK. Accordingly, the disposal will not fall within the temporary non-residence rules. Therefore, the disposal will not be subject to capital gains tax if Boson sells the house in a tax year prior to his again becoming resident or ordinarily resident in the UK. So Boson should sell the house in the tax year 2009/10 and again defer his return to the UK until after 5 April 2010.

(b)   (i)   **Rental income after deduction of all taxes**

	£	£
Rental income		11,000
Less: Higgsian income tax		
£11,000 x 30%	3,300	
UK income tax		
(£7,275 (W) x 20%) + (£3,725 x 40%)	2,945	
	6,245	
Less: DTR (lower of Higgsian/UK tax)	(2,945)	(3,300)
Income after deduction of all taxes		7,700

Working

	£
Basic rate band	34,800
Less: salary £(33,560 – 6,035)	(27,525)
Remaining basic rate band	7,275

(ii)   **Dividend income after deduction of all taxes**

	£
Dividends generated £200,000 x 4.3%	8,600
Less: UK income tax (W)	(513)
Income after deduction of all taxes	8,087

Working

	£9,556
Gross divided income £8,600 x $\dfrac{100}{90}$	
£(9,556 – 7,275) = £2,281 x 22½%	£513

Tutorial note

As only some of the dividend is taxable at the higher rate it is not possible to calculate the tax due on the dividend as simply the net dividend x 25%.

(iii) **Maximum fall in rate of return**

	£
Net income from dividends	8,087
Less: net income from rental	(7,700)
Maximum fall in net dividend income	387

This represents gross dividend income of

£387 x $\dfrac{100}{100-32\frac{1}{2}}$ 573

because all this income is taxed at the higher rate (32½% for dividends).

Therefore dividends received would be

£573 x $\dfrac{90}{100}$ 516

So the minimum dividends to be received to equal rental income will be
£(8,600 – 516)   8,084

Yield to produce this dividend income is

$\dfrac{8,084}{200,000}$ x 100   4.042%

So rate of return can fall by up to
4.3% – 4.042%   0.258%
before the after tax income generated from dividends would be less than the return from renting out the property.

Tax tables

The following tax rates and allowances are to be used in answering the questions

Income tax

Savings starting rate	£1 – £2,320	10%
Basic rate	£1 – £34,800	20%
Higher rate	£34,801 and above	40%

Personal allowances

	£
Personal allowance	6,035
Personal allowance aged 65 to 74	9,030
Personal allowance aged 75 and over	9,180
Income limit for age-related allowances	21,800

Car benefit percentage

The base level of CO_2 emissions is 135 grams per kilometre.

Car fuel benefit

The base figure for calculating the car fuel benefit is £16,900.

Pension scheme limits

Annual allowance	£235,000
Lifetime allowance	£1,650,000

The maximum contribution that can qualify for tax relief without any earnings is £3,600.

Authorised mileage allowances

All cars:

Up to 10,000 miles	40p
Over 10,000 miles	25p

Capital allowances

Plant and machinery	
Annual investment allowance	£50,000
Writing down allowance	20%
First year allowance – low emission motor cars (CO_2 emissions less than 110 g/km)	100%
Enhanced capital allowances on energy saving and water saving plant and machinery	100%
Special rate pool writing down allowance	10%

Industrial buildings

Writing-down allowance	3%

Corporation tax

Financial year	2006	2007	2008
Small companies (SC) rate	19%	20%	21%
Full rate	30%	30%	28%
Lower limit	300,000	300,000	300,000
Upper limit	1,500,000	1,500,000	1,500,000
Marginal relief fraction:			
Small companies' rate	11/400	1/40	7/400

Marginal relief

$$(M - P) \times I/P \times \text{marginal relief fraction}$$

Value Added Tax

Registration limit	£67,000
Deregistration limit	£65,000

Inheritance tax

First £312,000	Nil
Excess	40%

Capital gains tax

Annual exemption	£9,600
Rate of tax for individuals	18%
Entrepreneurs' relief	
Lifetime limit	£1,000,000
Reducing faction	4/9

National insurance (not contracted-out rates)

		%
Class 1 employee	£1 – £5,435 per year	Nil
	£5,436 – £40,040 per year	11.0
	£40,041 and above per year	1.0
Class 1 employer	£1 – £5,435 per year	Nil
	£5,436 and above per year	12.8
Class 1A		12.8
Class 2	£2.30 per week	
Class 4	£1 – £5,435 per year	Nil
	£5,436 – £40,040 per year	8.0
	£40,041 and above per year	1.0

Rates of Interest

Official rate of interest	6.25%
Rate of interest on underpaid tax	7.5% (assumed)
Rate of interest on overpaid tax	3.0% (assumed)

Stamp Duty and Stamp Duty Land Tax

	Rate
Ad valorem duty	
Residential property:	
£125,000 or less [(1)]	Nil
£125,001 to £250,000	1%
£250,001 to £500,000	3%
£500,001 or above	4%

[(1)] for non residential property, the nil rate is extended to £150,000

Shares	0.5%
Fixed duty	£5

Calculations and workings need only be made to the nearest £.

All apportionments may be made to the nearest month.

All workings should be shown.

Review Form & Free Prize Draw – Paper P6 Advanced Taxation (Finance Act 2008) (1/09)

All original review forms from the entire BPP range, completed with genuine comments, will be entered into one of two draws on 31 July 2009 and 31 January 2010. The names on the first four forms picked out on each occasion will be sent a cheque for £50.

Name: _____   Address: _____

_____

_____

How have you used this Kit?
(Tick one box only)

☐ Home study (book only)

☐ On a course: college _____

☐ With 'correspondence' package

☐ Other _____

Why did you decide to purchase this Kit?
(Tick one box only)

☐ Have used the complementary Study text

☐ Have used other BPP products in the past

☐ Recommendation by friend/colleague

☐ Recommendation by a lecturer at college

☐ Saw advertising

☐ Other _____

During the past six months do you recall seeing/receiving any of the following?
(Tick as many boxes as are relevant)

☐ Our advertisement in *Student Accountant*

☐ Our advertisement in *Pass*

☐ Our advertisement in *PQ*

☐ Our brochure with a letter through the post

☐ Our website www.bpp.com

Which (if any) aspects of our advertising do you find useful?
(Tick as many boxes as are relevant)

☐ Prices and publication dates of new editions

☐ Information on product content

☐ Facility to order books off-the-page

☐ None of the above

Which BPP products have you used?

Text	☐	Success CD	☐	Learn Online	☐
Kit	☑	i-Learn	☐	Home Study Package	☐
Passcard	☐	i-Pass	☐	Home Study PLUS	☐

Your ratings, comments and suggestions would be appreciated on the following areas.

	Very useful	Useful	Not useful
Passing ACCA exams	☐	☐	☐
Passing P6	☐	☐	☐
Planning your question practice	☐	☐	☐
Questions	☐	☐	☐
Top Tips etc in answers	☐	☐	☐
Content and structure of answers	☐	☐	☐
'Plan of attack' in mock exams	☐	☐	☐
Mock exam answers			

Overall opinion of this Kit	Excellent ☐	Good ☐	Adequate ☐	Poor ☐

Do you intend to continue using BPP products?   Yes ☐   No ☐

The BPP author of this edition can be e-mailed at: suedexter@bpp.com

Please return this form to: Lesley Buick, ACCA Publishing Manager, BPP Learning Media, FREEPOST, London, W12 8BR

Review Form & Free Prize Draw (continued)

TELL US WHAT YOU THINK

Please note any further comments and suggestions/errors below.

Free Prize Draw Rules

1   Closing date for 31 July 2009 draw is 30 June 2009. Closing date for 31 January 2010 draw is 31 December 2009.

2   Restricted to entries with UK and Eire addresses only. BPP employees, their families and business associates are excluded.

3   No purchase necessary. Entry forms are available upon request from BPP Learning Media. No more than one entry per title, per person. Draw restricted to persons aged 16 and over.

4   Winners will be notified by post and receive their cheques not later than 6 weeks after the relevant draw date.

5   The decision of the promoter in all matters is final and binding. No correspondence will be entered into.